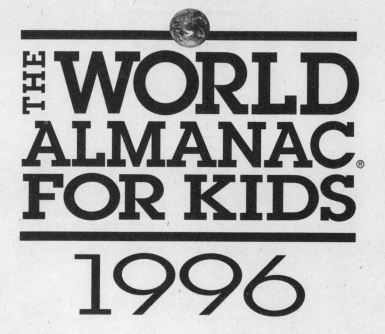

THE WORLD ALMANAC FOR KIDS 1996

WORLD ALMANAC BOOKS

AN IMPRINT OF FUNK & WAGNALLS CORPORATION

A K-III Communications Company

THE WORLD ALMANAC FOR KIDS 1996

EDITOR:
Judith S. Levey

CURRICULUM CONSULTANT:
Jean Craven
District Coordinator of Curriculum Development
Albuquerque, NM, Public Schools

CONTRIBUTORS (listed alphabetically):
Jim Anderson, Melanie Belkin (index), Christina Cheddar, Jerilyn Famighetti,
Joan Gampert, Robert Gampert, Irene Gunther, Bill Gutman, Bonny R. Hart,
Judith Leale, William A. McGeveran, Jr., Randi Metsch-Ampel,
Michael Northrop, Susan R. Norton, Terry Simon, Richard Steins
Religion Consultant: Dr. Anthony T. Padovano, S.T.D., Ph.D.

DESIGN:
Janice Edelman-Lee, Bill Smith Studio
Cover Design: Todd Cooper, Bill Smith Studio

WORLD ALMANAC BOOKS
Vice President and Publisher: Richard W. Eiger

| **Editor:** | **Sales Manager:** | **Director of Marketing:** |
| Robert Famighetti | James R. Keenley | Joyce J. Stein |

FUNK & WAGNALLS
Vice President and Editorial Director: Leon L. Bram
Vice President of Manufacturing: Sally McCravey
Director of Editorial Production: Andrea J. Pitluk

THE WORLD ALMANAC FOR KIDS 1996
Copyright © 1995 by Funk & Wagnalls Corporation
A K-III Communications Company

The World Almanac is a registered trademark of Funk & Wagnalls Corporation.

ISBN (softcover) 0-88687-770-9
ISBN (hardcover) 0-88687-771-7

Printed in the United States of America

The softcover and hardcover editions are distributed to the
trade in the United States by St. Martin's Press.

WORLD ALMANAC BOOKS
An Imprint of Funk & Wagnalls Corporation
One International Boulevard
Mahwah, New Jersey 07495-0017

CONTENTS

INTRODUCTION

A Note to Kids

Are you a young person who enjoys browsing through a book of facts and information? Do you hope to find something new and interesting there? Do you sometimes need just a little more information to finish your homework? Do you pride yourself on writing a good report that has a few surprises for the teacher? Do you like games and puzzles that put your knowledge to the test? If so, this book is for you.

In *The World Almanac for Kids* you will find information on many topics—from computers, inventions, health, and history to movies, TV, books, and sports—topics that kids are interested in and often study in school. And all of this information is easy to locate and use. You will find yourself moving from one subject to another—even exploring subjects you usually pass by. If you have sudden attacks of curiosity, this is a book you will want to keep handy.

Did you ever think that kids would be the source of information for an almanac? Some of you are! In the section called "What Kids Are Saying," we printed some of your answers to our questions about kids' interests. Now it is your turn to help *The World Almanac for Kids* select next year's questions.

A Word for Parents

When it's homework time and a science project or a social studies report is due, do you ever wish your child could use *The World Almanac*? Here's an answer to your wish—a World Almanac created just for kids! Turn the pages and notice the kid-friendly look. Yet each page is packed with interesting facts and information. After using this book for a few years, kids will be ready for *The World Almanac* and will already know how to use it.

How did we choose the topics for this book? We followed the curiosity of kids and the subjects in the school curriculum. The topics are good for reports and projects, and they include interesting diagrams, facts, and explanations to help kids get started. Many of the facts are not found in encyclopedias or in other sources that may not be updated every year. Kids will now learn what source to consult when the latest facts are needed.

There's another bonus for parents. Do you ever find yourself trying to help your child understand a topic you don't fully understand yourself? This almanac is a good source of basic information written for a reader who knows little—or nothing—about a subject. Sometimes that clear, straightforward information is as useful to you as it is to the kids. So, don't be surprised if you also learn something from *The World Almanac for Kids!*

Jean Craven
District Coordinator of Curriculum Development
Albuquerque, NM, Public Schools

The World Almanac for Kids wanted to know more about you, our readers. So to find out, we sent a questionnaire to fourth and fifth graders in schools all over the United States. We learned a lot about what today's kids are interested in, whom they admire, and what their hopes are for the future.

QUESTION: **If you could meet any real person or made-up character, who would you meet and why?** Most kids wanted to meet their idols or heroes, to ask questions, get a few tips, or simply meet someone famous.

WHO TOPPED THE LIST? Shaq is "cool"! Michael is "awesome"! Basketball players Michael Jordan and Shaquille O'Neal were hands-down winners. Football favorites were Emmitt Smith, Deion Sanders, and Jerry Rice. Jonathan Taylor Thomas from *Home Improvement* led the list of actors and entertainers. Whitney Houston, Garth Brooks, and Reba McEntire were tops among singers. Bill Clinton led the presidents, while Martin Luther King, Jr., was the favorite among historical figures. Many kids said they'd like to visit a friend who lived far away, or to meet relatives, whether dead or alive. Many wanted to meet God or Jesus.

I'd like to meet George Washington. Yes, our strong, brave, and very first president.
—Michele E. Quigley, Hilton Head, South Carolina

I would like to meet Jim Carrey because he is funny and I like his movies.
—Trey Preston, Edmond, Oklahoma

I would like to meet Martin Luther King, Jr. He helped make the world a better place. He treated everyone equally and wanted people to look on the inside of each other.
—Ashley J. Reeves, Jacksonville, Arkansas

Me? I would like to meet Garfield, the no. 1 funniest, laziest, sloppiest, and the biggest pig around, cat.
—Amanda Sidelinger, Memphis, Michigan

I would like to meet Michael Jordan because he could teach me how to play basketball better and teach me different skills.
—Bethany Joy Stagen, Paxton, Illinois

I would meet Reba McEntire because I think she is pretty and I love her music. Reba sings and acts, and I have always wanted to do that.
—Dorothy Richele Mitchell, Boston, Kentucky

I'd meet Laura Ingalls Wilder because I really like her books and TV series. I've always thought she was neat the way she was so mean, but so polite.
—Carolyn A. Giles, Bath, Maine

QUESTION: If you could go anywhere, real or imaginary, where would you go and why? Kids told us they would like to:

Travel to see new places, mostly within the United States, but also to Europe, Africa, Australia, and elsewhere. Hawaii was the favorite choice by far.

If I can go anywhere,...it would be Hawaii. I would walk on the sand shores and let the water touch my feet.... I would meet famous people, actors and actresses, models, athletes.

—Jason Boggs Atcheson,
Cherry Hill, New Jersey

I would go to Alaska to see the snow. I haven't seen snow since I was five and I think it would be exciting.

—Angela Goddard,
Clearwater, Florida

If I could go anywhere, it would be Africa...because most people that live there have a hard life. I would like to help the sick ones come back to health and give things to the poor.

—Amanda Campbell, Empire, Alabama

I would like to live in Arizona because I won't have to shovel the snow in the winter time and won't have to worry about my flowers dying in the cold.

—Mitchell K. Burnett, Le Claire, Iowa

I would go to the Bermuda Triangle because of all the stories you hear about it. I would like to see if it's really true that...you disappear or something bad happens to you.

—Anna Jasicki, Derby, Connecticut

Travel to meet relatives, dead or alive, or the place they came from.

I would go to Cuba to see my father's great-great grandfather's ranch.

—Alex Diaz, Rye, New York

Go to an imaginary or ideal place such as Narnia or Never Never Land.

I would love to go inside a person's body...because I want to learn more about organs and veins. I also want to learn about how people get sick.

—John Priest, Mt. Sinai, New York

I would go to a place called Paradise. Everything there would be perfect. There wouldn't be killing or people using drugs. Every single person that is homeless would have a home.... No one ever would make fun of others.

—Holly DiFebo,
Meyersdale, Pennsylvania

Explore outer space, go under the sea, or travel to the past or the future.

I would go back in time and be a fighter pilot and try to stop Japan from bombing Pearl Harbor.

—Nicholas Alan Baldock,
Holloman Air Force Base, New Mexico

I would go to an underwater city. I think it would be cool to make friends with a mermaid. You could swim to school, you could swim with the otters.

—Erica Goss,
Valdosta, Georgia

I would go to the future to see how I turn out as an adult.

—Ryan Galindo,
Ellensburg, Washington

Go to an amusement park, especially Disneyland or Disney World.

I would go to Disneyland and meet Mickey and Minnie Mouse. I would ride rides and go to places I've never been before. That would be neat!

—Rebekah Creasap, Wooster, Ohio

Go to the Super Bowl, or to see their favorite team play.

I would go to...watch the Dallas Cowboys play football because I haven't been there before. I would sit in the front row. I would try to get Troy Aikman's autograph.

—Matthew Neal Murphy III, Livingston, Texas

QUESTION: If you were going to outer space and could take only one thing, what would you take and why?

HOW WOULD I LIVE OUT THERE? Many kids weren't sure what would be provided on their imaginary trip, so they chose items that would help them survive, such as food, water, and oxygen. Some kids opted for a space suit. Others, thinking big, wanted to bring a house, a refrigerator, even a shopping mall.

I would bring an oxygen tank because it gives you air and you need oxygen to live.

—Travis Wiltse, Brewster, Washington

IT WOULD BE LONELY OUT THERE! Many kids said they'd want company, and chose to take a family member, a best friend, a beloved pet, a stuffed toy, or even a picture of their family.

I would take my family because I love them very much and I don't like outer space at all. I would rather eat 200 oranges than go to outer space.

—Laura Wells, Grand Island, Nebraska

IT MIGHT BE BORING OUT THERE! Not sure how long the trip would take, some kids decided to take items that would help them pass the time. Popular choices included video and other games, computers, books, cameras, TVs, radios, and telephones.

I would take checkers. It would be awesome! When you lay the checkers down they would float!

—Gregory Anderson, Dale City, Virginia

IT WOULD BE EXCITING OUT THERE! Kids were curious about space. They thought it would be neat, fun, cool, and awesome to go there, a chance to visit planets, experiment with gravity, or make discoveries.

A chemistry set because I could experiment in space. I could mix them and make a new chemical that I would name Space Formula.

—Ashraf Darwish, Dearborn, Michigan

I think I would take my diary... because you would know what day it was without a calendar and then you could write what happened.

—Jenna Bird, Grass Valley, Oregon

Help Us Choose Next Year's Questions. Do you have any questions that you would like to see answered by kids your age in the next *World Almanac for Kids?* If you do, send them to the address below. Thank you for your help.

Survey Editor, *The World Almanac for Kids*
One International Boulevard, Suite 444
Mahwah, NJ 07495

FEATS and FIRSTS in 1994 and 1995

You never know what you can do until you try. At least that's what these people would say:

12-YEAR-OLD PLAYS WITH THE PHILHARMONIC

In February 1995, pianist **Helen Huang**, 12, played for the first time with the New York Philharmonic Orchestra. She still wasn't very tall—a special gadget had to be used so her feet could reach the pedals.

◀ *Helen Huang playing with the New York Philharmonic*

UNUSUAL WAYS TO CROSS THE OCEAN

In early 1995, **Steve Fossett,** 50, became the first person to fly across the Pacific Ocean in a balloon by himself. He went farther in a balloon than anyone else ever did—5,400 miles. And Frenchman **Guy Delage,** 42, the "mad swimmer," finished a swim across the Atlantic. Delage didn't paddle continuously the whole way—he spent nights sailing along on a raft. He did have to swim past sharks.

HOW OLD IS OLD?

On February 21, 1995, a French woman named **Jeanne Calment** celebrated her 120th birthday. She was the oldest person in the world—if you count only those who have good records of their birth date. Asked what kind of future she expected, the woman replied, "A very short one."

MISS AMERICA FOR 1995

Heather Whitestone was the first deaf person to be crowned Miss America. She won the contest, in September 1994, after a talent competition where she danced to the "vibrations" of the music.

THE YOUNGEST FLYERS

In 1994, **Vicki Van Meter**, 12, of Meadville, Pennsylvania, became the youngest person to fly a plane all the way across the Atlantic Ocean. She did have an adult sitting next to her, but **Jimmy Mathis,** of Glen Arm, Maryland, didn't. At 16, he was the youngest person to fly all by himself across the United States.

A TEN-YEAR-OLD COLLEGE GRADUATE

Michael Kearney graduated from the University of South Alabama in June 1994 with an honors degree in anthropology—and he was only ten years old! Michael got an early start on his education. He was tutored at home by his parents and began high school at the age of five. Meanwhile, other young geniuses were coming along. For example, in England, **Michael Tan** got accepted into Cambridge University at the age of seven.

SCIENCE AND TECHNOLOGY

BABY PICTURES OF THE UNIVERSE

The **Hubble Space Telescope**, launched into space in 1990, is also a camera and a sort of time machine—some of the things it sees are so far away that the light from them took billions of years to get to the lens. Scientists are proud of the pictures Hubble took recently of a distant galaxy from about 12 billion years ago. They show part of the universe when it was very young— only a billion or two years old!

▲ *Hubble Space Telescope*

RUSSIAN COSMONAUT SETS RECORD IN SPACE

After spending 439 days in space, a record for time spent by humans in space, Russian cosmonaut (astronaut) Valery Polyakov returned to Earth from the Russian space station Mir in March 1995. During his 14½ months in space, he circled Earth more than 7,000 times.

PARTNERS IN SPACE

By the year 2002, if all goes well, an international **space station** bigger than a football field will be circling Earth. Inside, scientists from the United States, Russia, Japan, and Europe will work together. In March 1995, as a warm-up, an American astronaut went up in a Russian space capsule to join cosmonauts at Russia's Mir space station. American space shuttles were soon to begin docking with Mir and swapping crews. Building of the new space station was to start in 1997.

WATCH OUT BELOW!

A **comet** about 6 miles across, weighing some 500 billion tons, broke up and crash-landed on Jupiter in July 1994. The crash created fireballs hotter than the sun and huge, dark gas bubbles that could be seen from Earth with a small telescope. But it was no big deal for the giant planet, which is about 1,000 times bigger than Earth. Could this kind of thing happen here? Many scientists think it already did happen, wiping out the dinosaurs about 65 million years ago.

THERE WERE DINOSAURS IN ANTARCTICA, TOO

Scientists, for the first time, found dinosaur remains in Antarctica. The **meat-eating dinosaurs** were about 25 feet long and lived there some 200 million years ago—at a time when Antarctica had a nice warm climate. Dr. William Hammer said his group named this newly discovered animal the "*frozen* crested reptile"—because "we almost froze to death collecting it."

THEY THOUGHT HE WAS CRAZY

Automobiles, fax machines, subways, the electric chair—these are a few of the inventions French writer **Jules Verne** predicted back in the 1860s, in a long-lost science fiction novel called *Paris in the Twentieth Century*. Publishers wouldn't print his book; they said it was unbelievable. But the manuscript recently turned up in an attic, and in 1994, it got published for the first time, in France.

SPORTS

SUPERSTARS ON ICE

Nicole Bobek, 17, trained harder than ever before and captured the United States women's figure skating crown in February 1995. She edged out 14-year-old dynamo **Michelle Kwan**—who would have been the youngest champ ever. The next month, Bobek and Kwan placed third and fourth in the world championships—China's **Chen Lu** took the women's title, beating France's **Surya Bonaly** in a tie-breaking round.

▲ *Chen Lu at the 1994 Winter Olympics*

MIRACLE MAN RETURNS

In late 1993, **Michael Jordan** stunned the sports world by retiring from basketball. He wanted to play baseball instead. But the world's greatest hoopster was only so-so on the baseball diamond. Fans were delighted when he switched back to basketball early in 1995—and proved he could still play it like nobody else!

THE SUPER 49ers

The **San Francisco 49ers** won their fifth Super Bowl, swamping the San Diego Chargers, 49-26, in Miami, on January 29, 1995. Quarterback **Steve Young**, who was named Most Valuable Player, threw a record six touchdown passes, heading up a spectacular offense. Receiver **Jerry Rice** had a bad cold and injured his left shoulder—but still caught ten passes for 149 yards and three touchdowns.

◄ *Steve Young of the San Francisco 49ers*

UCONN WOMEN'S BASKETBALL VICTORY

On April 12, 1995, the Lady Huskies of the University of Connecticut made women's basketball history. They won the National Collegiate Athletic Association (NCAA) tournament with a perfect 35-0 record. The last and only other team to achieve a perfect season and win the NCAA women's tournament were the Lady Longhorns of the University of Texas in 1986.

BASEBALL STRIKES OUT

For the first time in 90 years there was no World Series in 1994. Players went on strike August 12, 1994, and everything stopped. A new season began on April 26, 1995, after the players agreed to return to work.

HOUSTON ROCKETS WIN AGAIN

In June 1995, the Houston Rockets won their second consecutive National Basketball Association championship, sweeping the Orlando Magic 4 games to 0 in the championship series. Houston center Hakeem Olajuwon was chosen as the Finals Most Valuable Player for a second year in a row.

ENTERTAINMENT: Rising Stars

▲ *Jim Carrey in The Mask*

JIM CARREY

When zany **Jim Carrey** was a kid, he loved to make his classmates and the teacher laugh. Now he has millions of fans breaking up at his antics in such films as *Ace Ventura: Pet Detective, The Mask,* and *Dumb and Dumber.* He recently took on the role of Batman's batty archfoe the Riddler in *Batman Forever.*

BRAD PITT

Brad Pitt once worked at a Pizza Hut restaurant, dressed up as a chicken. Now he dresses for big roles in movies like *Legends of the Fall, Interview With the Vampire,* and, more recently, the adventure film *Twelve Monkeys.*

CLAIRE DANES

Not long ago **Claire Danes** was an ordinary schoolkid. Then she got to play an ordinary teenager on TV—in the series *My So-Called Life.* Critics and kids thought she acted just like a real teenager. Claire also starred as Beth in the 1994 movie *Little Women,* based on a classic novel by Louisa May Alcott.

JONATHAN TAYLOR THOMAS

In 1995, teen actor **Jonathan Taylor Thomas** starred with Chevy Chase in the hit film *Man of the House.* He was already a hit on TV, where he plays Randy on the comedy *Home Improvement.* And he was the voice behind Simba in *The Lion King.*

MARY-KATE AND ASHLEY OLSEN

Do the names **Mary-Kate** and **Ashley Olsen** ring a bell? These twin stars have been gaining fans for years. When they were only babies, they started taking turns at playing the role of Michelle on TV's *Full House.* Now both of them also act in TV movies, make records and videos—and collect teddy bears. The twins turn ten years old in June 1996.

SHERYL CROW AND OTHER GRAMMY WINNERS

One of the biggest winners at the 1995 Grammy awards was rising star **Sheryl Crow.** She was named Best New Artist, and her song "All I Wanna Do" picked up two other awards. The San Francisco punk-pop band **Green Day** won Best Alternative Performance for *Dookie.* Other winners, to mention a few, included **Boyz II Men** (Best Rhythm and Blues Group) and the Seattle band **Soundgarden** (for both hard rock and metal performances).

▲ *Sheryl Crow*

OTHER EVENTS THAT MADE NEWS

DEADLY BLAST SHOCKS THE NATION

On April 19, 1995, the Alfred P. Murrah Federal Building in Oklahoma City was destroyed by a massive car bomb explosion. For 17 days, people around the country watched in shock and sadness as rescuers risked their own lives searching for survivors and victims of the blast. The nation mourned the loss of the 168 people who died. Officials called the attack the worst terrorist incident in U.S. history.

THE DAY THE EARTH SHOOK

Roads twisted like ribbons, and buildings crumbled and fell, as Japan's worst earthquake in 50 years hit the city of Kobe and its surroundings, in January 1995. Over 5,000 people died, 25,000 were hurt, and hundreds of thousands lost their homes. There was one piece of good news: most of the newest buildings constructed to withstand earthquakes were not badly damaged.

O.J. SIMPSON ON TRIAL

Police arrested former football star **O.J. Simpson** and charged him with the murder of his ex-wife, **Nicole Brown Simpson**, and **Ronald J. Goldman**, a friend of hers. O.J. was one of the most famous people ever charged with such a major crime, and millions of people watched his trial on TV, which started in January 1995.

A SWEEP FOR REPUBLICANS

On November 8, 1994, **Republicans** won a huge election victory, taking most of the seats in *both* houses of Congress—the Senate and the House of Representatives. It was a big blow to the Democrats and President Bill Clinton. When the new Congress met in early 1995, **Bob Dole,** a Republican from Kansas, became the majority leader of the Senate. He later said he would run for president in 1996. **Newt Gingrich,** a Georgia Republican, took over as Speaker of the House of Representitives. Republicans began to pass new laws based on the "Contract With America"—a plan many of them had agreed to before the election.

A NEW SOUTH AFRICA

South Africa has a black president for the first time. **Nelson Mandela** became the country's leader in May 1994, after elections that were open to people of all races. Before then, black people could not vote and had to live under very harsh laws. Mandela, who fought against these laws, was arrested by the government when he was young, and spent over 25 years of his life in prison.

ART IN A CAVE

Three explorers in France recently made an exciting discovery. They stumbled on a huge underground cave with colorful wall paintings of animals believed to be at least 30,000 years old. There are paintings of horses' heads, bears with their mouths open, rhinoceroses fighting, and lions and other beasts running through the woods. These are the world's oldest known paintings and can help give us a new view of life in the Stone Age.

ANNIVERSARIES in 1995

50TH ANNIVERSARY OF THE END OF WORLD WAR II

January 27, 1945: The Auschwitz prison camp, where millions of Jews and others were murdered, was freed from Nazi control.

May 7, 1945: Germany surrendered.

August 6 and 9, 1945: American planes dropped atomic bombs on Japan.

August 14, 1945: Japan surrendered, ending the war.

October 24, 1945: Hoping to prevent more wars, nations joined to create a new world organization, the United Nations. The charter, which the nations all agreed to, officially came into effect on October 24—now celebrated as United Nations Day.

The Diary of Anne Frank

In 1942, Anne Frank, a 13-year-old Jewish girl, and her family, were forced into hiding to escape arrest by the Nazis. While in hiding, Anne wrote a diary describing what it felt like to live in fear in a tiny, secret upstairs annex for two years. In 1944, Anne and her family were found and sent to a German concentration camp, where all but her father died in 1945. Anne Frank's diary, called *Anne Frank: The Diary of a Young Girl*, was first published in 1947. In 1995, it was published again, this time including entries that had been left out of the earlier publication.

OTHER MAJOR DATES in 1995:

February 6: Babe Ruth's 100th birthday.

April 20: the 25th annual Earth Day.

July 1-9: the World Special Olympic Games.

October 24: a total eclipse of the sun.

1996 HAPPENINGS

SOME BIG DATES IN 1996

July 19 to August 4: the Summer Olympics, in Atlanta, Georgia.

November 5: Election Day, when the United States picks a president.

December 11: The 50th birthday of UNICEF, a world organization to help children— first created to aid children who were victims of World War II.

100TH ANNIVERSARIES

There were many firsts in 1896:

- ☑ The first Tootsie Rolls were made in 1896 by candyman Leo Hirschfield. He named them after his six-year-old daughter, whom he called "Tootsie."
- ☑ The first comic strip was published. It was called "The Yellow Kid."
- ☑ The hit song "When the Saints Go Marching In" was introduced.
- ☑ The first box of Cracker Jack went on sale.
- ☑ The first motor cars were offered for sale.
- ☑ The first motion picture was shown to the public.

WHERE TO FIND IT:
From Animals to World History

 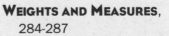

The LARGEST and the FASTEST

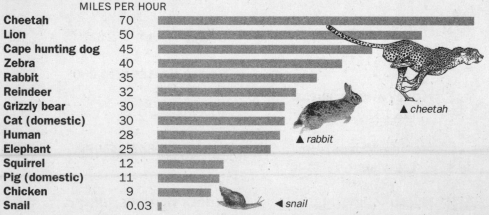

THE LARGEST ANIMALS

World's Largest Animal: blue whale (100 feet long, 150 tons)   ▲ *blue whale*
Largest Land Animal: African bush elephant (10 feet, 6 inches high, over 6 tons)
Tallest Animal: giraffe (20 feet tall)
Largest Reptile: saltwater crocodile (16 feet long, 1,150 pounds)
Largest Snake: anaconda (27 feet, 9 inches long, 500 pounds)
Longest Fish: whale shark (41½ feet long)
Largest Bird: ostrich (9 feet tall, 345 pounds)   ▼ *ostrich*
Largest Insect: stick insect (15 inches long)

▲ *anaconda snake*

THE FASTEST ANIMALS

World's Fastest Animal: swift, a bird (100–200 miles per hour)
Fastest Marine Animal: killer whale (34.5 miles per hour)
Fastest Land Animal: cheetah (70 miles per hour)
Fastest Fish: sailfish (68 miles per hour)
Fastest Bird: swift (100–200 miles per hour)
Fastest Insect: dragonfly (36 miles per hour)

▲ *dragonfly*

How Fast Do Animals Run?

Did you know that some animals can run as fast as a car can move or that a snail would need more than 30 hours just to go one mile? If you look at this table, you will see how fast some common land animals can move.

MILES PER HOUR

Cheetah	70
Lion	50
Cape hunting dog	45
Zebra	40
Rabbit	35
Reindeer	32
Grizzly bear	30
Cat (domestic)	30
Human	28
Elephant	25
Squirrel	12
Pig (domestic)	11
Chicken	9
Snail	0.03

▲ *cheetah*

▲ *rabbit*

◄ *snail*

Box turtle	100 years
Asian elephant	40 years
Grizzly bear	25 years
Horse	20 years
Gorilla	20 years
Polar bear	20 years
Rhinoceros (white)	20 years
Black bear	18 years
Lion	15 years
Rhesus monkey	15 years
Rhinoceros (black)	15 years
Camel	12 years
Cat (domestic)	12 years
Dog (domestic)	12 years
Leopard	12 years
Giraffe	10 years
Pig	10 years
Squirrel	10 years
Red fox	7 years
Kangaroo	7 years
Chipmunk	6 years
Rabbit	5 years
Guinea pig	4 years
Mouse	3 years
Opossum	1 year

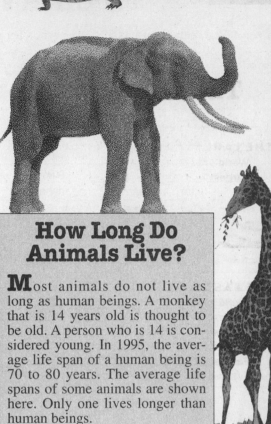

How Long Do Animals Live?

Most animals do not live as long as human beings. A monkey that is 14 years old is thought to be old. A person who is 14 is considered young. In 1995, the average life span of a human being is 70 to 80 years. The average life spans of some animals are shown here. Only one lives longer than human beings.

What Are GROUPS OF ANIMALS Called?

Groups or pairs of animals often have special names. The next time you see some of these animals, rather than saying that you saw a bunch of fish, sheep, or ants, use the expressions below.

▲ *gaggle of geese*

ants: *colony* of ants
bees: *swarm* of bees
chicks: *clutch* of chicks
clams: *bed* of clams
ducks: *brace* of ducks
elks: *gang* of elks
fish: *school* of fish
geese: *flock* or *gaggle*
gorillas: *band* of gorillas
hares: *down* of hares

hens: *brood* of hens
kangaroos: *troop* of kangaroos
leopards: *leap* of leopards
lions: *pride* of lions
monkeys: *troop* of monkeys
oxen: *yoke* of oxen
seals: *pod* of seals
sheep: *flock* of sheep
swans: *bevy* of swans
whales: *pod* of whales

What To Call ANIMALS and THEIR YOUNG

Below are some animals and the names for males, females, and their young.

ANIMAL	MALE	FEMALE	YOUNG
bear	boar	sow	cub
cattle	bull	cow	calf
deer	buck	doe	fawn
duck	drake	duck	duckling
elephant	bull	cow	calf
giraffe	bull	cow	calf
goat	billy-goat	nanny-goat	kid
goose	gander	goose	gosling
hippopotamus	bull	cow	calf
horse	stallion	mare	foal
lion	lion	lioness	cub
pig	boar	sow	piglet
rabbit	buck	doe	bunny, kit
sheep	ram	ewe	lamb
tiger	tiger	tigress	cub
whale	bull	cow	calf

HABITAT PUZZLE **W**here Do Animals Live? The area where an animal lives is called its **habitat**. Below are animals and their habitats. The habitats are written in code. Each letter of the habitat is one letter of the alphabet after the letter of the code (the letter following Z would be A). For example, if the habitat is EZQL, E = F, Z = A, Q = R, and L = M; so, EZQL = FARM. Can you now decode the habitats below? (Answers are on page 302.)

1. **These animals live in a dry place:** camel, bobcat, coyote, mule deer, kangaroo mouse, gila monster, scorpion, rattlesnake, roadrunner. **Habitat:** CDRDQSR

2. **These animals like warm weather:** orangutan, gibbon, leopard, crocodile, anteater, tapir, iguana, parrot, tarantula. **Habitat:** SQNOHBZK ENQDRSR

3. **These animals like flat, open land:** African elephant, kangaroo, Indian rhinoceros, giraffe, zebra, prairie dog, ostrich. **Habitat:** FQZRRKZMCR

4. **These animals like cold weather:** polar bear, musk ox, caribou, ermine, arctic fox, walrus, penguin, Siberian husky, snowy owl. **Habitat:** ONKZQ QDFHNMR

5. **These animals like water:** whale, dolphin, seal, manatee, shark, swordfish, crab, octopus, sting ray, coral, jellyfish, starfish, scallop, sponge. **Habitat:** NBDZMR

6. **These animals live high up:** yak, snow leopard, vicuna, bighorn sheep, chinchilla, pika, eagle, Rocky Mountain goat, Nepalese swift. **Habitat:** LNTMSZHMR

CLASSIFYING ANIMALS

There are so many different types of animals in the world that scientists had to find a way to organize them into groups. A man named Carolus Linnaeus, who lived in the 1700s, worked out a system for classifying both animals and plants. We still use that system today. All animals together are called the **animal kindgom**. Below is a simplified chart showing how a few animals in the animal kingdom are classified.

ANIMAL KINGDOM

The animal kingdom includes all the animals in the world. The animal kingdom is separated into two large groups—animals with backbones, called **vertebrates**, and animals without backbones, called **invertebrates**. These large groups are divided into smaller groups called *phyla*. And phyla are divided into even smaller groups called *classes*. The animals in each group are classified together when their bodies are similar in certain ways. Below are a few examples of some of the animals in these groups.

VERTEBRATES: Animals With Backbones

FISH: Sharks, skates, salmon, trout, halibut

AMPHIBIANS: Frogs, toads, mud puppies

REPTILES: Turtles, alligators, crocodiles, lizards

BIRDS: Sparrows, owls, turkeys, hawks

MAMMALS: Kangaroos, opossums, dogs, cats, bears, seals, rats, squirrels, rabbits, chipmunks, porcupines, horses, pigs, cows, deer, bats, whales, dolphins, monkeys, apes, humans

INVERTEBRATES: Animals Without Backbones

PROTOZOA The simplest form of animals.

COELENTERATES Jelly fish, sea anemones, coral, hydra

MOLLUSKS Clams, snails, squid, oysters

ANNELIDS Earthworms

ARTHROPODS
Crustaceans: Lobsters, crayfish
Centipedes and Millipedes
Arachnids: Spiders, scorpions
Insects: Butterflies, grasshoppers, bees, termites, cockroaches

ECHINODERMS Starfish, sea urchins, sea cucumbers

ENDANGERED SPECIES

WHAT IS AN ENDANGERED SPECIES?

When an animal becomes less and less plentiful on one part of the earth or in the entire world, the animal is said to be **endangered** or **threatened**. The U.S. Department of the Interior keeps track of endangered and threatened species. Throughout the world today, 954 species of animals are endangered or threatened. These include:

☑ 338 species of mammals   ☑ 112 species of reptiles   ☑ 58 other
☑ 243 species of birds   ☑ 58 species of clams   species
☑ 113 species of fish   ☑ 32 species of insects

HOW DO ANIMALS BECOME ENDANGERED?

Over very long periods of time, many kinds of animals and plants have disappeared from the earth (become extinct). This happens for several reasons:

☑ **Changes in Climate.** Animals are threatened when the climate of their habitat (where they live) changes in a major way. For example, if an area becomes very hot and dry and a river dries up, the fish and other plant and animal life that live in the river will die.

☑ **Habitat Destruction.** Sometimes animal habitats are destroyed when people need the land. For example, wetlands, which are the home to many types of waterfowl, fish, and insects, might be drained for a housing development or a mall. The animals that lived there would either have to find a new home or they would die out. Sometimes animals move to a nearby habitat, but even then their new home may become overcrowded and food may become scarce.

☑ **Over-hunting.** The bison or buffalo that once ranged over the entire Great Plains of the United States were hunted almost to extinction in the 19th century. Since then, they have been protected by laws, and their numbers are increasing. Sometimes, though, controlled hunting can protect the environment and improve the quality of life for the remaining animals. For example, if the deer population in a certain area is too large, the deer will eat all the small bushes and plants and eventually remove from their environment the very food they need to survive. But if controlled hunting takes place, the population may be reduced enough so that the surviving animals can live comfortably with the food available to them.

Some ENDANGERED SPECIES

Some animals are endangered in only one part of the world and remain fairly common in another part. Other species are endangered throughout the world. Below are a few species endangered in 1994 and where they are threatened.

MAMMALS

Asiatic lion, from Turkey to India
Cheetah, from Africa to India
Giant otter, South America
Giant panda, in China
Gorilla, in Central and West Africa
Gray whale, in North Pacific Ocean
Ozark big-eared bat, in the U.S.
   in Missouri, Oklahoma, Arkansas

BIRDS

Hooded crane, in Japan and Russia
Bald eagle, in most U.S. states,
   Canada, and northern Mexico
Hawaiian hawk, in the U.S. in Hawaii
Golden parakeet, in Brazil
Japanese crested ibis, in China,
   Japan, Russia, and Korea
Indigo macaw, in Brazil

FISH

Bonytail chub, in the U.S. in Arizona,
   California, Colorado, Nevada,
   Utah, Wyoming
Sockeye (red) salmon, in the North
   Pacific Basin from the U.S.
   (California) to Russia

REPTILES

Nile crocodile, in Africa and the
   Middle East
Plymouth red-bellied turtle, in the U.S.
   in Massachusetts
San Francisco garter snake, in the
   U.S. in California

ENDANGERED SPECIES PUZZLE

The names of endangered animal species are hidden in the puzzle below. Circle as many as of these as you can find: AMERICAN CROCODILE, ASIAN ELEPHANT, CALIFORNIA CONDOR, CAVE CRAYFISH, ESKIMO CURLEW, GRIZZLY BEAR, HOWLER MONKEY, INDIGO MACAW, LEOPARD, WEST AFRICAN OSTRICH, WILD YAK. Hint: Look for one word at a time. (Answers are on page 302.)

```
Q V N A H L M B S F Q X C U S A I F S H C O Z A
U P A O P A I L K D R A K E R N T B E F A G N Y
L E O P A R D H L E W R Y O U R A O V O L R C N
M Z L O R P F O I N I G T P W R I A E R I O A T
A G A R U I B W E S K I M O C U R L E W F C V A
T R S W I N C L V E C R J U L E S T M X O K E R
T I M A S E W E S T A F R I C A N O S T R I C H
E Z O E N T H R N Y L F O R T I L D E S N B R P
S Z T L U A Y M V B W F W E R T Y U I O I L A D
D L I N D I G O M A C A W C V B N M J H A F Y E
P Y K I J L V N I U M S B G R T Y C I O C Q F M
A B D F N E X K N V B W W I L D Y A K R O M I O
D E R E P D Q E A D R E W E R T H E Y O N R S T
O A E C R S X Y I H A B I T L R V E N T D O H L
C R E A M E R I C A N C R O C O D I L E O Z E U
K J H D R I W I N W E R T G H J P A L Y R T L N
A S I A N E L E P H A N T I L K J H S D G B V X
```

ANIMAL LIFE on Earth

This time line shows how animal life developed on earth and when land plants developed. The earliest animals are at the top of the chart. The most recent are at the bottom of the chart.

	YEARS AGO		ANIMAL LIFE ON EARTH
PRECAMBRIAN	4.5 billion		Formation of the earth. No forms of life.
	2.5 billion		First evidence of life in the form of bacteria and algae. All life was in water.
PALEOZOIC	570-500 million		Animals with shells (called trilobites) and some mollusks. Some fossils begin to form.
	500-430 million		Jawless fish appear, oldest known animals with backbones (vertebrates).
	430-395 million		Many coral reefs, jawed fishes, and scorpion-like animals. First land plants.
	395-345 million		Many fishes. Earliest known insect. Amphibians (animals living in water and on land) appear.
	345-280 million		Large insects appear. Amphibians increase in numbers. First trees appear.
	280-225 million		Reptiles and modern insects appear. Trilobites, many corals and fishes become extinct.
MESOZOIC	225-195 million		Dinosaurs and turtles appear. Many reptiles and insects develop further. Mammals appear.
	195-136 million		Many giant dinosaurs. Reptiles increase in number. First birds appear. Crablike animals appear.
	136-65 million		Dinosaurs develop further and then become extinct. Flowering plants begin to appear.
CENOZOIC	65-2.5 million		Modern-day land and sea animals began to develop, including such mammals as rhinoceroses, whales, elephants, cats, dogs, apes, bears, seals.
	2.5 million-10,000		Earliest humans appear. Mastodon, mammoths, and other huge animals become extinct.
	10,000-present		Modern human beings and animals.

FOSSIL MYSTERIES:
Learning About Extinct Animals

WHAT IS A FOSSIL?

A fossil is the remains of an animal or plant. Most fossils are formed from the hard parts of an animal's body, such as bones, shells, or teeth. Some are large, like dinosaur footprints. Some are so tiny that you need a microscope to see them. Most fossils are found in rocks formed from the mud or sand that collects at the bottom of oceans, rivers, and lakes.

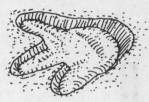

WHAT DO FOSSILS TELL US?

Scientists study fossils to help understand life in ancient periods of the world's history. The age and structure of the rocks in which fossils are found can help scientists tell how long ago certain kinds of animals or plants lived. For example, dinosaurs lived millions of years ago, but people have known about dinosaurs for less than 200 years. One of the first dinosaurs to be discovered was the fossil of an Iguanodon, which was discovered in England in 1822. And scientists believe that there were many species of dinosaurs that we don't even know about, and we won't learn about them until their fossils can be found.

WHERE ARE FOSSILS FOUND?

Fossils, including dinosaur fossils, are found on every continent on the earth. In eastern and southern Africa, people have found fossils that are ancestors of early humans. Insects that lived millions of years ago are sometimes found preserved in amber. Amber is hardened tree sap. Fossils have also been found in ice and tar. In 1991 a frozen corpse of a man believed to have lived over 5,000 years ago was found in the Austrian alps.

IF YOU LIKE DINOSAURS...

Dinosaur fossils are found in certain layers of sedimentary rock. From these fossils, we have learned that dinosaurs lived during the **Mesozoic Era**, from 225 to 65 million years ago. The Mesozoic Era is divided into three periods:

1. **The Triassic Period,** from 225 to 195 million years ago, when dinosaurs first appeared. These were small dinosaurs, rarely longer than 15 feet.
2. **The Jurassic Period,** from 195 to 136 million years ago, when many giant dinosaurs lived, including the Allosaurus, Tyrannosaurus, Apatosaurus, Iguanodon, Trachodon, Megalosaurus, Stegosaurus, and Diplodocus.
3. **Cretaceous Period,** from 136 to 65 million years ago, when horned dinosaurs, such as Triceratops, appeared, and dinosaurs from the Jurassic Period lived. By the end of the Cretaceous Period, all dinosaurs had died out.

WHY DID DINOSAURS BECOME EXTINCT?

So far, fossils have not told us for sure why dinosaurs died out. One theory is that an asteroid from space hit the earth 65 million years ago and that it blocked out the sunlight. This possibly caused the climate to change drastically, which may have caused plants and animals to die. If this happened, it could have led to the starvation of both plant-eating and meat-eating dinosaurs.

MUSEUMS of NATURAL HISTORY

A natural history museum contains exhibits of things that are found in nature. Some of the nonliving things you can see in a natural history museum are animals, plants, and rocks. You can see fossils of prehistoric animals and plants, too. Here are some museums with major exhibits of dinosaurs and other prehistoric animals.

Academy of Natural Sciences
1900 & Ben Franklin Parkway
Philadelphia, Pennsylvania 19103
Phone: (215) 299-1000
Displays: has some of the first fossil dinosaurs found in North America

American Museum of Natural History
Central Park West at 79th Street
New York, New York 10024
Phone: (212) 769-5100
Displays: No other museum contains as many dinosaurs. Exhibits include fossil eggs, tracks, and skin imprints.

Carnegie Museum of Natural History
4400 Forbes Avenue
Pittsburgh, Pennsylvania 15213
Phone: (412) 622-3131
Displays: Major fossil exhibits including displays of well-preserved Late Jurassic dinosaurs

Denver Museum of Natural History
City Park, Denver, Colorado 80205
Phone: (303) 370-6387
Displays: "Succession of Life" exhibit contains dinosaurs, marine reptiles, and 50 million years of mammal evolution

Field Museum of Natural History
Roosevelt Road at Lake Shore Drive
Chicago, Illinois 60605
Phone: (312) 922-9410
Displays: fossil invertebrates, vertebrates, and plants from South America and the western U.S., including dinosaurs

Museum of Comparative Zoology
Harvard University
26 Oxford Street
Cambridge, Massachusetts 02138
Phone: (617) 495-8149
Displays: major collection of fossil vertebrates, fossil fishes, South American prehistoric reptiles and amphibians, and North American dinosaurs

National Museum of Natural History Smithsonian Institution
10th St. & Constitution Ave, N.W.
Washington, D.C. 20560
Phone: (202) 357-1300
Displays: Has fossils representing most phases of prehistoric life

University of Nebraska State Museum
307 Morrill Hall, 14th and U Streets
Lincoln, Nebraska 68588
Phone: (402) 472-3779
Displays: over 13 million specimens from Central Plains states, many fossil mammals

WHERE ELSE TO FIND DINOSAURS:
- ☑ Dinosaur National Monument, Dinosaur, Colorado. Shows a hill partly dug away with dinosaur remains still in the earth.
- ☑ Museum of the Rockies, Bozeman, Montana
- ☑ New Mexico Museum of Natural History, Albuquerque, New Mexico
- ☑ Pratt Museum of Natural History, Amherst College, Amherst, Massachusetts
- ☑ Tyrrell Museum of Palaeontology, Drumheller, Alberta, Canada
- ☑ Utah Museum of Natural History, Salt Lake City, Utah

Which U.S. Zoos Have the
LARGEST NUMBERS of Species?

San Diego Zoo
2920 Zoo Drive
San Diego, California 92103
Phone: (619) 234-3153
Number of Species: 800
Popular Exhibits: Tiger River, Komodo
    dragons, koalas

Cincinnati Zoo
3400 Vine Street
Cincinnati, Ohio 45220
Phone: (513) 281-4700
Number of Species: 761
Popular Exhibits: Gorilla World, white
    Bengal tigers, Jungle Trails

**San Antonio Zoological Gardens
and Aquarium**
3903 N. St. Mary's Street
San Antonio, Texas 78212
Phone: (210) 734-7184
Number of Species: 700
Popular Exhibits: Australian Walkabout,
    Amazonia, Aquarium

Bronx Zoo/Wildlife Conservation Park
Fordham Road and Bronx River Pkwy.
Bronx, New York 10460
Phone: (718) 367-1010
Number of Species: 670
Popular Exhibits: Himalayan Highlands,
    Jungle World, endangered species

St. Louis Zoological Park
Forest Park
St. Louis, Missouri 63110
Phone: (314) 781-0900
Number of Species: 665
Popular Exhibits: Living World, Bear Pits,
    Jungle of the Apes

Houston Zoological Gardens
1513 North MacGregor
Houston, Texas 77030
Phone: (713) 523-5888
Number of Species: 605
Popular Exhibits: Bird Garden, white
    tigers, African lion savannah

Denver Zoological Gardens
City Park
Denver, Colorado 80205
Phone: (303) 331-4100
Number of Species: 600
Popular Exhibits: Tropical Discovery,
    Northern Shores

Cleveland Metroparks Zoo
3900 Brookside Drive
Cleveland, Ohio 44109
Phone: (216) 661-7511
Number of Species: 564
Popular Exhibits: Rain Forest with 600
    animals and 7,000 plants

National Zoological Park
3000 block of Connecticut Ave. N.W.
Washington, D.C. 20008
Phone: (202) 673-4800
Number of Species: 509
Popular Exhibits: Giant pandas, Komodo
    dragon lizards, koalas

Audubon Park and Zoological Garden
6500 Magazine Street
New Orleans, Louisiana 70118
Phone: (504) 861-2537
Number of Species: 500
Popular Exhibits: White alligators,
    Louisiana Swamp, Reptile Encounter

Milwaukee County Zoological Garden
10001 W. Bluemound Road
Milwaukee, Wisconsin 53226
Phone: (414) 771-5500
Number of Species: 500
Popular Exhibits: sea lions, wolf woods,
    bear dens

Oklahoma City Zoo
2101 N.E. 50th Street
Oklahoma City, Oklahoma 73111
Phone: (405) 424-3344
Number of Species: 500
Popular Exhibits: Great EscApe, dolphin,
    sea lion shows

PAINTING:
Landscape, Portrait, and Still Life

Art can be real or imaginary, funny or sad, beautiful or disturbing. Before photography was invented, most artists tried to show things as they saw them or as they imagined them to look. Throughout history, artists have painted pictures of nature (called **landscapes**); or pictures of people (called **portraits**); or pictures of flowers in vases, food, and other objects (called **still lifes**). When artists paint people and things to look as they do in real life, their art is called **realistic**, or **representational**.

SOME FAMOUS PAINTERS AND LANDSCAPES

A drawing or painting of nature is called a **landscape**. A picture of the sea is called a **seascape**. A picture of city buildings is called a **cityscape**. Below are a few famous painters, when they lived, their nationality, and the name of one of their landscapes.

▲ *A landscape*

El Greco (1541-1614), Spanish painter: "View of Toledo" (cityscape)
Jan Vermeer (1632-1675), Dutch painter: "View of Delft" (cityscape)
Katsushika Hokusai (1760-1849), Japanese painter: "Views of Mount Fuji" (landscape)
John Constable (1776-1837), English painter: "The Cornfield" (landscape)
Winslow Homer (1836-1910), American painter: "Northeaster" (seascape)
Georgia O'Keeffe (1887-1986), American painter: "Grey Hills" (landscape)

SOME FAMOUS PAINTERS AND PORTRAITS

A painting of a person (or more than one person) is called a **portrait**. When a person paints a picture of himself or herself, it is called a **self-portrait**. Below are a few famous painters, when they lived, their nationality, and the name of one of their portraits.

Leonardo da Vinci (1452-1519), Italian painter:
   "The Mona Lisa"
Rembrandt (1606-1669), Dutch painter: "Self Portrait"
John Singleton Copley (1737-1815), American painter:
   "Paul Revere"
Edouard Manet (1832-1883), French painter: "The Fifer"
Pierre Auguste Renoir (1841-1919), French painter:
   "Madame Charpentier and Her Children"
Mary Cassatt (1844-1926), American painter: "The Bath"

▲ *A portrait*

SOME FAMOUS PAINTERS AND STILL LIFES

A picture of small objects—like flowers, bottles, books, food, and other things—is called a **still life**. Below are a few famous painters, when they lived, their nationality, and the name of one of their still-life paintings.

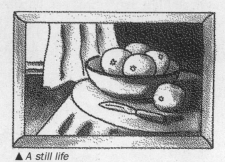

▲ *A still life*

Henri Fantin-Latour (1836-1904), French painter: "Still Life with Flowers and Fruit"
Paul Cezanne (1839-1906), French painter: "Apples and Pears"
William Michael Harnett (1848-1892), American painter: "Still Life—Violin and Music"
Vincent van Gogh (1853-1890), Dutch painter: "Sunflowers"

 DID YOU KNOW? Thousands of years ago, people painted pictures on the walls of caves. In December of 1994, prehistoric paintings from about 30,000 years ago were discovered in an underground cave in France by three French explorers. These works of art are the oldest cave paintings ever found.

Modern Art

Many artists still paint pictures that can be recognized as landscapes and portraits. But many artists today create pictures using shapes or colors or textures in interesting ways that do not look like anything in the real world. These paintings are called **abstract**, or **nonrepresentational**. Abstract art is also called **modern art**.

Some Famous MODERN ARTISTS and ABSTRACT PAINTINGS

Below are a few famous painters known for their abstract paintings, including their names, when they lived, their nationality, and the name of one of their paintings. Sometimes an abstract painting has a name that sounds realistic—like Picasso's "Three Musicians"—even though the painting is abstract.

Pablo Picasso (1881-1973), Spanish painter: "Three Musicians"
Joan Miró (1893-1983), Spanish painter: "Composition"
Helen Frankenthaler (born 1928), American painter: "Blue Territory"
Wassily Kandinsky (1866-1944), Russian painter: "Impression No. 30"
Piet Mondrian (1872-1944), Dutch painter: "Composition"
Jackson Pollack (1912-1956), American painter: "Number 1"

▲ *Abstract art*

SCULPTURE

Sculpture is a three-dimensional form made from clay, stone, metal, or other material. Many sculptures stand freely so that you can walk around them. Some are mobiles that hang from the ceiling. Sculptures can be large, like the Statue of Liberty or the statue of Lincoln in the Lincoln Memorial, or they can be small. Some sculpture is representational (looks like the person or animal it represents). Some modern sculpture is abstract and has no form that can be recognized.

SOME FAMOUS SCULPTORS AND SCULPTURE

Below is a list of a few sculptors, their names, when they lived, their nationality, and the name of one of their sculptures.

Michelangelo Buonarroti (1475-1564), Italian sculptor
and painter: "Pieta" (representational)
Edgar Degas (1834-1917), French painter and sculptor:
"Little Fourteen-Year-Old Dancer" (representational)
Auguste Rodin (1840-1917), French sculptor:
"The Thinker" (representational)
Henry Moore (born 1898), English sculptor:
"Family Group" (abstract)
Louise Nevelson (1899-1988), American sculptor:
"Royal Tide II" (abstract)
Isamu Noguchi (born 1904), American sculptor,
"Unidentified Object" (abstract)

WHERE TO LOOK AT ART

There are art museums in many cities in the United States. Some of them are general art museums, where you can see art from many different countries and from many different time periods—sometimes from early Egyptian art to modern art. Many cities also have museums of American art, museums of modern art, and other special collections. For museums that focus on ethnic art, culture, and history, such as African or Asian culture, see the section called MUSEUMS, page 142. A few general art museums are listed below.

Art Institute of Chicago
Baltimore Museum of Art
Boston Museum of Fine Arts
Cleveland Museum of Art
Dallas Museum of Art
Denver Art Museum
Detroit Institute of Arts
Houston Museum of Fine Arts
Los Angeles County Museum of Art
Kansas City Art Institute

Metropolitan Museum of Art
  (New York City)
Minneapolis Institute of Arts
National Gallery of Art
  (Washington, D.C.)
North Carolina Museum of Art (Raleigh, NC)
Philadelphia Museum of Art
San Antonio Museum of Art
San Francisco Museum of Art
Seattle Art Museum

Ten ALL-TIME FAVORITE Books

Anne of Green Gables, by Lucy Maud Montgomery. The adventures of Anne Shirley, an orphaned girl who is adopted by a couple in Prince Edward Island, in Canada.

The Black Stallion, by Walter Farley. A proud Arabian stallion becomes a champion racehorse.

The Chronicles of Narnia, by C.S. Lewis. The four Pevensy children visit a magical world called Narnia.

Island of the Blue Dolphins, by Scott O'Dell. The true story of a 12-year-old Indian girl who learns to survive alone on an island in the Pacific Ocean.

Little House on the Prairie, by Laura Ingalls Wilder. A story about a family homesteading in Wisconsin.

The Pinballs, by Betsy Byers. A friendship develops when three misfits—two boys and a girl—find themselves in the same foster home.

Sarah, Plain and Tall, by Patricia MacLachlan. When Sarah answers their father's call for a mail-order bride, young Anna and Caleb fall in love with her. But what about their father?

The Secret Garden, by Frances Hodgson Burnett. Everyone thinks Mary is just a mean girl and Colin is just a sick boy—until they become best friends.

Tuck Everlasting, by Natalie Babbitt. Living forever isn't all Tuck wishes.

A Wrinkle in Time, by Madeleine L'Engle. With the help of witches, Meg and Charles Wallace Murry travel through time to rescue their father.

BEST BOOKS of 1994

(Recommended by the American Library Association)

Misoso, by Verna Aardema

Coming Home, by Floyd Cooper

Sister Shako and Kolo the Goat, by Vedat Dalokoy, translated by Güner Ener

The Big Bug Book, by Margery Facklam, illustrated by Paul Facklam

Beast Feast, by Douglas Florian

Meet Danitra Brown, by Nikki Grimes, illustrated by Floyd Cooper

Sweet and Sour Animal Book, by Langston Hughes

Russian Girl, by Russ Kendall

The Three Princes, by Eric A. Kimmel, illustrated by Leonard Everett Fisher

Three Terrible Trins, by Dick King-Smith, illustrated by Mark Teague

The Librarian Who Measured the Earth, by Kathryn Lasky, illustrated by Kevin Hawkes

John Henry, by Julius Lester, illustrated by Jerry Pinkney

Seven Spiders Spinning, by Gregory Maguire

Outside and Inside Birds, by Sandra Markle

Hob and the Goblins, by William Mayne, illustrated by Norman Messenger

Coyote, by Gerald McDermott

My Rotten Redheaded Older Brother, by Patricia Polacco

Cleopatra, by Diane Stanley and Peter Vennema

Other BOOKS YOU MAY ENJOY Reading

The books listed on this page and the next one have won awards for excellence. For books that won awards for 1994, see page 178 under PRIZES.

FICTION

Fiction books are stories that come out of the writer's imagination. Some stories are realistic. Others, such as stories about talking animals or mysterious kingdoms, are fantasy.

Abel's Island, by William Steig. A spoiled mouse is swept away in a violent storm while picnicking with his wife and finds himself marooned on an island.

Across Five Aprils, by Irene Hunt. A story of a nine-year-old boy whose brothers are fighting on opposite sides of the Civil War.

Bridge to Terabithia, by Katherine Paterson. In a rural community, two new friends, a boy and a girl, build a secret kingdom of wooden boards and call it Terabithia.

Dear Mr. Henshaw, by Beverly Cleary. A lonely 12-year-old boy writes letters about himself to his favorite author.

Dragonwings, by Lawrence Yep. Set in a Chinese community of San Francisco, this story is about a boy's love for a father who has dreams about flying.

The Friendship, by Mildred Taylor. What happens when, in Mississippi in the 1930s, a black man refuses to call his white friend "Mister."

Maniac Magee, by Jerry Spinelli. An unhappy orphaned boy runs away from home at age eight and tries to survive on his own.

Missing May, by Cynthia Rylant. A 12-year-old girl learns to accept the death of her beloved aunt.

Morning Girl, by Michael Dorris. The story of a brother and sister who grow up on an island.

Mrs. Frisby and the Rats of NIMH, by Robert C. O'Brien. When Mrs. Frisby, the mother of a family of field mice, sees her home threatened by the farmer's plow, she seeks help from some super-bright rats who have escaped from a laboratory.

Number the Stars, by Lois Lowry. In World War II, in Denmark, AnneMarie Johansen bravely hides her Jewish friend Ellen Rosen to keep her from being taken away by the Germans.

Scooter, by Vera B. Williams. Elana Rose Rosen moves to a big apartment building in New York City and discovers an amazingly varied new world.

Shiloh, by Phyllis Reynolds Naylor. When a beagle, who is being mistreated by his owner, follows him home, Marty, a West Virginia boy, wants to keep the dog. His parents help him understand that it isn't an easy decision.

Sign of the Beaver, by Elizabeth Speare. Set in the backwoods of Maine in the 18th century, this is the story of the friendship that develops between a 12-year-old boy and the chief of the Beaver clan.

The Dark-Thirty: Southern Tales of the Supernatural, by Patricia McKissack. Ten hair-raising stories rooted in the history of African Americans.

Toning the Sweep, by Angela Johnson. When Emily, a 14-year-old African American, finds out that her Grandmama Ola is very sick, she begins to videotape the people and places in the California desert that Ola loved.

NONFICTION

Nonfiction books are factual books that provide information about what is real, from aardvarks to zithers. Many are about science or history or are biographies (books that tell the story of a real person, either living or dead). Reference books, like almanacs and encyclopedias, are also nonfiction. Below are some outstanding nonfiction books you might enjoy reading.

The Big Beast Book: Dinosaurs and How They Got That Way, by Jerry Booth. How did scientists find out about these huge beasts who lived so long ago? The story of dinosaurs and their fossil remains.

The Book of Eagles, by Helen Roney Sattler. All about eagles in words and pictures and about the attempts to save them from dying out.

Christopher Columbus: Voyage to the Unknown, by Nancy Smiler Levinson. An account of the explorer's childhood and his voyages to the New World, with excerpts from his letters and diaries.

Good Queen Bess: The Story of Elizabeth I of England, by Diane Stanley and Peter Vennema. This biography describes how the first Queen Elizabeth grew up and tells of the times in which she lived.

Inspirations: Stories About Women Artists, by Leslie Sills. The lives of four very different women artists, Georgia O'Keeffe, Frida Kahlo, Alice Neel, and Faith Ringold, and how they found their inspiration.

Lincoln: A Photobiography, by Russell Freedman. This profile reveals the many sides of President Abraham Lincoln and describes both his successes and his failures.

Maggie by My Side, by Beverly Butler. The author is a blind teacher, and Maggie is the German shepherd who becomes her Seeing Eye dog and her friend.

The Origin of Life on Earth: An African Creation Myth, retold by David Anderson, illustrated by Kathleen Atkins. An African myth about how the world began.

REFERENCE BOOKS: Where the Answers Are

Would you know where to find answers to the following questions? Which is the correct spelling, *receive* or *recieve*? In what part of Africa is Egypt? Which team won the Super Bowl in 1994? How much can the blue whale, the largest animal in the world, weigh? When did North Dakota become a state? Can you figure out which type of reference book below would have the answer? In some cases, the answer can be found in more than one book.

Almanac: A one-volume book of facts and statistics. Almanacs cover sports, the government, countries of the world, the planets, states, prize winners, and many other subjects.

Atlas: A collection of maps. Political maps help us locate towns and cities and roads and show borders between countries or states. Physical maps show features like mountains, rivers, and forests.

Dictionary: A book of words in alphabetical order. A dictionary gives the meanings and spelling of words and shows how they are pronounced.

Encyclopedia: The place to go for information on almost every subject you can think of. Encyclopedias cover the past and the present, the arts and sciences, and the countries of the world, either in one volume or several.

The 7 WONDERS of the Ancient World

These were considered the most remarkable structures of ancient times. Only one of them—the pyramids in Egypt—has survived and can be visited today.

Pyramids of Egypt

At Giza, Egypt, built as royal tombs from 3000 to 1800 B.C. The largest is the **Great Pyramid of Khufu** (or Cheops), a mass of limestone blocks covering 13 acres.

Hanging Gardens of Babylon

Terraced gardens built by King Nebuchadnezzar II around 600 B.C. for his wife.

Temple of Artemis

At Ephesus (now part of Turkey), built mostly of marble around 550 B.C. in honor of the Greek goddess Artemis.

Statue of Zeus

At Olympia, Greece. The statue, made about 462 B.C. by the ancient Greek sculptor Phidias from ivory and gold, showed the king of the gods sitting on a throne.

Mausoleum of Halicarnassus

(Now part of Turkey), built about 353 B.C. in honor of King Mausolus, a ruler of ancient Caria.

Colossus of Rhodes

Overlooking the harbor on the island of Rhodes (Greece), a bronze statue of the sun god Helios, built about 280 B.C. Probably 120 feet high.

Lighthouse of Alexandria, Egypt

Built about 270 B.C. during the reign of King Ptolemy II. It may have been around 500 feet tall.

TALLEST BUILDINGS in the United States

Sears Tower, Chicago, IL (built 1974) ....1,454 feet
World Trade Center, New York, NY (built 1973) ....1,368 feet
Empire State Building, New York, NY (built 1931) ....1,250 feet
Amoco, Chicago, IL (built 1974)................................1,136 feet
John Hancock Center, Chicago, IL (built 1969)...........1,127 feet
Nations Bank Tower, Atlanta, GA (built 1992) ....1,050 feet
Chrysler Building, New York, NY (built 1930) ....1,046 feet

 DID YOU KNOW? The tallest free-standing structure in the world is the CN Tower in Toronto, Canada, built in 1975 as a communications and observation tower. It is 1,821 feet high.

The LONGEST BRIDGES in the World

The **span** of a bridge is the distance between its supports. The three bridges below were the longest bridges in the world when this book was published. But bridges seem to be getting longer and longer. Some bridges now under construction in Denmark, Japan, and Italy will be longer than these when they are completed. (The Store Baelt, or East Bridge, in Denmark is scheduled to be finished in 1995.)

NAME OF BRIDGE	LOCATION	LONGEST SPAN
Humber	England	4,626 feet
Verrazano-Narrows	United States (New York)	4,260 feet
Golden Gate	United States (California)	4,200 feet

DID YOU KNOW? The oldest covered bridge in continuous use in the United States spans the Ammonoosuc River in New Hampshire. The bridge was completed in 1827. It is a wooden bridge, 278 feet long.

The LONGEST TUNNELS in the World

A **tunnel** is a long underground passageway, dug through rock or earth or built underwater. Vehicular tunnels (on land and under water) are for automobiles, trucks, and the like. Railroad tunnels are for trains and subway traffic. Water tunnels are for water mains, drainage, sewage, mining, and storage. These are the longest tunnels of each type:

TYPE OF TUNNEL	NAME	LOCATION	LENGTH
Land Vehicular	St. Gotthard	Switzerland	10.1 miles
Underwater Vehicular	Brooklyn-Battery	New York, USA	1.7 miles
Railroad	Seikan	Japan	33.5 miles
Water	Delaware Aqueduct	New York, USA	85.0 miles

DID YOU KNOW? Have you ever heard of the **Chunnel**? The "Chunnel" is the nickname for the English Channel Tunnel, which links England and France by railway underneath the English Channel. The Chunnel, which opened in 1994, is nearly 31 miles long and took six years to build.

How COMPUTERS are USED

Today's high-powered computers can do things in a few seconds that would take a person working by hand days, or even years, to do. Here are just a few of the many ways people are using computers today:

Computers Help People Learn.

- ☑ Educational games teach subjects like math, spelling, and geography.
- ☑ The computer can keep track of the student's progress.
- ☑ Pilots and astronauts practice their skills with computer flight simulators.

Computers Keep Information Organized.
- ☑ Computers can keep track of information in files called databases. All the names, addresses, and phone numbers in a telephone book are part of a telephone directory database. Police departments can get information about criminals or stolen merchandise from a database managed by the FBI.

Computers Help Make Predictions.
- ☑ Companies use computer programs to predict how the business decisions they make will affect them in the future.
- ☑ Special computer programs use data collected from satellites to help forecast the weather.

Computers Are Used to Manufacture Products.
- ☑ Engineers use Computer-Aided Design (CAD) software to create detailed drawings of an object and then test it to see how to make it stronger or cheaper.
- ☑ Computers can then be used to control machinery used to make parts or to control robots that assemble the parts.

Computers Help People Create.
- ☑ People are using computers to create artwork and music or to design buildings.
- ☑ Special effects in movies and television are created with the use of computers.

Computers Help People Communicate.
- ☑ People who cannot speak can type out messages that the computer can translate into speech.

Computers Aren't Just Found on Desks.
- ☑ Computers are used in automatic teller machines at the bank and with the price scanner at the supermarket checkout.
- ☑ Automobiles, microwave ovens, VCRs, and digital watches all have built-in computers.

COMPUTER TALK

artificial intelligence or AI
The development of computers and robots that are programmed to imitate human intelligence by learning and making decisions.

boot
To **boot** means to turn a computer on.

bug or glitch
An error in a program or in the computer itself.

database
A large collection of information organized electronically in a particular way, so that the information can be easily retrieved and used in a variety of ways. A directory of airlines or the names and addresses of everyone who is eligible to vote are examples of databases.

desktop publishing
The use of computers for combining text and pictures to design and produce magazines and books.

e-mail or electronic mail
Messages sent from one computer to another over a network, such as telephone lines.

hard copy
Computer output printed on paper or similar material.

mainframe
The largest type of computer. A mainframe stores large amounts of information and can be used by many people at the same time.

multimedia
Software that includes pictures, video, and sound, often on CD-ROMs. In multimedia books and encyclopedias, you can see pictures move and hear music and other sounds.

network
A group of computers linked together so that they can share information.

notebook or laptop
A portable personal computer that runs on batteries. It has a built-in keyboard and display screen.

password
A secret code that keeps unwanted people from using a computer or software.

program
A set of instructions for a computer to follow. Programs are written in languages called programming languages.

PC
Short for personal computer. PC is another name for a microcomputer, which is a small computer often used in homes, schools, offices, and small businesses.

RAM
One of the kinds of memory inside a computer, RAM is short for Random Access Memory. The person using a computer can use and change the programs and other information in RAM. The information in RAM disappears when the computer is turned off.

ROM
One of the kinds of memory inside a computer, ROM is short for Read Only Memory. ROM contains permanent instructions for the computer and cannot be changed. The information in ROM stays in the computer after it is turned off.

scanner
A device that can read words and pictures from a printed page into the computer without using a mouse or the keyboard. A scanner converts words and pictures into codes that the computer can use.

spreadsheet
Software used for doing many calculations quickly. Spreadsheet programs are used in accounting and bookkeeping.

user-friendly
Easy for the person using the computer to figure out without a lot of reading.

virtual reality
Three-dimensional images on a screen that are viewed using special equipment (like gloves and goggles). With virtual reality, the user feels as if he or she is part of the image and can interact with everything around.

virus
A program that causes damage to other computer programs and data. A virus gets into a computer through shared disks or telephone lines without the user's knowledge.

HOW COMPUTERS WORK

For a computer to work, three things are necessary:
1. **hardware**, the pieces of equipment that make up the computer;
2. **software** or **programs**, the instructions that tell the computer how to perform its tasks; and
3. **you**, the **user,** the person who tells the computer what tasks it should perform.

First, you enter **data,** or **information,** into the computer. This is called **input**. The computer then **processes** the data to perform the required task. When it is finished, the computer gives you the results. The results are called **output**. A computer also **stores** your work for you, so you can use it again or make changes in it at another time. If you want to write a story, here's how the computer can help.

INPUT:
Selecting the Right Software.
To write a story (or letter or school report) you need to use a type of software called a word-processing program. This can be selected by using the **keyboard** or a **mouse**.

Entering Data.
Once you are in the right program, you can begin to input the story by typing on the **keyboard**. The backspace and delete keys are like electronic erasers. In addition to letters and numbers, the keyboard has special keys (called **function keys**) for centering or underlining words, moving sentences around, checking spelling, printing out a page, and doing other tasks. When you hit one of these keys, the word-processing program tells the computer what to do.

PROCESSING:
Inside the Computer.
The instructions from the word-processing program are carried out inside the computer by the **central processing unit,** or **CPU.** The CPU is the computer's brain.

STORAGE:
Keeping Data To Use It Later.
A computer also stores information that you want to use later. Suppose you want to stop working on your story and eat lunch. You can save the work you've done so far and then go back to it later.

Floppy Disk.
Information can be saved on a small plastic **"floppy" disk** (many of these are not floppy anymore). The floppy disk goes into a slot in the computer called the **floppy drive**. If you use a floppy disk for your story, it can be moved and used on other computers.

Hard Disk.
Inside most computers is a **hard drive.** The hard drive contains a **hard disk** made of metal that cannot be removed. This disk holds much more information than a floppy disk and works faster. The hard disk stores the programs you need and also stores the information you want to save.

OUTPUT:
Getting the Results.

The **monitor** and **printer** are the most commonly used output devices. As you type your story, the words appear on a **monitor,** which is similar to a television screen. Your story can then be printed on paper by using a **printer.**

COMMUNICATIONS:
Computers Talk to Each Other.

When you finish writing your story, if you want to send it to a friend you can print it out and mail it. But if your computer has a **modem** and your friend's does too, the story can be sent from your computer directly to your friend's computer. A **modem** allows information from a computer to travel over telephone lines. With a modem, your friend can send you back a note, telling you how he or she liked the story.

SOFTWARE:
There Are Many Kinds.

Besides word-processing programs, there are many other types of software that people can use in their computers at home, in school, or at work. Some common types of software are programs for doing mathematics, keeping records, playing games, and creating pictures.

CD-ROMS

Many newer computers have a third type of drive (besides the floppy drive and the hard drive), called a CD-ROM drive. This allows you to play special disks called **CD-ROMs,** which are similar to music CDs. A CD-ROM can hold a huge amount of information, including pictures and sound. Almanacs, games, encyclopedias, dictionaries, and many other types of information and entertainment are on CD-ROMs.

A COMPUTER SYSTEM

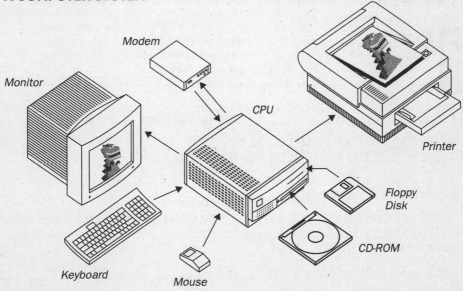

Monitor

Modem

CPU

Printer

Floppy Disk

CD-ROM

Keyboard

Mouse

The BINARY SYSTEM

A computer can do many impressive things, but one thing it cannot do is understand English. For a computer to do its work, every piece of information given to it must be translated into binary code. You are probably used to using ten digits, 0 through 9, when you do arithmetic. When the computer uses the **binary code**, it uses only two digits, 0 and 1. Think of it as sending messages to the computer by switching a light on and off.

Each 0 or 1 digit is called a **bit,** and most computers use a sequence of 8 bits (called a **byte**) to represent individual pieces of data. Almost all computers use the same code, called ASCII (pronounced "askey"), to represent letters of the alphabet, number digits, punctuation, and other special characters that control the computer's operation. Below is a list of ASCII bytes for the alphabet.

A	01000001	**J**	01001010	**S**	01010011
B	01000010	**K**	01001011	**T**	01010100
C	01000011	**L**	01001100	**U**	01010101
D	01000100	**M**	01001101	**V**	01010110
E	01000101	**N**	01001110	**W**	01010111
F	01000110	**O**	01001111	**X**	01011000
G	01000111	**P**	01010000	**Y**	01011001
H	01001000	**Q**	01010001	**Z**	01011010
I	01001001	**R**	01010010		

BINARY PUZZLE **L**ook at the clues below and try to get the answers by translating the binary code sequences. Be careful not to lose your place! (Clue: Start by putting a mark after every 8 numbers. Answers are on page 302.)

1. A __ __ __   __ __ __ __ can really make your computer "itch"!

0100001001010101010001111
010000100101100101010100010001000101

2. A cool rodent's house is a __ __ __ __ __   __ __ __.

0100110101001111010101010100110101000101
010100000100000101000100

3. Los Angeles to Honolulu is a very __ __ __ __   __ __ __ __ __!

0100100001000001010100100100100
01000100010100100100100101010110010001000101

Computing Gets FASTER and *FASTER*

1000 B.C.: In ancient times people did computing with a device called an **abacus,** which is made up of rods and beads. A modern version of the abacus is still used today in Japan. A person who is skilled with an abacus can add more than 15 numbers in one minute.

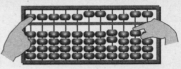

1946: The first electronic computer was introduced in 1946. Called ENIAC (short for Electronic Numerical Integrator and Computer), the computer could multiply around 3,000 numbers in one second.

1995: Today's high-powered computers can do in a few seconds calculations that would take a person working by hand days, or even years, to do. A modern personal computer can perform more than 10,000,000 mathematical operations in one second.

THE INTERNET

Did you know that computers all over the world can communicate with one another? Well, they can through the Internet, the world's largest computer network. The Internet connects government institutions, colleges, scientific laboratories, corporations, and individuals. Computers connected to the network can send and receive e-mail, copy software, participate in discussion groups on hundreds of different topics, and get access to all kinds of information, like news, sports, and stock market reports.

COMPUTER MUSEUMS

Some museums have sections where you can learn about computers and use them to do many fascinating things. A few museums are devoted entirely to the computer. Here are three:

THE COMPUTER MUSEUM, INC.	AMERICAN COMPUTER MUSEUM	TECH MUSEUM OF INNOVATION
300 Congress Street	234 East Babcock Street	145 West San Carlos Street
Boston, MA 02210	Bozeman, MT 59715	San Jose, CA 95113
Phone: (617) 426-2800	Phone: (406) 587-7545	Phone: (408) 279-7150

BEST-SELLING CD-ROMS

The following CD-ROMs were listed (by the organization PC Data) as the 10 best-sellers for 1994. The name of the manufacturer is shown in parentheses after the title.

1 Myst (Brøderbund)
2 Doom II (GT Interactive)
3 5Ft. 10 Pack (Sirius)
4 Star Wars Rebel Assault (LucasArts)
5 7th Guest (Virgin)
6 Microsoft Encarta (Microsoft)
7 The Lion King (Disney)
8 Print Shop Deluxe CD Ensemble (Brøderbund)
9 Quicken CD Rom Deluxe (Intuit)
10 Corel Gallery (Corel)

COUNTRIES of the World

There are 192 countries in the world. The information for each country goes across two pages. The left-hand page gives the **name** and **capital** of each country, where the country is **located**, and its **area** in both square miles (sq. mi.) and square kilometers (sq. km.). On the right-hand page, the **population** column tells approximately how many people lived in each country (as of 1994). The **currency** column tells you what the money is called and approximately how much it was worth in United States dollars or cents as of March 1, 1995 (if the information was available). If a country belongs to the **United Nations,** the column called "Joined UN" gives the date the country became a member of the UN.

COUNTRY	CAPITAL	LOCATION OF COUNTRY	AREA
Afghanistan	Kabul	Southern Asia, between Iran and Pakistan	251,825 sq. mi. (652,224 sq. km.)
Albania	Tiranë	Eastern Europe, north of Greece	11,100 sq. mi. (28,749 sq. km.)
Algeria	Algiers	North Africa on the Mediterranean Sea, between Libya and Morocco	919,595 sq. mi. (2,381,740 sq. km.)
Andorra	Andorra la Vella	Europe, in the mountains between France and Spain	181 sq. mi. (469 sq. km.)
Angola	Luanda	Southern Africa on the Atlantic Ocean, south of Zaire	481,354 sq. mi. (1,246,701 sq. km.)
Antigua and Barbuda	St. John's	Islands on eastern edge of the Caribbean Sea	171 sq. mi. (443 sq. km.)
Argentina	Buenos Aires	Fills up most of the southern part of South America	1,073,518 sq. mi. (2,780,399 sq. km.)
Armenia	Yerevan	Eastern Europe, north of Turkey and Iran	11,500 sq. mi. (29,784 sq. km.)
Australia	Canberra	Island south of Asia, between Indian and Pacific Oceans	2,966,200 sq. mi. (7,682,423 sq. km.)
Austria	Vienna	Central Europe, north of Italy	32,378 sq. mi. (83,859 sq. km.)
Azerbaijan	Baku	Eastern Europe, north of Iran	33,400 sq. mi. (86,506 sq. km.)

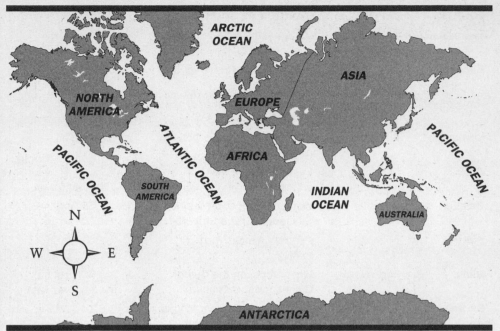

POPULATION	CURRENCY	JOINED UN	COUNTRY
16,903,000	Afghani 1 afghani = 2 cents	1946	**Afghanistan**
3,374,000	Lek 1 lek = ⁹⁄₁₀ of a cent	1955	**Albania**
27,895,000	Dinar 1 dinar = 4 cents	1962	**Algeria**
64,000	French franc or Spanish peseta	1993	**Andorra**
9,804,000	Kwanza 1 kwanza = ⅕ of a cent	1976	**Angola**
65,000	East Caribbean dollar 1 EC dollar = 37 cents	1981	**Antigua and Barbuda**
33,913,000	Peso 1 peso = 99 cents	1945	**Argentina**
3,522,000	Dram	1992	**Armenia**
18,077,000	Australian dollar 1 Australian dollar = 74 cents	1945	**Australia**
7,955,000	Schilling 1 schilling = 9 cents	1955	**Austria**
7,684,000	Manat	1992	**Azerbaijan**

COUNTRY	CAPITAL	LOCATION OF COUNTRY	AREA
The Bahamas	Nassau	Islands in the Atlantic Ocean, east of Florida	5,382 sq. mi. (13,939 sq. km.)
Bahrain	Manama	In the Persian Gulf, near the coast of Qatar	268 sq. mi. (694 sq. km.)
Bangladesh	Dhaka	Southern Asia, nearly surrounded by India	57,295 sq. mi. (148,393 sq. km.)
Barbados	Bridgetown	Island in the Atlantic Ocean, north of Trinidad	166 sq. mi. (430 sq. km.)
Belarus	Minsk	Eastern Europe, east of Poland	80,134 sq. mi. (207,546 sq. km.)
Belgium	Brussels	Western Europe, on the North Sea, south of the Netherlands	11,787 sq. mi. (30,528 sq. km.)
Belize	Belmopan	Central America, next to Mexico	8,867 sq. mi. (22,965 sq. km.)
Benin	Porto-Novo	West Africa, on the Gulf of Guinea, west of Nigeria	43,500 sq. mi. (112,665 sq. km.)
Bhutan	Thimphu	Asia, in the Himalaya Mountains, between China and India	18,147 sq. mi. (47,001 sq. km.)
Bolivia	La Paz	South America, in the Andes Mountains, next to Brazil	424,164 sq. mi. (1,098,580 sq. km.)
Bosnia and Herzegovina	Sarajevo	Southern Europe, on the Balkan Peninsula, west of Yugoslavia	19,741 sq. mi. (51,129 sq. km.)
Botswana	Gaborone	Southern Africa, between South Africa and Zambia	224,607 sq. mi. (581,730 sq. km.)
Brazil	Brasília	Occupies most of the eastern part of South America	3,286,470 sq. mi. (8,511,918 sq. km.)
Brunei	Bandar Seri Begawan	On the island of Borneo, northwest of Australia in the Pacific Ocean	2,226 sq. mi. (5,765 sq. km.)
Bulgaria	Sofia	Eastern Europe, on the Balkan Peninsula, bordering the Black Sea	42,855 sq. mi. (110,994 sq. km.)
Burkina Faso	Ouagadougou	West Africa, between Mali and Ghana	105,946 sq. mi. (274,399 sq. km.)
Burundi	Bujumbura	Central Africa, between Tanzania and Zaire	10,740 sq. mi. (27,816 sq. km.)
Cambodia	Phnom Penh	Southeast Asia, between Vietnam and Thailand	70,238 sq. mi. (181,916 sq. km.)
Cameroon	Yaoundé	Central Africa, between Nigeria and Congo	183,569 sq. mi. (475,442 sq. km.)
Canada	Ottawa	Occupies the northern part of North America, north of the United States	3,849,674 sq. mi. (9,970,610 sq. km.)
Cape Verde	Praia	Islands off the western tip of Africa	1,557 sq. mi. (4,033 sq. km.)

POPULATION	CURRENCY	JOINED UN	COUNTRY
273,000	Bahamas dollar Same value as U.S. dollar	1973	**The Bahamas**
586,000	Dinar 1 dinar = $2.65	1971	**Bahrain**
125,149,000	Taka 1 taka = 2½ cents	1974	**Bangladesh**
256,000	Barbados dollar 1 Barbados dollar = 50 cents	1966	**Barbados**
10,405,000	Belarus ruble	1945	**Belarus**
10,063,000	Franc 1 franc = 3 cents	1945	**Belgium**
209,000	Belize dollar 1 Belize dollar = 50 cents	1981	**Belize**
5,342,000	CFA franc 1 CFA franc = ⅕ of a cent	1960	**Benin**
1,739,000	Ngultrum 1 ngultrum = 3 cents	1971	**Bhutan**
7,719,000	Boliviano 1 Boliviano = 22 cents	1945	**Bolivia**
4,651,000	New Yugoslav dinar 1 dinar = 65 cents	1992	**Bosnia and Herzegovina**
1,359,000	Pula 1 pula = 38 cents	1966	**Botswana**
158,739,000	Cruzeiro real 1 cruzeiro real = $1.18	1945	**Brazil**
285,000	Brunei dollar 1 Brunei dollar = 61 cents	1984	**Brunei**
8,800,000	Lev 1 lev = 4 cents	1955	**Bulgaria**
10,135,000	Franc 1 franc = ⅕ of a cent	1960	**Burkina Faso**
6,125,000	CFA Franc 1 CFA franc = ⅜ of a cent	1962	**Burundi**
10,265,000	Riel 1 riel = 1/15 of a cent	1955	**Cambodia**
13,132,000	CFA franc 1 CFA franc = ⅕ of a cent	1960	**Cameroon**
28,114,000	Canadian dollar 1 Canadian dollar = 72 cents	1945	**Canada**
423,000	Escudo 1 escudo = 1 cent	1975	**Cape Verde**

COUNTRY	CAPITAL	LOCATION OF COUNTRY	AREA
Central African Republic	Bangui	Central Africa, north of Zaire	240,324 sq. mi. (622,436 sq. km.)
Chad	N'Djamena	North Africa, south of Libya	495,755 sq. mi. (1,284,000 sq. km.)
Chile	Santiago	Along the western coast of South America	292,135 sq. mi. (756,626 sq. km.)
China	Beijing	Occupies most of the mainland of eastern Asia	3,696,100 sq. mi. (9,572,855 sq. km.)
Colombia	Bogotá	Northwestern South America, southeast of Panama	440,831 sq. mi. (1,141,747 sq. km.)
Comoros	Moroni	Islands between Madagascar and the east coast of Africa	719 sq. mi. (1,862 sq. km.)
Congo	Brazzaville	Central Africa, west of Zaire	132,047 sq. mi. (342,000 sq. km.)
Costa Rica	San José	Central America, south of Nicaragua	19,730 sq. mi (51,100 sq. km.)
Côte d'Ivoire (Ivory Coast)	Abidjan	West Africa, on the Gulf of Guinea, west of Ghana	124,504 sq. mi. (322,464 sq. km.)
Croatia	Zagreb	Southern Europe, south of Hungary	21,829 sq. mi. (56,537 sq. km.)
Cuba	Havana	In the Caribbean Sea, south of Florida	42,804 sq. mi. (110,862 sq. km.)
Cyprus	Nicosia	Island in the Mediterranean Sea, off the coast of Turkey	3,572 sq. mi. (9,251 sq. km.)
Czech Republic	Prague	Central Europe, south of Poland, east of Germany	30,449 sq. mi. (78,863 sq. km.)
Denmark	Copenhagen	Northern Europe, between the Baltic Sea and North Sea	16,639 sq. mi. (43,095 sq. km.)
Djibouti	Djibouti	North Africa, on the Gulf of Aden, across from Saudi Arabia	8,950 sq. mi. (23,180 sq. km.)
Dominica	Roseau	Island in the Caribbean Sea	290 sq. mi. (751 sq. km.)
Dominican Republic	Santo Domingo	On an island, along with Haiti, in the Caribbean Sea	18,704 sq. mi. (48,443 sq. km.)
Ecuador	Quito	South America, on the equator, bordering the Pacific Ocean	105,037 sq. mi. (272,045 sq. km.)
Egypt	Cairo	Northeastern Africa, on the Red Sea and Mediterranean Sea	385,229 sq. mi. (997,739 sq. km.)
El Salvador	San Salvador	Central America, southwest of Honduras	8,124 sq. mi. (21,041 sq. km.)
Equatorial Guinea	Malabo	West Africa, on the Gulf of Guinea, off the west coast of Cameroon	10,831 sq. mi. (28,052 sq. km.)

POPULATION	CURRENCY	JOINED UN	COUNTRY
3,142,000	CFA franc 1 CFA franc = ⅕ of a cent	1960	**Central African Republic**
5,467,000	CFA franc 1 CFA franc = ⅕ of a cent	1960	**Chad**
13,951,000	Peso 1 peso = ¼ of a cent	1945	**Chile**
1,190,431,000	Yuan 1 yuan = 12 cents	1945	**China**
35,578,000	Peso 1 peso = ⅛ of a cent	1945	**Colombia**
530,000	CFA franc 1 franc = ¼ of a cent	1975	**Comoros**
2,447,000	CFA franc 1 CFA franc = ⅕ of a cent	1960	**Congo**
3,342,000	Colon 1 colon = ⅔ of a cent	1945	**Costa Rica**
14,296,000	CFA franc 1 CFA franc = ⅕ of a cent	1960	**Côte d'Ivoire (Ivory Coast)**
4,698,000	Croatian dinar 1 dinar = ¼ of a cent	1992	**Croatia**
11,064,000	Peso 1 peso = $1	1945	**Cuba**
730,000	Pound 1 pound = $1.96	1960	**Cyprus**
10,408,000	Koruna 1 koruna = 3½ cents	1993	**Czech Republic**
5,188,000	Krone 1 krone = 17 cents	1945	**Denmark**
413,000	Franc 1 franc = ⅗ of a cent	1977	**Djibouti**
88,000	East Caribbean dollar 1 EC dollar = 37 cents	1978	**Dominica**
7,826,000	Peso 1 peso = 8 cents	1945	**Dominican Republic**
10,677,000	Sucre 1 sucre = 1/24 of a cent	1945	**Ecuador**
59,325,000	Pound 1 pound = 30 cents	1945	**Egypt**
5,753,000	Colon 1 colon = 11 cents	1945	**El Salvador**
410,000	CFA franc 1 CFA franc = ⅕ of a cent	1968	**Equatorial Guinea**

COUNTRY	CAPITAL	LOCATION OF COUNTRY	AREA
Eritrea	Asmera	Northeast Africa, north of Ethiopia	45,300 sq. mi. (117,327 sq. km.)
Estonia	Tallinn	Northern Europe, on the Baltic Sea, north of Latvia	17,413 sq. mi. (45,099 sq. km.)
Ethiopia	Addis Ababa	East Africa, east of Sudan	437,794 sq. mi. (1,133,881 sq. km.)
Fiji	Suva	Islands in the South Pacific Ocean, east of Australia	7,056 sq. mi. (18,275 sq. km.)
Finland	Helsinki	Northern Europe, between Sweden and Russia	130,559 sq. mi. (338,146 sq. km.)
France	Paris	Western Europe, extending from the Atlantic Ocean to the Mediterranean Sea	210,026 sq. mi. (543,965 sq. km.)
Gabon	Libreville	Central Africa, on the Atlantic coast, west of the Congo	103,347 sq. mi. (267,668 sq. km.)
The Gambia	Banjul	West Africa, on the Atlantic Ocean, surrounded by Senegal	4,127 sq. mi. (10,689 sq. km.)
Georgia	Tbilisi	Eastern Europe, south of Russia, on the Black Sea	26,900 sq. mi. (69,671 sq. km.)
Germany	Berlin	Central Europe, northeast of France	137,735 sq. mi. (356,732 sq. km.)
Ghana	Accra	West Africa, on the southern coast	92,098 sq. mi. (238,533 sq. km.)
Great Britain (United Kingdom)	London	Off the northwest coast of Europe	94,251 sq. mi. (244,109 sq. km.)
Greece	Athens	Southern Europe, in the southern part of the Balkan Peninsula	50,949 sq. mi. (131,957 sq. km.)
Grenada	St. George's	Island on the eastern edge of the Caribbean Sea	133 sq. mi. (344 sq. km.)
Guatemala	Guatemala City	Central America, southeast of Mexico	42,042 sq. mi. (108,888 sq. km.)
Guinea	Conakry	West Africa, on the Atlantic Ocean, north of Sierra Leone	94,926 sq. mi. (245,857 sq. km.)
Guinea-Bissau	Bissau	West Africa, on the Atlantic Ocean, south of Senegal	13,948 sq. mi. (36,125 sq. km.)
Guyana	Georgetown	South America, on the northern coast, east of Venezuela	83,044 sq. mi. (215,083 sq. km.)
Haiti	Port-au-Prince	On an island, along with Dominican Republic, in the Caribbean Sea	10,695 sq. mi. (27,700 sq. km.)
Honduras	Tegucigalpa	Central America, between Guatemala and Nicaragua	43,277 sq. mi. (112,087 sq. km.)

POPULATION	CURRENCY	JOINED UN	COUNTRY
3,200,000	Birr 1 birr = 20 cents	1993	**Eritrea**
1,617,000	Kroon 1 kroon = 9 cents	1991	**Estonia**
58,710,000	Birr 1 birr = 20 cents	1945	**Ethiopia**
764,000	Fiji dollar 1 Fiji dollar = 67 cents	1970	**Fiji**
5,069,000	Markka 1 markka = 22 cents	1955	**Finland**
57,840,000	Franc 1 franc = 19 cents	1945	**France**
1,139,000	CFA franc 1 CFA franc = $\frac{1}{5}$ of a cent	1960	**Gabon**
959,000	Dalasi 1 dalasi = 11 cents	1965	**The Gambia**
5,681,000	Ruble	1992	**Georgia**
81,088,000	Mark 1 mark = 68 cents	1973	**Germany**
17,225,000	Cedi 1 cedi = $\frac{1}{2}$ of a cent	1957	**Ghana**
58,135,000	Pound 1 pound = $1.49	1945	**Great Britain** (United Kingdom)
10,565,000	Drachma 1 drachma = $\frac{2}{5}$ of a cent	1945	**Greece**
94,000	East Caribbean dollar 1 EC dollar = 37 cents	1974	**Grenada**
10,721,000	Quetzal 1 quetzal = 17 cents	1945	**Guatemala**
6,392,000	Franc 1 franc = $\frac{1}{8}$ of a cent	1958	**Guinea**
1,098,000	Peso 1 peso = $\frac{1}{120}$ of a cent	1974	**Guinea-Bissau**
729,000	Guyana dollar 1 Guyana dollar = $\frac{3}{4}$ of a cent	1966	**Guyana**
6,491,000	Gourde 1 gourde = 20 cents	1945	**Haiti**
5,315,000	Lempira 1 lempira = 14 cents	1945	**Honduras**

COUNTRY	CAPITAL	LOCATION OF COUNTRY	AREA
Hungary	Budapest	Central Europe, north of Yugoslavia	35,919 sq. mi. (93,030 sq. km.)
Iceland	Reykjavik	Island off the coast of Europe, in the North Atlantic Ocean, near Greenland	36,699 sq. mi. (95,050 sq. km.)
India	New Delhi	Southern Asia, on a large peninsula on the Indian Ocean	1,222,559 sq. mi. (3,166,413 sq. km.)
Indonesia	Jakarta	Islands south of Southeast Asia, along the equator	741,052 sq. mi. (1,919,316 sq. km.)
Iran	Tehran	Southern Asia, between Iraq and Pakistan	632,457 sq. mi. (1,638,056 sq. km.)
Iraq	Baghdad	In the Middle East, between Syria and Iran	167,975 sq. mi. (435,053 sq. km.)
Ireland	Dublin	Off the coast of Europe, in the Atlantic Ocean, west of Great Britain	27,137 sq. mi. (70,285 sq. km.)
Israel	Jerusalem	In the Middle East, between Jordan and the Mediterranean Sea	7,992 sq. mi. (20,699 sq. km.)
Italy	Rome	Southern Europe, jutting out into the Mediterranean Sea	116,333 sq. mi. (301,301 sq. km.)
Jamaica	Kingston	Island in the Caribbean Sea, south of Cuba	4,244 sq. mi. (10,992 sq. km.)
Japan	Tokyo	Four big islands and many small ones, off the east coast of Asia	145,850 sq. mi. (377,750 sq. km.)
Jordan	Amman	In the Middle East, south of Syria, east of Israel	34,342 sq. mi. (88,945 sq. km.)
Kazakhstan	Almaty (Alma-Ata)	Central Asia, south of Russia	1,049,200 sq. mi. (2,717,416 sq. km.)
Kenya	Nairobi	East Africa, on the Indian Ocean, south of Ethiopia	224,961 sq. mi. (582,646 sq. km.)
Kiribati	Tarawa	Islands in the middle of the Pacific Ocean, near the equator	313 sq. mi. (811 sq. km.)
Korea, North	Pyongyang	Eastern Asia, in the northern part of the Korean Peninsula; China is to the north	47,399 sq. mi. (122,763 sq. km.)
Korea, South	Seoul	Eastern Asia, south of North Korea, on the Korean Peninsula	38,330 sq. mi. (99,274 sq. km.)
Kuwait	Kuwait City	In the Middle East, on the northern end of the Persian Gulf	6,880 sq. mi. (17,819 sq. km.)
Kyrgyzstan	Bishkek	Western Asia, between Kazakhstan and Tajikistan	76,642 sq. mi. (198,502 sq. km.)
Laos	Vientiane	Southeast Asia, between Vietnam and Thailand	91,429 sq. mi. (236,800 sq. km.)

POPULATION	CURRENCY	JOINED UN	COUNTRY
10,319,000	Forint 1 forint = 1 cent	1955	**Hungary**
264,000	Krona 1 krona = 1 cent	1946	**Iceland**
919,903,000	Rupee 1 rupee = 3 cents	1945	**India**
200,410,000	Rupiah 1 rupiah = $\frac{1}{22}$ of a cent	1950	**Indonesia**
65,612,000	Rial 1 rial = $\frac{1}{17}$ of cent	1945	**Iran**
19,890,000	Dinar 1 dinar = $3.20	1945	**Iraq**
3,539,000	Punt 1 punt = $1.58	1955	**Ireland**
5,051,000	New shekel 1 new shekel = 33 cents	1949	**Israel**
58,138,000	Lira 1 lira = $\frac{1}{17}$ of a cent	1955	**Italy**
2,555,000	Jamaican dollar 1 Jamaican dollar = 3 cents	1962	**Jamaica**
125,107,000	Yen 1 yen = 1 cent	1956	**Japan**
3,961,000	Dinar 1 dinar = $1.44	1955	**Jordan**
17,268,000	Ruble	1992	**Kazakhstan**
28,241,000	Shilling 1 shilling = 1½ cents	1963	**Kenya**
78,000	Australian dollar 1 Australian dollar = 74 cents	not in UN	**Kiribati**
23,067,000	Won 1 won = 47 cents	1991	**Korea, North**
45,083,000	Won 1 won = $\frac{1}{8}$ of a cent	1991	**Korea, South**
1,819,000	Dinar 1 dinar = $3.36	1963	**Kuwait**
4,698,000	Som 1 som = 24 cents	1992	**Kyrgyzstan**
4,702,000	New kip 1 new kip = $\frac{1}{7}$ of a cent	1955	**Laos**

COUNTRY	CAPITAL	LOCATION OF COUNTRY	AREA
Latvia	Riga	On the Baltic Sea, between Lithuania and Estonia	24,900 sq. mi. (64,491 sq. km.)
Lebanon	Beirut	In the Middle East, between the Mediterranean Sea and Syria	3,950 sq. mi. (10,230 sq. km.)
Lesotho	Maseru	Southern Africa, surrounded by the nation of South Africa	11,716 sq. mi. (30,344 sq. km.)
Liberia	Monrovia	Western Africa, on the Atlantic Ocean, southeast of Sierra Leone	38,250 sq. mi. (99,067 sq. km.)
Libya	Tripoli	North Africa, on the Mediterranean Sea, to the west of Egypt	679,359 sq. mi. (1,759,532 sq. km.)
Liechtenstein	Vaduz	Southern Europe, in the Alps between Austria and Switzerland	62 sq. mi. (161 sq. km.)
Lithuania	Vilnius	Northern Europe, on the Baltic Sea, north of Poland	25,213 sq. mi. (65,301 sq. km.)
Luxembourg	Luxembourg	Western Europe, between France and Germany	999 sq. mi. (2,587 sq. km.)
Macedonia	Skopje	Southern Europe, north of Greece	9,928 sq. mi. (25,713 sq. km.)
Madagascar	Antananarivo	Island in the Indian Ocean, off the east coast of Africa	226,658 sq. mi. (587,042 sq. km.)
Malawi	Lilongwe	Southern Africa, south of Tanzania and Zaire	45,747 sq. mi. (118,484 sq. km.)
Malaysia	Kuala Lumpur	Southeast Asia, on the island of Borneo	127,584 sq. mi. (330,441 sq. km.)
Maldives	Male	Islands in the Indian Ocean, south of India	115 sq. mi. (298 sq. km.)
Mali	Bamako	West Africa, between Algeria and Mauritania	482,077 sq. mi. (1,248,574 sq. km.)
Malta	Valletta	Island in the Mediterranean Sea, south of Italy	122 sq. mi. (316 sq. km.)
Marshall Islands	Majuro	Chain of small islands in the middle of the Pacific Ocean	70 sq. mi. (181 sq. km.)
Mauritania	Nouakchott	West Africa, on the Atlantic Ocean, north of Senegal	398,000 sq. mi. (1,030,815 sq. km.)
Mauritius	Port Louis	Islands in the Indian Ocean, east of Madagascar	788 sq. mi. (2,041 sq. km.)
Mexico	Mexico City	North America, south of the United States	756,066 sq. mi. (1,958,202 sq. km.)
Micronesia	Palikir	Islands in the Western Pacific Ocean	271 sq. mi. (702 sq. km.)
Moldova	Chisinau	Eastern Europe, between Ukraine and Romania	13,012 sq. mi. (33,701 sq. km.)

POPULATION	CURRENCY	JOINED UN	COUNTRY
2,749,000	Lat	1991	**Latvia**
3,620,000	Pound 1 pound = 1/16 of a cent	1945	**Lebanon**
1,944,000	Maloti 1 maloti = 28 cents	1966	**Lesotho**
2,973,000	Liberian dollar Same as U.S. dollar	1945	**Liberia**
5,057,000	Dinar 1 dinar = $3.16	1955	**Libya**
30,000	Swiss franc 1 Swiss franc = 81 cents	1990	**Liechtenstein**
3,848,000	Litas 1 litas = 25 cents	1991	**Lithuania**
402,000	Franc 1 franc = 3 cents	1945	**Luxembourg**
2,214,000	Denar Value not available	1993	**Macedonia**
13,428,000	Franc 1 franc = 1/20 of a cent	1960	**Madagascar**
9,732,000	Kwacha 1 kwacha = 22 cents	1964	**Malawi**
19,283,000	Ringgit 1 ringgit = 39 cents	1957	**Malaysia**
252,000	Rufiyaa 1 rufiyaa = 9 cents	1965	**Maldives**
9,113,000	Franc 1 franc = 1/5 of a cent	1960	**Mali**
367,000	Maltese lira 1 Maltese lira = $2.79	1964	**Malta**
54,000	U.S. dollar	1991	**Marshall Islands**
2,193,000	Ouguiya 1 ouguiya = 1/5 of a cent	1961	**Mauritania**
1,117,000	Mauritian rupee 1 Mauritian rupee = 5 cents	1968	**Mauritius**
92,202,000	New peso 1 new peso = 17 cents	1945	**Mexico**
120,000	U.S. dollar	1991	**Micronesia**
4,473,000	Ruble	1992	**Moldova**

COUNTRY	CAPITAL	LOCATION OF COUNTRY	AREA
Monaco	Monaco	Europe, on the Mediterranean Sea, surrounded by France	3/4 of a sq. mi. (1.9 sq. km.)
Mongolia	Ulaanbaatar	Central Asia between Russia and China	604,800 sq. mi. (1,566,425 sq. km.)
Morocco	Rabat	Northwest Africa, on the Atlantic Ocean and Mediterranean Sea	177,117 sq. mi. (458,731 sq. km.)
Mozambique	Maputo	Southeastern Africa, on the Indian Ocean	313,661 sq. mi. (812,378 sq. km.)
Myanmar (Burma)	Yangôn	Southern Asia, to the east of India and Bangladesh	261,228 sq. mi. (676,577 sq. km.)
Namibia	Windhoek	Southwestern Africa, on the Atlantic Ocean, west of Botswana	318,146 sq. mi. (823,994 sq. km.)
Nauru	Yaren	Island in the western Pacific Ocean, just below the equator	8 sq. mi. (21 sq. km.)
Nepal	Kathmandu	Asia, in the Himalaya Mountains, between China and India	56,827 sq. mi. (147,181 sq. km.)
The Netherlands	Amsterdam	Northern Europe, on the North Sea, to the west of Germany	16,033 sq. mi. (41,525 sq. km.)
New Zealand	Wellington	Islands in the Pacific Ocean east of Australia	104,454 sq. mi. (270,535 sq. km.)
Nicaragua	Managua	Central America, between Honduras and Costa Rica	50,880 sq. mi. (131,779 sq. km.)
Niger	Niamey	North Africa, south of Algeria and Libya	497,000 sq. mi. (1,287,224 sq. km.)
Nigeria	Abuja	West Africa, on the southern coast between Benin and Cameroon	356,669 sq. mi. (923,769 sq. km.)
Norway	Oslo	Northern Europe, on the Scandinavian Peninsula, west of Sweden	125,050 sq. mi. (323,878 sq. km.)
Oman	Muscat	On the Arabian Peninsula, southeast of Saudi Arabia	118,150 sq. mi. (306,007 sq. km.)
Pakistan	Islamabad	South Asia, between Iran and India	339,697 sq. mi. (879,811 sq. km.)
Palau	Koror	Islands in North Pacific Ocean, southeast of Philippines	179 sq. mi. (464 sq. km.)
Panama	Panama City	Central America, between Costa Rica and Colombia	29,157 sq. mi. (75,516 sq. km.)
Papua New Guinea	Port Moresby	Part of the island of New Guinea, north of Australia	178,704 sq. mi. (462,841 sq. km.)
Paraguay	Asunción	South America, between Argentina and Brazil	157,048 sq. mi. (406,753 sq. km.)

POPULATION	CURRENCY	JOINED UN	COUNTRY
31,000	French franc 1 franc = 19 cents	1993	**Monaco**
2,430,000	Tughrik 1 tughrik = $\frac{5}{6}$ of a cent	1961	**Mongolia**
28,559,000	Dirham 1 dirham = 11 cents	1956	**Morocco**
17,346,000	Metical 1 metical = $\frac{1}{54}$ of a cent	1975	**Mozambique**
44,277,000	Kyat 1 kyat = 16 cents	1948	**Myanmar (Burma)**
1,596,000	Rand 1 rand = 29 cents	1990	**Namibia**
10,000	Australian dollar 1 Australian dollar = 74 cents	not in UN	**Nauru**
21,042,000	Rupee 1 rupee = 2 cents	1955	**Nepal**
15,368,000	Guilder 1 guilder = 61 cents	1945	**The Netherlands**
3,389,000	New Zealand dollar 1 NZ dollar = 63 cents	1945	**New Zealand**
4,097,000	Cordoba 1 cordoba = 20 cents	1945	**Nicaragua**
8,635,000	CFA franc 1 CFA franc = $\frac{1}{5}$ of a cent	1960	**Niger**
98,091,000	Naira 1 naira = 5 cents	1960	**Nigeria**
4,315,000	Krone 1 krone = 15 cents	1945	**Norway**
1,701,000	Rial Omani 1 rial Omani = $2.63	1971	**Oman**
121,856,000	Rupee 1 rupee = 3 cents	1947	**Pakistan**
16,000	U.S. Dollar	1994	**Palau**
2,630,000	Balboa Same value as U.S. dollar	1945	**Panama**
4,197,000	Kina 1 kina = 98 cents	1975	**Papua New Guinea**
5,214,000	Guarani 1 guarani = $\frac{1}{19}$ of a cent	1945	**Paraguay**

COUNTRY	CAPITAL	LOCATION OF COUNTRY	AREA
Peru	Lima	South America, along the Pacific coast, north of Chile	496,225 sq. mi. (1,285,217 sq. km.)
Philippines	Manila	Islands in the Pacific Ocean, off the coast of Southeast Asia	115,860 sq. mi. (300,076 sq. km.)
Poland	Warsaw	Central Europe, on the Baltic Sea, east of Germany	120,727 sq. mi. (312,682 sq. km.)
Portugal	Lisbon	Southern Europe, on the Iberian Peninsula, west of Spain	35,672 sq. mi. (92,390 sq. km.)
Qatar	Doha	Arabian Peninsula, on the Persian Gulf	4,412 sq. mi. (11,427 sq. km.)
Romania	Bucharest	Southern Europe, on the Black Sea, north of Bulgaria	91,699 sq. mi. (237,499 sq. km.)
Russia	Moscow	Stretches from Eastern Europe across northern Asia to the Pacific Ocean	6,592,800 sq. mi. (17,075,274 sq. km.)
Rwanda	Kigali	Central Africa, between Zaire and Tanzania	10,169 sq. mi. (26,338 sq. km.)
Saint Kitts and Nevis	Basseterre	Islands in the Caribbean Sea, near Puerto Rico	104 sq. mi. (269 sq. km.)
Saint Lucia	Castries	Island on eastern edge of the Caribbean Sea	238 sq. mi. (616 sq. km.)
Saint Vincent and the Grenadines	Kingstown	Islands on eastern edge of the Caribbean Sea, north of Grenada	150 sq. mi. (388 sq. km.)
San Marino	San Marino	Southern Europe, surrounded by Italy	24 sq. mi. (62 sq. km.)
São Tomé and Príncipe	São Tomé	In the Gulf of Guinea, off the coast of West Africa	386 sq. mi. (1,000 sq. km.)
Saudi Arabia	Riyadh	Western Asia, occupying most of the Arabian Peninsula	865,000 sq. mi. (2,240,340 sq. km.)
Senegal	Dakar	West Africa, on the Atlantic Ocean, south of Mauritania	75,951 sq. mi. (196,712 sq. km.)
Seychelles	Victoria	Islands off the coast of Africa, in the Indian Ocean, north of Madagascar	176 sq. mi. (456 sq. km.)
Sierra Leone	Freetown	West Africa, on the Atlantic Ocean, south of Guinea	27,699 sq. mi. (71,740 sq. km.)
Singapore	Singapore	Mostly on one island, off the tip of Southeast Asia	247 sq. mi. (640 sq. km.)
Slovakia	Bratislava	Eastern Europe, between Poland and Hungary	18,933 sq. mi. (49,036 sq. km.)

POPULATION	CURRENCY	JOINED UN	COUNTRY
23,651,000	New sol 1 new sol = 45 cents	1945	**Peru**
69,809,000	Peso 1 peso = 4 cents	1945	**Philippines**
38,655,000	Zloty 1 zloty = 41 cents	1945	**Poland**
10,524,000	Escudo 1 escudo = $\frac{2}{3}$ of a cent	1955	**Portugal**
513,000	Riyal 1 riyal = 27 cents	1971	**Qatar**
23,181,000	Lei 1 lei = $\frac{1}{16}$ of a cent	1955	**Romania**
149,609,000	Ruble 1 ruble = $\frac{1}{10}$ of a cent	1945	**Russia**
population figures not available	Franc 1 franc = $\frac{7}{10}$ of a cent	1962	**Rwanda**
41,000	East Caribbean dollar 1 EC dollar = 37 cents	1983	**Saint Kitts and Nevis**
145,000	East Caribbean dollar 1 EC dollar = 37 cents	1979	**Saint Lucia**
115,000	East Caribbean dollar 1 EC dollar = 37 cents	1980	**Saint Vincent and the Grenadines**
24,000	Italian lira 1 lire = $\frac{1}{17}$ of a cent	1992	**San Marino**
137,000	Dobra 1 dobra = $\frac{2}{5}$ of a cent	1975	**São Tomé and Príncipe**
18,197,000	Riyal 1 riyal = 27 cents	1945	**Saudi Arabia**
8,731,000	CFA franc 1 CFA franc = $\frac{1}{5}$ of a cent	1960	**Senegal**
72,000	Rupee 1 rupee = 19 cents	1976	**Seychelles**
4,630,000	Leone 1 leone = $\frac{1}{5}$ of a cent	1961	**Sierra Leone**
2,859,000	Singapore dollar 1 Singapore dollar = 69 cents	1965	**Singapore**
5,404,000	Koruna 1 koruna = 3 cents	1993	**Slovakia**

COUNTRY	CAPITAL	LOCATION OF COUNTRY	AREA
Slovenia	Ljubljana	Eastern Europe, between Austria and Croatia	7,821 sq. mi. (20,256 sq. km.)
Solomon Islands	Honiara	Western Pacific Ocean	10,954 sq. mi. (28,371 sq. km.)
Somalia	Mogadishu	East Africa, east of Ethiopia	246,300 sq. mi. (637,914 sq. km.)
South Africa	Pretoria	At the southern tip of Africa	473,290 sq. mi. (1,225,815 sq. km.)
Spain	Madrid	Europe, south of France, on the Iberian Peninsula	194,898 sq. mi. (504,784 sq. km.)
Sri Lanka	Colombo	Island in the Indian Ocean, southeast of India	25,332 sq. mi. (65,610 sq. km.)
Sudan	Khartoum	North Africa, south of Egypt, on the Red Sea	966,757 sq. mi. (2,503,889 sq. km.)
Suriname	Paramaribo	South America, on the northern shore, east of Guyana	63,251 sq. mi. (163,819 sq. km.)
Swaziland	Mbabane	Southern Africa, almost surrounded by South Africa	6,704 sq. mi. (17,363 sq. km.)
Sweden	Stockholm	Northern Europe, on the Scandinavian Peninsula, east of Norway	173,732 sq. mi. (449,964 sq. km.)
Switzerland	Bern	Central Europe, in the Alps, north of Italy	15,943 sq. mi. (41,292 sq. km.)
Syria	Damascus	In the Middle East, on the Mediterranean Sea, north of Jordan and Iraq	71,498 sq. mi. (185,179 sq. km.)
Taiwan	Taipei	Island off southeast coast of China	13,969 sq. mi. (36,180 sq. km.)
Tajikistan	Dushanbe	Asia, west of China, south of Kyrgyzstan	55,300 sq. mi. (143,226 sq. km.)
Tanzania	Dar-es-Salaam	East Africa, on the Indian Ocean, south of Kenya	364,017 sq. mi. (942,800 sq. km.)
Thailand	Bangkok	Southeast Asia, west of Laos	198,115 sq. mi. (513,116 sq. km.)
Togo	Lomé	West Africa, between Ghana and Benin	21,925 sq. mi. (56,785 sq. km.)
Tonga	Nku'alofa	Islands in the South Pacific Ocean	301 sq. mi. (780 sq. km.)
Trinidad and Tobago	Port-of-Spain	Islands off the north coast of South America	1,980 sq. mi. (5,128 sq. km.)
Tunisia	Tunis	North Africa, on the Mediterranean, between Algeria and Libya	63,378 sq. mi. (164,148 sq. km.)

POPULATION	CURRENCY	JOINED UN	COUNTRY
1,972,000	Tolar 1 tolar = ⅘ of a cent	1992	**Slovenia**
386,000	Solomon Islands dollar 1 Solomon dollar = 31 cents	1978	**Solomon Islands**
6,667,000	Shilling 1 shilling = 1/42 of a cent	1960	**Somalia**
43,931,000	Rand 1 rand = 28 cents	1945	**South Africa**
39,303,000	Peseta 1 peseta = ⅘ of a cent	1955	**Spain**
18,033,000	Rupee 1 rupee = 2 cents	1955	**Sri Lanka**
29,420,000	Pound 1 pound = ⅘ of a cent	1956	**Sudan**
423,000	Guilder 1 guilder = 56 cents	1975	**Suriname**
936,000	Lilangeni 1 lilangeni = 28 cents	1968	**Swaziland**
8,778,000	Krona 1 krona = 13 cents	1946	**Sweden**
7,040,000	Franc 1 franc = 81 cents	participant, not a member	**Switzerland**
14,887,000	Pound 1 pound = 9 cents	1945	**Syria**
21,299,000	New Taiwan dollar 1 new Taiwan dollar = 4 cents	not in UN	**Taiwan**
5,995,000	Ruble	1992	**Tajikistan**
27,986,000	Shilling 1 shilling = ⅕ of a cent	1961	**Tanzania**
59,510,000	Baht 1 baht = 4 cents	1946	**Thailand**
4,255,000	CFA franc 1 CFA franc = ⅕ of a cent	1960	**Togo**
105,000	Pa'anga 1 pa'anga = 74 cents	not in UN	**Tonga**
1,328,000	Trinidad and Tobago dollar 1 Trinidad dollar = 18 cents	1962	**Trinidad and Tobago**
8,727,000	Dinar 1 dinar = 96 cents	1956	**Tunisia**

COUNTRY	CAPITAL	LOCATION OF COUNTRY	AREA
Turkey	Ankara	On the southern shore of the Black Sea, partly in Europe and partly in Asia	300,948 sq. mi. (779,452 sq. km.)
Turkmenistan	Ashgabat	Western Asia, north of Afghanistan and Iran	188,417 sq. mi. (487,998 sq. km.)
Tuvalu	Funafuti	Chain of islands in the South Pacific Ocean	9 sq. mi. (24 sq. km.)
Uganda	Kampala	East Africa, south of Sudan	93,070 sq. mi. (241,050 sq. km.)
Ukraine	Kiev	Eastern Europe, south of Belarus and Russia	233,100 sq. mi. (603,726 sq. km.)
United Arab Emirates	Abu Dhabi	Arabian Peninsula, on the Persian Gulf	30,000 sq. mi. (77,700 sq. km.)
United States	Washington, D.C.	48 (of 50) states in North America, between Canada and Mexico	3,787,319 sq. mi. (9,809,109 sq. km.)
Uruguay	Montevideo	South America, on the Atlantic Ocean, south of Brazil	68,037 sq. mi. (176,215 sq. km.)
Uzbekistan	Tashkent	Central Asia, south of Kazakhstan	172,700 sq. mi. (447,291 sq. km.)
Vanuatu	Vila	Islands in the South Pacific Ocean	4,707 sq. mi. (12,191 sq. km.)
Vatican City		Surrounded by the city of Rome, Italy	1/5 sq. mi. (2/5 sq. km.)
Venezuela	Caracas	On the northern coast of South America, east of Colombia	352,144 sq. mi. (912,049 sq. km.)
Vietnam	Hanoi	Southeast Asia, south of China, on the eastern coast	127,246 sq. mi. (329,566 sq. km.)
Western Samoa	Apia	Islands in the South Pacific Ocean	1,093 sq. mi. (2,831 sq. km.)
Yemen	Sanaa	Asia, on the southern coast of the Arabian Peninsula	205,356 sq. mi. (531,870 sq. km.)
Yugoslavia	Belgrade	Southern Europe, on the Balkan Peninsula, west of Romania and Bulgaria	39,449 sq. mi. (102,172 sq. km.)
Zaire	Kinshasa	Central Africa, north of Angola and Zambia	905,446 sq. mi. (2,345,094 sq. km.)
Zambia	Lusaka	Southern Africa, south of Zaire	290,586 sq. mi. (752,614 sq. km.)
Zimbabwe	Harare	Southern Africa, south of Zambia	150,872 sq. mi. (390,757 sq. km.)

POPULATION	CURRENCY	JOINED UN	COUNTRY
62,154,000	Turkish lira 1 Turkish lira = $\frac{1}{204}$ of a cent	1945	**Turkey**
3,995,000	Manat	1992	**Turkmenistan**
10,000	Tuvaluan (Australian) dollar 1 Tuvaluan (Australian) dollar = 74 cents	not in UN	**Tuvalu**
19,859,000	Shilling 1 shilling = $\frac{1}{11}$ of a cent	1962	**Uganda**
51,847,000	Karbovanet 1 karbovanet = $\frac{1}{30}$ of a cent	1945	**Ukraine**
2,791,000	Dirham 1 dirham = 27 cents	1971	**United Arab Emirates**
260,341,000	U.S. dollar	1945	**United States**
3,199,000	Peso 1 peso = 17 cents	1945	**Uruguay**
22,609,000	Som	1992	**Uzbekistan**
170,000	Vatu 1 vatu = 81 cents	1981	**Vanuatu**
811	Lira 1 lira = $\frac{1}{17}$ of a cent	not in UN	**Vatican City**
20,562,000	Bolivar 1 bolivar = $\frac{3}{5}$ of a cent	1945	**Venezuela**
73,104,000	Dong 1 dong = $\frac{1}{109}$ of a cent	1977	**Vietnam**
204,000	Tala 1 tala = 39 cents	1976	**Western Samoa**
11,105,000	Rial 1 rial = 6 cents	1947	**Yemen**
10,760,000	Yugoslav new dinar 1 Yugoslav new dinar = $\frac{5}{9}$ of a cent	1945 (suspended in 1992)	**Yugoslavia**
42,684,000	Zaire 1 zaire = 1 cent	1960	**Zaire**
9,188,000	Kwacha 1 kwacha = 1 cent	1964	**Zambia**
10,975,000	Zimbabwe dollar 1 Zimbabwe dollar = 12 cents	1980	**Zimbabwe**

COUNTRY PUZZLE

Mixed-Up Countries: Here are some scrambled country names, plus a clue to help you figure each one out. The first letter of the scrambled name is correct. If you have trouble, look up the countries starting with that letter in the table of countries that begins on page 44. (Answers are on page 302.)

MCOXEI — This is in North America, but it's not the United States or Canada.

ANGEINRTA — This nation is in the southern part of South America.

TEKYUR — This country is partly in Europe, but mostly in Asia.

ATRUAALIS — This nation is a continent all by itself.

SNRWETLDAIZ — This is one of the only countries in Europe that does not belong to the United Nations.

ZIREA — This nation is in Africa, on the equator.

NELPA — This country is in Asia, in the mountains between China and India.

CAPITAL CITY CROSSWORD

In this crossword puzzle, all the clues are names of countries. The answers are the names of their capital cities. Can you fill in all the boxes? (Answers are on page 302.)

Clues for Solving the Puzzle:

ACROSS
1. Uganda
7. Egypt
8. United States
9. Spain
10. Russia
11. Cuba
12. Ecuador

DOWN
2. France
3. Afghanistan
4. Japan
5. Kenya
6. Great Britain

MAPS and FLAGS of the COUNTRIES of the WORLD

Maps showing the continents and countries of the world appear on pages 65 through 76. Flags of the countries appear on pages 77 through 80.

Maps of the United States appear on pages 241-256

Australia

⊛ National Capital

★ State Capital

• Other City

1:40,886,000

| 0 | 250 | 500 mi |
| 0 | 250 | 500 km |

Two-Point Equidistant Projection

SWEDEN

NORWAY

GREAT BRITAIN

ICELAND

Arctic Circle

Spitsbergen

Greenland Sea

Denmark Strait

Cape Farvel

Tasiilaq

GREENLAND (KALAALLIT NUNAAT) (Den.)

Nuuk (Godthaab)

Labrador Sea

NEWFOUNDLAND

St. Anthony

Island of Newfoundland

St. John's

St. Pierre & Miquelon Is. (Fr.)

Corner Brook

Anticosti I.

Happy Valley Goose Bay

QUÉBEC

Hebron

Sept-Îles

Scheffeville

Labrador City

Nord

Cape Morris Jessup

North Pole

Arctic Ocean

Knud Rasmussen Land

Qaanaaq (Thule)

Qibe Fiord

Alert

Ellesmere I.

Queen Elizabeth Islands

Resolute

Baffin Bay

Arctic Bay

Pond Inlet

Baffin Island

Davis Strait

Pangnirtung

Iqaluit

Hudson Strait

Ungava Peninsula

Povungnituk

Belcher Is.

Mooseonee

James Bay

CANADIAN SHIELD

Repulse Bay

Southampton I.

Hudson Bay

Churchill

York Factory

L. Winnipeg

Victoria I.

Cambridge Bay

Holmann

Coppermine

NORTHWEST TERRITORIES

CANADA

Yellowknife

Ft. Smith

Uranium City

Thompson

Flin Flon

MANITOBA

Banks I.

Sachs Harbour

Great Bear L.

Fort Franklin

Great Slave L.

Ft. Simpson

Hay River

Athabasca

SASK.

La Loche

Ft. McMurray

L. Athabasca

La Range

Prince Albert

Beaufort Sea

Inuvik

Fort McPherson

Mackenzie

Fort Yukon

ALBERTA

Peace River

Edmonton

L. Winnipeg

Saskatchewan

Point Barrow

Barrow

BROOKS RANGE

Yukon

Dawson

Mayo

YUKON

Carmacks

Whitehorse

Watson Lake

Prince George

Jasper

BRITISH COLUMBIA

ROCKY

GREAT

Point Hope

Kotzebue

Fairbanks

ALASKA

ALASKA RANGE

Anchorage

Valdez

Mt. McKinley 6,194 m (20,320 ft.)

Mt. Logan 5,951 m (19,524 ft.)

Yakutat

Skagway

Juneau

Sitka

COAST MOUNTAINS

Williams Lake

Vancouver I.

RUSSIA

Bering Strait

Nome

Bethel

Kenai

Seward

Kodiak

Gulf of Alaska

Arctic Circle

Ketchikan

Prince Rupert

Queen Charlotte Is.

Kitimat

Bering Sea

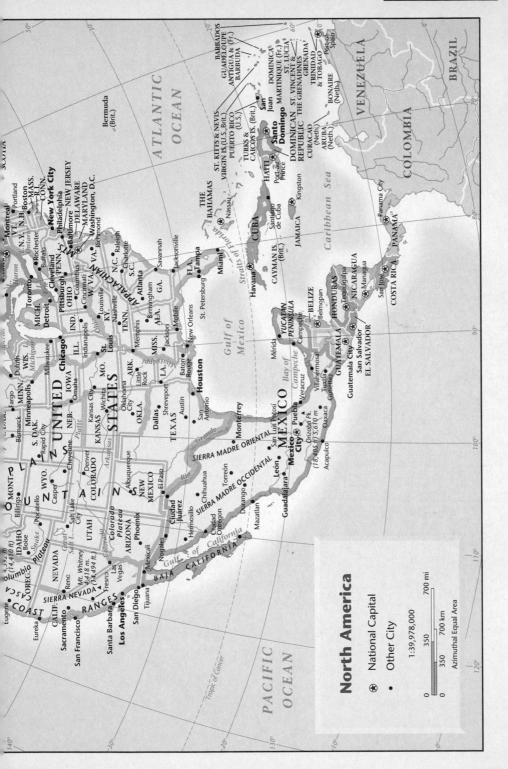

BRAZIL

VENEZUELA

COLOMBIA

BARBADOS
GUADELOUPE (Fr.)
ANTIGUA & BARBUDA
DOMINICA
MARTINIQUE (Fr.)
ST. LUCIA
ST. VINCENT & GRENADA
THE GRENADINES
TRINIDAD & TOBAGO
BONAIRE (Neth.)
CURACAO (Neth.)
ARUBA (Neth.)

ST. KITTS & NEVIS
VIRGIN IS.(U.S. Brit.)
PUERTO RICO (U.S.)
TURKS & CALCOS IS. (Brit.)

San Juan

HAITI
Port-au-Prince

DOMINICAN REPUBLIC

Santo Domingo

Caribbean Sea

Santiago de Cuba

Kingston

JAMAICA

CAYMAN IS. (Brit.)

Havana

CUBA

THE BAHAMAS

Nassau

Straits of Florida

Bermuda (Brit.)

Miami

FLA.

Tampa

St. Petersburg

Jacksonville

Savannah

GA.

S.C.

Charleston

N.C.

Raleigh

Atlanta

Birmingham

ALA.

Mobile

New Orleans

LA.

Baton Rouge

Houston

Gulf of Mexico

Bay of Campeche

Mérida

YUCATAN PENINSULA

Campeche

Villahermosa

BELIZE

Belmopan

GUATEMALA

Guatemala City

San Salvador

EL SALVADOR

HONDURAS

Tegucigalpa

NICARAGUA

Managua

COSTA RICA

San José

PANAMA

Panama City

Veracruz

Tuxtla Gutiérrez

Oaxaca

Acapulco

Puebla

Mexico City

Orizaba Pk. (18,405 ft) 5,610 m

León

San Luis Potosí

Guadalajara

MEXICO

Monterrey

SIERRA MADRE ORIENTAL

Torreón

Durango

SIERRA MADRE OCCIDENTAL

Chihuahua

Ciudad Juárez

El Paso

Rio Grande

San Antonio

Austin

Dallas

TEXAS

Shreveport

Little Rock

ARK.

Oklahoma City

OKLA.

Wichita

KANSAS

Kansas City

MO.

St. Louis

Memphis

TENN.

Nashville

MISS.

Jackson

KY.

Louisville

Indianapolis

IND.

ILL.

Chicago

IOWA

Omaha

NEB.

Des Moines

Platte

Cheyenne

Denver

COLORADO

Colorado Plateau

Albuquerque

NEW MEXICO

ARIZONA

Phoenix

Tucson

Nogales

Hermosillo

Ciudad Obregón

Mazatlán

Gulf of California

BAJA CALIFORNIA

Mexicali

Tijuana

San Diego

Los Angeles

Santa Barbara

SIERRA NEVADA

Fresno

Mt. Whitney 4,418 m. (14,494 ft.)

Las Vegas

Salt Lake City

UTAH

Great Salt L.

NEVADA

CALIF.

San Francisco

Sacramento

Eureka

Reno

COAST RANGES

Eugene

OREGON

COLUMBIA

IDAHO

Boise

Pocatello

WYO.

Casper

MONT.

Billings

S. DAK.

Rapid City

Bismarck

N. DAK.

Fargo

MINN.

Duluth

Minneapolis

WIS.

Milwaukee

Madison

MICH.

Detroit

Toronto

OHIO

Columbus

Cincinnati

Cleveland

Pittsburgh

PENN.

W. VA.

VA.

Richmond

Washington, D.C.

MARYLAND

DELAWARE

Baltimore

Philadelphia

NEW JERSEY

New York City

N.Y.

CONN.

R.I.

MASS.

Boston

N.H.

VT.

Portland

Montreal

Rochester

Buffalo

APPALACHIAN MTS.

Columbus

Louisville

Nashville

Charlotte

ROCKY MOUNTAINS

GREAT PLAINS

UNITED STATES

Mississippi

Missouri

Arkansas

Snake

Columbia 4,392 m (14,410 ft)

Lake Michigan

Lake Huron

Lake Ontario

Lake Erie

PACIFIC OCEAN

Tropic of Cancer

North America

⊛ National Capital
• Other City

1:39,978,000

0   350   700 mi
0   350   700 km

Azimuthal Equal Area

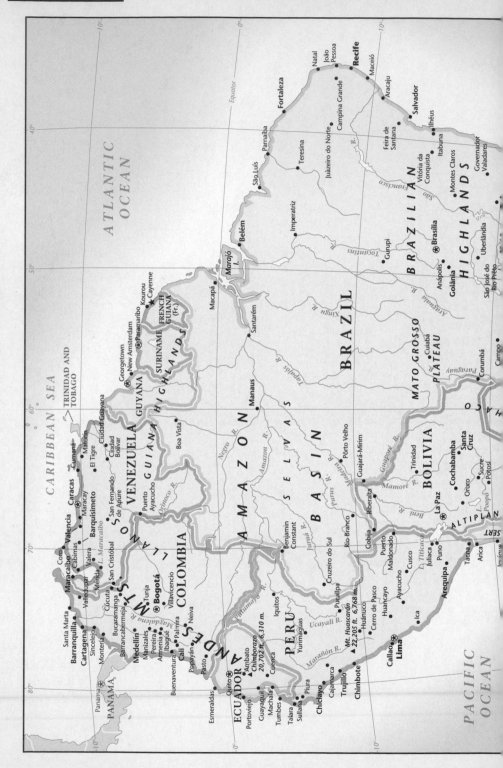

ATLANTIC OCEAN

CARIBBEAN SEA

PACIFIC OCEAN

Equator

TRINIDAD AND TOBAGO

VENEZUELA

GUYANA

SURINAME

FRENCH GUIANA (Fr.)

GUIANA HIGHLANDS

COLOMBIA

PANAMA

ECUADOR

PERU

BRAZIL

AMAZON BASIN

SELVAS

BOLIVIA

BRAZILIAN HIGHLANDS

MATO GROSSO PLATEAU

ALTIPLANO

LLANOS

ANDES MTS.

CHACO

Recife
Natal
João Pessoa
Maceió
Aracaju
Salvador
Ilhéus
Itabuna
Campina Grande
Feira de Santana
Vitória da Conquista
Montes Claros
Governador Valadares
Natal
Fortaleza
Parnaíba
São Luís
Teresina
Juàzeiro do Norte
Imperatriz
Belém
Gurupi
Anápolis
Goiânia
Brasília
Uberlândia
São José do Rio Preto
Campo
Corumbá
Cuiabá
Pôrto Velho
Guajará-Mirim
Trinidad
Santa Cruz
Cochabamba
Oruro
Sucre
Potosí
La Paz
Riberalta
Cobija
Puerto Maldonado
Cusco
Ayacucho
Juliaca
Puno
Tacna
Arica
Arequipa
Ica
Cerro de Pasco
Huancayo
Huánuco
Mt. Huascarán ▲22,205 ft. 6,768 m.
Cruzeiro do Sul
Rio Branco
Pucallpa
Benjamin Constant
Iquitos
Manaus
Boa Vista
Santarém
Macapá
Marajó I.
Cayenne
Kourou
Paramaribo
New Amsterdam
Georgetown
Ciudad Guayana
Ciudad Bolívar
El Tigre
Maturín
Cumaná
Caracas
Valencia
Maracay
Barquisimeto
Coro
Maracaibo
Cabimas
Valera
Mérida
San Cristóbal
Cúcuta
San Fernando de Apure
Puerto Ayacucho
Bucaramanga
Barrancabermeja
Santa Marta
Barranquilla
Cartagena
Sincelejo
Montería
Valledupar
Medellín
Manizales
Pereira
Armenia
Ibagué
Bogotá
Tunja
Villavicencio
Neiva
Cali
Palmira
Buenaventura
Popayán
Pasto
Quito
Ambato
Chimborazo ▲20,702 ft. 6,310 m.
Cuenca
Esmeraldas
Portoviejo
Guayaquil
Machala
Tumbes
Talara
Sullana
Piura
Cajamarca
Chiclayo
Trujillo
Chimbote
Callao
Lima
Yurimaguas
Yurimaguas

Amazon R.
Negro R.
Xingu R.
Tapajós R.
Tocantins R.
São Francisco R.
Araguaia R.
Paraguay R.
Guaporé R.
Mamoré R.
Beni R.
Madeira R.
Purus R.
Juruá R.
Ucayali R.
Marañón R.
Putumayo R.
Magdalena R.
Orinoco R.
L. Maracaibo
L. Titicaca
L. Poopó

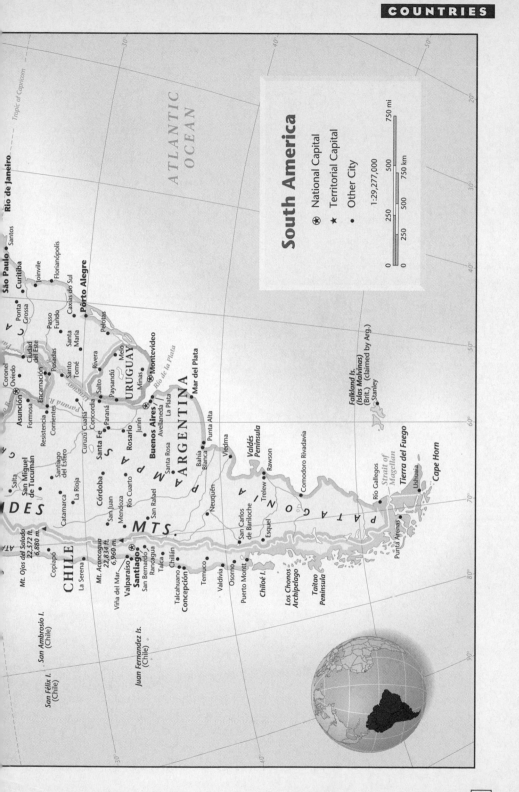

South America

- ⊛ National Capital
- ★ Territorial Capital
- • Other City

1:29,277,000

0   250   500   750 mi
0   250   500   750 km

ATLANTIC OCEAN

Tropic of Capricorn

Río de Janeiro

São Paulo   Santos
Curitiba   Joinvile
Ponta   Florianópolis
Grossa
Passo   Caxias do Sul
Fundo
Porto Alegre
Santa   Passo
Maria   Fundo
Pelotas

Coronel   Santo
Oviedo   Tomé   Rivera   Melo
Asunción ⊛   Salto   Montevideo ⊛
Formosa   Encarnación Paysandú   Minas
Resistencia Posadas   URUGUAY
Corrientes   Curuzú Cuatiá Concordia
Santiago   Santa Fe   Paraná   La Plata
del Estero   Rosario   Avellaneda Mar del Plata
Córdoba   Junín
San Juan   Santa Rosa Punta Alta
Mendoza   ARGENTINA   Bahía
Río Cuarto   Blanca
San Rafael   Viedma
Neuquén   Valdés
San Carlos   Peninsula
de Bariloche Rawson
Esquel   Comodoro Rivadavia
Trelew   PATAGONIA

Salta
San Miguel
de Tucumán
Catamarca   La Rioja

CHILE
Mt. Ojos del Salado
22,572 ft.
6,880 m.
Copiapó
La Serena
Mt. Aconcagua
22,834 ft.
6,960 m.
Valparaíso ⊛
Viña del Mar   Santiago ⊛
San Bernardo
Rancagua
Talca
Chillán
Talcahuano
Concepción   Temuco
Valdivia
Osorno
Puerto Montt
Chiloé I.
Los Chonos
Archipelago
Taitao
Peninsula

MTS.

Río Gallegos
Strait of
Magellan
Punta Arenas
Tierra del Fuego
Ushuaia
Cape Horn

Falkland Is.
(Islas Malvinas)
(Brit.)   (claimed by Arg.)
★ Stanley

San Ambrosio I.
(Chile)
San Félix I.
(Chile)
Juan Fernández Is.
(Chile)

69

Europe

⊛ National Capital

● Other City

1:22,107,000

| 0 | 250 | 500 mi |
| 0 | 250 | 500 km |

Azimuthal Equal Area Projection

ICELAND
Reykjavík Akureyri

Arctic Circle

Norwegian   Sea

Faroe Is.
(Den.)

Troedheim

Shetland Is.
(Brit.)

NORWAY

SWED

Bergen

Orkney
Is.

Oslo

Uppsa

Stavanger

Stockho

Linköping

Go

Aberdeen

Hebrides

Skagerrak

Göteborg

Glasgow   Edinburgh

Jutland   Århus

Belfast

GREAT BRITAIN

Newcastle

Copenhagen Helsingborg

Dublin

Liverpool   Leeds

DENMARK   Odense Malmö

IRELAND

Manchester   Sheffield

North

Cork

Birmingham

Sea

Hamburg

Cardiff   Bristol

NETHERLANDS

Bremen

Szczecin

Portsmouth

Amsterdam

Hannover

Land's End

London

Rotterdam

Essen   GERMANY   Berlin   Po

English Channel

Antwerp

Channel Is.
(Brit.)   Le Havre

Brussels

Cologne   Leipzig   Dresden

BELGIUM   Bonn

ATLANTIC

Lille

Liège

Frankfurt

Oder

Brest

Rouen

LUXEMBOURG

Mannheim   Prague

OCEAN

Paris

Luxembourg

CZECH. REP.   Kato

Nantes

Loire

Strasbourg

Stuttgart   Brno   O

Dijon

Munich   Linz   SL

FRANCE

Bern   Zürich

Vienna   Bra

Cabo Finisterre

Geneva

LIECHTENSTEIN

AUSTRIA

Bay
of
Biscay

Lyon

SWITZERLAND

ALPS   Graz

B

Bordeaux

Mt. Blanc
4807 m
(15,771 ft)

Milan

SLOVENIA   HU

Verona   Ljubljana   Zag

Vigo

Bilbao

Turin

Venice   DINARIC

Porto

Toulouse

Nice

Genoa

Bologna   CROATIA   BOS

Valladolid

Ebro

Marseille

Florence

SAN   HERZE

PORTUGAL   IBERIAN

Pico de Aneto

Toulon

MONACO

MARINO

Split

Lisbon

Zaragoza

3404 m
(11,168 ft)

ANDORRA

Ligurian Sea

Corsica

Elba

Adriatic

Dubrovn

Badajoz

Tagus

Madrid

Barcelona

(Fr.)

VATICAN

Rome

Po

PENINSULA

Valéncia

Balearic Sea

CITY

ITALY

Bar

SPAIN

Majorca

Minorca

Naples   Salerno

Córdoba

Alicante

Palma

Sardinia

Cabo de
São Vicente

Sevilla

Granada

Balearic
(Sp.)   Is.

(It.)

Tyrrhenian
Sea

Cádiz

Málaga

Cagliari

Strait of
Gibraltar

GIBRALTAR (Brit.)

Mediterra-n   Palermo

Catania   Mt. Etna
3323 m
(10,902 ft)

Rabat

Algiers

Sicily

Casablanca

Tunis

Valletta
MALTA

MOROCCO

ATLAS   MOUNTAINS   ALGERIA

TUNISIA

Sea

Pyrenees

Rhône

Rhine

Danube

Apennines

North
Cape
Hammerfest

Barents
Sea

Nar'yan-Mar

Ob

30°   40°   50° 70°   80°   70°   80° 60°

APLAND

na

Murmansk
KOLA
PENINSULA
Apatity

Pechora

Pechora

Arctic Circle

Irtysh

R U S S I A

Ukhta

Luleå

Oulu

White Sea

Arkhangel'sk

Serov

Gulf of
Bothnia

eå

FINLAND

Belomorsk

Syktyvkar

Bereziki

Petropavl

Vaasa

Lake
Onega

Kotlas

Yekaterinburg

Tampere
Lahti
Helsinki
ku

Petrozavodsk

Divina

Kirov

Izhevsk

Perm'

M
O
U
N
T
A
I
N
S

Chelyabinsk

Qostanay

Vologda

Naberezhnyye
Chelny

Ufa

Magnitogorsk

Lake
Ladoga

St.
Petersburg

Cherepovets

U
R
A
L

Kama

Novgorod

nd

Gulf of
Finland

Tallinn

ESTONIA

Tartu

Yaroslavl'

Kazan

Nizhniy
Novgorod

Ivanovo

PLAIN

Pskov

EUROPEAN

Tver

Ul'yanovsk

Tol'yatti

Orenburg

Orsk

50°

Riga

LATVIA

Daugavpils

Moscow

Ryazan'

Saransk

Samara

Aqtöbe

LITHUANIA

Vitsyebsk

Penza

Oral

KAZAKHSTAN

Kaunas
USSIA
ningrad

Vilnius

Smolensk

Tula

Tambov

Mahilyow

Lipetsk

Saratov

Volga

Ural

RTHERN

Hrodna

Minsk

Bryansk

Voronezh

Aral
Sea

Warsaw

Brest

BELARUS

Homyel'

Kursk

Volgograd

Atyraū

UZBEKISTAN

OLAND

L'viv

UKRAINE

Dnieper

Kharkiv

Luhans'k

Don

Astrakhan

ów

Chernivtsi

Dnipropetrovs'k

Donets'k

Aqtaū

RPATHIAN

Dniester

Zaporizhzhya

Kryvyy Rih

Mariupol'

Rostov na Donu

Caspian

Kosice

MOLDOVA

Chişinău

Mykolayiv

Sea of
Azov

Stavropol'

Makhachkala

TURKMENISTAN

Debrecen

Iaşi

Odesa

CRIMEA

Krasnodar

Groznyy

Sea

40°

ROMANIA

Timişoara

Ploieşti

Sevastopol'

Simferopol'

CAUCASUS

Krasnowodsk

i Sad

elgrade

Bucharest

Constanţa

Black Sea

GEORGIA

T'bilisi

ARMENIA

AZERBAIJAN

Baku

OSLAVIA

Danube

BULGARIA

Varna

Trabzon

Yerevan

Sofia

Burgas

Skopje

Plovdiv

CEDONIA

ane

Istanbul

Tabriz

Tehran

NIA

LKAN

NSULA

Lárisa

Thessaloníki

Ankara

TURKEY

IRAN

GREECE

trai

Izmir

Athens

Adana

IRAQ

LOPONNESUS

Cyclades

Sea

Rhodes

Nicosia

SYRIA

Baghdad

Sea of Crete

Crete

Iráklion

CYPRUS

LEBANON

Beirut

Damascus

Euphrates

50°

30°

Persian
Gulf

30°   40°   30°

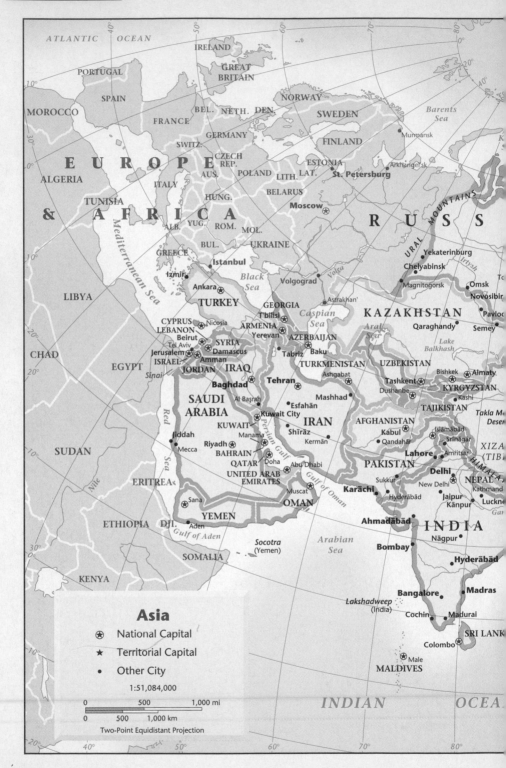

ATLANTIC OCEAN
IRELAND
GREAT BRITAIN
PORTUGAL
SPAIN
MOROCCO
NORWAY
BEL. NETH. DEN.
FRANCE
SWEDEN
Barents Sea
Murmansk
GERMANY
FINLAND
SWITZ.
CZECH REP.
AUS.
ESTONIA
Arkhangel'sk
EUROPE
ALGERIA
ITALY
POLAND
LITH. LAT.
St. Petersburg
HUNG.
BELARUS
Moscow
TUNISIA
& AFRICA
ALB. YUG. ROM.
UKRAINE
MOL.
RUSS
Mediterranean Sea
BUL.
GREECE
Izmir
Istanbul
Black Sea
Volgograd
Volga
URAL MOUNTAINS
Yekaterinburg
Chelyabinsk
Irtysh
Ankara
TURKEY
GEORGIA
Magnitogorsk
Omsk
Novosibir
LIBYA
CYPRUS
Nicosia
T'bilisi
Caspian Sea
KAZAKHSTAN
Pavlo
LEBANON
ARMENIA
Astrakhan'
Aral Sea
Qaraghandy
Semey
Beirut
SYRIA
Yerevan
AZERBAIJAN
Lake Balkhash
CHAD
Tel Aviv
Damascus
Tabriz
Baku
TURKMENISTAN
UZBEKISTAN
Bishkek
Almaty
Jerusalem
Amman
ISRAEL
JORDAN
IRAQ
Tehran
Ashgabat
Tashkent
KYRGYZSTAN
EGYPT
Sinai
Baghdad
TAJIKISTAN
Kashi
Takla M Dese
Dushanbe
SAUDI ARABIA
Al Başrah
Esfahān
Mashhad
ARABIA
Kuwait City
IRAN
AFGHANISTAN
Islāmābād
Srīnagar
Red Sea
KUWAIT
Manama
Shīrāz
Kermān
Kābul
Qandahār
Amritsar
Lahore
XIZA (TIB)
HIMALA
Jiddah
Riyadh
BAHRAIN
QATAR
Doha
Abu Dhabi
PAKISTAN
Delhi
NEPAL
Mecca
UNITED ARAB EMIRATES
Gulf of Oman
Sukkur
Karāchi
New Delhi
Kathmand
Jaipur
Kānpur
Luckn
Sana
Muscat
OMAN
Hyderābād
SUDAN
ERITREA
YEMEN
Ahmadābād
INDIA
Gar
ETHIOPIA
DJI.
Aden
Gulf of Aden
Arabian Sea
Socotra (Yemen)
Bombay
Nāgpur
Hyderābād
SOMALIA
KENYA
Lakshadweep (India)
Bangalore
Madras
Cochin
Madurai
SRI LANK
Colombo
Male
MALDIVES
INDIAN OCEA

Asia

⊛ National Capital

★ Territorial Capital

• Other City

1:51,084,000

| 0 | 500 | 1,000 mi |

| 0 | 500 | 1,000 km |

Two-Point Equidistant Projection

North Pole
180°
80°
70°
60°
50°
40°
170°

CTIC
CEAN

Chukchi
Sea

Bering
Sea

ALASKA

East
Siberian
Sea

•Anadyr

160°
140°
120°
100°

Laptev
Sea

KAMCHATKA
PENINSULA

180°

Magadan•

Petropavlovsk-
Kamchatskiy

170°

•Yakutsk

Sea of
Okhotsk

30°

Sakhalin

Kuril
Islands
(Russia)

S I B E R I A

Komsomol'sk
na Amure

Khabarovsk•

Sapporo•

160°

oyarsk•   •Bratsk

Lake
Baikal

Blagoveshchensk•

Amur

JAPAN

Sendai

znetsk   •Chita

Irkutsk•

Harbin•

Vladivostok•

Sea of
Japan

Tokyo•
Yokohama•

Kyōto

20°

•Ulan-Ude

Changchun•

Ulaanbaatar✪

Shenyang

N. KOREA

Pyongyang✪

Kōbe• •Ōsaka

MONGOLIA

GOBI DESERT

Beijing✪

Dalian•

Seoul✪
S. KOREA

Hiroshima

IANG

Hohhot•

Tianjin•

Huang

Jinan•

Qingdao•

Nagasaki•

Taiyuan•

Zhengzhou•

Yellow
Sea

CHINA

Lanzhou•

Xi'an•

Nanjing•

Shanghai•

PACIFIC
OCEAN

rest
n.
8 ft.)
•Lhasa

Chengdu•

Chongqing•

Changsha•

Wuhan•

Wenzhou•

Fuzhou•

East
China
Sea

Islands

Okinawa (Japan)

150°

Ryukyu

10°

UTAN
aphu

Kunming•

Xiamen•

Taipei✪

ADESH
haka
tta

Mandalay•

Nanning•

Guangzhou•

Macau•★Victoria
HONG KONG
(Brit.)
MACAU
(Port.)

TAIWAN

Philippine
Sea

LUZON

MYANMAR
(BURMA)

Hanoi✪

LAOS

Gulf
of
Tonkin

Mekong

Manila✪

PHILIPPINES

al

Vientiane✪

Da Nang•

South
China
Sea

Cebu•

0°

Yangon•

THAILAND

VIETNAM

MINDINAO

an
nds
dia)

Bangkok•

CAMBODIA

Phnom
Penh• •Ho Chi Minh City

Davao•

Andaman
Sea

Gulf of
Thailand

Kota Kinabalu•

Sulu
Sea

Celebes
Sea

Manado•

obar
nds
dia)

Medan•

Bandar Seri Begawan✪

BRUNEI

Kuching•

BORNEO

Manila✪

I N D O N E S I A

Banda
Sea

Arafura
Sea

10°

Kuala
Lumpur✪
SUMATRA

SINGAPORE
•Singapore

Padang•

Banjarmasin•

Java
Sea

Ujungpandang•

Timor
Sea

Palembang•

Jakarta•

Bandung•

JAVA

Surabaya•

Kupang•

AUSTRALIA

100°   110°   120°   130°   140°

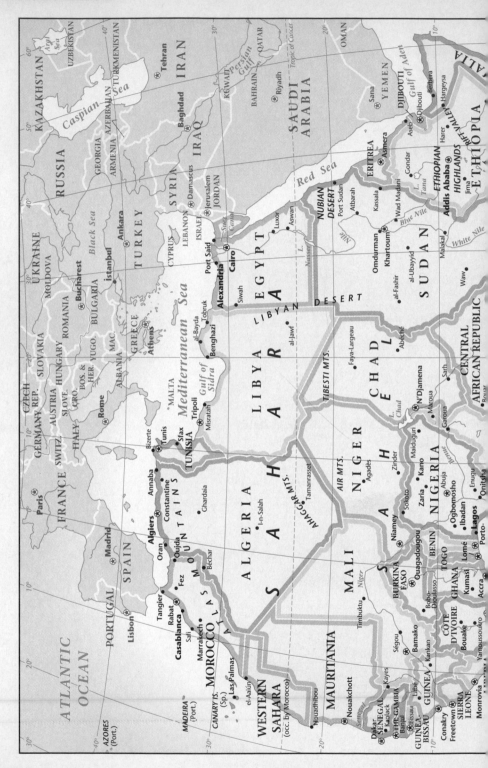

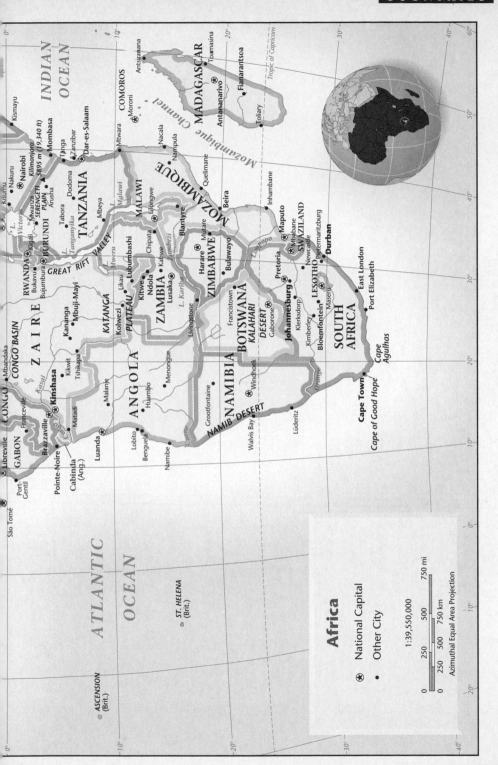

INDIAN OCEAN

Kismayu

Kismayu

MADAGASCAR

COMOROS
Moroni

Antsiranana

Toamasina

Antananarivo ⊛

Fianarantsoa

Toliary

Mozambique Channel

Tropic of Capricorn

Nakuru
Nairobi ⊛
Kilimanjaro
5895 m (19,340 ft) ▲
Kisumu
L. Victoria
Mwanza
SERENGETI PLAIN
BURUNDI
RWANDA ⊛ Kigali
Bukavu
Bujumbura ⊛
L. Tanganyika
Mombasa
Tanga
Zanzibar
Dar-es-Salaam
Mtwara
Dodoma ⊛
Arusha
TANZANIA
Tabora
Mbeya
L. Malawi
MALAWI
Lilongwe ⊛
GREAT RIFT VALLEY

Nacala
Nampula
Quelimane

MOZAMBIQUE

Inhambane
Beira

Maputo ⊛

SWAZILAND
Mbabane ⊛
Pietermaritzburg
Durban

L. Mweru
Luluba
Bukama
Likasi
Kolwezi
Ndola
Kabwe
Lubumbashi
Kitwe
Chipata
Blantyre
ZAMBIA
Lusaka ⊛
PLATEAU
Livingstone
L. Kariba

Harare ⊛
Mutare
ZIMBABWE
Bulawayo

Francistown

Pretoria ⊛
Newcastle
Pietermaritzburg

LESOTHO
Maseru ⊛
East London

SOUTH
AFRICA

East London
Port Elizabeth

RWANDA
ZAIRE
Mbandaka
CONGO BASIN
Kananga
Mbuji-Mayi
Kikwit
Tshikapa
KATANGA
Kinshasa ⊛
Matadi

Kasai

Brazzaville ⊛
GABON
Libreville ⊛
Franceville
CONGO
Pointe-Noire
Cabinda (Ang.)
Port-Gentil

São Tomé

Luanda ⊛

Lobito
Benguela
Namibe

ANGOLA
Malanje
Huambo
Menongue

Cuanza
Cunene

Grootfontein

NAMIBIA
NAMIB DESERT

Windhoek ⊛

Walvis Bay

Lüderitz

Orange

BOTSWANA
KALAHARI DESERT
Gaborone ⊛

Johannesburg ⊛
Klerksdorp
Kimberley
Bloemfontein ⊛

Limpopo

Cape Agulhas

Cape of Good Hope
Cape Town ⊛

ATLANTIC
OCEAN

ST. HELENA
(Brit.)

ASCENSION
(Brit.)

Africa

⊛ National Capital

• Other City

1:39,550,000

750 mi
0   250   500   750 km
Azimuthal Equal Area Projection

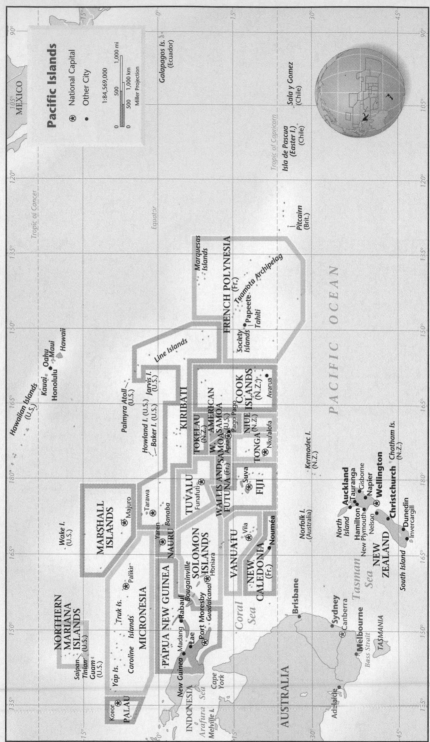

Pacific Islands

⊛ National Capital
• Other City

1:84,569,000

0   500   1,000 mi
0   500   1,000 km
Miller Projection

Galapagos Is.
(Ecuador)

Sala y Gomez (Chile)

Tropic of Cancer

Tropic of Capricorn

Isla de Pascua (Easter I.) (Chile)

MEXICO

Equator

Pitcairn (Brit.)

Marquesas Islands

FRENCH POLYNESIA (Fr.)

Tuamota Archipelago

PACIFIC OCEAN

Society Islands   Papeete
Tahiti

Line Islands

Hawaiian Islands (U.S.)

Kauai   Oahu   Maui   Hawaii
Honolulu

Palmyra Atoll (U.S.)

Howland I. (U.S.)
Baker I. (U.S.)

Jarvis I. (U.S.)

KIRIBATI

Pago Pago   COOK ISLANDS (N.Z.)
AMERICAN SAMOA (U.S.)   Avarua
TOKELAU (N.Z.)   W. SAMOA
Apia   NIUE (N.Z.)
TONGA   Nukualofa

Wake I. (U.S.)

MARSHALL ISLANDS

Majuro

Tarawa
Banaba

TUVALU
Funafuti

WALLIS AND FUTUNA (Fr.)

Suva
Nuku'alofa

Kermadec I. (N.Z.)

NORTHERN MARIANA ISLANDS
Saipan   (U.S.)
Tinian   (U.S.)
Guam   (U.S.)

Truk Is.
Yap Is.   Caroline Islands

MICRONESIA

Yaren
NAURU

SOLOMON ISLANDS
Bougainville   Honiara
Rabaul   Guadalcanal

VANUATU
Vila

FIJI

NEW CALEDONIA (Fr.)   Noumea

Norfolk I. (Australia)

North Island   Auckland   Tauranga
Hamilton   Gisborne
New Plymouth   Napier
Nelson   Wellington
Christchurch   Chatham Is. (N.Z.)
South Island   Dunedin
Invercargill

Palikir

PAPUA NEW GUINEA
New Guinea   Madang   Lae
Port Moresby

Koror
PALAU

INDONESIA

Melville I.

Arafura Sea

Cape York

AUSTRALIA

Coral Sea

Brisbane

Sydney
Canberra

Tasman Sea

NEW ZEALAND

Adelaide

Melbourne

TASMANIA

Bass Strait

FLAGS of the
COUNTRIES of the WORLD
(Afghanistan-Ecuador)

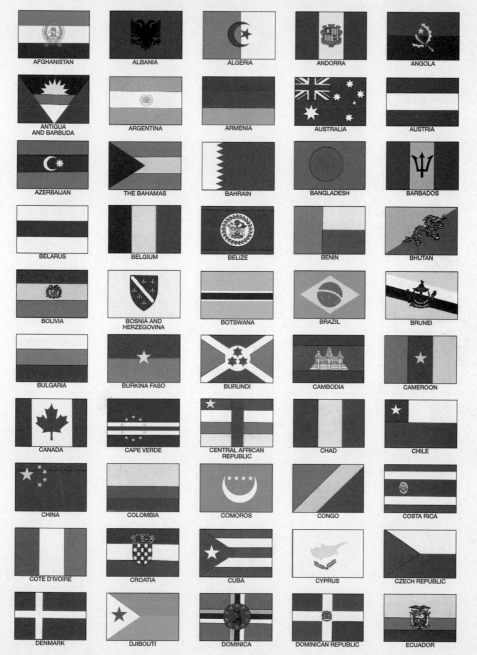

AFGHANISTAN · ALBANIA · ALGERIA · ANDORRA · ANGOLA
ANTIGUA AND BARBUDA · ARGENTINA · ARMENIA · AUSTRALIA · AUSTRIA
AZERBAIJAN · THE BAHAMAS · BAHRAIN · BANGLADESH · BARBADOS
BELARUS · BELGIUM · BELIZE · BENIN · BHUTAN
BOLIVIA · BOSNIA AND HERZEGOVINA · BOTSWANA · BRAZIL · BRUNEI
BULGARIA · BURKINA FASO · BURUNDI · CAMBODIA · CAMEROON
CANADA · CAPE VERDE · CENTRAL AFRICAN REPUBLIC · CHAD · CHILE
CHINA · COLOMBIA · COMOROS · CONGO · COSTA RICA
COTE D'IVOIRE · CROATIA · CUBA · CYPRUS · CZECH REPUBLIC
DENMARK · DJIBOUTI · DOMINICA · DOMINICAN REPUBLIC · ECUADOR

77

FLAGS of the COUNTRIES of the WORLD
(Egypt-Luxembourg)

EGYPT	EL SALVADOR	EQUATORIAL GUINEA	ERITREA	ESTONIA
ETHIOPIA	FIJI	FINLAND	FRANCE	GABON
THE GAMBIA	GEORGIA	GERMANY	GHANA	GREECE
GRENADA	GUATEMALA	GUINEA	GUINEA-BISSAU	GUYANA
HAITI	HONDURAS	HUNGARY	ICELAND	INDIA
INDONESIA	IRAN	IRAQ	IRELAND	ISRAEL
ITALY	JAMAICA	JAPAN	JORDAN	KAZAKHSTAN
KENYA	KIRIBATI	NORTH KOREA	SOUTH KOREA	KUWAIT
KYRGYZSTAN	LAOS	LATVIA	LEBANON	LESOTHO
LIBERIA	LIBYA	LIECHTENSTEIN	LITHUANIA	LUXEMBOURG

FLAGS of the COUNTRIES of the WORLD

(Macedonia-Sierra Leone)

MACEDONIA

MADAGASCAR

MALAWI

MALAYSIA

MALDIVES

MALI

MALTA

MARSHALL ISLANDS

MAURITANIA

MAURITIUS

MEXICO

MICRONESIA

MOLDOVA

MONACO

MONGOLIA

MOROCCO

MOZAMBIQUE

MYANMAR (BURMA)

NAMIBIA

NAURU

NEPAL

NETHERLANDS

NEW ZEALAND

NICARAGUA

NIGER

NIGERIA

NORWAY

OMAN

PAKISTAN

PALAU

PANAMA

PAPUA NEW GUINEA

PARAGUAY

PERU

PHILIPPINES

POLAND

PORTUGAL

QATAR

ROMANIA

RUSSIA

RWANDA

ST. KITTS AND NEVIS

ST. LUCIA

ST. VINCENT AND THE GRENADINES

SAN MARINO

SÃO TOMÉ AND PRÍNCIPE

SAUDI ARABIA

SENEGAL

SEYCHELLES

SIERRA LEONE

FLAGS of the COUNTRIES of the WORLD

(Singapore-Zimbabwe)

SINGAPORE	SLOVAKIA	SLOVENIA	SOLOMON ISLANDS	SOMALIA
SOUTH AFRICA	SPAIN	SRI LANKA	SUDAN	SURINAME
SWAZILAND	SWEDEN	SWITZERLAND	SYRIA	TAIWAN
TAJIKISTAN	TANZANIA	THAILAND	TOGO	TONGA
TRINIDAD AND TOBAGO	TUNISIA	TURKEY	TURKMENISTAN	TUVALU
UGANDA	UKRAINE	UNITED ARAB EMIRATES	UNITED KINGDOM (GREAT BRITAIN)	UNITED STATES
URUGUAY	VANUATU	VANUATU	VATICAN CITY	VENEZUELA
VIETNAM	WESTERN SAMOA	YEMEN	YUGOSLAVIA	ZAIRE
ZAMBIA	ZIMBABWE			

A QUICK VISIT to Some COUNTRIES of the WORLD

Suppose you got a free round-trip ticket to visit any spot in the whole world. Where would you like to go? Here are a few sights you might want to see.

AUSTRALIA
In Australia is **Ayers Rock,** the biggest exposed rock in the world. Located in a remote desert, it is about 1½ miles long and shines bright red when the sun sets. Australia's first people, the Aborigines, thought it was sacred.

CANADA
Want to feel like you're in France without leaving North America? Visit **Quebec City.** You'll see a high, walled fortress (the Citadel), a hotel that looks like a French castle (Château Frontenac), and people who speak French. In **Toronto,** however, English is the main language. You can get a view of that fast-growing city by going to the top of the **CN Tower,** the tallest free-standing structure in the world.

CANADA—UNITED STATES
On the border between Canada and the United States is the famous waterfall **Niagara Falls.** About 20,000 bathtubs of water pour over the falls every second. You can put on a slicker and look at the falls from an observation deck—or ride by in a boat.

CHINA
Some 2,400 years ago, workers started putting up the **Great Wall.** It became the world's longest struc-ture, with a main section 2,150 miles long. It was built to keep out invaders, but didn't stop Genghis Khan from conquering much of China in the 1200s.

DENMARK
One of the world's oldest and most charming amusement parks is Denmark's **Tivoli Gardens.** There you will find everything from a mouse circus to the world's oldest roller coaster.

ECUADOR
The **Galapagos Islands**, which belong to Ecuador, are remote islands in the Pacific Ocean, about 600 miles off South America. They are filled with wildlife (such as cormorants and penguins, giant tortoises and lizards) and odd plants.

EGYPT
In Egypt you can see the **Great Sphinx,** a stone figure with a man's head and a lion's body. Carved in the desert 4,500 years ago, it's still there, despite wear and tear. Nearby, at Giza, are the great **pyramids** of ancient Egyptian pharaohs.

FRANCE
A high point of a trip to France would be the **Eiffel Tower.** You get to the top of this open, cast-iron tower in four elevators, one after another. Then you can look down 1,000 feet on the beautiful city of Paris below.

GERMANY
Though it was built in the 1800s, the mad King Ludwig II planned **Neuschwanstein Castle** to look just like a fairy-tale castle from the Middle Ages, complete with turrets and drawbridges.

Eiffel Tower ▶

GREECE

On the **Acropolis**, you will find the ruins of the Parthenon and other public buildings from ancient Athens. The remains of the buildings, some partly rebuilt, stand high on a hill overlooking the city.

GREAT BRITAIN

The regular London home of the queen of England is **Buckingham Palace**. When she's there a royal flag is flying. Outside you can see the Changing of the Guard. Another attraction is the **Tower of London**, where many famous people were jailed, tortured, and killed. The crown jewels are shown there.

INDIA

One of the world's biggest and richest tombs is the **Taj Mahal**, which took about 20,000 workers to build. A ruler of India had it built for his wife after her death in 1631.

IRELAND

If you kiss the **Blarney Stone**, which is in the tower of Blarney Castle, legends say you'll be able to throw words around and get people to agree with you—even if what you say is nonsense.

ISRAEL

In Israel you can visit **Jerusalem**—a Holy City for three faiths. You can see the **Dome of the Rock**, built over the rock where Muhammad, founder of Islam, is said to have risen to heaven. You can stop at the **Western Wall**, where Jews pray; it is said to contain stones from Solomon's Temple. And you can see the **Church of the Holy Sepulcher**, built where it is believed that Jesus was crucified and buried.

ITALY

The **Leaning Tower of Pisa** is proof that kids aren't the only ones who make mistakes. Long before it was finished, the bell tower began sinking into the soft ground and leaning to one side. Every year, it leans ½₀ of an inch more.

KENYA

Here and in other countries of East Africa, you can visit **National Parks**. You can go on safaris to see lions, zebras, giraffes, elephants, and other animals in their natural home.

MEXICO

On the Yucatán peninsula, you can visit remains of the city of **Chichén Itzá**, where the Mayan people settled in the sixth century. Abandoned before the Spanish came, it's now partly rebuilt. You can see stone pyramids and temples and a Mayan ballfield.

▲ *Kremlin in Moscow, Russia*

RUSSIA

A famous place to visit here is the **Kremlin**, a walled fortress in Moscow, with old churches, palaces, and towers with onion-shaped gold domes, dating back to the Middle Ages. Today the Kremlin is the headquarters for the Russian government.

UNITED STATES

Yellowstone National Park was the world's first natural park and is one of the best. (See U.S. NATIONAL PARKS section of this book for more details.) There are many other places to visit in Washington, DC, and the 50 states (see U.S. STATES section for more information).

ENERGY: What It Is and Where It Comes From

You can't touch or smell or taste energy, but you can observe what energy can *do*. You can feel that sunlight warms objects, and you can see that electricity lights up a light bulb, even if you can't see the heat or the electricity.

What Is Energy? Things that you see and touch every day use some form of energy to work: your body, a bike, a basketball, a car. Energy enables things to move. Scientists define **energy** as the ability to do work.

Why Do We Need Energy To Do Work? Scientists define **work** as a force moving an object. Scientifically speaking, throwing a ball is work, but studying for a test isn't! When you throw a ball, you use energy from the food you eat to do work on the ball. The engine in a car uses energy from gasoline to make the car move.

Are There Different Kinds of Energy? Yes, there are. When we rest or sleep we still have the ability to move. We do not lose our energy. We simply store it for another time. Stored energy is called **potential energy**. When we get up and begin to move around, we are using stored energy. As we move around and walk, our stored (potential) energy changes into **kinetic energy**, which is the energy of moving things. A parked car has potential energy. A moving car has kinetic energy. A sled stopped at the top of the hill has potential energy. As the sled goes down the hill, its potential energy changes to kinetic energy.

potential energy

kinetic energy

How Is Energy Created? Energy cannot be created or destroyed, but it can be changed or converted into different forms. **Heat**, **light**, and **electricity** are forms of energy. Other forms of energy are **sound**, **chemical energy**, **mechanical energy**, and **nuclear energy**.

Where Does Energy Come From? All of the forms of energy we use come from the energy stored in **natural resources**. Sunlight, water, wind, petroleum, coal, and natural gas are natural resources. From these resources, we get heat and electricity.

Turning NATURAL RESOURCES Into Energy

THE SUN AND ITS ENERGY

Most of our energy comes from the sun. The sun is a big ball of glowing gases, made up mostly of hydrogen. Inside the sun, hydrogen atoms join together (through a process called nuclear fusion) and become helium. During the fusion process, large amounts of energy are released. This energy works its way to the sun's surface and then radiates out into space in the form of waves. These waves give us heat and light. The energy from the sun is stored in our food, which provides fuel for our bodies.

1. Plants absorb energy from the sun (solar energy) and convert absorbed energy to chemical energy for storage.

2. Animals eat plants and gain the stored chemical energy.

3. People eat plants and meat.

4. Food provides the body with energy to work and play.

THE SUN STORES ITS ENERGY IN FOSSIL FUELS

The sun also provides the energy stored in fossil fuels. Coal, petroleum, and natural gas are **fossil fuels**. Fossil fuels come from the remains of ancient plants and animals over millions and millions of years. This is how it happened:

1. Hundreds of millions of years ago, before people lived on Earth, trees and other plants absorbed energy from the sun, just as they do today.

2. Animals ate plants and smaller animals.

3. After the plants and animals died, they slowly became buried deeper and deeper underground.

4. After millions of years, they eventually turned into coal and petroleum.

Although the buried prehistoric plants and animals changed form over time, they still contained stored energy.

When we burn fossil fuels today, the stored energy from the sun is released in the form of heat. The heat is used to warm our homes and other buildings and produce electricity for our lights and appliances.

How Does ENERGY GET TO YOU?

ENERGY FROM FOSSIL FUELS

Most of our energy comes from fossil fuels. Your home may be heated with oil or natural gas. You may have a kitchen stove that uses natural gas. Cars need gasoline to run. The diagram below shows how energy goes from a primary source (like coal or other fossil fuels) to a form of energy that you can use (like electricity).

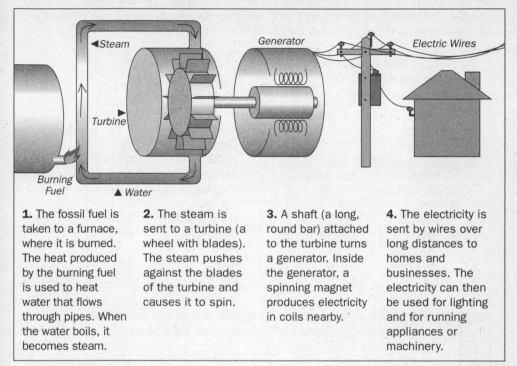

1. The fossil fuel is taken to a furnace, where it is burned. The heat produced by the burning fuel is used to heat water that flows through pipes. When the water boils, it becomes steam.

2. The steam is sent to a turbine (a wheel with blades). The steam pushes against the blades of the turbine and causes it to spin.

3. A shaft (a long, round bar) attached to the turbine turns a generator. Inside the generator, a spinning magnet produces electricity in coils nearby.

4. The electricity is sent by wires over long distances to homes and businesses. The electricity can then be used for lighting and for running appliances or machinery.

ENERGY FROM WATER

For centuries, people have been getting energy from rushing water. In a hydroelectric plant, water from rivers or dams is used to drive machinery like a turbine. The turbine is connected to a generator, which produces electricity.

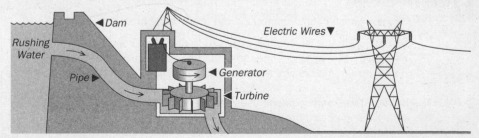

NUCLEAR ENERGY

In nuclear reactors, uranium atoms are split into smaller atoms to produce heat. The heat is then used to produce electricity, just as the heat from burning coal is used.

Who PRODUCES and USES the Most Energy?

The chart below shows which countries produced the most energy in 1992 and which ones used the most. A unit that is often used to measure energy is the British Thermal Unit, abbreviated Btu. A 60-watt light bulb uses about 205 Btus of energy in the form of electricity every hour. In these charts, the amounts of energy are written in quadrillions of Btus. One quadrillion is written as 1,000,000,000,000,000.

COUNTRIES THAT PRODUCE THE MOST ENERGY (in quadrillion Btus)		COUNTRIES THAT USE THE MOST ENERGY (in quadrillion Btus)	
United States	66.68	United States	82.19
Russia	45.66	Russia	32.72
China	30.18	China	29.22
Saudi Arabia	20.63	Japan	19.01
Canada	14.36	Germany	14.11
Great Britain	9.23	Canada	10.97
Iran	8.53	France	9.71
Mexico	7.76	Great Britain	9.68
India	6.94	Ukraine	8.75
Norway	6.8	India	8.51
Venezuela	6.8	Italy	7.0
		Brazil	6.07

ENERGY PUZZLE

Can you find the three countries (in the chart above) that produce energy and use *more* energy than they produce? (Answers are on page 303.)

1. _ _ _ _ _ _ _   _ _ _ _ _ _ _

2. _ _ _ _ _   3. _ _ _ _ _ _   _ _ _ _ _ _ _ _

? DID YOU KNOW?

☑ Do you know which countries produce the most fossil fuels?

The country that produces the most crude oil is Saudi Arabia.
The country that produces the most natural gas is Russia.
The country that produces the most coal is China.

☑ The United States produces and uses more energy than any other country in the world. It also uses more energy than it produces. To meet its energy needs, the United States imports fossil fuels from other countries.

The United States gets crude oil mainly from Saudi Arabia, West Africa, Mexico, and Venezuela. It also gets both crude oil and natural gas from Canada.

WILL WE HAVE ENOUGH ENERGY?

SOME ENERGY SOURCES ARE LIMITED

In 1993, 88% of the energy used in the United States came from fossil fuels (40% from petroleum, 25% from natural gas, and 23% from coal). The rest came from hydropower (water power) and nuclear energy.

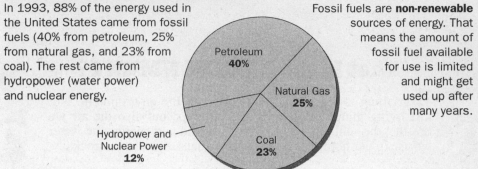

Petroleum
40%

Natural Gas
25%

Coal
23%

Hydropower and
Nuclear Power
12%

Fossil fuels are **non-renewable** sources of energy. That means the amount of fossil fuel available for use is limited and might get used up after many years.

LOOKING FOR RENEWABLE RESOURCES

Scientists are trying to find more sources of energy that will reduce pollution and save some of the fossil fuels. People are using several types of **renewable resources**. Some of these forms of energy exist in an unlimited supply.

☑ **Solar power.** Solar power uses energy from sunlight. Solar panels can collect the sun's rays for heating. Solar cells can convert light energy directly into electricity.

☑ **The wind.** Old-fashioned windmills were used to drive machinery. Today, some people are using wind turbines to generate electricity.

☑ **Water from the ocean.** Ocean waves and tides can be used to drive generators to produce electricity.

☑ **Geothermal energy.** Geothermal energy is energy that comes from the hot, molten rock inside Earth. In certain parts of the world, people use this kind of energy for electricity and to heat buildings.

☑ **Biomass energy.** Biomass includes wood from trees and other plants, animal wastes, and garbage. When these are burned or allowed to decay, they produce natural gas. Biomass energy is widely available and used in some parts of the world, although it is not unlimited.

SAVING ENERGY FOR TOMORROW

☑ Many businesses are trying to find ways to reuse heat from steam turbine generators.
☑ Recycling reduces the energy that would be used for making new products.
☑ Riding buses and trains, car pooling, and driving fuel-efficient cars reduces fossil fuel usage (and also air pollution).
☑ Using less heat, less hot water, and less air conditioning also helps save energy.

What Is the ENVIRONMENT?

Everything that surrounds us is part of the environment. Not just living things like plants and animals, but also the air we breathe, the sunlight that provides warmth and energy, the water we use in our homes, schools, and businesses, and even rocks.

People and the Environment. People have been a part of the environment for thousands and thousands of years. For a long time people thought the earth was so huge that it would always absorb any kind of pollution. And they thought that its natural resources would never be used up.

Even prehistoric people affected the environment. They killed animals for food. They built fires to cook food and keep themselves warm. They cut down trees for fuel, and their fires released gases into the air. In prehistoric times, though, there were so few people that their activities had little impact on the environment.

Today, there are an enormous number of people in the world—we've had a population explosion. Because there are so many people on earth, the things we do affect the environment more dramatically. Look at the table below to see how fast the population of the world has grown.

YEAR	WORLD POPULATION	
1650	550,000,000	🧍
1750	725,000,000	🧍🧍
1850	1,175,000,000	🧍🧍
1950	2,564,000,000	🧍🧍🧍🧍🧍
1994	5,607,000,000	🧍🧍🧍🧍🧍🧍🧍🧍🧍🧍

The Earth Belongs to Everyone. Many people are becoming aware that some of the things people do could seriously damage the planet and the animals and plants that live on it. Sometimes this damage can be fixed over a long period of time. But sometimes it is permanent. On the following pages there are facts about some of the parts of the environment, how they are being affected, and what can be done to clean up and protect the environment. People are an important part of the environment because they have the unique ability to change it.

ENVIRONMENT GLOSSARY

climate
The average weather in a region of the world.

compost heap
A pile of food scraps and yard waste that is broken down by worms and tiny insects. The result looks like dirt. It can be used to enrich the soil.

deforestation
The cutting down of most of the trees from forested land, usually so that the land can be used for something besides a forest.

ecosystem
A community of living things and the place where they live, such as a forest or pond.

environment
All living and non-living things in an area at a given time. The environment affects the growth of living things.

extinction
The disappearance of a type (species) of plant or animal from the earth. Some species become extinct because of natural forces, but many others are becoming endangered or threatened with extinction because of the activities of people.

fossil fuel
Anything that comes from once-living matter deep in the earth, such as oil, gas, and coal.

global warming
An increase in the earth's temperature due to a buildup of certain gases in the atmosphere.

greenhouse effect
Warming of the earth caused by certain gases (called **greenhouse gases**) that form a blanket in the atmosphere high over the earth. Small amounts of these gases keep the earth warm so we can live here, but the larger amounts produced by factories, cars, and burning trees may hold in too much heat and cause global warming.

habitat
The natural home of an animal or plant.

incinerator
A large furnace in which garbage is burned.

landfill (or dump)
A low area of land that is filled with garbage.

pollution
Contamination of air, water, or soil by materials that can injure health, the quality of life, or the working of ecosystems.

recycling
Using something more than once, either just the way it is, or treated and made into something else.

soil erosion
The washing or blowing away of topsoil. Trees and other plants hold the soil in place and help reduce the force of the wind. Soil erosion can happen when trees and plants are removed.

GARBAGE and RECYCLING

Look around. Everything you see will probably be replaced or thrown away someday. Skates, clothes, the toaster, the refrigerator, furniture—they may break or wear out, or you may get tired of them and want new ones sooner or later. Where will they go when they are thrown out? What kinds of waste will they create, and how will it affect the environment? The average person in the United States today produces more than 4 pounds of trash every day. In 1960, it was less than 3 pounds.

What HAPPENS to the THINGS We THROW AWAY?

Landfills

Most of our trash goes to places called landfills. A **landfill** (or dump) is a low area of land that is filled with garbage. Most modern landfills are lined with a layer of plastic or clay to try to keep dangerous liquids from seeping out. The garbage is spread in layers and packed down by a bulldozer so that it takes up less space.

The Problem with Landfills

There is so much trash that we are quickly running out of room for it. In less than ten years, all the landfills in more than half of the states of the United States will be full.

Incinerators

Another way to get rid of trash is to burn it. Trash is burned in a device like a furnace called an **incinerator**. Because incinerators can get rid of almost all of the bulk of the trash, some communities would rather use incinerators than landfills.

The Problem with Incinerators

Leftover ash and smoke from burning trash may contain harmful chemicals, called **pollutants**. These pollutants can harm plants, animals, and people.

Look at what is now in landfills

Metal **6%**

Plastic **10%**

Food and Yard Waste **13%**

Other Trash **21%**

Paper **50%**

WHAT CAN WE DO?

We are very good at producing waste, but we are not good at getting rid of it. What can we do?

Paper

Use both sides of a piece of paper. Recycle newspapers, magazines, comic books, and catalogs. Try to buy paper products made of recycled paper. When possible, use cloth towels instead of paper towels.

Plastic

Return soda bottles to the store. Refill or recycle detergent bottles and milk jugs. Wash food containers and use them to store leftovers or to store your collections. Reuse plastic bags.

Glass

Reuse or recycle glass bottles and jars.

Metal

Recycle aluminum cans and foil trays. Give the dry cleaner any wire clothes hangers you don't need.

Food and Yard Waste

If you have a yard, make a compost heap for food scraps and grass clippings and leaves. A **compost heap** is a pile of food scraps, leaves, and other natural materials that decompose (rot) with the help of earthworms and tiny organisms. The decomposed material, called humus, can be used to fertilize soil.

Clothes

Give clothes to younger relatives, or donate used clothes to thrift shops. Cut torn, unwearable old clothes into rags to use instead of paper towels.

Batteries

Use rechargeable batteries for toys and games, radios, tape players, and flashlights.

REDUCE, REUSE, RECYCLE

We can reduce the amount of garbage we create by reusing containers, batteries, and many other things we now throw away. We can recycle as many things as possible. Many communities have laws that require recycling. In other communities, volunteers provide a center where people can take paper, glass, and plastic trash to be recycled.

? DID YOU KNOW? Plastics are good for many things because they are indestructible, but they turn into a problem when they are thrown away. Something plastic—a bottle, a six-pack holder, a toy—may take more than 400 years to rot away.

The largest amount of American trash is packaging, such as plastic containers, glass bottles, aluminum cans, and cardboard boxes. Americans throw out 57 million tons of packaging every year.

Every ton of paper we recycle saves 17 trees and keeps over 9 cubic feet of garbage out of landfills.

THE AIR WE BREATHE

All human beings and animals need air to survive. Without air we would all die. Plants also need air to live. Plants use sunlight and the carbon dioxide in air to make food, and then give off oxygen.

We all breathe the air that surrounds the earth. The air is composed mainly of gases: around 78% nitrogen, 21% oxygen, and 1% carbon dioxide, other gases, and water vapor. Human beings breathe more than 6 quarts of air every minute. Because air is so basic to life, it is very important to keep the air clean by reducing or preventing air pollution. Today, air pollution causes problems worldwide, such as **acid rain, global warming,** and the **breakdown of the ozone layer.**

Nitrogen
78%

Oxygen
21%

▲ Carbon Dioxide,
Other Gases,
Water Vapor
1%

What Is Air Pollution and Where Does It Come From? Air pollution is dirtying the air with chemicals or other materials that can injure health, the enjoyment of life, or the working of ecosystems. The major sources of air pollution are cars, trucks and buses, waste incinerators, factories, and some electric power plants, especially those that burn fossil fuels.

What Is Acid Rain and Where Does It Come From? Acid rain is a kind of air pollution. It is caused by chemicals that are released into the air and cause rain, snow, and fog to be more acidic than usual. The main sources of these chemicals are power plants that burn coal to create the electricity we use. When these chemicals mix with moisture and other particles in the air, they create sulfuric acid and nitric acid. The wind often carries these acids many miles before they fall to the ground in rain, snow, and fog, or even as dry particles.

Why Worry About Air Pollution and Acid Rain? Air pollution and acid rain can harm people, animals, and plants. Air pollution can cause our eyes to sting and can make some people sick. It can also damage crops and trees.

Air pollution (especially acid rain) is also harmful to water in lakes, often killing plants and fish that live there. Hundreds of lakes in the northeastern United States and 14,000 lakes in Canada are so acidic that fish can no longer live there. Acid rain has affected trees in U.S. national parks. In the Appalachian Mountains, for example, it has harmed spruce trees growing in the Shenandoah and Great Smoky Mountain National Parks. And it can turn buildings and statues black and damage them by eating away at metal, stone, and paint. Monuments and statues that have survived hundreds of years are suddenly disintegrating.

Global Warming and the Greenhouse Effect

Many scientists believe that gases in the air are causing the earth's climate to become warmer. This is called **global warming.** If the climate becomes so warm that a great deal of ice near the north and south poles melts and more water goes into the oceans, many areas along the coasts may be flooded.

In the earth's atmosphere there are tiny amounts of gases called **greenhouse gases.** These gases let the rays of the sun pass through to the planet, but they hold in the heat that comes up from the sun-warmed earth—just like the glass of a greenhouse holds in the warmth of the sun.

As cities increased in size and population, factories and businesses also grew. People needed more and more electricity, cars, and other things that had to be manufactured. As industries in the world have increased, greenhouse gases have been added to the atmosphere. These gases increase the thickness of the greenhouse "glass," causing too much heat to be trapped. This is called **the greenhouse effect.**

DID YOU KNOW? Americans contribute 21% of the greenhouse gases that enter the atmosphere. That is more than any other country.

Good and Bad Ozone

Good Ozone. Another problem caused by air pollution involves a layer in the atmosphere high above the earth, called the **ozone layer.** The ozone layer protects us from the harsh rays of the sun. When refrigerators, air conditioners, and similar items are thrown away, gases from them (called chlorofluorocarbons or CFCs) rise into the air and destroy some of the ozone in this layer.

Bad Ozone. There is also ozone near the ground that forms when sunlight hits air pollutants from cars and smokestacks, causing smog. This ozone near the ground can be harmful.

What Are We Doing To Reduce Air Pollution?

Many countries, including the United States, are trying to reduce air pollution. Today's cars can go farther on a gallon of gasoline than cars of 20 or 30 years ago, so that less gasoline has to be burned to get people where they want to go. In the United States, cars must have a special device to remove harmful chemicals from their smoke before it comes out of the tailpipe. More and more power plants and factories are putting devices on their smokestacks to catch harmful chemicals before they can enter the air. Many people are trying not to use more electricity than they really need, so that less coal will have to be burned to produce electricity. And in some places, power companies are using windmills or other equipment that does not pollute the air to make some of their electricity.

PROTECTING OUR WATER

Every plant and animal needs water for its body to work. Fish, frogs, and many other animals depend on water as a place to live. Besides drinking, people use water to cook, to clean, to cool machinery in factories, to produce power, to irrigate farm land, and for swimming and boating.

Around two thirds of the earth's surface is water. About 97% of that is seawater, and 2% is frozen in glaciers and the ice around the north and south poles. Only 1% is fresh water, and only part of that is close enough to the earth's surface for us to use. If all of the water on earth fit in a two gallon bucket, just over two tablespoons would be available as fresh water.

A DROP IN THE BUCKET?

How Do Americans Use Fresh Water?

People in the United States use 338 billion gallons of fresh water every day.

Gallons Used Every Day	How Fresh Water Is Used in the United States
137 billion	To water crops on farms
131 billion	To produce electricity
28 billion	In factories
24 billion	In homes, for drinking, cooking, flushing toilets, etc.
7 billion	In hotels, restaurants, offices
4 billion	For farm animals
4 billion	Public use in parks, firefighting, street washing
3 billion	For mining
Total water used every day: 338 billion gallons	

What Is Threatening Our Water and What Are We Doing About It?

Water pollution and overuse of water are the major threats to our water.

Water Pollution. Water is said to be polluted when it is not fit for its intended uses, such as drinking, swimming, watering crops, or serving as a habitat. Polluted water can cause disease and kill fish and other animals. Some major water pollutants include sewage, chemicals from factories, fertilizers and weed killers, and leaking landfills. But water pollution is also being reduced in some areas. Some lakes are being cleaned up enough to restore plants and fish to them. Companies continue to look for better ways to get rid of wastes, and many farmers are trying new ways to grow crops without using fertilizers or chemicals that kill weeds or bugs.

Overuse of Water. Another major threat to our water supply is overuse—using up so much water that not enough is left. It is important to try to conserve as much water as possible. Some modern plumbing supplies (like toilets and shower heads) are now designed to use less water. Many people are taking shorter showers, and they don't let the water run when they brush their teeth or wash dishes by hand. People concerned about water are also running dishwashers or washing machines only when they have a full load. They fix faucets that drip and don't water the lawn unless it really needs it.

The IMPORTANCE of FORESTS

Trees and forests are very important to the environment. In addition to holding water, trees hold the soil in place. Trees use carbon dioxide and give off oxygen, which animals and plants need for survival. And they provide homes and food for millions of types of animals.

Why Do We Cut Down Trees? People cut down trees for many reasons. When the population grows, people cut down trees to clear space to build houses, schools, factories, and other buildings. People may clear land to plant crops and graze livestock. Sometimes all the trees in an area are cut and sold for lumber and paper. Cutting down trees—usually to use the land for something besides a forest—is called **deforestation.**

What Happens When Trees Are Cut Down? Although people often have good reasons for cutting down trees, deforestation can have serious effects. If animal habitats are destroyed, many species will become extinct. Because of deforestation, thousands of species in the Amazon rain forest in South America are being lost before scientists can even learn about them.

Cutting down trees can also affect the climate. After rain falls on a forest, mist starts rising and new rain clouds are created. When forests are cut down, this cycle is disrupted, and the area eventually grows drier, causing a change in the local climate.

If huge areas of trees are cut down, the carbon dioxide they would have used builds up in the atmosphere and contributes to the greenhouse effect. And without trees to hold the soil and absorb water, rain washes topsoil away into rivers and reservoirs, a process called **soil erosion**. Farming on the poorer soil that is left can be very hard.

What Are We Doing To Save Forests? In 24 European countries, trees are being planted faster than they are being cut down. Also, trees are being planted to restock woodland areas and to create forests in some countries where timber is scarce. In addition, communities and individuals are helping to save forests by recycling paper.

TEST YOUR TREE SMARTS: TRUE OR FALSE? *(Answers on page 302)*

T F 1. Scientists can tell what the climate was like thousands of years ago by studying trees.

T F 2. Pollution harms all trees equally.

T F 3. Nearly 50% of the original forests of the United States are still standing.

T F 4. Half of the world's plant and animal species come from tropical forests.

T F 5. Americans throw out more than 70,000,000 tons of paper each year.

 DID YOU KNOW? Twenty years ago, the Chinese people who live in Beijing planted more than 300 million fast-growing trees along the path of the Great Wall of China. It was the largest reforestation project ever attempted. They were hoping the trees would help prevent the terrible dust storms that hit Beijing every year. Now those trees are big. Because they hold the soil in place and slow down the winds, they have nearly eliminated Beijing's dust storms.

Sharing the Earth: BIODIVERSITY

Trees, flowers, insects, fish, whales, dogs, cats, human beings—all of us share the planet Earth. Each type (species) of animal or plant has its place on Earth, and each one is dependent on the others. Plants give off oxygen that animals need to breathe. Animals pollinate plants and spread their seeds. Animals eat plants and are in turn eaten by larger animals. When plants and animals die, they become part of the soil in which plants, in their turn, can take root and grow.

What Is Biodiversity? Our planet, Earth, is shared by more than 5 million species. Human beings of all colors, races, and nationalities make up just one species, *Homo sapiens*. All of the species together form the variety of life we call *biodiversity* (*bio* means "life" and *diversity* means "variety").

How Many Species Are There? The list of species below is a small sampling of how diverse Earth is.

BEETLES: 290,000 species
Fascinating Fact ▶
There are more kinds of beetles than any other animal on earth.

FLOWERING PLANTS: 250,000 species
Fascinating Fact ▶ The 750,000 species of insects and the 250,000 species of flowering plants depend on one another. The insects need the plants for food, the plants need the insects for pollination.

EDIBLE PLANTS: 30,000 species
Fascinating Fact ▶ Although 30,000 are edible, 90% of the world's food comes from only 20 species.

ANTS: 20,000 species
Fascinating Fact ▶
If you were to weigh all the insects on earth, ants would make up almost half of the total.

BIRDS: 9,040 species
Fascinating Fact ▶ More than 1,000 of these species are in danger of becoming extinct.

BATS: 1,000 species
Fascinating Fact ▶ There are more species of bats than of any other mammal.

PET DOGS: 1 species
Fascinating Fact ▶ Even though they can look very different, all dogs belong to the same species.

HUMAN BEINGS: 1 species
Fascinating Fact ▶ This one species holds the fate of all the others in its hands. People can affect the environment more than any other type of living thing.

Threats to Biodiversity. All of the threats to the other areas of the environment affect the lives and habitats of plants and animals. Deforestation, farming, and construction contribute to the destruction of habitats of plants and animals. Plants and animals are also harmed by air, water, and land pollution. Another threat to biodiversity is overharvesting, or the use of too many animals for food or other products. Whales, for example, have been overharvested.

Protecting Biodiversity. All of the efforts to reduce pollutants in air, water, and soil, and to limit deforestation and overharvesting will help to preserve biodiversity. A few species that were endangered have increased sufficiently in number, so that they are no longer in danger of becoming extinct.

PROTECTING the ENVIRONMENT

Many adults and children are working very hard to learn how to protect the environment and save the earth.

People Throughout the World Are Working Together

Most countries now have people in the government whose job it is to protect the environment. In the United States, the Environmental Protection Agency (EPA) is responsible for protecting the environment.

In 1992, the governments of nearly 180 countries met in Brazil to talk about the environment. They tried to find ways to protect the earth.

Every year on April 22nd, people throughout the world celebrate Earth Day. They have ecology fairs, tree plantings, parades, rallies, and demonstrations to educate people about the environment and to show them ways to conserve.

Many groups, large and small, are working on specific problems like the rain forests, endangered species, and recycling. Groups are also working together to clean up shores. On International Coastal Cleanup Day in 1993, over 150,000 volunteers from 13 countries collected more than 3 million pounds of trash from 4,600 miles of beaches.

Children and grown-ups alike can make a huge difference by doing simple things like disposing of trash correctly, recycling, and not wasting electricity and water.

How Kids Can Protect the Environment

☑ *Recycle* as many things as possible: plastic, glass, and papers.

☑ *Save electricity* by turning off lights when you leave the room. Close the refrigerator door as quickly as possible. Don't stand with it open.

☑ *Take care of things made from wood.* When you buy or get anything made from wood, remember that it came from a tree. When you're finished with it, give it to someone else.

☑ *Save water* by not letting the water run when you brush your teeth. Take shorter showers. Don't leave water running when you're not using it.

WHAT IS A GLOBE?

Did you ever travel on a spaceship? Whether you know it or not, you're traveling right now on the spaceship called Planet Earth. Earth is always zooming through space and around the sun at very fast speeds.

A tiny model of Earth is called a **globe**. Like Earth, a globe is shaped like a ball or **sphere**. Although Earth isn't exactly a sphere because it gets flat at the top and bottom and bulges a little in the middle, a globe gives us the best idea of what Earth looks like. Because Earth is round, most flat maps do not show the shapes of the land masses exactly right. The shapes at the top and bottom usually look too big. For example, on a flat map the island of Greenland, which is next to North America, looks bigger than Australia, but it is really much smaller.

When you look at a ball or sphere, you can see only the half of it that is facing toward you. The drawing here shows half of a globe.

Which Hemisphere Do You Live In?
You can draw an imaginary line around the middle of Earth, like a belt. This is called the **equator**. The closer you get to the equator, the hotter it gets. The equator splits Earth into two halves called **hemispheres**. The part that's north of the equator is called the **northern hemisphere**. The part that's south of the equator is called the **southern hemisphere**. You can also divide Earth into the **western hemisphere** and the **eastern hemisphere**. The western hemisphere is the part shown on the globe above.

▼ North Pole

◄ 40 degrees north latitude

North America

◄ 20 degrees north latitude

◄ Equator

◄ 20 degrees south latitude

South America

◄ 40 degrees south latitude

▲ South Pole

Lines of LATITUDE and LONGITUDE

Imaginary lines that run east and west around the earth, parallel to the equator, are called **parallels**. They tell you the **latitude** of a place, or how far it is from the equator. The equator is at 0 degrees latitude. As you go farther north or south, the latitude increases. The North Pole is at 90 degrees **north latitude**. The South Pole is at 90 degrees **south latitude**.

Imaginary lines that run north and south around the globe, from one pole to the other, are called **meridians**. These meridians tell you the degree of **longitude**, or how far east or west a place is from an imaginary line called the **Greenwich meridian** or **prime meridian**. That line runs through the city of Greenwich in England.

The CONTINENTS and OCEANS of the World

Almost two-thirds of Earth's surface is made up of water. The rest is land. The largest areas of water are called **oceans**, and the largest pieces of land are called **continents**. The Earth has seven continents and four oceans. Below are some basic facts about the continents and oceans. See pages 65-75 for maps of the continents.

CONTINENTS

The facts about the continents include their highest place (top of the highest mountain) and lowest place (the number of feet below sea level).

NORTH AMERICA
Area: 9,400,000 square miles
Population: 432,232,000
(including Central America and Caribbean islands)
Highest Point: Mount McKinley (Alaska), 20,320 feet
Lowest Point: Death Valley (California), 282 feet below sea level

SOUTH AMERICA
Area: 6,900,000 square miles
Population: 302,212,000
Highest Point: Mount Aconcagua (Argentina), 22,834 feet
Lowest Point: Valdes Peninsula (Argentina), 131 feet below sea level

EUROPE
Area: 3,800,000 square miles
Population: 727,234,000
Highest Point: Mount Elbrus (Russia), 18,510 feet
Lowest Point: Caspian Sea (Russia, Azerbaijan; eastern Europe and western Asia), 92 feet below sea level

ASIA
Area: 17,200,000 square miles
Population (1994): 3,291,269,000
Highest Point: Mount Everest (Nepal, Tibet), 29,028 feet
Lowest Point: Dead Sea (Israel, Jordan), 1,312 feet below sea level

AFRICA
Area: 11,700,000 square miles
Population: 656,108,000
Highest Point: Mount Kilimanjaro (Tanzania), 19,340 feet
Lowest Point: Lake Assal (Djibouti), 512 feet below sea level

AUSTRALIA
(including Australia and New Zealand)
Area: 3,071,000 square miles
Population: 21,466,000
Highest Point: Mount Kosciusko (New South Wales), 7,310 feet
Lowest Point: Lake Eyre (South Australia), 52 feet below sea level

ANTARCTICA
Area: 5,400,000 square miles
Population: Zero
Highest Point: Vinson Massif, 16,864 feet
Lowest Point: Not known

OCEANS

The facts about the oceans include their size and average depth.

Pacific Ocean: 64,186,300 square miles; 12,925 feet deep
Atlantic Ocean: 33,420,000 square miles; 11,730 feet deep
Indian Ocean: 28,350,500 square miles; 12,598 feet deep
Arctic Ocean: 5,105,700 square miles; 3,407 feet deep

FAMOUS REGIONS
of the World

When you watch the news on television or read the newspaper, you will see the names of many different regions of the world. Do you know where the Middle East is? Can you name the countries that make up the region known as the Balkans? Below are some of the major regions of the world.

BALKANS. A region often in the news is the Balkans, in southeastern Europe. This region consists of Yugoslavia, Slovenia, Croatia, Bosnia and Herzegovina, Macedonia, and Albania. Bulgaria, southeastern Romania, northern Greece, and the portion of Turkey in Europe are also part of the Balkans. All the Balkan states were once part of the Ottoman Empire.

CARIBBEAN. The Caribbean region is centered on the Caribbean Sea, an arm of the Atlantic Ocean that lies south of the United States, east of Central America, and north of South America. The Caribbean has thousands of islands. The largest groups are the Greater Antilles and the Lesser Antilles. Among the countries in the Greater Antilles are Cuba, Haiti, the Dominican Republic, Jamaica, and the U.S. Commonwealth of Puerto Rico. The Lesser Antilles include Dominica, Barbados, Grenada, and Trinidad and Tobago.

CENTRAL AMERICA. Central America is the region between Mexico and South America. It consists of Belize, Guatemala, Honduras, El Salvador, Nicaragua, Costa Rica, and Panama.

EASTERN EUROPE. Countries of Eastern Europe include Poland, the Czech Republic, Slovakia, Hungary, Romania, and Bulgaria. Three other Eastern European countries (Estonia, Latvia, and Lithuania) form a region known as the Baltic States.

MIDDLE EAST. One of the most famous regions in the news is the Middle East. The Middle East refers to Egypt and Libya (in northeast Africa), to Israel, Jordan, Lebanon, Syria, and Iraq, and to countries of the Arabian Peninsula: Saudi Arabia, Kuwait, Bahrain, Qatar, United Arab Emirates, Oman, and Yemen (all in southwestern Asia). The term "Middle East" sometimes also includes the other Islamic countries of North Africa: Morocco, Algeria, and Tunisia.

POLYNESIA. Polynesia is a region in the central and southern Pacific Ocean. It consists of a number of large island groups. The Hawaiian Islands make up the 50th state of the United States. Western Samoa and Tonga are independent countries. American Samoa is a territory of the United States administered by the U.S. Department of the Interior. French Polynesia, which includes Tahiti, is an overseas territory of France.

SCANDINAVIA. Scandinavia is in northern Europe. Its countries are Norway, Sweden, Denmark, and Finland. Iceland, in the north Atlantic Ocean, is also considered a Scandinavian country.

SOUTHEAST ASIA. The region of Southeast Asia lies east of India and south of China. It consists of 10 independent countries: Myanmar (Burma), Thailand, Vietnam, Laos, Cambodia, Malaysia, Singapore, the Philippines, Indonesia, and Brunei.

VOLCANOES

A **volcano** is a mountain or hill with an opening on top. Every once in a while, hot melted rock (**magma**), gases, ash, and other material from inside the earth may blast out, or erupt, through the opening. The magma is called **lava** when it reaches the air. This red-hot lava may have a temperature of more than 2,000 degrees Fahrenheit. The hill or mountain is made out of lava and other materials that come out of the opening, and then cool off and harden. The top of the volcano often has a big dent, known as a **crater**. Some islands are really the tops of volcanoes. The Hawaiian islands developed when volcanoes erupted under the Pacific Ocean.

SOME FAMOUS VOLCANIC ERUPTIONS

YEAR	VOLCANO (PLACE)	DEATHS (Approximate)
79	Mount Vesuvius (Italy)	16,000
1169	Mount Etna (Sicily)	15,000
1669	Mount Etna (Sicily)	20,000
1792	Mount Unzen-Dake (Japan)	10,400
1815	Tambora (Indonesia)	10,000
1883	Krakatau or Krakatoa (Indonesia)	36,000
1902	Mount Pelee (Martinique)	28,000
1980	Mount St. Helens (U.S.)	57
1985	Nevada del Ruiz (Colombia)	23,000
1994	Merapi (Indonesia)	60

Why Do Volcanoes Erupt?

There are about 850 active volcanoes in the world. Some have erupted many times. Volcanic eruptions come from pools of magma and other materials a few miles underground. The pools come from rock far below. After the rock melts and mixes with gases, it rises up through cracks and weak spots in the mountain.

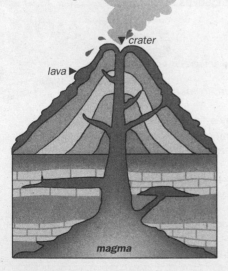

ash and gas ▶

▼ crater

lava ▶

magma

Where Is the Ring of Fire?

There are volcanoes on the bottom of the ocean and on every continent. Many of the active volcanoes are found on land along the edges of the Pacific Ocean. These volcanoes are often called the **Ring of Fire.**

The Ring of Fire marks the boundary between the plates under the Pacific Ocean and the plates under the continents around the Pacific Ocean (North America, South America, Asia). The plates of the earth are explained on page 102 and can be seen on a map on page 103, under the section on Earthquakes.

EARTHQUAKES

Earthquakes may be so weak that they are hardly felt, or they may be strong enough to do tremendous damage. There are thousands of earthquakes each year, but most of them are too small to be felt. About 1 in 5 can be felt, and about 1 in 500 causes damage.

What Causes Earthquakes?

The Earth's outer layer, called the **crust**, is divided into huge pieces called **plates**. These plates, which are made of rock, are constantly moving in different directions—away from each other, toward each other, or past each other. A crack in Earth's crust between two

plates is called a **fault**. Many earthquakes occur along faults where two plates collide as they move toward each other or grind together as they move past each other. Earthquakes along the famous **San Andreas Fault** in California are caused by the grinding of two plates moving past each other.

How Are Earthquakes Measured?

The strength of an earthquake is called its **magnitude**. The magnitude of an earthquake is registered on an instrument called a **seismograph** and is given a number on a scale called the **Richter scale**.

RICHTER SCALE

The Richter scale goes from zero to more than 9. These numbers are used to describe the strength of an earthquake. Each number on the Richter scale is 10 times greater than the one before it. An earthquake measuring 6 on the Richter scale is 10 times stronger than an earthquake measuring 5 and 100 times stronger than one measuring 4. Earthquakes that register below 4 on the Richter scale are considered minor. Those of 4 or above are considered major.

A seismograph ▶

MAGNITUDE	EFFECTS
0-2	Earthquake is recorded by instruments but is not felt by people.
2-3	Earthquake is felt slightly by a few people.
3-4	People feel tremors. Hanging objects like ceiling lights swing.
4-5	Earthquake causes some damage; walls crack; dishes and windows may break.
5-6	Furniture moves; earthquake seriously damages weak buildings.
6-7	Furniture may overturn; strong buildings are damaged; walls and buildings may collapse.
7-8	Many buildings are destroyed; underground pipes break; wide cracks appear in the ground.
Above 8	Total devastation, including buildings and bridges; ground wavy.

MAJOR EARTHQUAKES
of the 20th Century

The earthquakes listed below are among the largest and most destructive recorded in the 20th century. The list begins with the most recent earthquakes.

YEAR	LOCATION	MAGNITUDE	DEATHS
1995	Japan (Kobe)	7.2	5,000+
1994	United States (Los Angeles area)	6.6	61
1992	Indonesia (Flores)	7.5	2,500
1990	Iran (northwestern)	7.7	40,000+
1989	United States (San Francisco area)	6.9	62
1988	Armenia (northwestern)	6.8	55,000+
1985	Mexico (Mexico City)	8.1	4,200+
1976	China (Tangshan)	8.2	242,000
1976	Guatemala	7.5	22,778
1970	Peru (northern)	7.7	66,794
1960	Chile (southern)	8.3	5,000
1950	India (Assam)	8.7	1,530
1946	Japan (Honshu)	8.4	2,000
1939	Chile (Chillan)	8.3	28,000
1934	India (Bihar) - Nepal	8.4	10,700
1933	Japan	8.9	2,990
1927	China (Nanshan)	8.3	200,000
1923	Japan (Yokohama)	8.3	200,000
1920	China (Gansu)	8.6	100,000
1906	Chile (Valparaiso)	8.6	20,000
1906	United States (San Francisco)	8.3	503

? DID YOU KNOW? Between December 16, 1811, and February 7, 1812, a series of earthquakes near New Madrid, Missouri, caused enormous damage to much of the Midwest. These earthquakes (estimated at about 8.7 on the Richter scale) were so powerful that they caused the Mississippi River to change its course.

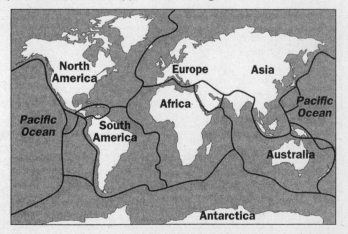

The Earth's surface is divided into huge pieces called plates that are constantly moving.

103

The TALLEST, LONGEST, HIGHEST, DEEPEST in the World

Tallest Mountain: Mount Everest, in Tibet and Nepal (29,028 feet)

Longest River: Nile, in Egypt and Sudan (4,160 miles)

Highest Waterfall: Angel Falls, in Venezuela (3,212 feet)

Deepest Lake: Lake Baykal, in Asia (5,315 feet)

Biggest Lake: Caspian Sea, in Europe and Asia (143,244 square miles)

Biggest Island: Greenland, in the Atlantic Ocean (840,000 square miles)

Biggest Swamp: Grand Pantanal, in Brazil (42,000 square miles)

Biggest Desert: Sahara, in Africa (3,500,000 square miles)

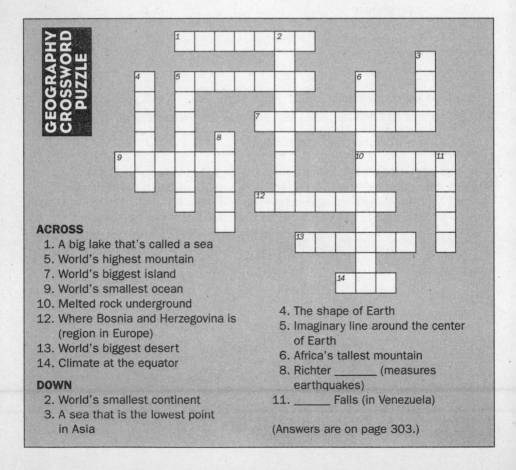

GEOGRAPHY CROSSWORD PUZZLE

ACROSS
1. A big lake that's called a sea
5. World's highest mountain
7. World's biggest island
9. World's smallest ocean
10. Melted rock underground
12. Where Bosnia and Herzegovina is (region in Europe)
13. World's biggest desert
14. Climate at the equator

DOWN
2. World's smallest continent
3. A sea that is the lowest point in Asia
4. The shape of Earth
5. Imaginary line around the center of Earth
6. Africa's tallest mountain
8. Richter _____ (measures earthquakes)
11. _____ Falls (in Venezuela)

(Answers are on page 303.)

How To READ a MAP

There are many different kinds of maps. **Physical maps** mainly show features that are part of nature, such as mountains, deserts, jungles, and grasslands. **Political** maps show features such as states and countries and the **boundaries** between them.

DISTANCE

Of course the distances on a map are much smaller than the distances in the real world. The **scale** shows you how much smaller they are. In the map below, every inch on paper means a real distance of 2 miles.

DIRECTION

Maps usually have a compass rose that shows you which way is north. On most maps, north is toward the top. On the map below, north is straight up. If you went from Westwood to Lake City you would be going almost exactly north. When north is straight up, east is to the right, and west is to the left.

LOCATING PLACES

To help you locate places on a map, there often is a list, giving you a letter and number for each city or town. In the map below, you can find the first city on the list, Centerville, by drawing a straight line down from the letter E on top, and another line going across from the number 3 on the side. Centerville should be near the area where these two lines meet.

SYMBOLS

Maps usually have different **symbols** in them. If you look along the side or bottom, you can find out what these symbols mean. At the bottom of this map, you can see the symbols for towns, roads, railroads tracks, and airports. Can you tell which are the two biggest cities or towns on the map? Can you find the airport and railroad? How would you get from the airport to Centerville by car?

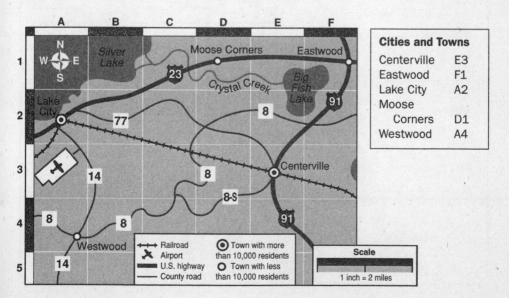

What's INSIDE Your BODY?

Your body is made up of many different parts that work together every minute of every day and night. It is more amazing than any machine or computer. Machines don't eat, run, have feelings, read and learn, or do other things that you do. Even though everyone's body looks different outside, people have the same parts inside.

Your body is made up of billions of tiny living units called **cells**. Different kinds of cells have different tasks to do in the body. Cells that do similar work form **tissue**, like nerve tissue or bone tissue. And tissues that work together form **organs**, like the heart, lungs, and kidneys. Organs work together as **systems**, and each system has a separate job to do. The human body has many different systems. Six of the largest systems are the Circulatory System, Respiratory System, Skeletal System, Muscular System, Digestive System, and Nervous System.

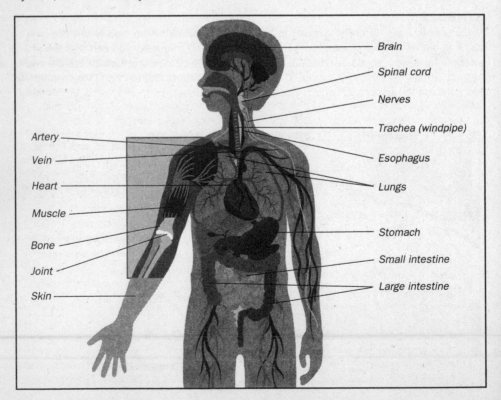

What Do the BODY'S SYSTEMS Do?

Each system of the body has its own job to do. Some of the systems also work together in teams to keep you healthy and strong.

CIRCULATORY SYSTEM

In the circulatory system, the **heart** pumps **blood**, which then travels through tubes, called **arteries**, to all parts of the body. The blood carries the oxygen and food that the body needs to stay alive. **Veins** carry the blood back to the heart.

RESPIRATORY SYSTEM

The respiratory system allows us to breathe. Air comes into the body through the nose and mouth. It goes through the windpipe (or trachea) to two tubes (called bronchi), which carry air to the **lungs**. Oxygen from the air is absorbed by tiny blood vessels in the lungs. The blood carries oxygen to the cells of the body.

SKELETAL SYSTEM

The skeletal system is made up of the **bones** that hold your body upright. Some bones protect organs, such as the ribs that cover the lungs.

MUSCULAR SYSTEM

Muscles are made up of elastic fibers that help the body move. We use large muscles to walk and run, and small muscles to smile. Muscles also help protect organs inside your body.

DIGESTIVE SYSTEM

The digestive system moves food through parts of the body called the **esophagus**, **stomach**, and **intestines**. As the food passes through the digestive system, some of it is broken down into tiny particles called nutrients, which the body needs. Nutrients enter the bloodstream, which carries them to all parts of the body. The digestive system then changes the remaining food into waste that is eliminated from the body.

NERVOUS SYSTEM

The nervous system enables us to think, feel, move, hear, and see. It includes the **brain**, the **spinal cord**, and **nerves** in all parts of the body. Nerves in the spinal cord carry signals back and forth between the brain and the rest of the body. The brain tells us what to do and how to respond. The brain has three major parts. The **cerebrum** controls thinking, speech, and vision. The **cerebellum** is responsible for physical coordination. The **brain stem** controls the respiratory, circulatory, and digestive systems.

OTHER SYSTEMS

Endocrine System

The endocrine system includes **glands** that are needed for some body functions. There are two kinds of glands. Exocrine glands produce liquids such as sweat and saliva. Endocrine glands produce chemicals called **hormones**. Hormones control body functions, such as growth.

Urinary System

This system, which includes the **kidneys**, cleans waste from the blood and regulates the amount of water in the body.

Reproductive System

Through the reproductive system, adult human beings create new human beings. Reproduction begins when a sperm cell from a man fertilizes an egg cell from a woman.

Skin

The skin is the body's largest organ. It protects the internal organs from infection, injury, and harmful sunlight. It also helps control the temperature of the body.

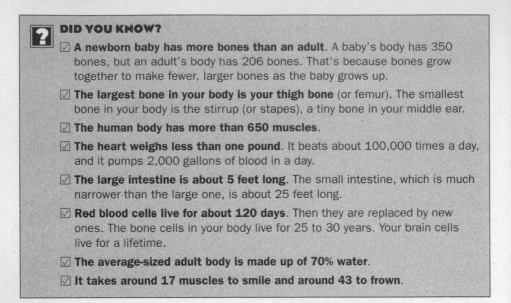

? **DID YOU KNOW?**

☑ **A newborn baby has more bones than an adult**. A baby's body has 350 bones, but an adult's body has 206 bones. That's because bones grow together to make fewer, larger bones as the baby grows up.

☑ **The largest bone in your body is your thigh bone** (or femur). The smallest bone in your body is the stirrup (or stapes), a tiny bone in your middle ear.

☑ **The human body has more than 650 muscles.**

☑ **The heart weighs less than one pound**. It beats about 100,000 times a day, and it pumps 2,000 gallons of blood in a day.

☑ **The large intestine is about 5 feet long**. The small intestine, which is much narrower than the large one, is about 25 feet long.

☑ **Red blood cells live for about 120 days**. Then they are replaced by new ones. The bone cells in your body live for 25 to 30 years. Your brain cells live for a lifetime.

☑ **The average-sized adult body is made up of 70% water**.

☑ **It takes around 17 muscles to smile and around 43 to frown**.

Tips for TIPTOP TEETH

If you want to chew food properly and speak clearly, it is important to keep your teeth healthy. Here are some tips for keeping your teeth in tiptop shape.

◀ **Brush your teeth at least twice a day.** If possible, brush after every meal.

◀ **Floss.** Clean between your teeth regularly with dental floss.

◀ **Eat healthful foods.** Don't eat too many sweets or sugary foods and sodas. They cause cavities.

◀ **Visit your dentist** to have your teeth checked and cleaned every six months.

What Causes a Cavity in Your Tooth?

Cavities are caused by tiny pieces of food left on or between the teeth after eating. These pieces of food combine with the natural bacteria in your mouth to form an acid. The acid slowly eats away the tooth's enamel and causes tooth decay, or cavities.

How MUCH Should You WEIGH?

When reading a chart about weight, you need to know that weight is related to height. Although everyone's body is different, the taller people get, the more they will usually weigh. The chart below shows a range of heights and weights for girls and boys ages 8 to 12. The lower number in the range is for a smaller person; the higher number in the range is for a larger person. Remember that everyone is different, and these heights and weights are not exact. So yours may be a little more or less than these figures.

Age	GIRLS Height in inches	Weight in pounds	Age	BOYS Height in inches	Weight in pounds
8	46-54	41-68	8	47-53	45-65
9	48-57	50-75	9	49-55	50-74
10	50-59	55-85	10	51-57	55-80
11	53-62	62-96	11	53-59	60-90
12	56-64	70-110	12	54-61	65-100

If you are worried about being overweight, talk with your parents and your doctor. Ask about what foods to eat and how much exercise you need.

Staying Healthy With EXERCISE

Daily exercise is important for your good health, fitness, and appearance. Exercise makes you feel good. It helps you think better. And, believe it or not, it helps you sleep better and feel less tired and more relaxed. Once you start exercising regularly, you will feel stronger and get better and better at physical activities.

What Happens When You Exercise? When you exercise, you breathe more deeply and get more oxygen into your lungs with each breath. Your heart pumps more oxygen-filled blood to all parts of your body with each beat. Your muscles and joints feel more flexible. Exercise also helps you to stay at a healthy weight.

What About People Who Don't Exercise? People who don't exercise may have less strength and energy. They may not sleep well and may feel tired. And they may gain more weight than would be healthy.

What Kind of Exercise Is Good? Almost all kinds of activity that move the body around. Bicycling, dancing, skating, swimming, running, roller-blading, and playing soccer are a few ways to exercise and have fun at the same time.

Which Foods Are the RIGHT FOODS?

To stay healthy, it is important to eat the right foods and to exercise. To help people choose the right foods for good health and fitness, the U.S. government developed the food pyramid shown below. The food pyramid shows the groups of foods that should be eaten every day.

The foods shown at the bottom (or largest part) of the pyramid are the foods to be eaten in the largest amounts. At the top are the foods to be eaten in the smallest amounts. The number of servings a person should eat depends on the person's age and body size. Younger, smaller people may eat fewer servings. Older, larger people may eat more. The meaning of "serving" is explained below the pyramid.

FOOD GUIDE PYRAMID: A GUIDE TO DAILY FOOD CHOICES

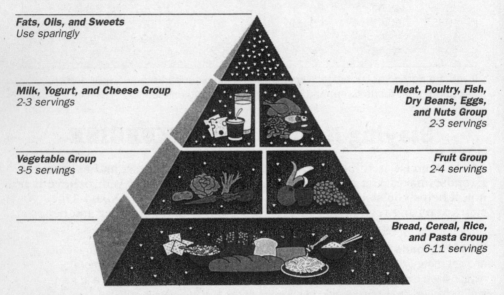

Fats, Oils, and Sweets
Use sparingly

Milk, Yogurt, and Cheese Group
2-3 servings

**Meat, Poultry, Fish,
Dry Beans, Eggs,
and Nuts Group**
2-3 servings

Vegetable Group
3-5 servings

Fruit Group
2-4 servings

**Bread, Cereal, Rice,
and Pasta Group**
6-11 servings

HOW MUCH FOOD IS IN A SERVING?

☑ **Milk, Yogurt, and Cheese Group**
1 serving = 1 cup of milk or yogurt; or 1½ to 2 ounces of cheese

☑ **Meat, Poultry, Fish Group**
1 serving = 2 to 3 ounces of cooked lean meat, fish, or poultry; 1 to 1½ cups of cooked dry beans; 2 eggs; or 4 to 6 tablespoons of peanut butter

☑ **Vegetable Group**
1 serving = 1 cup of raw, leafy vegetables; ½ cup of other vegetables (cooked or chopped raw); or ¾ cup vegetable juice

☑ **Fruit Group**
1 serving = 1 medium apple, banana, or orange; ½ cup of cooked, chopped, or canned fruit; or ¾ cup of fruit juice

☑ **Bread, Cereal, Rice and Pasta Group**
1 serving = 1 slice of bread; 1 ounce of ready-to-eat cereal; or ½ cup of cooked cereal, rice, or pasta

HEALTH TALK

Have you ever noticed the labels on the packages of food you and your family buy? The labels give information to help people make healthy choices about the foods they eat. Below are some words that will help you understand what the labels mean.

NUTRIENTS ARE NECESSARY

Nutrients are the parts of food that the body can use. The body needs nutrients for growth, for energy, and to repair itself when something goes wrong. Carbohydrates, fats, proteins, vitamins, minerals, and water are different kinds of nutrients that are found in food. **Carbohydrates** and **fats** provide energy. **Proteins** help with growth and help to maintain and repair the body. **Vitamins** help the body to use food, help eyesight and skin, and help fight off infections. **Minerals** help build bones and teeth and work with the chemicals in the body. **Water** helps with growth and repair of the body. It also works with the blood and chemicals, and helps the body get rid of wastes.

CALORIES COUNT

A **calorie** is a measure of the amount of energy we get from food. The government recommends the number of calories that should be taken in for different age groups. The number of calories recommended for children ages 7 to 10 is 2,400 a day. For ages 11 to 14, the government recommends 2,400 calories for girls every day and 2,800 calories for boys.

To maintain a **healthy weight**, it is important to balance the calories in the food you eat with the calories used by the body every day. Every activity uses up some calories. The more active you are, the more calories your body is burning. If you eat more calories than your body uses, you will gain weight.

A LITTLE FAT GOES A LONG WAY

A little bit of fat is important for your body. It keeps your body warm. It gives the muscles energy. It helps keep the skin soft and healthy. But the body needs only a small amount of fat to do all these things—just one tablespoon of fat each day is enough.

Cholesterol. Eating too much fat can cause some people's bodies to produce too much of a chemical called **cholesterol** (ko-LESS-ter-all). This is a waxy substance that can build up over the years on the inside of arteries. Too much cholesterol keeps blood from flowing freely through the arteries and can cause serious health problems like heart attacks.

To eat less fat, try eating these lower-fat foods instead of fatty foods:

Eat lower-fat foods	Instead of these fatty foods
chicken or turkey hot dog	beef or pork hot dog
broiled chicken breast	fried hamburger
tuna fish canned in water	tuna fish canned in oil
skim milk or 1% or 2% milk	whole milk
pretzels	potato chips
low-fat or nonfat frozen yogurt	ice cream
plain popcorn (without butter)	buttered popcorn

Understanding AIDS

What Is AIDS? AIDS is a disease that is caused by a virus called HIV. AIDS attacks the body's immune system. The immune system is made up of cells that usually help the body fight off infections and diseases, but it doesn't destroy the AIDS virus.

How Do Kids Get AIDS? A mother with AIDS may give it to her baby before the baby is born. Sometimes children (and adults, too) have gotten AIDS from blood transfusions. But this happens less and less, because blood banks now test all donations of blood for the AIDS virus.

How Do Adults Get AIDS? There are two main ways people get AIDS: Having sex with a person who has AIDS, or the use of drugs in which people share a needle to inject drugs into their bodies.

How Kids and Adults *Don't* Get AIDS. People *don't* get AIDS from everyday contact with infected people at school, at home, or other places. People *don't* get AIDS from clothes, telephones, or toilet seats, or from food prepared by someone with AIDS. Children *don't* get AIDS from sitting near AIDS victims or from shaking hands with them.

Is There a Cure for AIDS? Not yet. But researchers are hard at work trying to develop a vaccine to prevent AIDS or a drug to cure it.

WHICH DOCTOR DOES WHAT?

A doctor who takes care of children is called a **pediatrician.**
A doctor who fixes broken bones is called an **orthopedist.**
A doctor who takes general care of your teeth is called a **dentist.**
A doctor who straightens teeth is called an **orthodontist.**
A doctor who treats people who have allergies is called an **allergist.**
A doctor whose machines can see inside your body is called a **radiologist.**
A doctor who treats people who have cancer is called an **oncologist.**
A doctor who helps people with emotional problems is called a **psychiatrist.**

Saying NO to Harmful Substances

It's no secret that drugs, alcohol, and cigarettes can do serious damage to people's bodies and minds. Some kids try these harmful substances, but a lot of kids don't want to try them. And some kids don't know how to say "no" when someone wants them to say "yes." DARE, a program developed by the U.S. government to help young people say "no" to drugs, suggests some ways to refuse drugs, alcohol, and cigarettes:

☑ Say "No thanks." (Show that you mean it by saying it again and again if you have to.)

☑ Give reasons. ("I don't like beer" or "I'm going to soccer practice" or "I have asthma.")

☑ Change the subject or offer a better suggestion.

☑ Walk away. (Don't argue, don't discuss it. Just leave.)

☑ Avoid the situation. (If you are asked to a party where kids will be drinking, smoking, or using drugs, don't go. Make plans to do something else instead.)

☑ Find strength in numbers. (Do things with friends who don't use harmful substances.)

Keeping SAFE and
PREVENTING ACCIDENTS

When you are careful and use common sense, you're off to a good start at preventing accidents. Most accidents happen at home. Although no one can prevent every accident, there are some steps you can take to prevent many of them.

☑ **Safety in the Kitchen.** Sharp knives should be handled very carefully. Always cut away from your body. Be sure the knife is in a safe place when you put it down. To avoid fire, don't leave paper or cloth (like napkins or towels) near the stove. Keep sharp knives and matches away from babies and little children.

☑ **Safety in the Bathroom.** A rubber mat or other non-slip surface can keep you from slipping in the bathtub. Also, soap should be kept in a soap dish, so that no one will slip on it. Don't use hair dryers or other electrical appliances near water.

☑ **Other Safety Tips at Home.** Everyone in your family should know all the ways of getting out of your house or apartment in case there is a fire. If an accident happens, get an adult to help. When you are home, don't let strangers into your house or apartment. Don't give your name or address to strangers over the phone. Don't tell a stranger if you are home alone.

☑ **Riding Your Bike Safely.** Wear a helmet when riding your bike. Use reflectors and lights on your bike. Be alert—watch for traffic, other bikes, roller bladers, and people who are walking. Learn the safety laws for cars—bikes must obey the same laws.

☑ **Safety in the Car.** In the car always wear a seat belt. Don't distract the driver by making loud noise or jumping around.

☑ **Crossing the Street Safely.** When crossing a street, watch for traffic. Look both ways before crossing the street. Cross only at corners. Stay on the curb until the light turns green and the "Walk" sign is on. Don't fool around near traffic.

If There Is an Emergency

With your family, make a list of emergency telephone numbers and keep the list near the telephone or taped to the refrigerator. Here are some numbers to put on the list: your parent's or guardian's telephone numbers at work, the telephone number of a friend who lives nearby or a neighbor, your family doctor, hospital, fire department, police department. Phone numbers for emergencies can often be found inside the front cover of your telephone book.

Remember 911. The number 911 is a special phone number for emergencies. When a person who needs help calls 911, the 911 operator asks the caller for his or her name and address and what the emergency is. Then the 911 operator will quickly send the police, an ambulance, or the fire department. If your town doesn't have 911, dial 0 (operator) and ask the operator for help.

LEGAL or PUBLIC HOLIDAYS in the United States

The days shown below are legal or public holidays in the United States. Banks, schools, and offices are closed on most of these days. Each state decides which of the holidays it will celebrate, but most states celebrate most of the holidays below. Since 1971, Washington's Birthday (now Presidents' Day), Memorial Day, Columbus Day, and Veterans Day have been celebrated on a Monday so that many people who work can have a three-day weekend.

New Year's Day. Countries the world over celebrate the new year, although not always on January 1. The Chinese New Year falls between January 10 and February 19. In ancient Egypt, the New Year began around mid-June, when the Nile river overflowed and watered the crops.

Martin Luther King Day. Observed on the third Monday in January, this holiday marks the birth (January 15, 1929) in Atlanta of the African-American civil rights leader Martin Luther King, Jr.

Presidents' Day or Washington's Birthday. On the third Monday in February, Americans celebrate the births of both George Washington (born on February 22, 1732) and Abraham Lincoln (born on February 12, 1809).

Memorial Day or Decoration Day. Memorial Day, observed on the last Monday in May, is set aside to remember all those who died in United States wars.

Fourth of July or Independence Day. July 4 is the anniversary of the day in 1776 when the American colonies declared their independence from England. Kids and grownups celebrate with bands and parades, picnics, barbecues, and fireworks.

Labor Day. Labor Day, the first Monday in September, honors the workers of America. It was first celebrated in 1882.

Columbus Day. Celebrated on the second Monday in October, Columbus Day is the anniversary of October 12, 1492, the day when Christopher Columbus was traditionally thought to have discovered America.

Election Day. Election Day, the first Tuesday after the first Monday in November, is a legal holiday in most states every four years, when a U.S. president is elected.

Veterans Day. Veterans Day, November 11, honors the veterans of United States wars. First called Armistice Day, it marked the armistice (agreement) that ended World War I. It was signed on the 11th hour (11 A.M.) of the 11th day of the 11th month of 1918.

Thanksgiving. Celebrated on the fourth Thursday in November, Thanksgiving Day was first observed by the Pilgrims in 1621 as a harvest festival and a day for thanks and feasting.

Christmas. Christmas is both a religious holiday and a legal holiday. (See p. 183).

HOLIDAYS in 1996		
Holiday	**Date in 1996**	**Day**
New Year's Day	January 1	Monday
Martin Luther King Day	January 15	Monday
Presidents' Day	February 19	Monday
Memorial Day	May 27	Monday
Independence Day	July 4	Thursday
Labor Day	September 2	Monday
Columbus Day	October 14	Monday
Election Day	November 5	Tuesday
Veterans Day	November 11	Monday
Thanksgiving	November 28	Thursday
Christmas	December 25	Wednesday

SOME OTHER SPECIAL HOLIDAYS

Valentine's Day.
February 14
is a day for
sending cards
to people
you love.

Arbor Day.
Trees are planted on
Arbor Day, reminding us of the importance
of protecting the environment. Each state
observes the day at different times in the
spring, depending on the state's climate.

Mother's Day and Father's Day.
Mothers are honored on the second
Sunday in May. Fathers are honored on
the third Sunday in June.

Halloween. Did you
know that in
ancient Britain,
Druids lit fires
and wore
grotesque
costumes on
October 31 to
scare off evil spirits?

Today, "trick or treating" children collect
candy and other sweets. Some also
collect money for UNICEF, the United
Nations Children's Fund.

Kwanza. Originally an African harvest
festival, Kwanza is a week-long African-
American celebration beginning on
December 26. Candles are lit every night.

SOME HOLIDAYS AROUND THE WORLD

Children's Day. In Japan, May 5 is set aside to honor all the children of the country.

Cinco de Mayo. Mexicans remember May 5, 1867, when Mexico defeated its French
rulers and became independent.

Canada Day. Canada's national holiday, July 1, commemorates the union of
Canadian provinces under one government in 1867.

Bastille Day. July 14 is France's national holiday. It commemorates the storming of
the Bastille prison in 1789 at the beginning of the French Revolution.

Boxing Day. December 26 is a holiday in Britain, and also in Australia, Canada, and New
Zealand. The name is thought to date back to the time when Christmas
gifts were distributed in boxes to servants, tradespeople, and the poor.

INVENTIONS

Some of the world's most important inventions were developed before history was ever written. These include the invention of tools and the wheel, the ability to make and control fire, and the ability to make pottery. And these inventions led to others, which in turn helped create new and better and cheaper ways of doing things. For example, light bulbs replaced candles and oil lamps, and rocket engines made it possible to go to the moon.

INVENTIONS THAT TAKE US FROM ONE PLACE TO ANOTHER

Automobiles made travel easier, and jet planes allowed ordinary people to see the world.

Year	Invention	Inventor	Country
1785	parachute	Jean Pierre Blanchard	France
1807	steamboat	Robert Fulton	U.S.
1829	steam locomotive	George Stephenson	England
1852	safety elevator	Elisha G. Otis	U.S.
1885	bicycle	James Starley	England
1885	motorcycle	Gottlieb Daimler	Germany
1892	automobile (gasoline)	Charles E. Duryea & J. Frank Duryea	U.S.
1891	escalator	Jesse W. Reno	U.S.
1894	submarine	Simon Lake	U.S.
1895	diesel engine	Rudolf Diesel	Germany
1903	propeller airplane	Orville & Wilbur Wright	U.S.
1939	helicopter	Igor Sikorsky	U.S.
1939	turbojet airplane	Hans von Ohain	Germany

INVENTIONS THAT HELP US LIVE HEALTHIER AND LONGER LIVES

Antibiotics such as penicillin help fight some illnesses. CAT scanners and X-rays let doctors look inside our bodies to see what's wrong.

Year	Invention	Inventor	Country
1780	bifocal lenses for glasses	Benjamin Franklin	U.S.
1819	stethoscope	René T.M.H. Laënnec	France
1842	anesthesia (ether)	Crawford W. Long	U.S.
1895	X-ray	Wilhelm Roentgen	Germany
1922	insulin	Sir Frederick G. Banting	Canada
1929	penicillin	Alexander Fleming	Scotland
1954	antibiotic for fungal diseases	Rachel F. Brown & Elizabeth L. Hazen	U.S.
1955	polio vaccine	Jonas E. Salk	U.S.
1973	CAT scanner	Godfrey N. Hounsfield	England

INVENTIONS THAT HELP US COMMUNICATE WITH ONE ANOTHER

The pen and pencil and printing press, fax and phone and computer are all ways of exchanging messages, information, and ideas. Today, we use older inventions like the pencil along with newer ones like the computer.

Year	Invention	Inventor	Country
A.D. 105	paper	Ts'ai Lun	China
1447	movable type	Johann Gutenberg	Germany
1795	modern pencil	Nicolas Jacques Conté	France
1837	telegraph	Samuel F.B. Morse	U.S.
1845	rotary printing press	Richard M. Hoe	U.S.
1867	typewriter	Christopher L. Sholes, Carlos Glidden, & Samuel W. Soulé	U.S.
1876	telephone	Alexander G. Bell	U.S.
1913	modern radio receiver	Reginald A. Fessenden	U.S.
1937	xerography copies	Chester Carlson	U.S.
1943	ballpoint pen	Laszlo Biro	Argentina
1944	auto sequence computer	Howard H. Aiken	U.S.
1945	electronic computer	J. Presper Eckert & John W. Mauchly	U.S.
1947	transistor	William Shockley, Walter H. Brattain, & John Bardeen	U.S.
1955	fiber optics	Narinder S. Kapany	England
1965	word processor	IBM	U.S.

INVENTIONS THAT ENTERTAIN US

Books and games, the radio and television have entertained people in their homes for many years and continue to do so. Newer inventions like VCRs and CD players have brought more movies and concerts into homes.

Year	Invention	Inventor	Country
1709	piano	Bartolomeo Cristofori	Italy
1877	phonograph	Thomas A. Edison	U.S.
1877	microphone	Emile Berliner	U.S.
1888	portable camera	George Eastman	U.S.
1893	moving picture viewer	Thomas A. Edison	U.S.
1894	motion picture projector	Charles F. Jenkins	U.S.
1899	tape recorder	Valdemar Poulsen	Denmark
1924	television	Vladimir K. Zworykin	U.S.
1951	flexible kite	Gertrude Rogallo & Francis Rogallo	U.S.
1963	audiocassette	Phillips Corporation	Netherlands
1969	videotape cassette	Sony	Japan
1972	compact disc (CD)	RCA	U.S.
1972	video game (Pong)	Norman Buschnel	U.S.

INVENTIONS THAT MAKE OUR LIVES EASIER

Year	Invention	Inventor	Country
1589	flush toilet	John Harington	England
1800	electric battery	Alessandro Volta	Italy
1827	matches	John Walker	England
1831	lawn mower	Edwin Budding & John Ferrabee	England
1834	refrigeration	Jacob Perkins	England
1846	sewing machine	Elias Howe	U.S.
1849	safety pin	Walter Hunt	U.S.
1851	cylinder (door) lock	Linus Yale	U.S.
1879	electric light bulb	Thomas A. Edison	U.S.
1886	dishwasher	Josephine Cochran	U.S.
1891	zipper	Whitcomb L. Judson	U.S.
1903	windshield wipers	Mary Anderson	U.S.
1907	vacuum cleaner	J. Murray Spangler	U.S.
1911	air conditioning	Willis H. Carrier	U.S.
1924	frozen packaged food	Clarence Birdseye	U.S.
1938	Teflon	DuPont Corporation	U.S.
1947	microwave oven	Percy L. Spencer	U.S.
1948	Velcro	Georges de Mestral	Switzerland
1971	food processor	Pierre Verdon	France

INVENTIONS THAT HELP US EXPLORE AND UNDERSTAND THE WORLD AND THE UNIVERSE

Year	Invention	Inventor	Country
1250	magnifying glass	Roger Bacon	England
1590	microscope using two lenses	Zacharias Janssen	Netherlands
1593	water thermometer	Galileo Galilei	Italy
1608	telescope	Hans Lippershey	Netherlands
1714	mercury thermometer	Gabriel D. Fahrenheit	Germany
1730	alcohol thermometer	René de Réaumur	France
1926	rocket engine	Robert H. Goddard	U.S.
1930	cyclotron (atom smasher)	Ernest O. Lawrence	U.S.
1931	electron microscope	Max Knoll & Ernst Ruska	Germany
1943	Aqua Lung	Jacques-Yves Cousteau & Emile Gagnan	France
1953	bathyscaphe	August Piccard	France
1977	space shuttle	NASA	U.S.

INVENTORS HALL OF FAME

The U.S. Patent and Trademark Office has honored inventors since 1973 by naming them to the Inventors Hall of Fame. A few of the inventors in the Hall of Fame are Rachel F. Brown and Elizabeth L. Hazen (antibiotics for fungal diseases), George Washington Carver (process for organic dyes), Thomas Edison (electric light bulb), Henry Ford (automobile transmission), Herman Hollerith (calculator for compiling statistics), Elisha Otis (elevator), Igor Sikorsky (helicopter), Orville and Wilbur Wright (flying machine), An Wang (computer control device).

Making DISCOVERIES

Ever since ancient times, people have been exploring the world around them and making discoveries about it. Some people are inventors and provide us with new ways of doing things. Some are discoverers and reveal more about our world as it exists. Some people, like Jacques-Yves Cousteau, are both. Below are some of the different kinds of discoveries.

SCIENTIFIC DISCOVERIES

Scientists make discoveries about everything on earth and in the universe: plants and animals, oceans and rivers and mountains, planets and stars, the human body and how it works.

☑ In 1543, Copernicus discovered that the earth went around the sun.
☑ In 1687, the English mathematician Isaac Newton discovered the law of gravity.
☑ In the mid-19th century, French chemist Louis Pasteur discovered that some diseases were spread by germs, or microbes. This led to the first vaccines against illnesses.
☑ The discovery of DNA in 1953 helped explain how certain characteristics (such as eye or hair color or a certain disease) may be passed on from parent to child.

FAMOUS EXPLORERS

An explorer is another kind of discoverer. Exploration has also been going on for centuries. Sometimes people explore new lands to conquer them or for trade. And sometimes they have a sense of curiosity or a thirst for knowledge.

☑ In ancient times, the Greeks and the Phoenicians explored the Mediterranean.
☑ In 1911, Norwegian explorer Roald Amundsen was the first person to reach the South Pole.
☑ In 1969, U.S. astronauts Neil Armstrong and Edwin Aldrin were the first humans to land on the moon.
☑ In the mid-20th century, the French explorer Jacques-Yves Cousteau explored, studied, and photographed the world beneath the sea.

DISCOVERING THE PAST

Archeologists make other kinds of discoveries. They search for the remains of earlier cultures in an effort to understand them.

☑ In the late 19th century, Heinrich Schliemann, a German businessman, found the remains of the ancient city of Troy in Asia Minor. Until then, Troy was known only through the writings of the Greek poet Homer.
☑ In 1922, the tomb of King Tutankhamen, who lived more than 3,000 years ago, was discovered in Egypt.
☑ The discovery of cave paintings in France and Spain helped us know what life was like in the Stone Age.

Others who dig into the earth are paleontologists, who study life in prehistoric times. Their discoveries of bones and other fossils have revealed information about dinosaurs and other animals millions of years after they became extinct.

ABBREVIATIONS

Abbreviations are short forms of words or phrases. We use abbreviations all the time because they save us time in both writing and speaking. Isn't it quicker and easier to say or write VCR than videocassette recorder, CD instead of compact disk, TV rather than television, UN instead of United Nations?

Postal Abbreviations
When addressing an envelope, we use postal abbreviations for the U.S. states. If you were writing to a friend in Alabama, on the envelope you could write only AL instead of the whole state name. When addressing an envelope, you should always follow the state with the correct ZIP code. (ZIP is an abbreviation for Zone Improvement Plan.)

Titles
We almost always use abbreviations before and after people's names.
For example, Mr., Mrs., Ms., Miss, Jr., and Sr.

Technical Talk
Special fields have their own abbreviations.

Sports. Baseball players brag about their RBIs (runs batted in) or ERA (earned run average).

Another run scores! His third RBI of the day!

Cooking. Cooks measure their ingredients by the tsp. (teaspoon), tbs. or tbsp. (tablespoon), oz. (ounce), or lb. (pound).

Whoops! It says 2 tsp. of red peppers, not 2 tbs.!

Computers. Computer users talk about their PCs (personal computers), a CD-ROM (Compact Disk-Read Only Memory), and DOS (Disk Operating System), and some communicate electronically through a BBS (Bulletin Board Service).

Navigation. Navigators use N, S, E, and W to refer to compass directions.

ACRONYM PUZZLE

Acronyms are abbreviations that combine the first letters of several words and can be pronounced as a word. Can you match the acronym in the first column with the words it stands for in the second column? (Answers are on page 303.)

1. — MADD	a. National Aeronautics and Space Administration
2. — NOW	b. Special Weapons And Tactics
3. — NASA	c. Mothers Against Drunk Driving
4. — UNICEF	d. North Atlantic Treaty Organization
5. — SWAT	e. National Organization for Women
6. — NATO	f. United Nations International Children's Emergency Fund

Writing a LETTER

Did you know that there are different kinds of letters? When you write a letter to a friend, you can write it any way you like. It is an informal letter. But when you write to an official person, say, your school principal or mayor, you would write a formal letter or a business letter. This type of letter includes some specific elements: your name and address, the date, the address of the person you're writing to, and an ending or salutation such as "Sincerely," "Sincerely yours," or "Yours truly."

Here's how one fifth grader suggested writing to the President:

> 17 North Street
> New Phantom, MI 54321
>
> April 1, 1995
>
> The President
> The White House
> Washington, D.C. 20500
>
> Dear Mr. President:
>
> It makes me sad to see people on the street who are hungry and homeless. So I'm writing to suggest some ways to solve the problem.
>
> One way is to get kids involved. Maybe schools could start a program where kids would get together and raise money, then give it to a homeless shelter at the end of the year. Girl Scouts and Boy Scouts could also help, perhaps by selling cookies or doing chores.
>
> Maybe you could declare a Homeless Day once a year, when everyone in America would be asked to give something to the homeless. It could be money, clothes, or just a can of tuna fish or a box of cereal.
>
> Thank you for considering my ideas.
>
> Sincerely,
>
> *Harriet Helper*
> Harriet Helper

How Would You Address Them?

Here are the correct forms of address to use in writing to some officials or public figures.

OFFICIAL	FORM OF ADDRESS	SALUTATION
U.S. President	The President	Dear Mr. President
U.S. Senator	Senator Pete V. Domenici	Dear Mr. Domenici
Congressperson	Representative Maxine G. Waters	Dear Ms. Waters
Chief Justice	The Honorable William H. Rehnquist Chief Justice of the United States	Dear Mr. Chief Justice
Governor	Governor Mel Carnahan	Dear Governor Carnahan

Words That Sound Alike or Almost Alike

When words sound similar, sometimes their spellings and meanings are confusing. Here are some words that are often confused.

brake or break
A **brake** is a device for slowing or stopping a vehicle. A **break** is a brief rest period (a lunch break).

capital or capitol
A **capital** is the city where a country or state government is located. **Capitol** is the building where a legislative body meets.

The capitol in the capital Washington, D.C.

desert or dessert
A **desert** is a hot, sandy area where few plants can grow. **Dessert** is fruit, ice cream, or something else eaten at the end of a meal.

emigrate or immigrate
To **emigrate** means to move away from a country. To **immigrate** means to move to another country. (Ana emigrated from Brazil. She immigrated to the United States.)

fair or fare
A **fair** is an exhibition or show. **Fair** also means better than poor, but less than good. **Fare** is the cost of a ride on a public vehicle like a bus, train, plane, or taxi.

its or it's
Its is the possessive form of "it" (the bird flapped its wings). **It's** is a contraction of "it is."

principal or principle
A **principal** is the person in charge of a school. **Principal** also means first in importance. A **principle** is a basic idea that a person believes in deeply.

stationary or stationery
Stationary means fixed in one place. When you have **stationery**, you have paper and envelopes to write on.

their, they're, or there
Their is the possessive form of "they." **They're** is a contraction of "they are." **There** means at or in that place. (They're going to put their packages there on the table.)

WORDS THAT ARE HARD TO SPELL
The following words are frequently misspelled:

across	changeable	foreign	independent	parallel
address	desperate	friend	lightning	proceed
amateur	eighth	height	mischief	rhythm
bureau	embarrass	humorous	occurred	seize

Some Spelling Bee Winners
Every year children win prizes for spelling. The Scripps Howard National Spelling Bee is for children in eighth grade or below, under 16 years old. Here are some of the winning words in these spelling bees: croissant (1970), incisor (1975), sarcophagus (1981), luge (1984), milieu (1985), staphylococci (1987), lyceum (1992), kamikaze (1993), antediluvian (1994).

WORD PUZZLE **T**he word "staphylococci" (1987 Spelling Bee winner) has 13 letters. See how many words of three or more letters (no plurals!) you can make from these letters. How many 3-letter words? How many 4-letter words? How many 5-letter words? Can you find a 6-letter word? (Answers are on page 303.)

IDIOMS: Words That Are Not as They Seem

Idioms are groups of words (phrases) that cannot be understood just by knowing the meaning of each of the words. This often makes them particularly puzzling to people learning a new language. Some idioms are hard to understand even in your own language. Here are some common idioms, with their meanings.

BODY LANGUAGE

put your foot in your mouth: say something embarrassing or hurtful.

have a heart of stone: be cold and unfeeling.

to be on your last legs: to be so tired that you feel you are going to collapse.

down in the mouth: very sad or depressed.

right under your nose: easily seen or within plain view.

IT'S ALL IN THE GAME

to play games: to fool someone or keep the truth from someone.

to be on the ball: to be alert or quick to catch on or understand.

get the ball rolling: get something started.

to be off base: to be wrong.

right off the bat: immediately, first thing.

skate on thin ice: be in a dangerous or risky situation.

THE ANIMAL KINGDOM

straight from the horse's mouth: from the original, or most reliable, source.

let the cat out of the bag: reveal a secret, usually by mistake.

like a fish out of water: ill at ease or in unfamiliar surroundings.

rain cats and dogs: rain very hard.

the lion's share: the greatest amount, the largest portion.

take the bull by the horns: to deal courageously with a situation.

IDIOM PUZZLE

Look at the idioms in the left column. See if you can find the correct meaning for each one in the right column. (Answers are on page 304.)

MIXING COLORS

1. **in the black**

2. **out of the blue**

3. **to be green with envy**

4. **to see red**

5. **show the white flag**

a. to become very angry

b. to be extremely envious

c. indicate, in battle, that you wish to surrender

d. making a profit, not in debt

e. unexpectedly, without warning

LANGUAGES of the WORLD

Would you have guessed that Mandarin, the principal language of China, is the world's most spoken language? You may find more surprises in the chart below, which lists languages spoken by at least 50,000,000 native speakers (those for whom the language is their first language, or mother tongue).

PRINCIPAL LANGUAGES OF THE WORLD

LANGUAGE	NUMBER OF NATIVE SPEAKERS
Mandarin	836,000,000
Hindi*	333,000,000
Spanish	332,000,000
English	322,000,000
Bengali*	187,000,000
Arabic	186,000,000
Russian	170,000,000
Portuguese	170,000,000
Japanese	125,000,000
German	98,000,000
French	72,000,000
Malay-Indonesian	50,000,000

*Hindi and Bengali are spoken in different parts of India.

> Are you surprised to see that English ranks only fourth?

Which Languages Are Spoken in the United States?

Since the beginning of American history, immigrants have come to the United States from all over the world and brought their native languages with them. That's why so many Americans speak a language other than English at home. Here are some of the languages other than English that are spoken by 200,000 or more Americans.

> Hello! I'm Carmen!

> ¡Buenos días! ¡Soy Carmen!

LANGUAGE USED AT HOME	SPEAKERS OVER 5 YEARS OLD	LANGUAGE USED AT HOME	SPEAKERS OVER 5 YEARS OLD
1. Spanish	17,339,000	11. Japanese	428,000
2. French	1,703,000	12. Greek	388,000
3. German	1,547,000	13. Arabic	355,000
4. Italian	1,309,000	14. Hindu, Urdu, & related languages	331,000
5. Chinese	1,249,000		
6. Tagalog	843,000	15. Russian	242,000
7. Polish	723,000	16. Yiddish	213,000
8. Korean	626,000	17. Thai	206,000
9. Vietnamese	507,000	18. Persian	202,000
10. Portuguese	430,000		

Where in the WORLD Do ENGLISH WORDS Come From?

In addition to its language, each new ethnic group that immigrated to the United States brought its own traditions and customs. Immigrants brought their music, art, folk dances, style of dress, and special foods. Many of their customs were adopted by Americans, and so were the words that described them.

IMPORTED FOODS

Food is a good example. Foods from many cultures have become part of the American diet. Even words for typically American foods such as hamburgers and frankfurters have foreign origins. Here are some food and food-related words and the languages from which they came.

from Arabic:
apricot, candy, coffee, couscous, lime, sherbet, spinach, sugar, syrup, tuna

from Italian:
bologna, broccoli, lasagna, minestrone, pasta, pizza, salami, spaghetti

from Chinese:
chopsticks, chow, chow mein, soy, tea, wok, wonton

from Japanese:
sukiyaki, sushi, tempura, teriyaki, tofu

from French:
bouillon, casserole, chowder, crepe, croissant, croutons, mayonnaise, menu, mousse, omelette, quiche, tart

from Spanish:
avocado, burrito, chili, chocolate, cocoa, garbanzo, maize, tomato, tamale, tortilla

from German:
delicatessen, frankfurter, hamburger, pretzel, pumpernickel, sauerkraut, seltzer

from Yiddish:
bagel, blintze, knish, nosh

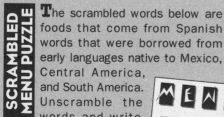

SCRAMBLED MENU PUZZLE

The scrambled words below are foods that come from Spanish words that were borrowed from early languages native to Mexico, Central America, and South America. Unscramble the words and write the answers to the right (one letter on each dash). Then insert the numbered letters on the line to find the name of a popular Mexican dish. (Answers are on page 304.)

1. OTTMAO ___ ___ ___ ___ ___ ___
                    1   4

2. ZEMIA ___ ___ ___ ___ ___
                 3   6

3. HILCI ___ ___ ___ ___ ___
                        5

4. ACCOO ___ ___ ___ ___ ___
                              2

___ ___ ___ ___ ___ ___
1   2   3   4   5   6

WHY DO WE NEED LAWS?

Did you ever wonder what your day would be like if there weren't any rules to follow? What if you could go to school any time you wanted? What if your teacher could also get to school any time he or she wanted? And what if there were no rules on the playground, or no traffic lights or stop signs for crossing the street?

Life would be difficult and confusing without rules. We all need them. Governments, businesses, organizations, and families make rules so that people don't get hurt and are not treated unfairly. The rules that a government makes are called laws. The government has the power to punish people who break a law.

Laws are made to:
- ☑ Protect people from getting hurt
- ☑ Help people to be treated fairly
- ☑ Help people do their jobs properly
- ☑ Help people know how to act in public

WHAT HAPPENS WHEN YOU BREAK THE LAW?

Kids. When children under 18 years old are caught breaking the law, they are arrested by the police and sometimes have to appear in a court called **juvenile court.** In this court, there is no jury. There is a judge who first decides whether or not there is strong enough evidence that the child has broken the law.

If there is enough evidence, the judge then decides what kind of help or punishment the child needs to get back on the right track. Sometimes the judge sends the child home, instructing him or her to follow certain rules. This is called **probation**. Sometimes the child is sent to a **foster home** or to another place where the judge thinks the child can more easily stay out of trouble or benefit from some training. In very serious cases, the child may be sent to a jail for kids, or a **reformatory**.

Adults. When an adult breaks the law, the offense may be minor or it may be serious. If the adult parks a car in a no-parking zone, this is considered a minor offense. The grown-up would be given a parking ticket, which may offer the choice of paying a fine by mail or going to court to argue against the ticket.

An adult who commits a serious crime would be arrested and have to appear in court. If there is strong evidence against him or her, there would be a trial. At the trial, a government lawyer, called a **prosecutor,** would present the case against the accused person (called the **defendant**). At the end of the trial, if the accused person is **acquitted,** or found "not guilty," he or she is free to go home. When the defendant is **convicted,** or found "guilty," he or she will get a punishment, or a **sentence,** such as having to go to jail for a specific length of time.

LAWS YOU CAN NO LONGER BREAK

Here are some state laws that people were supposed to follow a long time ago. You can see why these laws are no longer on the books.

☑ In California, a permit was needed to set a trap for a mouse.

☑ In Louisiana, it was illegal to lead a bear around with a rope.

☑ In Massachusetts, a dachshund could not be kept as a pet dog.

☑ In Michigan, it was illegal to hitch a crocodile to a fire hydrant.

☑ In West Virginia, it was illegal to sneeze on a train.

GROWN-UPS HAVE RIGHTS AND SO DO KIDS

All people have rights. This means that no one should be treated unfairly. It means that everyone should be free to do certain things. In the United States many years ago, the government made a list of these rights. This list is part of the U.S. Constitution and is called the **Bill of Rights**.

The Bill of Rights says that all the people in the United States should have the right to belong to any religion they choose and to say and write whatever they believe, even if it is against the government. It also says that the police cannot search people or go into their houses, unless they have a good reason and get special permission. And any person who is arrested has the right to a lawyer and a fair trial.

RIGHTS FOR CHILDREN

Under the laws in the United States, children do not have all the rights that grown-ups do. Children cannot drive a car or vote until they reach a certain age. They must go to school and live with their parents or legal guardian. Children have some special rights. They have the right to be taken care of by their parents.

Today, most countries in the world have laws to help children be taken care of properly and treated fairly. The United Nations has a **Declaration of the Rights of the Child,** which affirms, among other things, that:

☑ All children in the world have the same rights.

☑ All children should be protected by laws, so they can grow up normally.

☑ All children should have a name and a country to belong to.

☑ All children should have a decent place to live, enough food to eat, and whatever health care they need.

☑ Children who are handicapped should have the help they need.

☑ All children should have love and security.

☑ All children should be able to get an education.

☑ Children should be among the first to get help and protection in emergencies.

☑ Children should be protected against abuse and should learn to respect and help others.

☑ Children should be protected against unfair treatment because of race or religion.

HISTORY of MONEY

Why Did People Start Using Money? People first started using money in order to trade. A farmer who had cattle might want to have salt to preserve meat or cloth to make clothing. For this farmer, a cow became a "medium of exchange"—a way of getting things that the farmer did not make or grow. Cattle became a form of money. Whatever people agreed to use for trade became the earliest kinds of money.

What Objects Have Been Used as Money Throughout History? You may be surprised by some of the items that people have used every day as money. What does the form of money tell you about a society and its people?

- ☑ knives, rice, and spades in China around 3000 B.C.
- ☑ cattle and clay tablets in Babylonia around 2500 B.C.
- ☑ wampum (beads) and beaver fur by American Indians of the northeast around A.D. 1500
- ☑ tobacco by early American colonists around 1650
- ☑ whales' teeth by the Pacific peoples on the island of Fiji, until the early 1900s

The First Paper Money. By the time of the Middle Ages in Europe (A.D. 800-1100), gold had become a popular medium for trade. But gold was heavy and difficult to carry, and European cities and the roads of Europe at that time were dangerous places to carry large amounts of gold. So merchants and goldsmiths began issuing notes promising to pay gold to the person carrying the note. These "promissory notes" were the beginning of paper money in Europe. Paper money was probably also invented in China, where the explorer Marco Polo saw it in the 1280s.

Why Did Governments Get Interested in Issuing Money? The first government to make coins that looked alike and use them as money is thought to be the Greek city-state of Lydia in the 7th century B.C. These Lydian coins were actually bean-shaped lumps made from a mixture of gold and silver.

The first government in Europe to issue paper money that looked alike was France in the early 18th century. Governments were interested in issuing money because the money itself had value. If a government could gain control over the manufacture of money, it could increase its own wealth—often simply by making more money.

Today, money throughout the world is issued only by governments. In the United States, the Department of the Treasury and the U.S. Mint make all the paper money and coins we use. Nowadays, we also use credit cards and checks to pay for things we buy. These are not thought of as real money but more as "promises to pay."

MONEY TALK:
AN ECONOMICS GLOSSARY

ATM or automated teller machine
An electronic machine in a public place where customers of a bank can withdraw cash from their accounts or make deposits by using a special plastic card.

bank
A business establishment in which people and businesses keep money in savings accounts or checking accounts.

bond
A certificate issued by a government or a business to a person or business from whom it has borrowed money. A bond promises to pay back the borrowed money with interest.

CD or certificate of deposit
A kind of bank savings account that earns a fixed rate of interest over a specific period of time.

cost of living
The average cost of the basic needs of life, including food, clothing, housing, medical care, and other services.

debt
Something that is owed.

depression
A period of severe decline. During a depression, many people are unemployed, many businesses fail, and people buy less. The last depression in the United States occurred in the 1930s.

FDIC or Federal Deposit Insurance Corporation
A government agency created in 1933 to protect deposits when a bank fails. The FDIC guarantees to insure deposits up to $100,000 if they are in a bank that is a member of the FDIC.

GDP or Gross Domestic Product
The total value of all goods and services in the United States in one year, including government spending as well as spending by private individuals and companies.

goods and services
Goods refer to real items such as cars, TVs, VCRs, wristwatches, clothes, and so on. **Services** refer to work that is done for other people. Fire fighters, nurses, waiters, actors, lawyers all perform services

inflation
An increase in the level of prices.

1990
$5.95

1995
$6.50

interest
The amount of money a borrower pays to borrow money. A bank pays interest on a savings account.

money
Paper and coins that are issued by the government and are used in exchange for all goods and services.

recession
A period of economic decline. During a recession, more people become unemployed, some businesses fail, and people buy less than usual. A recession is not as severe as a depression.

stock
A share in a corporation. A corporation sells shares to individuals or other companies to raise money for investment. When the company makes money, it pays the stockholder a "dividend," or a portion of the profit.

Making Money: THE U.S. MINT

What Is the U.S. Mint?   The U.S. Mint is a federal government organization responsible for making all U.S. coins. It also safeguards the Treasury Department's stored gold and silver. The U.S. Mint was founded in 1792 and is today a part of the U.S. Treasury Department.

The U.S. Mint's headquarters are in Washington, D.C. Local branches that produce coins are located in Philadelphia, PA; Denver, CO; San Francisco, CA; and West Point, NY. Treasury Department gold and silver is stored at Fort Knox, KY.

Another division of the Treasury Department—the Bureau of Engraving and Printing, also in Washington, D.C —designs, engraves, and prints all U.S. paper money.

What Kinds of Coins Does the Mint Make?   The U.S. Mint makes all the pennies, nickels, dimes, quarters, half dollars, and dollar coins that Americans use each day. U.S. coins are made of a mixture of metals. For example, dimes, quarters, half dollars, and dollar coins look like silver but are a mixture of copper, nickel, and silver.

The U.S. Mint also makes special coins honoring famous people and special events. For example, between 1971 and 1978 the Mint produced a special $1 coin with the portrait of former president Dwight D. Eisenhower on it. From 1979 to 1981 it made a special $1 coin honoring Susan B. Anthony, a leader in the struggles for women's right to vote.

Where Can I Get Information About the Mint?   Information about the Mint and the coins it sells is available from the United States Mint, Customer Service Center, 10001 Aerospace Road, Lanham, MD 20706. Telephone: (301) 436-7400. The Mint offers free public tours at all its facilities.

Whose Portraits Are on Our Money?   On the front of all U.S. paper money are portraits of presidents and other famous people in American history. Presidents also appear on the most commonly used coins. How many of them do you recognize?

Denomination	Portrait
1¢	Abraham Lincoln, 16th U.S. President
5¢	Thomas Jefferson, 3rd U.S. President
10¢	Franklin Delano Roosevelt, 32nd U.S. President
25¢	George Washington, 1st U.S. President
$1	George Washington, 1st U.S. President
$2	Thomas Jefferson, 3rd U.S. President
$5	Abraham Lincoln, 16th U.S. President
$10	Alexander Hamilton, 1st U.S. Treasury Secretary
$20	Andrew Jackson, 7th U.S. President
$50	Ulysses S. Grant, 18th U.S. President
$100	Benjamin Franklin, colonial inventor and U.S. patriot

Bills larger than $100 stopped being made in 1969. Up until then, $500, $1,000, $5,000, $10,000, and even $100,000 bills were produced. Some of these large bills have been turned in to the U.S. government and taken out of circulation. Some are still in circulation, and some belong to private citizens who collect rare or outdated currency.

How Much MONEY Is in CIRCULATION in the United States?

As of March 31, 1994, the U.S. Treasury Department reported that the total amount of money in circulation was $350,493,954,160 (more than 350 billion dollars). The following chart shows the number of bills in circulation in each denomination. Which kinds of bills are most common?

Denomination	Amount of Money in Circulation	Number of Bills in Circulation	
$1 bills	$5,674,996,280	5,674,996,280	
$2 bills	$973,910,720	486,955,360	
$5 bills	$6,672,449,500	1,334,489,900	
$10 bills	$13,205,056,280	1,320,505,628	
$20 bills	$75,061,576,480	3,753,078,824	
$50 bills	$41,046,149,300	820,922,986	
$100 bills	$207,539,210,500	2,075,392,105	

CURRENCY in Other Countries

The money that a country uses is called its *currency*. The currency of the United States is based on the U.S. dollar. All money used in the United States is a fraction of the dollar (a quarter, dime, nickel, cent) or a multiple of the dollar (as $5, $10, $20, $50 bills). Listed below are names of some of the currencies used throughout the world. Although many countries have currency with the same name, each of the currencies is different and may have a different value.

Name of Currency	Country	Name of Currency	Country
bolivar	Venezuela	krone	Denmark, Norway
cruzeiro	Brazil	lira	Italy, Turkey
dinar	Algeria, Jordan, Kuwait, and others	mark	Germany
		peseta	Spain
dirham	Morocco, United Arab Emirates	peso	Argentina, Chile, Colombia, Mexico, Philippines, Uruguay, and others
dollar	Australia, Canada, Hong Kong, New Zealand, Singapore, United States, and others	pound	Egypt, Great Britain, Lebanon, and others
		rand	South Africa
drachma	Greece	riyal	Saudi Arabia
franc	Belgium, France, Switzerland, and others	ruble	Russia
		rupee	India, Pakistan, and others
guilder	Netherlands	schilling	Austria
koruna	Czech Republic, Slovak Republic	yen	Japan
		yuan	China
krona	Iceland, Sweden	zloty	Poland

BUDGETS

A budget is a plan that estimates how much money a person, a business, or a government will receive during a particular period of time, how much money will be spent and what it will be spent on, and how much money will be left over (if any).

A FAMILY BUDGET

Does your family have a budget? Do you know what your family spends money on? Do you know where your family's income comes from? The chart below shows some sources of income and typical yearly expenses for a family's budget.

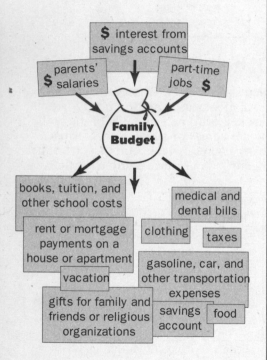

A Balanced Budget

A budget is **balanced** when the amount of money you receive equals the amount of money you spend. A budget is **unbalanced** when the amount of money you spend is greater than the amount of money you have.

MAKING YOUR OWN BUDGET

Imagine that you have been given a special allowance of $10. You may do anything you wish with the money but you must make a budget showing how you plan to spend it. Here are some of the things you may want to include in your budget:

Possible Purchases and Cost

A video rental of movie: $1.99
A candy bar: $.89
A poster of your favorite TV star: $4.99
A ball point pen: $.99
An audio cassette of your favorite
    music: $8.99
A visit to a museum: $4.00
A paperback book: $5.99

On the lines below, list the items you want along with their price. You may also add any other items that interest you— and their prices. And don't forget to include any money you want to save.

Item	Amount
_____	_____
_____	_____
_____	_____
_____	_____
Savings _____	_____

Now total all your
purchases and savings:_____

Is your budget balanced? Is the amount you plan to spend and save equal to the amount of your "income" ($10)?

The U.S. BUDGET

Not only do families and individuals have budgets, but businesses and governments have them too. Businesses take in money by making and selling products or by providing services. But what about the government? Where does the government's income come from? And what are the government's major expenses?

WHERE DOES THE GOVERNMENT GET MONEY?
The government gets much of its money from the taxes that Americans pay.

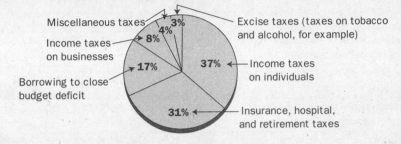

Miscellaneous taxes — 3%
4%
Excise taxes (taxes on tobacco and alcohol, for example)
Income taxes on businesses — 8%
17%
37% — Income taxes on individuals
Borrowing to close budget deficit
31% — Insurance, hospital, and retirement taxes

WHERE DOES THE GOVERNMENT SPEND MONEY?
The government spends money on a variety of programs.

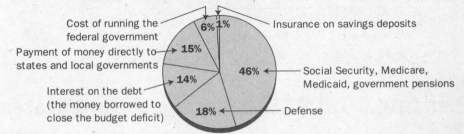

Cost of running the federal government — 6% 1% — Insurance on savings deposits
Payment of money directly to states and local governments — 15%
46% — Social Security, Medicare, Medicaid, government pensions
Interest on the debt (the money borrowed to close the budget deficit) — 14%
18% — Defense

THE GOVERNMENT'S UNBALANCED BUDGET
The U.S. government has not had a balanced budget since 1969. Every year since then, the government has spent more money than it has taken in through taxes. The difference between the higher amount spent and the amount taken in each year is called the **budget deficit.** The budget deficit went down a little in 1993 for the first time in many years.

YEAR	$ TAKEN IN	$ SPENT	DEFICIT
1990	$1.031 trillion	$1.252 trillion	$–220 billion
1992	$1.092 trillion	$1.382 trillion	$–290 billion
1993	$1.153 trillion	$1.408 trillion	$–255 billion
1994	$1.249 trillion	$1.484 trillion	$–235 billion

Since 1970 the U.S. government has borrowed money because taxes have not been sufficient to meet its expenses. Most economists believe that borrowing on such a huge scale hurts the economy. The interest payments on the debt will go on for years, and this money could otherwise be invested in private industry and programs to help citizens. But cutting the debt is also difficult, because that would mean cutting programs that citizens now depend on.

What Do AMERICANS BUY?

What do Americans spend their money on? The U.S. Department of Commerce publishes statistics each year on how Americans spend money. The following chart shows how much money Americans spent in 1993.

CATEGORY	AMOUNT SPENT
Medical and dental care, health insurance, drugs, hospital care	$760,500,000,000
Food	$649,800,000,000
Rent for housing	$629,000,000,000
Household expenses (telephone, electricity, furniture, kitchen supplies)	$508,200,000,000
Transportation expenses (cars, gasoline, taxis, train, bus, and plane tickets)	$504,200,000,000
Personal expenses (baby sitters, lawn care, house cleaning, lawyers)	$373,300,000,000
Recreation (books, magazines, toys, videos, sports events, amusement parks)	$339,900,000,000
Clothing	$293,900,000,000
Religious and charitable contributions	$123,000,000,000
School tuition and other educational expenses	$105,500,000,000
Personal care (haircuts, gyms and health clubs)	$ 65,800,000,000

Leading BUSINESSES in the United States

The United States is a leading manufacturer of many different kinds of products. The following chart lists the leading American business in each category that produces these products and the yearly sales in 1993.

Airplanes
Boeing, $25,285,000,000

Clothing
Levi Strauss, $5,892,000,000

Beverages
Pepsico, $25,021,000,000

Cars and Other Motor Vehicles
General Motors, $133,622,000,000

Chemicals
E.I. Du Pont De Nemours, $32,621,000,000

Computers and Office Equipment
IBM, $62,716,000,000

Electronics
General Electric, $60,823,000,000

Industrial and Farm Equipment
Tenneco, $13,255,000,000

Medicines and Drugs
Johnson & Johnson, $14,138,000,000

Petroleum Refining
Exxon, $103,547,000,000

Retail Stores
Wal-Mart Stores, $67,344,000,000

Rubber and Plastic Products
Goodyear Tire, $11,643,000,000

Supermarkets
Safeway, $15,214,000,000

Telecommunication
American Telephone & Telegraph (AT&T), $67,156,000,000

What Kinds of JOBS Do Americans Have?

How are Americans employed? Each year the U.S. Department of Labor publishes information on employment in the United States. The following chart shows the number of men and women employed in different kinds of jobs. The column showing yearly earnings shows the mid-range of earnings for a year. This means that many people in that category earn more than this amount and many earn less. This amount is in the middle of what people earned in 1992.

JOBS	NUMBER OF WORKERS	YEARLY EARNINGS
Managers and professionals (for example, business executives and supervisors, doctors, lawyers, teachers, nurses)		
Men	12,082,000	$40,500
Women	11,165,000	$29,000
Sales people, technicians, administrative workers (including clerical workers)		
Men	9,844,000	$27,000
Women	16,084,000	$19,000
People who repair things, precision workers, crafts people		
Men	9,581,000	$26,000
Women	854,000	$17,500
Machine operators and drivers of transportation equipment		
Men	10,618,000	$20,500
Women	3,383,000	$14,500
Service jobs (for example, waiters, guards, janitors, maids)		
Men	4,492,000	$17,000
Women	4,612,000	$13,000
Farming, forestry, and fishing		
Men	1,260,000	$14,000
Women	170,000	$11,500

OCCUPATIONS THAT ARE GROWING

Below is a list of some of the fastest-growing occupations in the United States:

Health and medical field: medical assistants and secretaries, physicians, technicians, licensed practical nurses, home health aides

Computer science field: computer programmers and scientists, systems analysts

Human services: social workers, child care workers, chefs and cooks, gardeners and groundskeepers

Correction officers

Teaching: elementary, secondary, and adult-education teachers

Travel: travel agents and flight attendants

TRADE

When companies or countries buy and sell their products or services to other companies or countries, we call this **trade. Exports** are goods that one country *sells* to another country. **Imports** are goods that one country *buys* from another country. The United States trades with many other countries. It exports and imports goods.

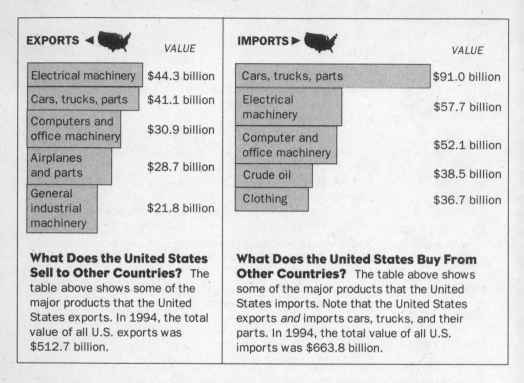

EXPORTS ◄	VALUE
Electrical machinery	$44.3 billion
Cars, trucks, parts	$41.1 billion
Computers and office machinery	$30.9 billion
Airplanes and parts	$28.7 billion
General industrial machinery	$21.8 billion

IMPORTS ►	VALUE
Cars, trucks, parts	$91.0 billion
Electrical machinery	$57.7 billion
Computer and office machinery	$52.1 billion
Crude oil	$38.5 billion
Clothing	$36.7 billion

What Does the United States Sell to Other Countries? The table above shows some of the major products that the United States exports. In 1994, the total value of all U.S. exports was $512.7 billion.

What Does the United States Buy From Other Countries? The table above shows some of the major products that the United States imports. Note that the United States exports *and* imports cars, trucks, and their parts. In 1994, the total value of all U.S. imports was $663.8 billion.

Who Are America's Leading Trading Partners? In 1994, the countries with which the United States traded most were: (1) Canada, (2) Japan, (3) Mexico, (4) Great Britain, (5) Germany.

Why Do Americans Buy Foreign-made Products? Americans buy products from abroad that (1) they do not make for themselves or (2) that are less expensive or better-made than products made in the United States. For example, the United States imports most of its clothing because foreign-made products are less expensive.

What Happens If a Country Imports More Than It Exports? When the United States sells to other countries (or exports), other countries pay the United States for the goods. When the United States buys from other countries (or imports), it makes payments to them. It is best for a country to export more than it imports, or to export and import an equal amount. When a country imports more than it exports, it has what is called a **trade deficit.** The United States imports more than it exports and has a trade deficit. That means it is spending more money abroad for foreign-made products than it is getting from selling American-made products overseas.

The BUSIEST PORTS in the United States

Can you guess where the busiest ports in the United States are? Most products that are imported into the United States and exported to other countries from the United States travel by ship over oceans and other bodies of water. The busiest U.S. ports are on the east coast (near the Atlantic Ocean), on the west coast (near the Pacific Ocean), and in the south (near the Gulf of Mexico). The table below lists the five busiest ports and the tons of cargo they handled in 1992.

Port	Tons of cargo in 1992
Port of South Louisiana	199.7 million tons
Houston, Texas	137.7 million tons
New York, New York (and New Jersey)	115.3 million tons
Valdez, Alaska	93.7 million tons
Baton Rouge, Louisiana	84.7 million tons

Some ports specialize in certain goods. Valdez, Alaska, for example, is known for oil from the Alaska pipeline. Long Beach, California, is noted as the arrival port for many Japanese cars being imported into the United States.

What Are EXCHANGE RATES?

When one country exports goods to another, the payment from the country buying the goods must be changed into the currency of the country selling the goods. An **exchange rate** is the price of one national currency in terms of another. For example, one U.S. dollar was equivalent to (or could buy) 5.24 French francs in 1994. The ratio of 1 to 5.24 is the exchange rate between the U.S. dollar and the French franc.

Exchange rates are not the same all the time. As a nation's economy becomes stronger or weaker, the exchange rates also change. The following chart shows a comparison of the exchange rates in 1970 and 1994 between the U.S. dollar and five of the country's most important trading partners. The more foreign currency the dollar can buy, the better the exchange rate for Americans.

$4 — U.S.

almost 21 francs — France

| | **$1 BOUGHT:** | |
COUNTRY	**IN 1970**	**IN 1994**
France	5.5 francs	5.24 francs
Germany	3.6 marks	1.53 marks
Great Britain	.42 pounds	.67 pounds
Japan	358 yen	97.3 yen
Italy	623 lira	1,542 lira

In 1994, products from France cost the United States a little more than they did in 1970. Products from Germany and Japan cost the United States much more than they did in 1970, and products from Great Britain and Italy cost less.

Some MOVIES Popular With KIDS

Snow White and the Seven Dwarfs (1937). This Disney classic was the first movie-length cartoon ever released. Since the late 1980s, Disney's new animated movies, such as *Beauty and the Beast, Aladdin, The Lion King,* and *Pocahontas* have been popular with adults almost as much as with kids.

The Wizard of Oz (1939). This movie made Judy Garland a star and "Over the Rainbow" a popular hit song. During the movie's filming, however, some people wanted to cut the song, thinking that it slowed down the action.

National Velvet (1944). This is the story of two kids and their beloved racehorse.

The Sound of Music (1965). Winner of five Academy Awards, including Best Picture, this musical tells the story of Maria Von Trapp, whose plans to become a nun change when she becomes the governess to seven children and falls in love with their father.

E.T. The Extra-Terrestrial (1982). A heartwarming tale about a boy and a space alien whose deep relationship helps them both to grow. "E.T., phone home" became the catchphrase for the year.

Anne of Green Gables (1985). This movie is based on the novel by L. M. Montgomery about the experience of a young girl who is adopted by a family living on Canada's isolated Prince Edward Island.

Some MOVIES Popular With Older KIDS

The movies below, which are rated PG or PG-13, have been popular with some of the older kids.

Star Wars (1977). Luke Skywalker, Princess Leia, and others battle Darth Vader and the forces of evil in a thriller set in outer space. Two sequels to *Star Wars, The Empire Strikes Back* (1980) and *The Return of the Jedi* (1983), were also huge hits. (PG)

Home Alone (1990). An 8-year-old kid left home alone by accident outwits the bad guys all by himself but decides that, in the end, he'd rather have his family back anyway. (PG)

Wayne's World (1992). Based on a *Saturday Night Live* skit about two wacky teenagers obsessed with rock 'n' roll and TV. Wayne and Garth match wits (as best they can) with a sleazy guy, who wants to get rich off their public-access cable TV show. (PG-13)

Jurassic Park (1993). A thriller about dinosaurs created in a lab from DNA found in fossils and put on a Caribbean island as the attraction in what is supposed to be a secure park. It's not. (PG-13)

10 MOVIE HITS of 1994

1. *The Lion King*
2. *Forrest Gump*
3. *The Santa Clause*
4. *The Flintstones*
5. *The Mask*

6. *Mrs. Doubtfire*
7. *Maverick*
8. *Ace Ventura: Pet Detective*
9. *Star Trek Generations*
10. *Beethoven's 2nd*

▲ *The Starship Enterprise from Star Trek Generations*

MOVIE-MAKING TALK

cameo
A brief appearance in a movie by a major star, usually in a small, rather unimportant role. Sometimes the star doing the cameo doesn't even receive billing (or listing) in the movie credits.

dubbing
Adding sound to a scene or a movie that has already been shot. Films are often dubbed when they are shown in countries where the language is different from the language in which the movie was originally shot. Another word for dubbing is *looping*.

editing
The process of choosing which of the scenes filmed will actually make it into the final movie and deciding on the order they should take. Editing also involves combining the finished movie with the sound track.

extra
An actor who is hired by the day to play a small non-speaking part, such as someone in a crowd or someone sitting in a park.

freeze-frame
A camera shot that seems to stop in an instant all the action on the screen.

outtake
A shot filmed by the camera operator but not used in the final movie, either because it just doesn't fit in or because one of the actors flubbed a line.

rushes
The first prints of a day's shooting. The prints are developed in a rush and given to the director, so that he or she can see how well the movie is coming along. Rushes are also called *dailies*.

Some BEST-SELLING VIDEOS in 1994

Aladdin
Free Willy
Mrs. Doubtfire
The Fugitive
Ace Ventura: Pet Detective
Beauty and the Beast
Beethoven's 2nd
Dennis the Menace

Homeward Bound: The Incredible
   Journey
The Secret Garden
Batman: Mask of the Phantasm
D2: The Mighty Ducks
Jurassic Park
Ren & Stimpy: The Classics
101 Dalmatians

Popular VIDEO GAMES in 1994

Super Nintendo Donkey Kong Country
Genesis NBA Jam
Super Nintendo NBA Jam
Genesis Sonic 3
Genesis Sonic & Knuckles
Genesis Madden NFL '95

Super Nintendo Aladdin
Genesis NHL '95
Super Nintendo Ken Griffey Jr. Presents:
   Major League Baseball
Genesis World Series Baseball
Genesis Mighty Morphin Power Rangers

Popular TV SHOWS in 1994-1995

▲ Home Improvement

AGES 6-11

1. Boy Meets World
2. Step by Step
3. Home Improvement
4. Hangin' with Mr. Cooper
5. Full House
6. Family Matters
7. Me and the Boys
8. Sister, Sister
9. On Our Own
10. Thunder Alley

AGES 12-17

1. Home Improvement
2. In the House
3. Blossom
4. Me and the Boys
5. Fresh Prince of Bel-Air
6. Grace Under Fire
7. Boy Meets World
8. Full House
9. Beverly Hills, 90210
10. Step by Step

(SOURCE: Nielsen Media Research)

Visiting the PAST and the FUTURE

If you like to learn new things and have fun at the same time, museums are the places to go. Some museums, like children's museums, have exhibits on many subjects. Some museums have exhibits in which you can learn a lot about one subject, such as people who share the same customs. In another kind of museum, you can walk in a village from an earlier time in history and watch people from another century work and go about their daily lives. This type of museum is called an historic restoration.

The ancient Greeks were the first people to have public museums open to everyone. The oldest museum in the United States in continuous existence is the Charleston Museum, founded in South Carolina in 1773 to gather material on the natural history of that colony. The United States now has more than 7,000 museums. A few children's museums, ethnic museums, museums of entertainment, and historic restorations are listed below. Look in the Index for museums of art, computers, natural history, and science.

CHILDREN'S MUSEUMS

Children's museums often have many different types of hands-on exhibits.

Children's Museum, Boston, Massachusetts
Has a full-size Japanese house, a Latino market, plus displays on Native Americans.
Visitors (1994), 430,000

Children's Museum of Indianapolis, Indianapolis, Indiana
Has natural science exhibits, including a walk-through limestone cave; computer center; old-fashioned railway depot with a 19th-century locomotive and caboose; exhibits about people around the world, including interactive videos.
Visitors (1994), 920,554

Children's Museum of Manhattan, New York, New York
Displays on natural history, science, and art. Visitors (1994), 250,000

Children's Museum of Portland, Portland, Oregon
Hands-on displays on transportation, natural history, and toys.
Visitors (1994), 120,000

Los Angeles Children's Museum, Los Angeles, California
Exhibits on health and city life; has a TV studio. Visitors (1994), 250,000

MUSEUMS OF ENTERTAINMENT

Country Music Hall of Fame and Museum, Nashville, Tennessee
Celebrates country music's history and stars, displaying costumes and instruments connected with country music. Visitors (1994), 290,559

Graceland, Memphis, Tennessee
The 14-acre estate of the King of Rock 'n' Roll, Elvis Presley. Visitors (1994), 670,000

Museum of Television and Radio, New York, New York
Contains 15,000 radio and 25,000 TV tapes from the 1920s to the present. Visitors (1994), 127,927

ETHNIC MUSEUMS

Below are some museums that show the culture or the history of groups of people who share traditions and customs.

Arthur M. Sackler Gallery and the **Freer Gallery of Art,** Washington, D.C.
Displays paintings and other art objects from China, Japan, Korea, India, Iran, and other Asian countries.
Visitors (1994), 637,108

California Afro-American Museum, Los Angeles, California
Displays art, books, and photographs on African-American culture. Visitors (1994), 241,936

Gilcrease Museum, Tulsa, Oklahoma
Exhibits on the Five Civilized Tribes (Cherokee, Choctaw, Chickasaw, Creek, and Seminole). Visitors (1994), 129,019

▲ *Chinese jar*

Heard Museum, Phoenix, Arizona
Displays art by Native Americans and artists from Africa, Asia, Oceania, and the Upper Amazon. Visitors (1994), 250,000

Institute of Texan Cultures, San Antonio, Texas
Exhibits on 24 ethnic groups showing historical and cultural contributions. Visitors (1994), 338,527

▲ *Native American bowl*

Jewish Museum, New York, New York
Exhibits covering 40 centuries of Jewish history and culture. Visitors (1994), 150,000

National Museum of African Art, Washington, D.C.
Displays African art made of many materials—wood, ivory, metal, and ceramic. Visitors (1994), 309,188

National Museum of the American Indian,
New York, New York
A branch of the Smithsonian Institution, this new museum features displays on the way of life and the history of Native Americans. Visitors (1994), 100,000

▲ *African sculpture*

HISTORIC RESTORATIONS

Historic restorations are often houses or parts of villages that have been restored to look the way they did many years ago. People in the village dress in costumes of an earlier time and show what daily life was like then.

Boot Hill Museum, Dodge City, Kansas
Historic buildings in this famous Western town, including the Fort Dodge jail. Visitors (1994), 147,003

Colonial Williamsburg, Williamsburg, Virginia
Restoration of the colonial capital of Virginia to its 18th-century appearance, with 88 original buildings. Visitors (1994), 900,000

Henry Ford Museum and Greenfield Village, Dearborn, Michigan
More than 80 historic buildings and more than 1 million artifacts on American history. Visitors (1994), 1,041,000

Mystic Seaport, Mystic, Connecticut
Re-creation of a 19th-century New England whaling village, including ships and a museum. Visitors (1994), 422,136

Old Sturbridge Village, Sturbridge, Massachusetts
Re-creation of a New England farming community of the 1830s, with more than 40 buildings. Visitors (1994), 432,523

Pioneer Arizona Living History Museum, Phoenix, Arizona
Twenty houses show pioneer life in a 19th-century rural town. Visitors (1994), 45,000

Plimoth Plantation, Plymouth, Massachusetts
Re-creation of the Pilgrims' first settlement in the New World. Visitors (1994), 450,000

Shelburne Museum, Shelburne, Vermont
Re-created New England village with 37 buildings and the *S.S. Ticonderoga*. Visitors (1994), 155,000

St. Augustine Historic District, St. Augustine, Florida
Includes the Oldest House (Gonzalez-Alvarez House), showing life in St. Augustine over 400 years. Visitors (1994), 53,300

Scene from a historic restoration ▶

MUSIC and MUSIC MAKERS

CLASSICAL MUSIC

People often think of classical music as serious music. Often more complex than other types of music, classical music is usually written to be listened to closely, as at a concert, rather than as background for another activity. Common forms of classical music include the symphony, chamber music, opera, and ballet music. **Famous early classical composers:** Johann Sebastian Bach, Ludwig van Beethoven, Johannes Brahms, Franz Joseph Haydn, Wolfgang Amadeus Mozart, Franz Schubert, Peter Ilyich Tchaikovsky, Richard Wagner. **Famous modern classical composers:** Aaron Copland, Virgil Thomson, Charles Ives, Igor Stravinsky.

CHAMBER MUSIC

Chamber music is written for a small group of musicians, often only three or four, to play together. In chamber music, each instrument plays a separate part. A string quartet (music written for two violins, viola, and cello) is an example of chamber music.

SYMPHONY

A symphony is music written for an orchestra. Symphonies usually have four parts called *movements*. The first movement is usually fast; the second is usually slow, and the last two are fast.

OPERA

An opera is a play whose words are sung to music. The music is played by an orchestra. The words of an opera are called the **libretto**, and a long song sung by one character (like a speech in a play) is called an **aria**. **Famous operas:** *Madama Butterfly* (Giacomo Puccini); *Aida* (Guiseppe Verdi).

VOICE

There are six common types of voices, three for men and three for women. Women's voices usually range from *soprano* (highest) to *mezzo-soprano* (middle) to *alto* (lowest). Men's voices range from *tenor* (highest) to *baritone* (middle) to *bass* (lowest).

MUSICAL NOTATION

These are some of the symbols composers use when they write music.

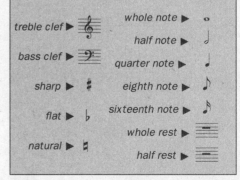

treble clef ▶	whole note ▶
bass clef ▶	half note ▶
	quarter note ▶
sharp ▶	eighth note ▶
flat ▶	sixteenth note ▶
natural ▶	whole rest ▶
	half rest ▶

❓ DID YOU KNOW?

Ludwig van Beethoven started to go deaf in his twenties. By the end of his life, he had completely lost his hearing, yet he continued to compose and play music.
Wolfgang Amadeus Mozart was eight years old when he wrote his first symphony.
Johann Sebastian Bach came from a well-known musical family. Over the course of about 300 years, more than 30 of his relatives made their living as musicians.

More MUSIC and MUSIC MAKERS

BLUES
The music called "the blues" developed from work songs and religious folk songs (called spirituals) sung by African-Americans. It was introduced early in the 1900s by African-American musicians, especially the composer W. C. Handy. The words of blues songs are usually sad.
Famous blues performers: Ma Rainey, Bessie Smith, Buddy Guy.
(A type of jazz is also called "the blues.")

JAZZ
Jazz is a type of American music that emphasizes rhythm and improvisation. Improvising means creating music as you play it, rather than performing written music. Jazz was created in the 1900s by African-Americans, mostly in large cities. **Famous jazz musicians:** Paul Whiteman, Louis Armstrong, Duke Ellington, Count Basie, Dizzy Gillespie, Benny Goodman, Fats Waller, Thelonious Monk, Jelly Roll Morton, Billie Holiday, Ella Fitzgerald, Sarah Vaughan, Dave Brubeck, Charlie Parker.

POP MUSIC
Pop music (short for popular music) puts more emphasis on melody (tune) than does rock and has a softer beat. It is often called "lite" music.
Famous pop singers: Barbra Streisand, Whitney Houston, Neil Diamond, Freddie Jackson, Peabo Bryson, Madonna.

▲ Whitney Houston

ROCK (also known as rock 'n' roll)
Rock is a form of popular American music that started in the 1950s. Rock music has a strong, rhythmic beat. It is based on black rhythm and blues and country music. Rock music often uses electronic instruments and equipment. Punk, heavy metal, alternative, and new wave music are types of rock music.
Famous rock musicians: Elvis Presley, Bob Dylan, the Beatles, the Rolling Stones, Aerosmith, Michael Jackson, R.E.M., Pearl Jam.

RAP MUSIC
Spoken, rhymed words backed by strong rhythm and music, rap was created by African-Americans living in inner cities. The words are often about violence and sex. **Famous rappers:** Salt-n-Pepa, Queen Latifah, Beastie Boys.

COUNTRY MUSIC
Country music is American music based on southern mountain music. It has also been influenced by blues, jazz, and other popular musical styles. Country music became well known through the *Grand Ole Opry* radio show in Nashville, Tennessee.
Famous country performers: Johnny Cash, Dolly Parton, Willy Nelson, Garth Brooks, Travis Tritt, Vince Gill, Reba McEntire.

▼ Ace of Base

TOP ALBUM ARTISTS FOR 1994
(Including rank, artist, title, and label)
1. Ace of Base, *The Sign,* Arista
2. Mariah Carey, *Music Box,* Columbia
3. Pearl Jam, *VS.,* Epic

INSTRUMENTS of the ORCHESTRA

The instruments of an orchestra are divided into four groups, or sections: string, woodwind, brass, and percussion. In an orchestra with 100 musicians usually more than 60 play string instruments. The rest play woodwinds, brasses, or percussion instruments.

STRINGS

Stringed instruments make sounds when the strings are either stroked with a bow or plucked with the fingers. The violin, viola, cello, bass, and harp are stringed instruments used in an orchestra. The guitar, banjo, balalaika, mandolin, koto, and dulcimer are other examples of stringed instruments.

WOODWINDS

Woodwind instruments are long and round and hollow inside. They make sounds when air is blown into them through a mouth hole or a reed. The clarinet, flute, oboe, bassoon, and piccolo are woodwinds.

BRASSES

Brass instruments are also hollow inside. They make sounds when air is blown into a mouthpiece shaped like a cup or a funnel. The trumpet, French horn, trombone, and tuba are brasses.

PERCUSSION INSTRUMENTS

Percussion instruments make sounds when they are struck. The most common percussion instrument is the drum, which comes in many forms. Other percussion instruments include cymbals, triangles, gongs, bells, and xylophone. Keyboard instruments, like the piano, are sometimes thought of as percussion instruments.

A TYPICAL ORCHESTRA

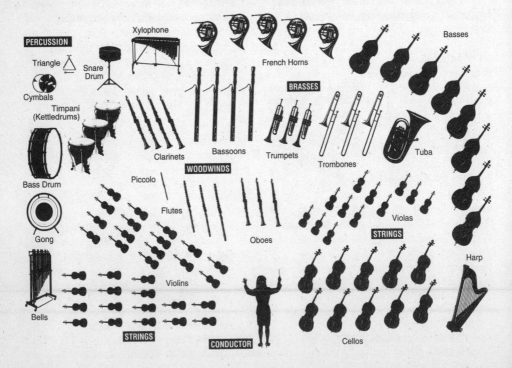

PERCUSSION — Triangle, Cymbals, Snare Drum, Timpani (Kettledrums), Bass Drum, Gong, Bells
Xylophone
French Horns
BRASSES
WOODWINDS — Clarinets, Bassoons, Piccolo, Flutes, Oboes
Trumpets, Trombones, Tuba
STRINGS — Basses, Violas, Violins, Cellos, Harp
CONDUCTOR

AMERICAN MUSICAL THEATER

American musicals are plays known for their lively music and songs, comedy routines, dancing, colorful costumes, and elaborate stage sets. In the early 1900s, most musicals did not tell a story. They were simply a series of songs, dances, and comedy skits and were called musical revues. These were written by George M. Cohan, Irving Berlin, Oscar Hammerstein II, Richard Rodgers, and others. By the 1930s and 1940s, it was more common for musicals to have plots, with songs and dances used to help tell the story and to express the characters' feelings.

Longest running American musical: *The Fantasticks,* by Tom Jones and Harvey Schmidt. Opened May 3, 1960. By May 1995, there had been more than 14,500 performances.

Longest running Broadway musical: *A Chorus Line,* by Marvin Hamlisch and Edward Kleban. The show ran for nearly 15 years, from July 25, 1975, to April 28, 1990, and played 6,137 performances. It won the Tony Award for best musical in 1976.

Tony (Antoinette Perry) Awards: Tony Awards are given every year to outstanding Broadway plays. **1995 Tony Award winner for best musical:** *Sunset Boulevard,* with music by Andrew Lloyd Webber and lyrics by Don Black and Christopher Hampton.

SOME OTHER FAMOUS MUSICALS

Note: The date after the name of the play is the year the play opened on Broadway.

Annie (1977), by Charles Strouse and Martin Charnin. Tony Award 1977.

Annie Get Your Gun (1946), by Irving Berlin.

Anything Goes (1930), by Cole Porter.

Brigadoon (1947), by Alan Jay Lerner and Frederick Loewe.

Cabaret (1966), by John Kander and Fred Ebb. Tony Award 1967.

Carousel (1945), by Richard Rodgers and Oscar Hammerstein II.

Cats (1982), by Andrew Lloyd Webber. Tony Award 1983.

Evita (1979), by Andrew Lloyd Webber and Tim Rice. Tony Award 1980.

Fiddler on the Roof (1964), by Jerry Bock and Sheldon Harnick. Tony Award 1964.

Grease (1972), by Jim Jacobs and Warren Casey.

Guys and Dolls (1950), by Frank Loesser. Tony Award 1951.

Hello, Dolly! (1964), by Jerry Herman. Tony Award 1964.

Kiss Me Kate (1948), by Cole Porter. Tony Award 1949.

Kiss of the Spider Woman (1993), by John Kander and Fred Ebb. Tony Award 1993.

My Fair Lady (1956), by Alan Jay Lerner and Frederick Loewe. Tony Award 1957.

Of Thee I Sing (1931), by George and Ira Gershwin.

Oklahoma! (1943), by Richard Rodgers and Oscar Hammerstein II.

Porgy and Bess (1935), by George Gershwin.

Show Boat (1927), by Jerome Kern and Oscar Hammerstein II.

South Pacific (1949), by Richard Rodgers and Oscar Hammerstein II. Tony Award 1950.

The King and I (1952), by Richard Rodgers and Oscar Hammerstein II. Tony Award 1952.

The Music Man (1957), by Meredith Willson. Tony Award 1958.

The Pajama Game (1954), by Richard Adler and Jerry Ross. Tony Award 1955.

The Sound of Music (1959), by Richard Rodgers and Oscar Hammerstein II.

West Side Story (1957), by Leonard Bernstein and Stephen Sondheim.

DANCE

In dance, the body performs patterns of movement, usually to music or rhythm. Dance may be a form of art, or it may be part of a religious ceremony. Dance may express feelings and ideas, or it may be done just for fun. Ballet, modern dance, folk dance, and social dance are major forms of dance.

BALLET

Dances in ballet are based on formal steps performed in graceful, flowing movements. Ballets are performed for an audience and often tell a story. In the 15th century, ballet was part of the elaborate entertainment that was performed for the rulers of Europe. In the 1600s, professional dance companies existed, but without women. Women's parts were danced by men wearing masks. In the 1700s dancers wore bulky costumes and shoes with high heels. Women danced in hoopskirts—and so did men! In the 1800s ballet steps and costumes began to look the way they do now. In fact, many of the most popular ballets today date back to the middle or late 1800s.

SOME FAMOUS BALLETS

Swan Lake. First danced in St. Petersburg, Russia, in 1895. Perhaps the most popular ballet ever, *Swan Lake* is the story of a prince and his love for a maiden who was turned into a swan by an evil magician.

The Nutcracker. When this ballet was first performed in St. Petersburg, Russia, in 1892, it was a colossal flop. It has since become so popular that it is danced in many places every year at Christmastime.

The Sleeping Beauty is based on the fairy tale *The Sleeping Beauty.* The ballet was first danced in St. Petersburg in 1890.

Jewels. This ballet by the American choreographer George Balanchine was first performed in New York City in 1967. In *Jewels,* the dancers do not dance to a story. They explore patterns and movement of the human body.

The River. This 1970 ballet by Alvin Ailey is danced to music by the famous jazz musician Duke Ellington. It has been described as a ballet of imaginative movement and a celebration of life.

NOTED BALLET DANCERS
Anna Pavlova (1885-1931)
Vaslav Nijinsky (1890-1950)
Margot Fonteyn (1919-1991)
Arthur Mitchell (born 1934)
Rudolf Nureyev (1938-1993)
Mikhail Baryshnikov (born 1948)

NOTED CHOREOGRAPHERS
Marius Petipa (1818-1910)
Michel Fokine (1880-1942)
George Balanchine (1904-1983)
Agnes de Mille (1908-1993)
Jerome Robbins (born 1918)
Kenneth MacMillan (1929-1992)

MODERN DANCE

Modern dance differs from classical ballet in many ways. It is less concerned with graceful, flowing movement and the appearance of weightlessness. Modern dance steps are often not ballet steps or positions. Dancers may put their bodies into awkward, angular positions and turn their backs on the audience. Many modern dances are based on ancient art, such as Greek sculpture, or on dance styles found in Africa and Asia.

Noted Modern Dancers and Choreographers. Many of the most important modern dance choreographers, including those on this list, are also dancers.

Alvin Ailey (1931-1989)
Trisha Brown (born 1936)
Merce Cunningham (born 1919)
Isadora Duncan (1878-1927)

Martha Graham (1894-1991)
Mark Morris (born 1956)
Paul Taylor (born 1930)
Twyla Tharp (born 1941)

FOLK DANCE. Folk dance is the term for a dance that is passed on from generation to generation and that in some way is part of the culture or way of life of people from a particular country or ethnic group. Virginia reel (American), czardas (Hungarian), jig, and the Israeli hora are some folk dances.

SOCIAL DANCE. Social dance is the name for dances done just for fun by ordinary people. They are not made up by professionals or danced by trained dancers for an audience. Instead, they are danced at parties and clubs. Social dancing has been around since at least the Middle Ages, when it was popular at fairs and festivals. In the 1400s social dance was part of fancy court pageants. It developed into dainty dances like the minuet and the waltz during the 1700s and eventually, in the 20th century, into such dances as the Charleston, the lindy, the twist, disco, and break dancing, as well as line dances such as the achy-breaky.

DANCE TALK

arabesque (ar-a-BESK)
A ballet pose in which the dancer balances on one leg, puts the other behind her, toes pointed, and extends one arm in front and the other behind her, creating the illusion of a straight line from fingertip in front to toe in back.

choreographer (core-e-OG-ra-fer)
The person who makes up the steps to be danced.

corps de ballet (core de bal-LAY)
The group of dancers, usually less experienced, who dance together, with or without the stars of the ballet.

position
The way that dancers place their arms and feet. In ballet there are 5 standard positions for the arms and 5 for the feet.

prima ballerina (PREE-ma)
In ballet, a woman who is one of the star dancers in her company and who takes on leading roles.

pas de deux (pa de DU)
A part of a ballet in which a man and a woman dance a duet.

Numerals in ANCIENT CIVILIZATIONS

People have been counting since the earliest of times. This is what some early numerals looked like.

Modern	1	2	3	4	5	6	7	8	9	10	20	50	100
Egyptian	I	II	III	IIII	III⁄II	III⁄III	IIII⁄III	IIII⁄IIII	IIIII⁄IIII	∩	∩∩	∩∩∩∩∩	9
Baby-lonian	𒁹	𒐀	𒐈	𒐲	𒐳	𒐴	𒐵	𒐶	𒐷	‹	‹‹	⫸	⫸‹
Greek	A	B	Γ	Δ	E	F	Z	H	θ	I	K	N	P
Mayan	•	••	•••	••••	—	•⁄—	••⁄—	•••⁄—	••••⁄—	=	⊙	⊙⊙	⊚
Chinese	一	二	三	四	五	六	七	八	九	十	二十	五十	百
Hindu	I	𑁨	𑁩	8	𑁪	𑁫	𑁬	𑁭	𑁮	10	𑁨0	𑁪0	100
Arabic	١	٢	٣	٤	٥	٦	٧	٨	٩	١٠	٢٠	٥٠	١٠٠

ROMAN NUMERALS

Roman numerals are still used today. The symbols used to represent different numbers are the letters I (1), V (5), X (10), L (50), C (100), D (500), and M (1000). If one roman numeral is followed by a larger one, the first is subtracted from the second. For example, the numeral IX means 10 − 1 = 9. Think of it as "one less than ten." Otherwise, if one roman numeral is followed by another that is equal or smaller, add them together. Therefore, VII means 5 + 1 + 1 = 7.

1	I	11	XI	30	XXX	400	CD
2	II	12	XII	40	XL	500	D
3	III	13	XIII	50	L	600	DC
4	IV	14	XIV	60	LX	700	DCC
5	V	15	XV	70	LXX	800	DCCC
6	VI	16	XVI	80	LXXX	900	CM
7	VII	17	XVII	90	XC	1,000	M
8	VIII	18	XVIII	100	C		
9	IX	19	XIX	200	CC		
10	X	20	XX	300	CCC		

Can you write the year on the front cover of this book in Roman numerals? The answer is on page 304.

The PREFIX Tells the Number

Each number listed below has one or more prefixes used to form words that include that number. Knowing which number the prefix stands for helps you to understand the meaning of the word. For example, a unicycle has 1 wheel. A triangle has 3 sides. An octopus has 8 tentacles. Next to the prefixes are some examples of words that use these prefixes.

1	uni-, mon-, mono-	unicycle, unicorn, monarch, monotone
2	bi-, di-	bicycle, binary, binoculars, bifocals, disect
3	tri-	tricycle, triangle, trilogy, triplet
4	quadr-, tetr-	quadrangle, quadruplet, tetrahedron
5	pent-, penta-	pentagon, pentathlon
6	hex-, hexa-	hexagon
7	hepta-	heptathlon
8	oct-, octa-, octo-	octave, octet, octopus, octagon
9	nona-	nonagon
10	dec-, deca-	decade, decibel, decimal
100	cent-	centipede, century
1000	kilo-	kilogram, kilometer
million	mega-	megabyte, megahertz
billion	giga-	gigabyte, gigawatt

Reading and Writing LARGE NUMBERS

Below is the name of a number and the number of zeros that would follow it when the number is written out.

> A googol! What's a googol?!

ten:	1 zero	10
hundred:	2 zeros	100
thousand:	3 zeros	1,000
ten thousand:	4 zeros	10,000
hundred thousand:	5 zeros	100,000
million:	6 zeros	1,000,000
ten million:	7 zeros	10,000,000
hundred million:	8 zeros	100,000,000
billion:	9 zeros	1,000,000,000
trillion:	12 zeros	1,000,000,000,000
quadrillion:	15 zeros	1,000,000,000,000,000
quintillion:	18 zeros	1,000,000,000,000,000,000
sextillion:	21 zeros	1,000,000,000,000,000,000,000
septillion:	24 zeros	1,000,000,000,000,000,000,000,000

Look below to see how numbers larger than these would be written:

octillion has 27 zeros   decillion has 33 zeros
nonillion has 30 zeros   googol has 100 zeros

How Many SIDES and FACES Do They Have?

When a figure is flat (two-dimensional), it is á **plane figure**. When a figure takes up space (three-dimensional), it is a **solid figure**. The flat surface of a solid figure is called a **face**. Plane and solid figures come in many different shapes.

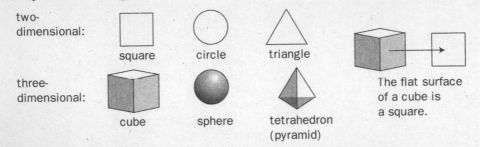

two-dimensional: square   circle   triangle

three-dimensional: cube   sphere   tetrahedron (pyramid)

The flat surface of a cube is a square.

WHAT ARE POLYGONS? A polygon is a two-dimensional figure that has three or more straight sides (called line segments). A square is a polygon. Polygons have different numbers of sides—and each has a different name. If the sides of a polygon are all the same length and all the angles between the sides are equal, the polygon is called regular. If the sides are of different lengths or the angles are not equal, the polygon is called irregular. Below are some regular and irregular polygons.

NAME AND NUMBER OF SIDES	REGULAR	IRREGULAR	NAME AND NUMBER OF SIDES	REGULAR	IRREGULAR
triangle - 3			heptagon - 7		
quadrilateral or tetragon - 4			octagon - 8		
pentagon - 5			nonagon - 9		
hexagon - 6			decagon - 10		

WHAT ARE POLYHEDRONS? A polyhedron is a three-dimensional figure with four or more faces. Each face on a polyhedron is a polygon. Below are some polyhedrons with many faces.

tetrahedron 4 faces   hexahedron 6 faces   octahedron 8 faces   dodecahedron 12 faces   icosahedron 20 faces

NUMBERS PUZZLES Can you solve the three numbers puzzles shown below? You can check your solutions with the answers on 304.

I. CALCULATORS CAN SPELL TOO

Did you know that a calculator can spell? Well, it can. If you press the sets of numbers on a calculator shown for each clue below and then turn the calculator upside-down, you will be able to fill in the puzzle.

Clues

1. 7738 (The fire station has one)   __ __ __ __

2. 5318804 (Do you have any of these?)   __ __ __ __ __ __ __

3. 0.7734 (A greeting)   __ __ __ __ __

4. 77345 (A clam has one)   __ __ __ __ __

5. 4614 (What mountains are)   __ __ __ __

6. 710 (A type of fuel)   __ __ __

7. 7108 (What water will do at 212° F)   __ __ __ __

8. 317.618 (A serious untruth)   __ __ __ __ __ __

2. MAGIC SQUARE

Can you place the numbers 1 through 9 (using each number only once) in the boxes below so that any three numbers in a row across, down, or diagonally will add up to 15? The number 5 has been placed to help you get started. One possible answer is given on page 304.

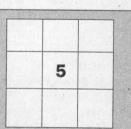

3. MATCHING NUMBERS

To the right are some numbers between 5 and 50 that you might want to know. Can you match the number on the left with the correct description on the right? (Answers are on page 304.)

5 continents
7 planets in the solar system
9 players on a basketball team
11 stripes on the American flag
13 players on a soccer team
26 ounces in a quart
27 presidents of the United States
32 states of the United States
42 letters in the English alphabet
50 amendments to the U.S. Constitution

The SOLAR SYSTEM

Nine planets, including Earth, travel around the sun. These planets, together with the sun, form the **solar system**.

THE SUN IS A STAR

Did you know that the sun is a star, like all the other stars you see at night? Although the sun is the brightest object in the sky, astronomers have found that as a star it is average in size, temperature, and brightness. The diameter of the sun is 864,000 miles. The gravity of the sun is nearly 28 times the gravity of Earth.

How Hot Is the Sun? The temperature of the sun's surface is close to 10,000°F, and the inner core may reach temperatures near 35 million degrees! The sun provides enough light and heat energy to support all forms of life on our planet.

THE PLANETS ARE IN MOTION

The planets move around the sun along oval-shaped paths called **orbits**. Each planet travels in its own orbit. One complete path around the sun is called a **revolution**. Earth takes one year for one revolution around the sun. Some planets have one or more **moons**. A moon orbits a planet in much the same way that the planets orbit the sun.

Each planet also spins (or rotates) on its axis. An **axis** is an imaginary line running through the center of a planet. The time it takes for one rotation of the planet Earth on its axis equals one day. Below are some facts about the planets and the symbol for each planet.

I. MERCURY

Average distance from the sun:
36 million miles
Diameter: 3,030 miles across
Time to revolve around the sun: 88 days
Time to rotate on its axis:
58 days, 15 hours, 30 minutes
Number of moons: 0

DID YOU KNOW? Like Earth's moon, Mercury is covered with craters. Astronomers have named the craters after famous writers, artists, and composers.

2. VENUS

Average distance from the sun:
68 million miles
Diameter: 7,520 miles across
Time to revolve around the sun:
224.7 days
Time to rotate on its axis: 243 days
Number of moons: 0

DID YOU KNOW? The surface of Venus is covered with thick clouds. Its atmosphere of carbon dioxide traps heat. The temperature of Venus can reach close to 900°F.

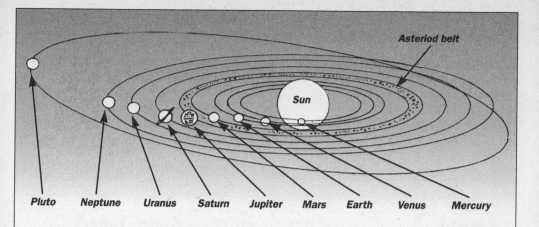

Asteriod belt

Sun

Pluto   Neptune   Uranus   Saturn   Jupiter   Mars   Earth   Venus   Mercury

3. EARTH

Average distance from the sun:
93 million miles
Diameter: 7,926 miles
Time to revolve around the sun:
365.3 days
Time to rotate on its axis:
23 hours, 56 minutes, 6.7 seconds
Number of moons: 1

DID YOU KNOW? Earth's path around the sun is nearly 600 million miles long. To make the trip in one year, Earth travels more than 66,000 miles per hour.

4. MARS

Average distance from the sun:
142 million miles
Diameter: 4,220 miles
Time to revolve around the sun:
687 days
Time to rotate on its axis:
24 hours, 37 minutes, 26 seconds
Number of moons: 2

DID YOU KNOW? Mars is the home of Olympus Mons, the largest volcano found in the solar system. It stands about 17 miles high, with a crater 50 miles wide.

5. JUPITER

Average distance from the sun:
484 million miles
Diameter: 88,800 miles
Time to revolve around the sun:
11.9 years
Time to rotate on its axis:
9 hours, 3 minutes, 30 seconds
Number of moons: 16

DID YOU KNOW? In the clouds over Jupiter, there is a gigantic swirling storm called the Great Red Spot. It is oval in shape and measures more than 20,000 miles long and 8,000 miles wide.

6. SATURN

Average distance from the sun:
888 million miles
Diameter: 74,900 miles
Time to revolve around the sun:
29.5 years
Time to rotate on its axis:
10 hours, 39 minutes, 22 seconds
Number of moons: 22

DID YOU KNOW? Saturn's famous rings are made of billions of chunks of ice. The rings stretch out to about 170,000 miles in diameter and range from a few meters to about one mile thick.

7. URANUS

Average distance from the sun:
1.8 billion miles
Diameter: 31,760 miles
Time to revolve around the sun: 84 years
Time to rotate on its axis:
17 hours, 14 minutes
Number of moons: 15

? DID YOU KNOW? Uranus was the first planet discovered with a telescope, by William Herschel in 1781. Its surface is covered with greenish clouds of methane gas.

8. NEPTUNE

Average distance from the sun:
2.8 billion miles
Diameter: 30,774 miles
Time to revolve around the sun:
164.8 years
Time to rotate on its axis:
16 hours, 6 minutes
Number of moons: 8

? DID YOU KNOW? Neptune's largest moon is called Triton. At –393°F, Triton is the coldest place in the solar system.

9. PLUTO

Average distance from the sun:
3.7 billion miles
Diameter: 1,430 miles
Time to revolve around the sun:
247.7 years
Time to rotate on its axis:
6 days, 9 hours, 17 minutes
Number of moons: 1

? DID YOU KNOW? Pluto's orbit is so strangely shaped, that since 1977, Pluto has been closer to the sun than Neptune. In March of 1999, Pluto will move beyond Neptune. So for the next few years, Pluto is actually the eighth planet from the sun.

FACTS ABOUT THE PLANETS

Largest planet: Jupiter
Smallest planet: Pluto
Planet closest to the sun: Mercury
Planet that comes closest to Earth:
Venus (Every 19 months, Venus gets closer to Earth than any other planet.)
Fastest-moving planet: Mercury (107,000 miles per hour)
Slowest-moving planet: Pluto (10,600 miles per hour)
Warmest planet: Mercury
Coldest planet: Pluto
Planet with the most moons: Saturn (at least 22 have been discovered)

THE MOON

Earth's satellite—the moon—is the only other body in the solar system that people have traveled to. The moon is about 238,900 miles from Earth. It is 2,160 miles in diameter and has no atmosphere. Its dusty surface is covered with deep craters. It takes the same amount of time for the moon to rotate on its axis as it does to orbit Earth (27 days, 7 hours, 43 minutes). For this reason, one side of the moon is always facing Earth. The moon has no light of its own, but it reflects light from the sun. The lighted part of the moon we can see from Earth is called a phase of the moon. It takes the moon 27 days to pass through all of its phases, from new moon to full moon and back to new moon. Below are some of these phases.

| New Moon | Crescent Moon | First Quarter | Full Moon | Last Quarter | Crescent Moon | New Moon |

COMETS, ASTEROIDS, and SATELLITES

Besides the planets and their moons, there are thousands of other objects in space that travel around the sun. These include comets, asteroids, and satellites.

Comets are fast-moving chunks of ice, dust, and rock that form long tails of gas as they move nearer to the sun. One of the most well-known is **Halley's Comet**. It can be seen every 76 years and will appear again in the year 2062.

Asteroids (or minor planets) are solid chunks of rock or metal that range in size from very small, like grains of sand, to very large. **Ceres**, the largest, is about 600 miles across. Thousands of asteroids orbit the sun between the planets Mars and Jupiter.

Satellites are objects that move in an orbit around a planet. Moons are natural satellites. Satellites made by humans are used to photograph Earth's surface and to transmit communications signals.

What Is an ECLIPSE?

An eclipse takes place when one heavenly body (like Earth or the moon) passes another heavenly body and blocks out the light.

SOLAR ECLIPSE. A **solar eclipse** occurs when the moon moves between the sun and Earth, casting a shadow over part of Earth. When the moon completely blocks out the sun, it is called a **total solar eclipse**. When this happens, a halo of gas can be seen around the sun. This halo of gas is called the **corona**.

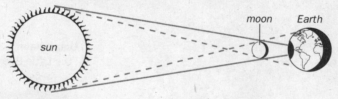

LUNAR ECLIPSE. Sometimes Earth casts a shadow on the moon. This is called a **lunar eclipse**. Usually, a lunar eclipse lasts longer than a solar eclipse. The moon remains visible, but becomes dark, often with a reddish tinge (from sunlight that is bent through Earth's atmosphere).

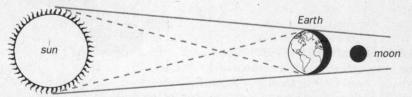

Some 1995-1996 Eclipses and Where They Can Be Seen

Oct. 24, 1995: Total solar eclipse. Visible mainly in southern Asia and the South Pacific Ocean.

April 4, 1996: Total lunar eclipse. The end of this eclipse will be visible in North America, except the Yukon Territory and Alaska.

September 27, 1996: Total lunar eclipse. All of this eclipse will be visible from eastern North America. The end of it can be seen from the rest of North America.

CONSTELLATIONS: Pictures in the Sky

Thousands of years ago ancient astronomers grouped stars together to form pictures. These groupings are called **constellations**. Astronomers all over the world named the constellations after animals or mythological figures or tools. Many of the constellations we know today were named by the people living in ancient Greece and Rome. But many constellations could not be seen from that part of the world. Some constellations were named later, when Europeans began traveling to different parts of the world and saw many other constellatons. Also, cultures in different parts of the world sometimes grouped the same stars into different constellations.

In 1930, the International Astronomical Union established a standard set of 88 constellations, which cover the entire sky visible from Earth. Astronomers use constellations as a quick way to locate other objects. For example, from Earth, the other planets moving around the sun appear in different constellations at different times.

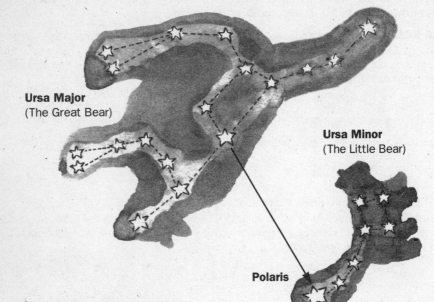

Ursa Major
(The Great Bear)

Ursa Minor
(The Little Bear)

Polaris

THE BIG AND LITTLE DIPPERS

The picture shows stars in the constellations
thought to resemble bears—Ursa Major (Great Bear)
and Ursa Minor (Little Bear). The tail and hips of the Great Bear are also
known as the Big Dipper. Ursa Minor is also known as the Little Dipper.

THE NORTH STAR

The last star in the handle of the Little Dipper is called Polaris, or the North Star.
Polaris always shines to the north. Throughout history, people have been using
Polaris to guide them in their travels. The two stars at the end of the bowl of the
Big Dipper always point in the direction of Polaris, making it easy to find.

The ZODIAC

The **zodiac** is an imaginary belt (or path) that goes around the sky. The orbits of the sun, the moon, and most of the planets are within the zodiac. Twelve of the constellations can also be found within the belt of the zodiac. The zodiac is divided into 12 equal sections. Each section is named for the constellation that occupies most of its space. Below are the symbols and signs of the zodiac.

Aries (Ram)	**Taurus** (Bull)	**Gemini** (Twins)	**Cancer** (Crab)
Leo (Lion)	**Virgo** (Maiden)	**Libra** (Balance)	**Scorpio** (Scorpion)
Sagittarius (Archer)	**Capricorn** (Sea-Goat)	**Aquarius** (Water Bearer)	**Pisces** (Fishes)

WHO IS INTERESTED IN THE SIGNS OF THE ZODIAC?

The stars in the constellations interest both astronomers and astrologers. **Astronomers** are scientists who study the sky, including the stars, planets, moons, comets, asteroids, and meteors. Astronomers study what these are made of, how they behave, what they measure, how fast they move, and what gases they are made up of. Astrologers are not scientists. **Astrologers** believe that the positions and movements of the sun, the moon, and the planets have an influence on the lives of people on earth and can be used to predict the future.

Some Heavenly
QUESTIONS and ANSWERS

WHAT IS A GALAXY?

A **galaxy** is a group of billions of stars that are held together by gravity. The galaxy we live in is called the **Milky Way**. The sun and every star we see at night are just a few of the 200 billion stars in the Milky Way. The Milky Way is so large that the light from a star along the edge of the galaxy does not reach the other side for about 100,000 years.

WHAT ARE METEORS AND METEORITES?

On a clear night, you may see a sudden streak of light in the sky. It may be caused by chunks of rock or metal called **meteoroids** speeding through space. When a meteoroid enters Earth's atmosphere, friction with air molecules causes it to burn brightly. The streak we see is called a **meteor**. Meteors are also called **shooting stars**. If the meteoroid is large enough to reach the ground without burning up completely, it is called a **meteorite**.

How Big Is the Largest Meteorite?

The largest known meteorite was found in Namibia in 1920. It is 9 feet long, 8 feet wide, and is estimated to weigh around 65 tons. The largest meteorite that can be seen in a museum is at the American Museum of Natural History in New York City. This meteorite weighs over 68,000 pounds. It was found in Greenland in 1897.

What Are Meteor Showers?

Many meteoroids follow in the path of a comet as it orbits the sun. As these meteoroids enter Earth's atmosphere, large numbers of meteors can be seen coming from about the same point in the sky. These are called **meteor showers.** There are about 10 major meteor showers every year. Two yearly meteor showers have approximately 50 meteors falling every hour. Look for the Perseid shower from August 10-14 and the Geminid shower from December 10-13. A meteor shower is named after the constellation that is near it in the sky.

WHAT IS A BLACK HOLE?

Black holes cannot be seen, but astronomers know they are there. A **black hole** is what remains at the end of the life of a star. Stars have limited life spans. Our sun, which is a star, is about 5 billion years old. It is expected to last another 5 billion years.

Stars are created in clouds of gas and dust called **nebulas**. Eventually a star runs out of hydrogen fuel. Some stars merely stop shining, while others explode. Many astronomers believe that when a star explodes it may leave behind a chunk of matter as heavy as our sun yet only a few miles across. The force of gravity of this tiny star is so strong that nothing that comes close to it can escape its pull, not even light. These objects, which cannot be observed directly, are called **black holes**.

HOW DID THE UNIVERSE BEGIN?

Most astronomers believe that the universe began in a massive explosion 10 to 20 billion years ago and that it has been expanding ever since. This is called the **big bang theory**. Some believe that the universe will keep expanding forever. Others believe that the expansion will slow down over billions of years and that gravity will begin to cause the universe to collapse.

TRAVELING INTO OUTER SPACE

American exploration into space began in January 1958, when the United States launched the *Explorer 1* satellite into orbit. Several months later, on October 1, 1958, NASA (National Aeronautics and Space Administration) was formed to explore space for peaceful and scientific purposes. The rapid entry of the United States into space was in response to the Soviet Union's launching of its satellite *Sputnik 1* into orbit on October 4, 1957. In 1961, President John F. Kennedy promised Americans that the U.S. would land a person on the moon by the end of the 1960s. The "space race" between the United States and the Soviet Union continued throughout the 1960s and 1970s.

The following time line gives some of the major flights of astronauts into space, including the U.S. Apollo flights to the moon.

1961 On April 12, Soviet cosmonaut Yuri Gagarin, in Vostok 1, became the **first human to orbit Earth**. On May 5, U.S. astronaut Alan B. Shepard Jr. of the Mercury 3 mission became the **first American in space**.

1962 On February 20, U.S. astronaut John H. Glenn Jr. of Mercury 6 became the **first American to orbit Earth**.

1963 From June 16 to 19, the Soviet spacecraft Vostok 6 carried the **first woman in space,** Valentina V. Tereshkova.

1965 On March 18, Soviet cosmonaut Aleksei A. Leonov became the **first person to walk in space.** He spent 10 minutes outside the spaceship. On December 15, U.S. Gemini 6A and 7, (with astronauts), became the **first vehicles to rendezvous** (approach and see each other) **in space**.

1966 On March 1, the Soviet probe Venera 3 crashed into Venus and became the **first humanmade object to land on another planet**. On March 16, U.S. Gemini 8 became the **first craft to dock with** (become attached to) **another vehicle** (an unmanned Agena rocket).

1967 On January 27, a fire in a U.S. Apollo spacecraft killed astronauts Virgil I. Grissom, Edward H. White, and Roger B. Chaffee. On April 23, Soyuz 1 crashed to the ground, killing Soviet cosmonaut Vladimir Komarov.

1969 On July 20, after successful flights of Apollo 8, 9, and 10, **U.S. Apollo 11's lunar module Eagle landed on the moon's surface** in the area known as the Sea of Tranquillity. Neil Armstrong became the **first person to walk on the moon**.

1970 In April, Apollo 13's moon landing ended after an explosion, but the astronauts returned safely to Earth.

1971 In July and August, U.S. Apollo 15 astronauts tested an electric vehicle called the **Lunar Rover** on the moon's surface.

1972 In December, Apollo 17 was the sixth and **final U.S. mission to land successfully on the moon**.

1973 On May 14, the U.S. put the **first space station, Skylab, into orbit**. Crews worked in Skylab until January 1974, when the last crew left.

▲ *Lunar Rover on the Moon*

1975 On July 15, the U.S. launched Apollo 18 and the U.S.S.R. launched Soyuz 19. Two days later, the **American and Soviet spacecraft docked**, and for several days their crews worked and spent time together in space. This was NASA's last space mission with astronauts until the Space Shuttle.

COOPERATION IN SPACE: The Space Shuttle and the Space Station

In an effort to reduce costs, NASA developed the space shuttle program during the 1970s. The U.S. space shuttle became the first reusable spacecraft. Earlier space capsules could not be used again after returning to Earth, but the space shuttle lands on a runway like an airplane and can be launched again at a later date. On space shuttle missions, astronauts perform many experiments, test equipment, and sometimes place satellites into orbit.

The European Space Agency, which was formed by some European countries in 1975, constructed the Spacelab scientific laboratory. Spacelab first rode a space shuttle in 1983. In 1986, the Soviet Union launched its successful Mir space station. By 1995, the United States and Russia were sharing projects in space.

1977 — On August 12, the first shuttle, **Enterprise**, took off from the back of a 747 jet airliner.

1981 — On April 12, **Columbia** was launched and became the first shuttle to reach Earth orbit.

▲ U.S. Space Shuttle

1983 — In April, NASA began using a third shuttle, **Challenger**. Two more **Challenger** flights in 1983 included astronauts Sally K. Ride and Guion S. Bluford, Jr., the first American woman and African-American man in space. On November 28, **Columbia** was launched carrying Spacelab, a scientific laboratory built by the European Space Agency.

1984 — In August, the shuttle **Discovery** was launched for the first time.

1985 — In October, the shuttle **Atlantis** was launched for the first time.

1986 — On January 28, after 24 successful shuttle missions, **Challenger** exploded 73 seconds after takeoff. Astronauts Dick Scobee, Michael Smith, Ellison Onizuka, Judith Resnick, Greg Jarvis, and Ron McNair, and teacher Christa McAuliffe all died. In March, the Soviet space station **Mir** was launched into orbit.

▲ Mir Space Station

1987 — On December 21, Soyuz TM-4 cosmonauts Vladimir Titov, Muso Manarov, and Anatoly Levchenko arrived at **Mir**. They stayed for one year, until December 21, 1988.

1988 — On September 29, nearly two years after the Challenger disaster, new safety procedures led to the successful launch of **Discovery**.

1990 — On April 24, the **Hubble Space Telescope** was launched from **Discovery**. Named for astronomer Edwin P. Hubble, the solar-powered telescope was placed into orbit. Due to a poorly shaped mirror, the images sent back to Earth were fuzzy.

1992 — In May, NASA launched a new shuttle, **Endeavor**.

1993 — In December, a crew aboard Endeavor successfully repaired the Hubble telescope.

1995 — On February 6, the U.S. shuttle **Discovery** approached within 40 feet of the orbiting Russian **Mir** station. In March, an American astronaut traveled in a Russian spacecraft and joined cosmonauts on the Russian space station **Mir**.

SENDING ROBOTS TO WORK

Another way to learn about our solar system is to send machines instead of people into space. Since the 1960s, dozens of robotic space probes have been launched. These are unmanned spacecraft that collect information to send back to Earth. These are less expensive and much less dangerous than space missions with astronauts. Some of these probes remain in space, orbiting or flying by a planet. Others are designed to land on the surface of a planet and perform certain tasks. Below are the names, launch dates, and missions of some successful U.S. unmanned probe missions.

Mariner 2 (August 27, 1962):
First successful flyby of Venus. Reached Venus in December 1962.

Mariner 4 (November 28, 1964): First probe to reach Mars. Reached Mars July 1965.

Ranger 7 (July 28, 1964):
Sent back over 4,000 close-up pictures of the moon.

Pioneer 10 (March 2, 1972):
First probe to reach Jupiter. Reached Jupiter in December 1973.

Mariner 10 (November 3, 1973):
Only U.S. probe to reach Mercury. Reached Mercury in March 1974.

Viking 1 (August 20, 1975):
Landed on Mars July 20, 1976. Followed soon after by Viking 2.

Voyager 1 (September 5, 1977):
Reached Jupiter in March 1979. Reached Saturn in November 1980.

Voyager 2 (August 20 1977):
Reached Jupiter in July 1979, Saturn in August 1981, Uranus in January 1986, and Neptune in August 1989.

Pioneer Venus 1 (May 20, 1978):
Operated in Venus orbit for 14 years, until October 1992.

Magellan (May 4, 1989):
After extensive mapping of Venus, *Magellan* burned up in its atmosphere on October 11, 1994.

Galileo (October 18, 1989):
Scheduled to reach Jupiter in late 1995.

SPACE TRAVEL PUZZLE

Look on page 162 to complete the sentences below. Then, write the answers in the blanks. The letters on the numbered blanks can be used to find the name of the probe that is planned to orbit Saturn early in the next century. (Answers are on page 304.)

The first American woman and African-American man went into space on the shuttle

___ ___ ___ ___ ___ ___ ___ .
 1   2

The name of the first American woman in space is

___ ___ ___ ___   ___ ___ ___ .
3

The Hubble Space Telescope was launched from

___ ___ ___ ___ ___ ___ ___ ___ .
  4

The Russian space station is called

___ ___ ___ .
 5

___ ___ ___ ___ ___ ___ ___ ___ ___ ___
  6   7
is the name of the first space shuttle.

The upcoming Saturn probe is called

___ ___ ___ ___ ___ ___ ___ .
 1 2 3 4 5 6 7

What Makes a PLANT a PLANT?

Plants were the first living things on earth. They appeared around three billion years ago, long before animals appeared. The first plants, called algae, grew in or near water. Years later—about 300 or 400 million years ago—the first land plants appeared. These were ferns, club mosses, and horsetails. After these came plants that bear cones (called "conifers") and trees that were ancestors of palms.

Flowers, grass, weeds, oak trees, palm trees, and poison ivy have certain things in common with each other and with every other plant. All plants have the following three important characteristics:

- ☑ Plants create their own food from air, sunlight, and water.
- ☑ Plants are rooted in the earth—they cannot move around.
- ☑ Plant cells contain cellulose, a substance that keeps plants rigid and upright.

In order to grow, plants need air, soil, water, light, and warmth. Not all plants need the same climate or the same kind of soil, or the same amount of light, warmth, and water to grow. A cactus plant needs a lot of heat and light but not much water, while a fir tree will grow in a northern forest where it is cold much of the year and light is limited.

 DID YOU KNOW? You can grow plants from some common foods, such as a sweet potato, an avocado pit, grapefruit seeds, or the tops of carrots.

RECORD-BREAKING PLANTS
World's Oldest Living Plants: Bristlecone pine trees in the California mountains (4,700 years old)
World's Tallest Plants: The tallest tree ever measured was a eucalyptus tree in Victoria, Australia, measuring 435 feet tall in 1872. The tallest tree now standing is a giant sequoia tree in Redwood National Park, Humboldt County, California, standing at 365 feet.

 DID YOU KNOW? Do you know that you can tell how old a tree is by looking at its rings? Rings are the irregularly shaped circles you see on the stump of a tree that has been cut down. As trees get taller, they also get wider, and each year that the tree grows outward is marked by a ring. A year with a good growing season leaves a thicker ring than a year that is too dry or cold.

PLANT TALK

agronomy
The growing of plants for food.

fertilizer
A natural or chemical substance applied to the soil to help plants grow bigger and faster.

herb
A plant used for flavoring or seasoning, for its scent, or as medicine. Mint, lavender, and rosemary are all herbs.

horticulture
The growing of plants for beauty.

house plant
A plant that is grown indoors. Many plants that are grown outdoors in tropical and desert regions have become popular as house plants.

hybrid
A plant that has been scientifically combined with another plant or has been changed to make it more beautiful, larger, stronger, or better in some other way. Many roses are hybrids.

hydroponics
A way of growing plants in a nutritional liquid rather than in soil.

mulch
A covering of bark, compost (decomposed garbage), hay, or other substance used to conserve water and control weeds. Mulch can also provide nutrients for plants and keep plants warm in winter.

native
A plant that has always grown in a certain place, rather than being brought there from somewhere else. Corn is native to North America.

photosynthesis
The process that allows plants to make their own food from air, sunlight, and water.

phototropism
The turning of plants toward the light.

propagation
The reproduction of plants. Plants can be reproduced from seeds, or by dividing the roots of a plant, or sometimes by simply placing a piece of the leaf on soil.

terrarium
A glass box containing small plants and animals, such as moss, ferns, lizards, and turtles.

transplant
A plant that is dug up and moved from one place to another.

wildflower
A flowering plant that grows on its own in the wild rather than being planted by a person.

evergreen
A tree that keeps its leaves or needles all year long.

deciduous
A tree that loses its leaves in autumn and gets new ones in the spring.

annual
A plant that grows, flowers, and dies in one year. Most annuals produce seeds that can be planted the following spring.

biennial
A plant that takes two years to mature. The first year the plant produces a stem and leaves, and the second year it produces flowers and seeds.

perennial
A plant that stops growing and may look dead in the fall, but comes back year after year.

WHERE DO PLANTS GROW?

Plants grow almost everywhere on earth. Even the highest mountaintops and the driest deserts have plant life. In fact, the only places on earth where plants don't grow are in most of Antarctica and near the North Pole. Plants can't grow there because the ground stays frozen all year round. The earth is sometimes divided into plant-growing regions.

TUNDRA and ALPINE REGION

The northernmost regions of North America, Europe, and Asia surrounding the Arctic Ocean are called the **tundra**. The temperature rarely rises above 45 degrees Fahrenheit, and it is too cold for trees to grow there. Most tundra plants are mosses and lichens that hug the ground for warmth. A few wildflowers and small shrubs also grow where the soil thaws for about two months of the year. This kind of climate and plant life also exist on top of the highest mountains (the Himalayas, Alps, Andes, Rockies), where small Alpine flowers also grow.

What Is the Tree Line? On mountains in the north (such as the Rockies) and in the far south (such as the Andes), there is an altitude above which trees will not grow. This is called the **tree line** or **timberline.** Above the tree line, low shrubs and small plants, like Alpine flowers, can be seen. As you move farther from the poles to the edge of the tundra, small dwarfed and twisted trees begin to appear just below the tree line. This is the beginning of the forest region.

FORESTS

Where Evergreens Grow. Forests cover much of the earth's land surface. Evergreen trees, such as pines, hemlocks, firs, and spruces, grow in the forest regions farthest from the equator. These trees are called **conifers** because they produce cones. Here the summers are longer than in the tundra, and temperatures reach 50 degrees Fahrenheit or a little warmer.

Temperate Forests. Between the cool evergreen forests and the hotter tropical rainforests, there are temperate forests with warm, rainy summers and cold, snowy winters. Here **deciduous trees** (trees that lose their leaves in the fall and grow new ones in the spring) join the evergreens in the forest. Temperate forests are home to such trees as maples, oaks, beeches, and poplars, and to many kinds of wildflowers and shrubs. Temperate forests are found in the eastern United States, southeastern Canada, northern Europe and Asia, and southern Australia.

Tropical Rainforests. Moving still closer to the equator, we come to the tropical rainforests, where the greatest variety of plants on earth can be found. The temperature never falls below freezing except on the mountain slopes, and there is plenty of rain all year long. Trees there stay green throughout the year. There are also many climbing vines, orchids, and tree ferns. Other typical plants of the moist tropics are cacao, coffee, sugarcane, bananas, pineapples, and cashews. Woods such as mahogany and teak also come from the tropics. Tropical rainforests are found in Central America, South America, Asia, and Africa.

GRASSLAND

The areas of the world that are too dry to have green forests, but not dry enough to be deserts, are called **grasslands.** The most common plants found there are grasses. Cooler grasslands are found in the Great Plains of the United States and Canada, in the steppes of Europe and Asia, and in the pampas of Argentina. The drier grasslands are used for grazing cattle and sheep. In the **prairies**, where there is a little more rain, important grains, such as wheat, rye, oats, and barley are grown. The warmer grasslands, called **savannas,** are found in central and southern Africa, Venezuela, southern Brazil, and Australia. Most savannas have moist summers and cool, dry winters.

DESERTS

The driest areas of the world are the **deserts.** They can be hot or cold, but they also contain an amazing number of plants. Cactuses and sagebrush are native to dry regions of North and South America, while the deserts of Africa and Asia contain plants called euphorbias. Dates have grown in the deserts of the Middle East and North Africa for thousands of years. In the southwestern United States and northern Mexico, there are many types of cactuses, including prickly pear, barrel, and saguaro.

FASCINATING PLANTS
Plants That "Eat" Bugs

You probably know that bugs sometimes eat plants. But did you know that some plants trap insects and use them as food? These are known as "carnivorous plants." The **pitcher-plant**, *Venus's*-**flytrap**, and **sundew** are three examples. Most carnivorous plants live in poor soils where they don't get enough nourishment. They digest their prey very slowly over a long period of time.

Flowering Stones

Did you know that plants have ways of protecting themselves, just as animals do? **Lithops** (or flowering stones) are plants in the South African desert that look like small, gray stones. They are much less likely to be eaten by animals than something that looks green and delicious.

Plants That Give Us Colors

Many natural dyes that are used to color fabrics come from plants. **Indigo** was grown by the American colonists in the South for the beautiful blue dye produced from its leaves. Weavers in Mexico still use indigo dyes. And people living in the Himalayan mountains in Asia use **rhubarb** to produce yellow dye. In Japan, some of the finest silks are dyed with barks and roots from several plants. In Australia, the leaves of the **eucalyptus tree** are used to make a dye for wool. Common garden flowers that can be boiled to produce dyes are **black-eyed Susans**, **coreopsis**, **dahlias**, **goldenrod**, and **marigolds**.

The LARGEST and SMALLEST PLACES in the World

If someone asks you what the largest country is, you would have to ask that person another question before you can answer: The largest country in area, or the largest in population (the one with the most people)? The world's largest country in area is Russia. The world's largest country in population is China. Vatican City is the smallest country in area and population. Below are lists of the most and least populous countries and the world's largest cities, with their populations in 1994.

LARGEST COUNTRIES (Most People)

Population	Country
1,190,431,000	China
919,903,000	India
260,714,000	United States
200,410,000	Indonesia
158,739,000	Brazil
149,609,000	Russia
125,149,000	Bangladesh
125,107,000	Japan
121,856,000	Pakistan
98,091,000	Nigeria
92,202,000	Mexico
81,088,000	Germany
73,104,000	Vietnam
69,809,000	Philippines
65,612,000	Iran
62,154,000	Turkey
59,510,000	Thailand
58,710,000	Ethiopia
58,138,000	Italy
58,135,000	Great Britain
57,840,000	France
51,847,000	Ukraine
45,083,000	South Korea
44,277,000	Myanmar (Burma)
43,931,000	South Africa

SMALLEST COUNTRIES (Fewest People)

Population	Country
811	Vatican City
10,000	Nauru
10,000	Tuvalu
15,000	Palau
24,000	San Marino
30,000	Liechtenstein

LARGEST CITIES (Most People)

Below are the 10 cities in the world that have the most people. It includes the cities themselves and the built-up areas around them (called the metropolitan area).

City, Country	Population
Tokyo-Yokohama, Japan	27,245,000
Mexico City, Mexico	20,899,000
Sao Paulo, Brazil	18,701,000
Seoul, South Korea	16,792,000
New York City, U.S.	14,625,000
Osaka-Kobe-Kyoto, Japan	13,872,000
Bombay, India	12,101,000
Calcutta, India	11,898,000
Rio de Janeiro, Brazil	11,688,000
Buenos Aires, Argentina	11,657,000

POPULATION of the UNITED STATES

Total Population of the United States in 1994: 260,340,990

Population of the STATES and DISTRICT OF COLUMBIA in 1994			
Rank & State Name	**Population**	**Rank & State Name**	**Population**
1. California	31,430,697	27. Connecticut	3,275,251
2. Texas	18,378,185	28. Oklahoma	3,258,069
3. New York	18,169,051	29. Oregon	3,086,188
4. Florida	13,952,714	30. Iowa	2,829,252
5. Pennsylvania	12,052,367	31. Mississippi	2,669,111
6. Illinois	11,751,774	32. Kansas	2,554,047
7. Ohio	11,102,198	33. Arkansas	2,452,671
8. Michigan	9,496,147	34. Utah	1,907,936
9. New Jersey	7,903,925	35. West Virginia	1,822,021
10. North Carolina	7,069,836	36. New Mexico	1,653,521
11. Georgia	7,055,336	37. Nebraska	1,622,858
12. Virginia	6,551,522	38. Nevada	1,457,028
13. Massachusetts	6,041,123	39. Maine	1,240,209
14. Indiana	5,752,073	40. Hawaii	1,178,564
15. Washington	5,343,090	41. New Hampshire	1,136,820
16. Missouri	5,277,640	42. Idaho	1,133,034
17. Tennessee	5,175,240	43. Rhode Island	996,757
18. Wisconsin	5,081,658	44. Montana	856,047
19. Maryland	5,006,265	45. South Dakota	721,164
20. Minnesota	4,567,267	46. Delaware	706,351
21. Louisiana	4,315,085	47. North Dakota	637,988
22. Alabama	4,218,792	48. Alaska	606,276
23. Arizona	4,075,052	49. Vermont	580,209
24. Kentucky	3,826,794	50. District of Columbia	570,175
25. South Carolina	3,663,984	51. Wyoming	475,981
26. Colorado	3,655,647		

THE LARGEST CITIES IN THE UNITED STATES IN 1994

Cities grow and shrink in population. Below is a list of the largest cities in the United States in 1994 compared with their populations in 1950. Can you find the 6 cities that increased in population? And the 4 that decreased?

Rank & City	1994	1950
1. New York, NY	7,322,564	7,891,957
2. Los Angeles, CA	3,485,557	1,970,358
3. Chicago, IL	2,783,726	3,620,962
4. Houston, TX	1,629,902	596,163
5. Philadelphia, PA	1,585,577	2,071,605
6. San Diego, CA	1,110,554	334,387
7. Detroit, MI	1,027,974	1,849,568
8. Dallas, TX	1,007,618	434,462
9. Phoenix, AZ	983,403	106,818
10. San Antonio, TX	935,393	408,442

Taking the Census: EVERYONE COUNTS

WHAT IS A CENSUS?

Every ten years the United States government counts the people who live in the United States. This is called taking the census. The census is taken to find out how many people live in the United States, where they live, how old they are, what they do, how much money they earn, the number of children in families, and many other things about them.

WHEN WAS THE FIRST U.S. CENSUS TAKEN?

The first census was taken in 1790, after the American Revolution. That year there were 3,929,200 people in the United States. Most of the people then lived in the eastern part of the country, on farms or in small towns.

WHY DO WE NEED TO BE COUNTED?

Census information is important for many reasons.

- ☑ **Congress.** The number of representatives from each state in the U.S. House of Representatives is determined by the population of each state.

- ☑ **National government.** Census information helps the national government make plans to provide public services such as health care, highways, and parks.

- ☑ **State and local governments.** Census information helps state and local governments decide local questions, such as whether to build more schools for children or homes for elderly people.

- ☑ **Private companies.** It gives private companies information that helps them—such as how many people use cars, refrigerators, baby food, and other products; how many people read newspapers; and where these people live.

WHAT DOES THE LATEST CENSUS TELL US ABOUT THE UNITED STATES?

- ☑ By 1990, the population had increased to 248,709,873.

- ☑ More than half of the people in the United States live in the southern and western sections of the country.

- ☑ About 80% of Americans live in cities or suburbs.

- ☑ The United States is known for its large population that includes people of different races and nationalities.

The chart below shows how many Americans called themselves white, black, Asian, American Indian, and Hispanic in the 1990 census. The percentages add up to more than 100% because Hispanics may be of Mexican, Puerto Rican, Cuban or Spanish decent, or have roots in other Spanish-speaking countries of the Caribbean, or Central or South America. Hispanics may be of any race.

White, 199,686,070 ....80%

Black, 29,986,060 ....12%

Hispanic, 22,354,059 ....9%

Asian, 7,276,662....................................3%
(including the Pacific Islands)

American Indian, 1,959,234.....................1%
(including Eskimo, or Aleut)

Other race, 9,804,847 ....4%
(people who said "other race")

COUNTING THE FIRST AMERICANS

WHERE DID THEY COME FROM?
American Indians, also called Native Americans, lived in North and South America long before the first European explorers arrived. Their ancestors are thought to have come from northeast Asia more than 20,000 years ago. American Indians are not one people, but many different peoples, each with their own traditions and way of life.

HOW MANY WERE THERE IN THE BEGINNING?
No one knows for sure, but it is believed that many millions of Indians lived in the Americas before Columbus came. About 850,000 lived in what is now the United States.

HOW MANY ARE THERE NOW?
During the 17th, 18th, and 19th centuries, disease and wars with white settlers and soldiers caused the death of thousands of American Indians. By 1910 there were only about 220,000 left in the United States. Since then, the American Indian population has increased dramatically. In 1990, the last year a census was taken, the total number of Native Americans was close to 2 million.

WHERE DO NATIVE AMERICANS LIVE?
Below are the states with the largest Native American populations.

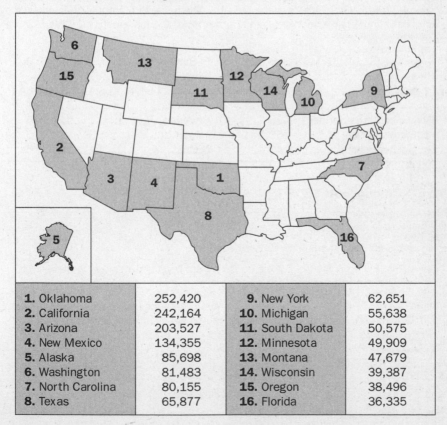

1. Oklahoma	252,420		**9.** New York	62,651
2. California	242,164		**10.** Michigan	55,638
3. Arizona	203,527		**11.** South Dakota	50,575
4. New Mexico	134,355		**12.** Minnesota	49,909
5. Alaska	85,698		**13.** Montana	47,679
6. Washington	81,483		**14.** Wisconsin	39,387
7. North Carolina	80,155		**15.** Oregon	38,496
8. Texas	65,877		**16.** Florida	36,335

The MANY FACES of America: IMMIGRATION

You have probably heard it said that America is a nation of immigrants. Many Americans are descended from Europeans or from Africans or from Asians. Do you know someone who was born in another country?

Why Do People Come to the United States?

Have you ever wondered why so many people want to leave their native country and come and live in the United States? It isn't usually because they don't love their own country. Most people are very attached to the place where they were born. Immigrants come to America for many reasons: to live in freedom, to worship as they choose, to escape poverty, to make a better life for themselves and their children.

Millions of people have immigrated to the United States from all over the world—more than 40 million since 1820. Much of the art we see or the music we hear, and many of the scientific discoveries and inventions we use, foods we eat, and languages we speak were introduced to us by people who came from other countries.

What Countries Do Immigrants Come From?

Immigrants come to the United States from many countries. Below are some of the countries from which immigrants came in 1993. The name of the country is followed by the number of immigrants. In 1993, immigration from all countries to the United States totaled 904,292.

Mexico	126,561	El Salvador	26,818
China	65,578	Great Britain	18,783
Philippines	63,457	North and South Korea	18,026
Vietnam	59,614	Jamaica	17,241
Russia and other former Soviet republics	58,571	Canada	17,156
Dominican Republic	45,420	Taiwan	14,329
India	40,121	Cuba	13,666
		Ireland	13,590

Where Do Immigrants Settle?

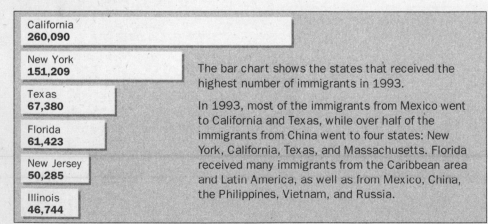

California
260,090

New York
151,209

Texas
67,380

Florida
61,423

New Jersey
50,285

Illinois
46,744

The bar chart shows the states that received the highest number of immigrants in 1993.

In 1993, most of the immigrants from Mexico went to California and Texas, while over half of the immigrants from China went to four states: New York, California, Texas, and Massachusetts. Florida received many immigrants from the Caribbean area and Latin America, as well as from Mexico, China, the Philippines, Vietnam, and Russia.

Becoming an AMERICAN CITIZEN: NATURALIZATION

When a foreign-born person becomes a citizen of the United States, we say the person has become *naturalized.* To apply for American citizenship, a person

- ☑ Must be at least 18 years old.
- ☑ Must have lived legally in the United States for at least 5 years.
- ☑ Must have an understanding of English if under the age of 50.
- ☑ Must be of good moral character.
- ☑ Must demonstrate a knowledge of the history and form of government of the United States.

ELLIS ISLAND and THE STATUE OF LIBERTY

ELLIS ISLAND: THE GATEWAY TO AMERICA

Until this century, people could immigrate freely to the United States. They piled on to ships and came, hoping to find a better life. Between 1892 and 1924, more than 12 million people came into the country by passing through Ellis Island, a huge immigration center in New York harbor. There they were screened for certain contagious diseases and some sick people were sent back, but most immigrants were allowed to stay.

Immigrants who passed through Ellis Island came from many places—Italy, Russia, Hungary, Austria, Germany, England, Ireland, Sweden, Greece, Norway, Turkey, Scotland, the West Indies, Poland, Portugal, France, and others.

Ellis Island as a Museum. As an immigration center, Ellis Island was closed in 1954. But in 1990, it reopened as a museum to tell the story of the immigrants who helped make the United States a great country. The names of many of the immigrants who came through Ellis Island are inscribed on a wall in their memory.

THE STATUE OF LIBERTY. Many of the immigrants who steamed into New York harbor passed by the Statue of Liberty. Set on her own island, the "Lady With the Lamp" was given to the United States by France and has served as a symbol of freedom and a welcome to Americans-to-be since she was erected in 1886. In 1903, a sonnet by the U.S. poet Emma Lazarus was inscribed at the base of the statue. Two of its lines read: "Give me your tired, your poor, your huddled masses yearning to breathe free...."

ENTERTAINMENT

Who is your favorite movie actor or actress? What is your all-time favorite film? If you are interested in the movies, you probably know that an Oscar is a golden statuette that is given every year by the Academy of Motion Picture Arts and Sciences for the best movie, best actor, best actress, and so on. The Oscar presentations are watched on television by millions of people all over the world. Among other awards given each year for the best in entertainment are Grammys, Emmys, and Tonys. Here are some recent winners.

ACADEMY AWARDS: THE OSCARS

The Oscars are given every year by the Academy of Motion Picture Arts and Sciences for the best movie, best actor and actress, best supporting actor and actress, best director, best original song, and so on. Here are some of the films and people who won an Oscar in 1995.

▲ Tom Hanks in Forrest Gump

Best Picture: *Forrest Gump*

Best Actor: Tom Hanks in *Forrest Gump*

Best Actress: Jessica Lange in *Blue Sky*

Best Supporting Actor: Martin Landau in *Ed Wood*

Best Supporting Actress: Dianne Wiest in *Bullets Over Broadway*

Best Director: Robert Zemeckis, for *Forrest Gump*

Best Original Song: Hans Zimmer, for "Can You Feel the Love Tonight" from the movie *The Lion King*

Best Original Score (music): Hans Zimmer, for *The Lion King*

Best Visual Effects: *Forrest Gump*

Best Makeup: *Ed Wood*

? DID YOU KNOW? An eleven-year-old girl named Anna Paquin won an Oscar in 1994 for best supporting actress in the movie *The Piano*.

THE GRAMMYS

Grammys are awards given out each year by the National Academy of Recording Arts & Sciences for the best in popular music. Among the latest winners are:

1995: Best Record: Sheryl Crow, "All I Wanna Do"
Best Album: Tony Bennett, "MTV Unplugged"
1994: Best Record: Whitney Houston, "I Will Always Love You"
Best Album: Whitney Houston, "The Bodyguard"
1993: Best Record: Eric Clapton, "Tears in Heaven"
Best Album: Eric Clapton, "Unplugged"
1992: Best Record: Natalie Cole, with Nat "King" Cole, "Unforgettable"
Best Album: Natalie Cole, with Nat "King" Cole, "Unforgettable"

THE EMMYS

The Emmy Awards are given each year by the Academy of Television Arts and Sciences for the best of television. These include the best series, best actors and actresses, and best writers and directors. Here are some of the major winners for the 1993-1994 season for prime-time television. (Prime time is the evening hours when the TV audience is the largest.)

Best Drama Series: *Picket Fences* (CBS)
Best Actor in a Drama Series: Dennis Franz, in *N.Y.P.D. Blue* (ABC)
Best Actress in a Drama Series: Sela Ward, in *Sisters* (NBC)
Best Comedy Series: *Frasier* (NBC)
Best Actor in a Comedy Series: Kelsey Grammer, in *Frasier*
Best Actress in a Comedy Series: Candice Bergen, in *Murphy Brown*
Best Miniseries: *Mystery, Prime Suspect 3*
Best Talk Show: *The Oprah Winfrey Show*
Best Game Show: *Jeopardy!*

THE TONYS

The Antoinette Perry Awards, known as the "Tonys," are annual awards given to the best Broadway plays and to those who write them, act in them, and direct them. Winners for the 1994-1995 season:

Best Play: *Love! Valour! Compassion!*, by Terrence McNally
Best Musical: *Sunset Boulevard*, with music by Andrew Lloyd Webber and lyrics by Don Black and Christopher Hampton
Best Musical Revival: *Show Boat*, the 1927 musical by Jerome Kern and Oscar Hammerstein 2nd
Leading Actor in a Play: Ralph Fiennes in *Hamlet*
Leading Actress in a Play: Cherry Jones in *The Heiress*, a play based on Henry James's novel *Washington Square*
Leading Actor in a Musical: Matthew Broderick in *How To Succeed in Business Without Really Trying*
Leading Actress in a Musical: Glenn Close in *Sunset Boulevard*

Other PRIZES and AWARDS

You may be familiar with entertainment awards, but did you know that prizes are given each year to exceptional people in many other fields? There are prizes for people who make important scientific and medical discoveries, prizes for writers, poets, and musicians, prizes for artists and architects. Here are some of the famous ones.

NOBEL PRIZES

The Nobel Prizes are named after Alfred B. Nobel (1833-1896), a Swedish scientist who left money to be awarded every year to people who have done something important to help humankind. The world-famous German-born physicist Albert Einstein won the physics prize in 1921, and the Polish-French scientist Marie Curie won two Nobel Prizes—one in physics in 1903 (with Pierre Curie, her husband, and Henry Becquerel) and one in chemistry in 1911. There are also prizes for medicine-physiology, literature, economics, and peace.

The Nobel Peace Prize goes to the person who has done the most the previous year to help achieve peace between nations. Sometimes the prize goes to a group of people.

1994: Yasir Arafat, head of the Palestine Liberation Organization, Yitzhak Rabin, Israel's Prime Minister, and Shimon Peres, Israel's Foreign Minister, won the Nobel Peace Prize in 1994 for their efforts to create peace in the Middle East.

▲ *Yasir Arafat*

▲ *Yitzhak Rabin*

▲ *Shimon Peres*

1993: F.W. de Klerk, then the president of South Africa, and Nelson Mandela, then the head of the African National Congress, won the Nobel Peace Prize in 1993 for their efforts to get rid of the system of apartheid and achieve racial equality for blacks in South Africa. Mandela became president of South Africa in 1994, in an election in which blacks were allowed to vote for the first time.

◄ *Nelson Mandela (right) with F.W. de Klerk*

DID YOU KNOW? Two American presidents have won the Nobel Peace Prize: Theodore Roosevelt in 1906 and Woodrow Wilson in 1919.

PULITZER PRIZES

The Pulitzer Prizes are named after Joseph Pulitzer (1847-1911), a journalist and publisher, who gave the money to set them up. The prizes are given yearly in the United States for journalism, literature, and music. Categories in journalism include international reporting, editorial writing, photography, and cartooning.

SPINGARN MEDAL

The Spingarn Medal was established in 1914 by Joel Elias Spingarn, then the chairperson of the National Association for the Advancement of Colored People (NAACP). It is awarded every year by the NAACP for the highest achievement by a black American. Here are some well-known winners and the year they won.

1994: Writer and poet Maya Angelou
1991: General Colin L. Powell, then the
      Chairman of the Joint Chiefs of Staff
1989: Political leader Jesse Jackson
1985: Actor Bill Cosby
1983: Singer Lena Horne
1979: Civil rights activist Rosa L. Parks
1975: Baseball player Hank Aaron
1968: Actor and singer Sammy Davis, Jr.
1965: Opera singer Leontyne Price
1959: Dance band leader and composer
      Duke Ellington
1957: Civil rights leader Martin Luther King, Jr.

▲ Maya Angelou

THE MEDAL OF HONOR

The Congressional Medal of Honor is the highest award that is given by the government of the United States. It is a military award for extraordinary personal bravery in war against an enemy. The first Medals of Honor were awarded in 1863. By the beginning of 1995, 3,420 Medals of Honor had been awarded.

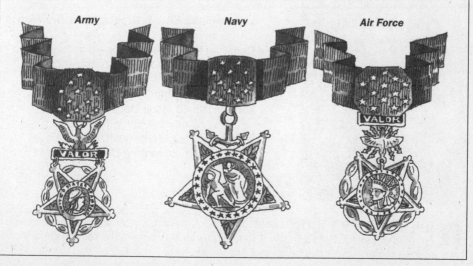

Army   *Navy*   *Air Force*

BOOK AWARDS:
1994 Winning Children's Books

In addition to Nobel and Pulitzer Prizes for fine writing, there are other awards for books. Many awards are also given each year for children's books and their illustrators. Some of the awards are listed below. You may want to look for some of these books in your library.

Boston Globe-Horn Book Award—Given every year for outstanding fiction, nonfiction, and illustration.
>   **1994 winners:** Vera B. Williams, *Scooter* (fiction)
>   Russell Freedman, *Eleanor Roosevelt: A Life of Discovery* (nonfiction)
>   Allen Say, *Grandfather's Journey* (illustration)

Caldecott Medal—Given for the most distinguished American illustrated book.
>   **1994 winner:** illustrator David Diaz for *Smoky Night*, written by Eve Bunting

Coretta Scott King Awards—Given to artists and authors who promote the cause of peace and world brotherhood.
>   **1994 winners:** Patricia C. and Frederick L. McKissack, *Christmas in the Big House, Christmas in the Quarters*

Golden Kite Awards—Given every year for the best children's fiction, nonfiction, and illustration.
>   **1994 winners:** Karen Cushman, *Catherine, Called Birdy* (fiction)
>   Russell Freedman, *Kids at Work: Lewis Hine and the Crusade Against Child Labor* (nonfiction)
>   Keith Baker, *Big Fat Hen* (picture illustration)

Newbery Award—Given for the most distinguished contribution to children's literature in the United States.
>   **1994 winner:** Sharon Creech, *Walk Two Moons*

Hans Christian Andersen Awards—Given every two years to an author and an illustrator whose complete works have made an important contribution to children's literature.
>   **Author:** Michio Mado (Japan) for *The Animals* and other books
>   **Illustrator:** Jörg Müller (Switzerland) for *The Changing City* and others

◄ *Walk Two Moons*
by Sharon Creech

? DID YOU KNOW? Did you know that a book by a teenager was on the bestseller list during 1994? *Zlata's Diary: A Child's Life in Sarajevo* is the touching story of one young girl's experience in the Bosnian war.

HALLS of FAME

Halls of fame are special museums created to honor people who are best in their field. The first hall of fame was opened in 1900 in New York. In a beautiful building with pillars set on a hill, this hall of fame honors great Americans from President George Washington to agricultural scientist George Washington Carver (who developed peanut butter), from early feminist Susan B. Anthony to composer and marching band leader John Philip Sousa. Some halls of fame have special exhibits; some run contests; some have lectures and tours. Below are some halls of fame. For others, look at the pages on SPORTS and INVENTIONS.

Conservation Hall of Fame

National Wildlife Federation
1400 16th St. NW
Washington, DC 20036-2266
Contains a wildlife gallery of art.

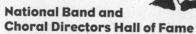

Hall of Fame for Great Americans

University Avenue and
W. 181st St.
Bronx, NY 10453

National Band and Choral Directors Hall of Fame

519 N. Halifax Ave.
Daytona Beach, FL 32118
Honors outstanding school band and choral directors. Holds national marching band and choral music contests.

National Cowboy Hall of Fame and Western Heritage Center

1700 NE 63rd St.
Oklahoma City, OK 73111
Honors the pioneers who developed the American West. Offers exhibitions, lectures, and tours.

National Women's Hall of Fame

76 Fall Street
Seneca Falls, NY 13148
Honors American women who have made great contributions to their country. Has essay and poster contests and special activities for school groups.

Orators Hall of Fame

International Platform Association
PO Box 250
Winnetka, IL 60093
Gives annual awards to people who speak in public.

Rock and Roll Hall of Fame

c/o Suzan Evans
Atlantic Records
75 Rockefeller Plaza, 2nd Fl.
New York, NY 10019
Honored in 1995 were the Allman Brothers Band, Al Green, Janis Joplin, Led Zeppelin, Martha and the Vandellas, Neil Young and Frank Zappa.

RELIGION
AROUND THE WORLD

Have you ever asked yourself questions like these: How did the universe begin? Why are we here on earth? What happens to us after we die? For many people, religion is a way of answering such questions. Believing in a God or gods, or in a Divine Being, is one way of making sense of the world around us. Religions can also give people principles for guiding their lives. More than 5 billion people all over the world belong to some religious group. Different religions have different beliefs. For example, Christians, Jews, and Muslims believe in one God, while Hindus believe in many gods. Here are some facts about the world's major religions.

CHRISTIANITY

Who Started Christianity? Jesus Christ, in the first century. He was born in Bethlehem between 8 B.C. and 4 B.C. and died about A.D. 29.

What Do Christians Believe? That there is one God. That Jesus Christ is the Son of God, who came on earth to save humankind.

How Many Christians Are There? Christianity is the world's biggest religion. In 1994 there were almost 2 billion Christians, in nearly all parts of the world. One billion of the Christians were Roman Catholics.
Among the Christians are:

Roman Catholics, for whom the pope in Rome is the leader of their church.

Orthodox Christians, who accept most Catholic teachings, but follow their bishop as their spiritual leader.

Protestants, who accept the Bible, as well as insights of the laity (members of the church who are not ordained as clergy). They are divided into many different groups.

JUDAISM

Who Started Judaism? Abraham is considered the founder of Judaism. He lived around 1300 B.C.

What Do Jews Believe? That there is one God who created the universe and rules over it. That they should be faithful to God and carry out God's commandments.

How Many Are There? In 1994, there were more than 13 million Jews, spread around the world. Many live in Israel and the United States.

What Kinds Are There? In the United States there are three main kinds: **Orthodox**, **Conservative**, and **Reform**. Orthodox Jews are the most traditional. Traditional means that they follow strict laws about how they dress, what they can eat, and how they conduct their lives. Conservative Jews follow many of the traditions. Reform Jews are the least traditional.

ISLAM

Who Started Islam? Muhammad, the Prophet, in A.D. 622.

What Do Muslims Believe? People who believe in Islam are called Muslims. They believe: That there is one God. That Muslims should follow the laws of God, as told to Muhammad. That they should pray five times a day. That they should try, during their lives, to make at least one trip to the holy city of Mecca in Saudi Arabia.

How Many Muslims Are There? In 1994, there were about 1 billion Muslims, mostly in parts of Africa and Asia. The two main kinds of Muslims are: **Sunni Muslims**, who make up about 85 percent of Muslims today, and **Shiite Muslims**, who broke away in a dispute over who should lead them.

HINDUISM

Who Started Hinduism? No single person. Aryan invaders of India, around 1500 B.C., brought their own beliefs with them, which were mixed with the beliefs of the people who already lived in India.

What Do Hindus Believe? That there are many gods and many ways of worshipping. That people die and are reborn many times as another living thing. That there is a universal soul or principle known as *Brahman*. That the goal of life is to escape the cycle of birth and death and become part of the *Brahman*. This is achieved by leading a pure and good life.

How Many Are There? In 1994, there were about 760 million Hindus, mainly in India and places where people from India have gone to live.

What Kinds Are There? There are many kinds of Hindus, who worship different gods or goddesses.

BUDDHISM

Who Started Buddhism? Gautama Siddhartha (the Buddha), around A.D. 525.

What Do Buddhists Believe? Buddha taught that life is filled with suffering. In order to be free of that suffering, believers have to give up worldly possessions and worldly goals and strive to achieve a state of perfect peace known as *nirvana*.

How Many Are There? In 1994, there were about 338 million Buddhists, mostly in Asia.

What Kinds Are There? There are two main kinds. **Theravada** ("Path of the Elders") **Buddhism,** the older kind, is more common in southern Asia. **Mahayana** ("Great Vessel") **Buddhism** is more common in northern Asia.

RELIGIOUS MEMBERSHIP
in the United States

All the Protestant groups together amount to nearly 81 million people, making Protestants the biggest religious group in the United States. Catholics come next, with almost 60 million people. All other religions have fewer members.

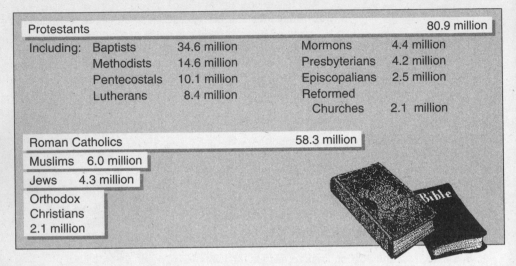

Protestants				80.9 million
Including:	Baptists	34.6 million	Mormons	4.4 million
	Methodists	14.6 million	Presbyterians	4.2 million
	Pentecostals	10.1 million	Episcopalians	2.5 million
	Lutherans	8.4 million	Reformed Churches	2.1 million

Roman Catholics	58.3 million

Muslims	6.0 million

Jews	4.3 million

Orthodox Christians 2.1 million

RELIGIOUS TEXTS

Every religion has its writings or sacred texts that set out its laws and beliefs. Among them are:

THE BIBLE

The Old Testament. Also known as the Hebrew Bible, this is a collection of laws, history, and other writings that are holy books for Jews and also for Christians. The first five books of the Old Testament are known by Jews as the Torah. These contain the stories of creation and the beginnings of human life, as well as the laws handed down by the prophet Moses.

The New Testament. A collection of Gospels (stories about Jesus), epistles (letters written to guide the early Christians), and other writings. The Old Testament and New Testament together make up the Bible that is read by Christians.

THE KORAN

The Koran sets out the central beliefs of Islam, the religion of Muslims. Muslims believe that the Koran was revealed by God to the prophet Muhammad through the angel Gabriel. The Koran is also spelled "Qur'an."

THE BHAGAVAD GHITA

The Bhagavad Ghita is one of several Hindu religious texts. Part of a long poem about war, it is familiar to almost every Hindu. In it the god Krishna, in the form of a man, drives the chariot of Prince Arjuna into battle and instructs him on how to live his life.

Major HOLY DAYS
for Christians, Jews, and Muslims

CHRISTIAN HOLY DAYS

	1995	1996	1997
Ash Wednesday	March 1	February 21	February 12
Good Friday	April 14	April 5	March 28
Easter Sunday	April 16	April 7	March 30
Easter for Orthodox Churches	April 23	April 14	April 7
Christmas	December 25	December 25	December 25

JEWISH HOLY DAYS

The Jewish holy days begin at sundown and end at sundown. The days listed below are the first full day of the holy day.

	1995 (5755-56)	1996 (5756-57)	1997 (5757-58)
Passover	April 15	April 4	April 22
Rosh Hashanah (New Year)	September 25	September 14	October 2
Yom Kippur	October 4	September 23	October 11
Chanukah	December 18	December 6	December 24

ISLAMIC (MUSLIM) HOLY DAYS

	1995-96 (1416)	1996-97 (1417)	1997-98 (1418)
Muharram 1 (New Year)	May 30	May 18	May 8
Mawlid (Birthday of Muhammad)	August 8	July 28	July 17
Ramadan 1	January 21	January 10	December 31
al-Adha Dhu al-Hijjah 10	April 28	April 17	April 7

CHEMICAL ELEMENTS

People, dogs, butterflies, flowers, rocks, CDs, baseball cards, telephones—everything we see and use is made up of "basic ingredients" called **elements**. Most of the elements—about 108 in all—have been found in nature. Some have been created in laboratories. The charts below show the elements found in Earth's crust and those found in the atmosphere:

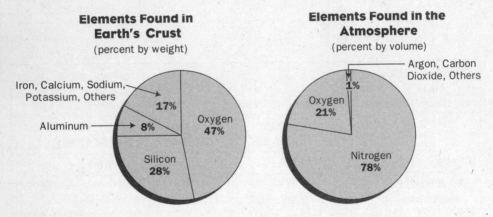

Elements Found in Earth's Crust
(percent by weight)

Iron, Calcium, Sodium, Potassium, Others — 17%
Aluminum — 8%
Oxygen 47%
Silicon 28%

Elements Found in the Atmosphere
(percent by volume)

Argon, Carbon Dioxide, Others — 1%
Oxygen 21%
Nitrogen 78%

Elements Are All Around Us. Neon signs light up store windows. Car batteries contain lead. Soda cans are made from aluminum. Chips using silicon are found in computers. Jewelry is made from gold and silver. Water is made up of hydrogen and oxygen. Salt is made up of sodium and chlorine.

How Can Scientists Tell One Element From Another? The smallest possible piece of an element that has all the properties of the original element is called an **atom**. Each tiny atom is made up of even smaller particles called **protons**, **neutrons**, and **electrons**.

To tell one element from another, scientists count the number of protons, neutrons, and electrons. The total number of protons is called the element's **atomic number**. The average weight of all the protons, neutrons, and electrons in an atom is called the element's **atomic weight**. Every element has a different atomic number and a different atomic weight.

Chemical Symbols Are Scientific Shorthand. When scientists write the names of elements, they often use a symbol instead of spelling out the full name. Just as we sometimes use $ instead of writing "dollars," scientists write O for oxygen and He for helium. The symbol for each element is one or two letters. The symbols usually come from the English name for the element (C for carbon). The symbols for some of the elements come from the element's Latin name. For example, the symbol for gold is Au, which is short for *Aurum,* the Latin word for gold.

A LOOK at Some COMMON ELEMENTS

The table below shows some common elements with their symbol, atomic number, atomic weight, the year they were discovered, and some of their common uses.

NAME OF ELEMENT	SYMBOL	ATOMIC NUMBER	ATOMIC WEIGHT	YEAR FOUND	COMMON USE
Helium	He	2	4.00	1868	inflate balloons
Carbon	C	6	12.01	B.C.	pencils, diamonds
Nitrogen	N	7	14.01	1772	fertilizers
Oxygen	O	8	16.00	1774	breathing
Fluorine	F	9	19.00	1771	toothpastes
Sodium	Na	11	22.99	1807	salt
Aluminum	Al	13	26.98	1825	soda cans
Sulfur	S	16	32.06	B.C.	matches
Chlorine	Cl	17	35.45	1774	purifies water, in salt
Calcium	Ca	20	40.08	1808	in bones
Iron	Fe	26	55.85	B.C.	steel
Copper	Cu	29	63.55	B.C.	water pipes, wire
Silver	Ag	47	107.87	B.C.	jewelry, dental fillings
Gold	Au	79	196.97	B.C.	jewelry, coins
Mercury	Hg	80	200.59	B.C.	thermometers
Lead	Pb	82	207.19	B.C.	car batteries

 DID YOU KNOW?

☑ Diamond, the hardest substance, and graphite, one of the softest substances, are different forms of the same element—carbon.

☑ The "lead" in pencils is not really lead. It is made of graphite (a form of carbon) and clay.

☑ The most abundant element in the universe is hydrogen. Scientists estimate that over 90% of the universe is made up of hydrogen atoms.

 ELEMENTS PUZZLE

Many elements are named after gods in Greek or Roman or Norse mythology. Some are named after planets. And others are named after famous scientists. Can you match the name of the element with the god, planet, or scientist the element is named after? (Answers are on page 305.)

ELEMENT	ELEMENT IS NAMED AFTER
Curium	the planet Pluto
Einsteinium	Norse god Thor
Neptunium	French chemists Marie and Pierre Curie
Nobelium	Greek god Prometheus
Plutonium	Nobel Prize winner Albert Einstein
Promethium	the planet Uranus
Thorium	the planet Neptune
Uranium	Swedish inventor Alfred Nobel

Some ANSWERS to
SCIENCE QUESTIONS

WHAT IS A MAGNET?

Have you ever seen paper clips or pins sliding toward a magnet and then sticking to it? Magnets have two areas, called **poles**, where magnetic effects are strongest. A bar magnet has a pole at each end. Around each pole is a region called a **magnetic field**. A magnetic field cannot be seen, but it can be felt when a another magnet enters the field or when an object that has iron in it, such as a paper clip or a pin, enters the magnetic field. Such an object will be attracted to one of the poles of the magnet.

HOW DO MAGNETS REACT TO OTHER MAGNETS?

Magnets have two poles. One is called the north pole and the other is called the south pole. The north pole of one magnet will attract the south pole of another magnet—in other words, opposites attract. But when the north poles of two magnets are brought near each other, they will push away (repel) each other. Magnets can have different shapes and can be made of different materials. But they all attract or repel other magnets.

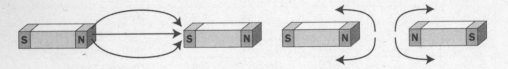

DID YOU KNOW? Did you know that Earth is a giant magnet whose magnetic field exists at all locations? Like a bar magnet, Earth has two magnetic poles—one of them is near the geographical north pole and the other is near the geographical south pole. If you have ever used a compass, you have seen that the compass needle always points in the same direction—toward the north—no matter which way you turn. The needle is a small bar magnet that can rotate easily. The needle points north because the north pole of the magnet is attracted to the magnetic pole of Earth near the geographical north pole.

WHEN DOES WATER MELT AND FREEZE?

We usually think of water as a liquid. But it can also be a solid or a gas, depending on its temperature. At low temperatures, below freezing (32 degrees Fahrenheit or 0 degrees Celsius), water is a solid called **ice**. At warmer temperatures, it is a **liquid**. At very high temperatures (212 degrees Fahrenheit or 100 degrees Celsius or higher), water boils and becomes a **gas** called steam. It also becomes a gas called vapor when it evaporates, as it does when wet clothes are hung out to dry.

WHAT CAUSES FROST PATTERNS ON WINDOWS IN WINTER?

Have you ever seen feathery patterns of frost on windows in very cold weather? When water vapor in the air comes in contact with the extremely cold glass of a window, the water vapor immediately turns to ice. The ice forms on the windows in patterns of ice crystals.

Some LIGHT and SOUND Subjects

WHAT IS LIGHT?

Light is a form of energy that travels in **rays**. Light rays generally move in straight lines, at a speed of 186,000 miles per second through empty space. It takes over 8 minutes for the light from the sun to reach Earth. Light also moves through materials like water and glass, but more slowly.

WHAT IS A RAINBOW?

The light we usually see (visible light) is made up of colors called the **spectrum**. The colors of the spectrum are red, orange, yellow, green, blue, indigo, and violet. White light is formed from a mixture of all the colors of the spectrum. A prism can separate the colors in a beam of white light. When you see a rainbow, the tiny water droplets in the air are separating the white light into the spectrum.

WHERE DOES SOUND COME FROM?

When objects vibrate quickly back and forth in the air, they create **sound**. The vibrating objects cause the molecules in the air around the objects to move. As the molecules move, the vibrations travel through the air in **waves**. These sound waves move outward in every direction from the place where they started—like ripples in a pond moving away from the point where a pebble is dropped.

WHAT CAN YOU HEAR IN OUTER SPACE?

Sound waves have to have a medium to move through. Usually air serves as the medium. But sounds can also travel through water, wood, glass, and other materials. In outer space, where there is no air or other medium for sound waves to travel through, there is no sound. Astronauts in space communicate with Earth over radio waves, not sound waves.

HOW LOUD ARE THOSE SOUNDS?

The loudness of a sound (called **volume**) is measured in **decibels**. The volume depends on how many air molecules are vibrating and how strongly they are vibrating. The quietest sound that can be heard has a value of zero decibels. The louder the sound, the higher the decibel level.

0 decibels
faintest sound heard

10-20 decibels
rustling leaves

20-30 decibels
whispering

50-70 decibels
conversation

80-100 decibels
heavy traffic and trains

100-120 decibels
loud music

140-150 decibels
neaby jet engine

Some FAMOUS SCIENTISTS

Archimedes (about 287 B.C.-212 B.C.), a Greek mathematician who discovered that heavy objects could be moved with little force. He was one of the first people to test his ideas with experiments.

Moving heavy blocks ▶ with a wheelbarrow.

Nicolaus Copernicus (1473-1543), a Polish scientist known as the founder of modern astronomy. He believed that Earth and other planets revolved around the sun. His ideas were not accepted during his lifetime.

Galileo Galilei (1564-1642), an Italian astronomer who, like Copernicus, believed that the sun was at the center of the solar system, and that the planets revolved around it. He also proved that all objects, whether heavy or light, fall at the same rate.

Sir Isaac Newton (1642-1727), a British scientist famous for discovering the laws of gravity. He also discovered that sunlight is made up of all the colors of the rainbow.

Edward Jenner (1749-1823), a British doctor who discovered a way to prevent smallpox by injecting healthy people with cowpox vaccine. Today's vaccines work in a similar way.

Michael Faraday (1791-1867), a British scientist who discovered that magnets can be used to create electricity in copper wires. His discoveries enable us to produce massive amounts of electricity.

Charles Darwin (1809-1882) was a British scientist best known for his theory of evolution. According to Darwin's theory of evolution, living creatures slowly develop and change over millions of years.

Gregor Johann Mendel (1822-1884), an Austrian monk who discovered the laws of heredity by showing how characteristics are passed from one generation of plants to the next.

Louis Pasteur (1822-1895), a French chemist who discovered a process called pasteurization, in which heat is used to kill germs. This process is still used to purify milk and many other food products.

Marie Curie (1867-1934), a Polish-French physical chemist known for discovering radium, which is used to treat some diseases. She won the Nobel Prize for chemistry in 1911. She and her husband, **Pierre Curie,** also won the Nobel Prize for physics in 1903 for their work in radiation.

▲ Pasteurized milk

Albert Einstein (1879-1955), a German-American physicist who developed a revolutionary theory about the relationships between time, space, matter, and energy. He won a Nobel Prize in 1921.

Francis Crick (born 1916) and **Maurice Wilkins** (born 1916) of England and **James D. Watson** (born 1928) of the United States won a Nobel Prize in 1962 for their discoveries about DNA, the basic chemical that controls inheritance in all living cells.

SCIENCE MUSEUMS

Seeing is believing—and you made it happen! If you like hands-on exhibits and like to learn about robots, computers, the Ice Age, dinosaurs, the brain, how the body works, and many other areas of science, a visit to a science museum is in order. There are many science museums in the United States. Below are a few of them.

National Air and Space Museum, Washington, D.C. Houses the Wright brothers' plane, Charles Lindbergh's *Spirit of St. Louis*, and *Skylab*, as well as many other planes and rockets. Visitors (1994), 8,668,213.

American Museum of Natural History, New York, New York. Famous for its dinosaur skeletons; also has displays on minerals, history of life, and the relationships between organisms and their environment. Includes the Hayden Planetarium. Visitors (1994), 3,000,000.

Museum of Science and Industry, Chicago, Illinois. Includes a reproduction of a coal mine, as well as displays on health, human intelligence, and how people live. Visitors (1994), 1,900,000.

Fort Worth Museum of Science and History, Fort Worth, Texas. Exhibits on dinosaurs, plants, insects, and humans. Visitors (1994), 1,130,761.

Liberty Science Center, Liberty State Park, Jersey City, New Jersey. Features more than 250 interactive exhibits and an OMNIMAX theater. The ferry to the Statue of Liberty and Ellis Island Museum is also in Liberty State Park. Visitors (1994), 1,000,000.

Bishop Museum, Honolulu, Hawaii. Contains exhibits on the natural history of Hawaii. Visitors (1994), 541,810.

Museum of Science and Discovery, Ft. Lauderdale, Florida. Displays on Florida's natural environment, human health and nutrition; aquarium. Visitors (1994), 534,000.

Signs and symbols give us information at a glance. Some signs indicate where something is located, such as Hospitals or Rest Rooms. Others give commands, such as Stop or Yield. Still others warn us of danger. Long ago, when most people did not know how to read, simple pictures and symbols were used on signs to help strangers find the shops in a town. Each sign shown here uses a symbol to describe something in a simple way, so you do not have to read the language to understand the sign.

Telephone	Gasoline	Hospital	First Aid	Drug Store
Handicapped Access	Men's Restroom	Women's Restroom	Food	Lodging
Airport	Information	Lost and Found	School Zone	No Bicycles
Picnic Area	Camping	Swimming	Fishing	Hiking Trail
No Smoking	Flammable	Poison	Radioactive	Explosives

ROAD SIGNS

Stop

One Way

No Entry

No Parking

Right Turn

No Left Turn

Hill

Signal Ahead

No U Turn

Pedestrian Crossing

Deer Crossing

Railroad Crossing

Road Work Ahead

Cross Road

Winding Road

Slippery Road

Divided Highway

Yield

Merging Traffic

SOME USEFUL SYMBOLS

$ Dollar

¢ Cent

% Percent

& Ampersand (and)

℞ Prescription

© Copyright

® Registered Trademark

♂ Male

♀ Female

± Plus or Minus

= Is Equal To

≠ Is Not Equal To

< Is Less Than

> Is Greater Than

( ) Parentheses

BRAILLE

Blind people read with their fingers using a system of raised dots called Braille. Braille was developed by Louis Braille (1809-1852) in France in 1826, when he was in his teens. The Braille alphabet, numbers, punctuation, and speech sounds are represented by 63 different combinations of 6 raised dots arranged in a grid like this:

```
1   4
2   5
3   6
```

The letters in the basic alphabet are lowercase. Special symbols are placed before the lowercase letters to form capital letters and numbers. The dark dots show the grid. The light dots show the raised dots.

BRAILLE ALPHABET AND NUMBERS

a b c d e f g h i j k l m

n o p q r s t u v w x y z

1 2 3 4 5 6 7 8 9 0

SIGN LANGUAGE

Many people who are deaf or hearing-impaired, and cannot hear spoken words, talk with their fingers instead of their voices. To do this, they use a system of manual signs (the manual alphabet) or fingerspelling in which the fingers are used to form letters and words. Originally developed in France by Abbe Charles Michel De l'Epee in the late 1700s, the manual alphabet was later brought to the United States by Laurent Clerc (1785-1869), a Frenchman who taught people who were deaf.

AMERICAN MANUAL ALPHABET

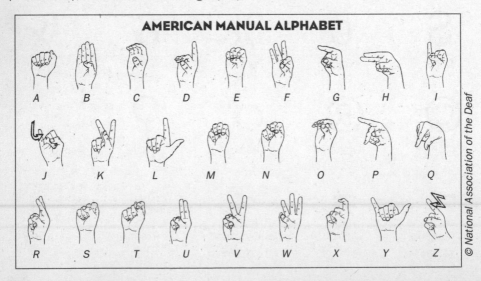

A B C D E F G H I

J K L M N O P Q

R S T U V W X Y Z

© National Association of the Deaf

SEMAPHORE CODE

Semaphore is a system of communication using two hand flags or two flashlights, one in each hand. It is used to send messages to people who are too far away to be heard but can be seen. The U.S. Navy uses semaphores when it needs to send messages between ships (up to 15 miles apart) in a fast, safe, and silent manner. A number is shown by making the numeral sign before and after spelling out the number.

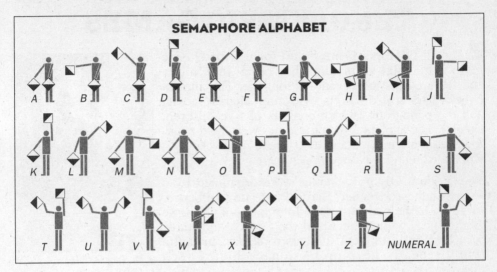

SEMAPHORE ALPHABET

MORSE CODE

Morse Code is a system of letters and numbers used by amateur radio operators, ships at sea, and the military. Letters and numbers are changed into short signals (dots) and long signals (dashes), which can be sent by radio or lights in an evenly timed series to spell out long messages. It was named after the inventor Samuel F.B. Morse (1791-1872), who developed the first successful telegraph in 1838.

INTERNATIONAL MORSE CODE

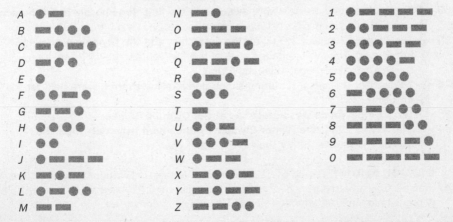

The OLYMPIC GAMES

The first Olympic Games were played in Greece more than 2,500 years ago. They began in 776 B.C. and featured just one event—a footrace. The ancient Greeks later added boxing, wrestling, chariot racing, and the pentathlon (which consists of five different events). The ancient Olympic Games were held every four years for more than 1,000 years, until A.D. 393, when a Roman Emperor stopped them.

The modern Olympic Games were organized by a French educator named Baron Pierre de Coubertin. In 1894, he helped set up the International Olympic Committee, which organized the Games and made sure that only amateur athletes took part in them. (Only recently have professional athletes been allowed to compete.)

▲ Running with the Olympic flame

OLYMPIC FIRSTS

1896 **The first modern Olympic Games were held in Athens, Greece.** Thirteen countries and 311 athletes took part. The athletes were all men, and they competed in nine sports: cycling, fencing, gymnastics, swimming, lawn tennis, track and field, wrestling, weight lifting, and shooting. The winners received a silver medal and a crown of olive branches.

1900 **Women competed in the Olympic Games for the first time.** Eleven women competed that year, out of a total of 1,330 competitors. The sports included women's golf, women's lawn tennis, and mixed-doubles tennis.

1908 **For the first time, medals were awarded to the first three people to finish each event**—a gold medal for first place, silver for second, and bronze for third.

1920 **The Olympic flag was raised for the first time, and the Olympic oath was introduced.** The five interlaced rings of the flag represent: North America, South America, Europe, Asia, and Africa.

1924 **The Winter Olympics, featuring skiing and skating events, were held for the first time.**

1928 **The Olympic flame was introduced at the Olympic Games.**

1994 **Starting in 1994, the Winter Olympics will be held two years after the Summer Olympics,** rather than in the same year.

DID YOU KNOW? During the 1992 Summer Games in Barcelona, Spain, more than 10,000 athletes from 172 countries competed in 257 events. In the 1994 Winter Games in Lillehammer, Norway, 67 countries competed.

SITES OF OLYMPIC GAMES

Winter Games:

1994 Lillehammer, Norway
1998 Nagano, Japan
2002 Salt Lake City, Utah, U.S.

Summer Games:

1992 Barcelona, Spain
1996 Atlanta, Georgia, U.S.
2000 Sydney, Australia

OLYMPIC SPORTS

Summer Olympic Sports

Archery

Badminton

Baseball

Basketball

Boxing

Canoe/Kayak

Cycling

Diving

Equestrian
(dressage,
show
jumping,
3-day event)

Fencing

Field Hockey

Football (Soccer)

Gymnastics

Rhythmic
Gymnastics

Judo

Modern Pentathlon
(cross-country
riding, fencing,
pistol shooting,
swimming,
cross-country
running—one
event per day for
5 days)

Rowing

Shooting

Softball

Swimming

Synchronized
Swimming

Table Tennis

Team Handball

Tennis

Track and Field

Volleyball

Water Polo

Weight Lifting

Wrestling

Yachting

Winter Olympic Sports

Biathlon
(cross-country
skiing, rifle
marksmanship)

Bobsled

Ice Hockey

Luge (Toboggan)

Figure Skating

Speed Skating

Alpine Skiing

Freestyle Skiing

Nordic Skiing
Cross-Country
Ski Jumping
Nordic Combined

THE OLYMPIC FLAME

The Olympic flame is carried by runners in a relay, from Olympia in Greece to the site of the Games. It was introduced to the modern Games at Amsterdam (the Netherlands) in 1928. The Olympic flame was first carried in 1936 for the Summer Games and in 1964 for the Winter Games. It traveled by air for the first time in 1956, when the Games were held in Australia.

BASEBALL

Major League Baseball struck out in 1994. The players went on strike on August 12, and the owners officially canceled the rest of the season on September 14. The World Series was canceled for the first time since 1904, and many fans were angry at both the players and the teams for not settling the strike quickly. After a court ruled in favor of the players, the players went back to work early in April 1995. The season began on April 26, 1995, and was shortened from the customary 162 games to 144 games. Major League Baseball will have to work hard for continued fan support in the future.

FINAL 1994 STANDINGS

AMERICAN LEAGUE

Eastern Division	Won	Lost
New York Yankees	70	43
Baltimore Orioles	63	49
Toronto Blue Jays	55	60
Boston Red Sox	54	61
Detroit Tigers	53	62

Central Division	Won	Lost
Chicago White Sox	67	46
Cleveland Indians	66	47
Kansas City Royals	64	51
Minnesota Twins	53	60
Milwaukee Brewers	53	62

Western Division	Won	Lost
Texas Rangers	52	62
Oakland Athletics	51	63
Seattle Mariners	49	63
California Angels	47	68

NATIONAL LEAGUE

Eastern Division	Won	Lost
Montreal Expos	74	40
Atlanta Braves	68	46
New York Mets	55	58
Philadelphia Phillies	54	61
Florida Marlins	51	64

Central Division	Won	Lost
Cincinnati Reds	66	48
Houston Astros	66	49
Pittsburgh Pirates	53	61
St. Louis Cardinals	53	61
Chicago Cubs	49	64

Western Division	Won	Lost
Los Angeles Dodgers	58	56
San Francisco Giants	55	60
Colorado Rockies	53	64
San Diego Padres	47	70

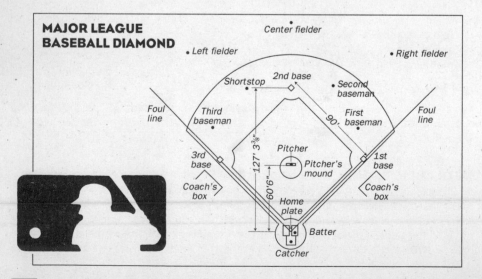

MAJOR LEAGUE BASEBALL DIAMOND

Center fielder

Left fielder

Right fielder

Shortstop

2nd base

Second baseman

Foul line

Third baseman

First baseman

Foul line

90'

127' 3⅜"

60'6"

3rd base

Pitcher

Pitcher's mound

1st base

Coach's box

Coach's box

Home plate

Batter

Catcher

1994 MAJOR LEAGUE LEADERS

Most Valuable Players
   American League: Frank Thomas, Chicago White Sox
   National League: Jeff Bagwell, Houston Astros
Cy Young Award Winners (Top Pitcher)
   American League: David Cone, Kansas City Royals
   National League: Greg Maddux, Atlanta Braves
Rookie of the Year
   American League: Bob Hamelin, Kansas City Royals
   National League: Raul Mondesi, Los Angeles Dodgers
Batting Champs
   American League: Paul O'Neill, New York Yankees, .359
   National League: Tony Gwynn, San Diego Padres, .394
Home Run Leaders
   American League: Ken Griffey, Jr., Seattle Mariners, 40
   National League: Matt Williams, San Francisco Giants, 43
Runs Batted In (RBI) Leaders
   American League: Kirby Puckett, Minnesota Twins, 112
   National League: Jeff Bagwell, Houston Astros, 116
Most Pitching Victories
   American League: Jimmy Key, New York Yankees, 17
   National League: Ken Hill, Montreal Expos, 16; Greg Maddux, Atlanta Braves, 16

▲ *Frank Thomas*

 DID YOU KNOW?
   ☑ A baseball has a cork and rubber core that is tightly wrapped with yarn and then covered with white leather. It is sewn together with raised seams. The ball weighs 5 ounces and has a circumference of 9 inches.
   ☑ A big league baseball bat is made from hardwood. The bat cannot be larger than 2¾ inches in diameter and cannot be longer than 42 inches.

BASEBALL HALL OF FAME

The National Baseball Hall of Fame and Museum opened on June 12, 1939, in Cooperstown, New York. To be nominated for membership, players must be retired from baseball for five years. **Address:** Post Office Box 590, Cooperstown, NY 13326. **Phone:** (607) 547-7200.

LITTLE LEAGUE

Little League baseball began in 1939 in Williamsport, Pennsylvania, with 30 boys playing on 3 teams. By 1994, 2.8 million boys and girls aged 5 to 18 played on 190,000 teams in 81 countries, making the Little League the largest youth sports program in the world.

DID YOU KNOW?
   ☑ Little League bats cannot be longer than 33 inches with a maximum diameter of 2¼ inches. In the 1990s, aluminum bats have almost replaced wood in Little League, high school, and college baseball.
   ☑ A Little League baseball field is smaller than a Major League field. The distance between the bases is 60 feet (instead of 90 feet), and the distance from home plate to the outfield wall is 200 feet (much shorter than in the majors).

BASKETBALL

Basketball began in 1891 in Springfield, Massachusetts, when Dr. James Naismith invented it using peach baskets as hoops. In 1936, it became part of the Olympics. Big-time professional basketball was born in 1949, when the National Basketball Association (NBA) was formed. In the 1994-1995 season, there were 27 NBA teams.

PROFESSIONAL BASKETBALL

FINAL 1994-1995 NBA STANDINGS

EASTERN CONFERENCE

Atlantic Division	Won	Lost
Orlando Magic	57	25
New York Knicks	55	27
Boston Celtics	35	47
Miami Heat	32	50
New Jersey Nets	30	52
Philadelphia 76ers	24	56
Washington Bullets	21	61

Central Division	Won	Lost
Indiana Pacers	52	30
Charlotte Hornets	50	32
Chicago Bulls	47	35
Cleveland Cavaliers	43	39
Atlanta Hawks	42	40
Milwaukee Bucks	34	48
Detroit Pistons	28	54

WESTERN CONFERENCE

Midwest Division	Won	Lost
San Antonio Spurs	62	20
Utah Jazz	60	22
Houston Rockets	47	35
Denver Nuggets	41	41
Dallas Mavericks	36	46
Minnesota Timberwolves	21	61

Pacific Division	Won	Lost
Phoenix Suns	59	23
Seattle SuperSonics	57	25
Los Angeles Lakers	48	34
Portland Trail Blazers	44	38
Sacramento Kings	39	43
Golden State Warriors	26	56
Los Angeles Clippers	17	65

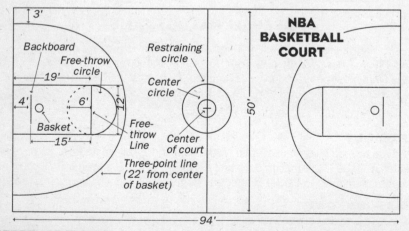

CONFERENCE FINALS

Eastern Conference: Orlando Magic defeated Indiana Pacers, 4 games to 3.
Western Conference: Houston Rockets defeated San Antonio Spurs, 4 games to 2.

CHAMPIONSHIP SERIES

Houston Rockets defeated Orlando Magic, 4 games to 0.

HIGHLIGHTS OF THE 1994-1995 BASKETBALL SEASON

Most Valuable Player: David Robinson, San Antonio Spurs
Defensive Player of the Year: Dikembe Mutombo, Denver Nuggets
Rookie of the Year: (co-winners) Grant Hill, Detroit Pistons;
Jason Kidd, Dallas Mavericks
Coach of the Year: Del Harris, Los Angeles Lakers
Most Valuable Player in the Finals: Hakeem Olajuwon
Scoring Leader: Shaquille O'Neal, Orlando Magic
   Games: 79   **Points:** 2,315   **Average:** 29.3
Rebounding Leader: Dennis Rodman, San Antonio Spurs
   Games: 49   **Rebounds:** 823   **Average:** 16.8
Assists Leader: John Stockton, Utah Jazz
   Games: 82   **Assists:** 1,011   **Average:** 12.3
Steals Leader: Scottie Pippen, Chicago Bulls
   Games: 79   **Steals:** 232   **Average:** 2.94
Blocked Shots Leader: Dikembe Mutombo, Denver Nuggets
   Games: 82   **Blocks:** 321   **Average:** 3.91

BASKETBALL HALL OF FAME

The Naismith Memorial Basketball Hall of Fame was founded in 1959 to honor great basketball players, coaches, referees, and other people who have made important contributions to the game. Named after the inventor of basketball, the museum features exhibits on the history of the game. **Address:** 1150 West Columbus Avenue, Springfield, MA 01101-0179. **Phone:** (413) 781-5759.

DID YOU KNOW?

☑ The Boston Celtics have won 16 NBA championships, most of any team. The Celtics won 8 titles in a row from 1959 to 1966 and 11 championships in 13 years.

☑ In the 1961-1962 season, the legendary Wilt Chamberlain averaged an incredible 50.4 points per game over an 80-game season. During the season, Wilt had a game against the New York Knicks in which he scored a record 100 points.

☑ When he retired in 1989 after 20 NBA seasons, Kareem Abdul-Jabbar had set an all-time record by scoring 38,387 points.

☑ A basketball is made from an inflated bladder with a cemented leather or rubber cover. It weighs 20-22 ounces and has a circumference of 30 inches.

HE'S BACK

One of the biggest sports stories of 1995 was the return of Michael Jordan to the NBA. Jordan had retired at the end of the 1993 season after leading the Chicago Bulls to three straight NBA championships and winning seven scoring titles in a row. He played minor league baseball in 1994. Then, on March 10, 1995, he retired from baseball, rejoined the Bulls, and led them into the playoffs.

▲ *Michael Jordan*

COLLEGE BASKETBALL

College basketball has become a huge sport. The National Collegiate Athletic Association (NCAA) Tournament began in 1939. Today, it is a spectacular 64-team extravaganza that is considered the national championship tournament. The Final Four weekend, when the semi-finals and finals are played, is one of the most watched sports events in America. The NCAA Tournament for women's basketball began in 1982. Since then, the popularity of the women's game has grown by leaps and bounds.

THE 1994-1995 NCAA TOURNAMENT RESULT

MEN'S FINAL FOUR RESULTS

Semi-Finals:

UCLA 74	Oklahoma State 61
Arkansas 75	North Carolina 68

Championship Game:

UCLA 89	Arkansas 78

DID YOU KNOW? By winning the national championship, the UCLA Bruins extended their record for most NCAA titles to 11. The Bruins won their first 10 in just 12 years (from 1964 to 1975) under legendary coach John Wooden, including an amazing 7 in a row. Their victory in 1995 was their first in 20 years.

WOMEN'S FINAL FOUR RESULTS

Semi-Finals:

Connecticut 87	Stanford 60
Tennessee 73	Georgia 51

Championship Game:

Connecticut 70	Tennessee 64

DID YOU KNOW? When the Lady Huskies of the University of Connecticut won the national championship with a perfect, 35-0 record, they became just the second women's team in history to achieve championship perfection. The only other unbeaten team to win the title was the 1986 Lady Longhorns of the University of Texas, who finished at 34-0.

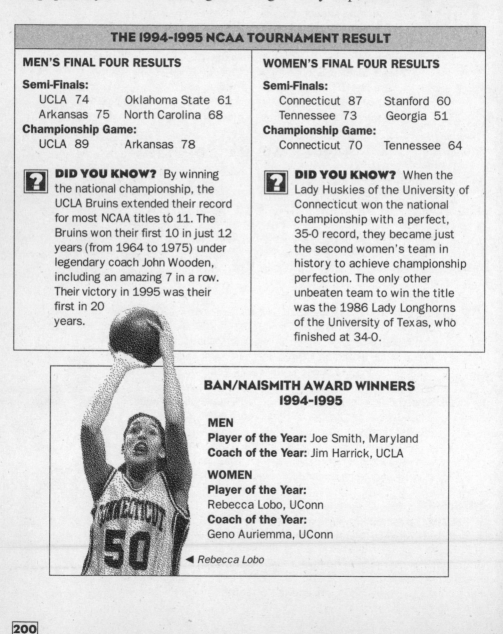

BAN/NAISMITH AWARD WINNERS 1994-1995

MEN
Player of the Year: Joe Smith, Maryland
Coach of the Year: Jim Harrick, UCLA

WOMEN
Player of the Year:
Rebecca Lobo, UConn
Coach of the Year:
Geno Auriemma, UConn

◀ Rebecca Lobo

FOOTBALL

American football began as a college sport. The first game that was like today's football took place between Yale and Harvard in New Haven, Connecticut, on November 13, 1875. The sport was largely shaped by Walter Camp in the 1880s. He reduced the number of players to 11 on each side and introduced the idea of each play beginning from the line of scrimmage. He also introduced the concept of "downs" and was the first to have the field lined with chalk every five yards.

By the turn of the century, college football was established throughout the United States. By the early 1900s professional teams began appearing. The National Football League (NFL) was formed in 1920 with 13 teams. As late as 1965 the NFL had just 14 teams. There are now 30 teams, including the Carolina Panthers and Jacksonville Jaguars, which began play at the beginning of the 1995 season.

PROFESSIONAL FOOTBALL

FINAL NFL STANDINGS FOR THE 1994 SEASON

National Football Conference

American Football Conference

Eastern Division	Won	Lost	Eastern Divison	Won	Lost
Dallas Cowboys	12	4	Miami Dolphins	10	6
New York Giants	9	7	New England Patriots	10	6
Arizona Cardinals	8	8	Indianapolis Colts	8	8
Philadelphia Eagles	7	9	Buffalo Bills	7	9
Washington Redskins	3	13	New York Jets	6	10

Central Division	Won	Lost	Central Division	Won	Lost
Minnesota Vikings	10	6	Pittsburgh Steelers	12	4
Green Bay Packers	9	7	Cleveland Browns	11	5
Detroit Lions	9	7	Cincinnati Bengals	3	13
Chicago Bears	9	7	Houston Oilers	2	14
Tampa Bay Buccaneers	6	10			

Western Division	Won	Lost	Western Division	Won	Lost
San Francisco 49ers	13	3	San Diego Chargers	11	5
New Orleans Saints	7	9	Kansas City Chiefs	9	7
Atlanta Falcons	7	9	Los Angeles Raiders	9	7
Los Angeles Rams	4	12	Denver Broncos	7	9
			Seattle Seahawks	6	10

1994 Conference Championship Games
National Football Conference: San Francisco 49ers 38, Dallas Cowboys 28
American Football Conference: San Diego Chargers 17, Pittsburgh Steelers 13

Super Bowl XXIX, January 29, 1995, Joe Robbie Stadium, Miami, Florida
San Francisco 49ers 49, San Diego Chargers 26

NFL FOOTBALL FIELD

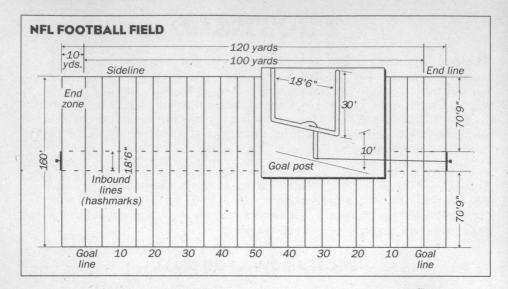

TOP NFL PERFORMERS OF 1994

Rushing Leader: Barry Sanders, Detroit Lions
   Carries: 331; **Yards:** 1,883; **Average:** 5.7
Passing Leader: Steve Young, San Francisco 49ers
   Passing Attempts: 461; **Passing Completions:** 324;
   Passing Yards: 3,969;
   Passing Completion Percentage: 70.3;
   Touchdown Passes: 35; **Passes Intercepted:** 10;
   Quarterback rating: 112.8 (new record)
Pass Receiving Leader: Cris Carter, Minnesota Vikings
   Catches: 122 (new record); **Yards:** 1,256; **Average:** 10.3

The following awards were all chosen by the Associated Press
   Most Valuable Player: Steve Young, San Francisco 49ers
   Offensive Player of the Year: Barry Sanders, Detroit Lions
   Defensive Player of the Year: Deion Sanders, San Francisco 49ers
   Coach of the Year: Bill Parcells, New England Patriots

▲ Barry Sanders

PRO FOOTBALL HALL OF FAME

Football's Hall of Fame was founded in 1963 by the National Football League to honor the game's outstanding players, coaches, and contributors. To be nominated, players must be retired from football for five years.
Address: Football Hall of Fame, 2121 George Halas Drive, Canton, OH 44708. **Phone:** (216) 456-8207.

DID YOU KNOW? A football is 11 to 11¼ inches long and weighs 14-15 ounces. It is oval in shape and somewhat pointed at the ends. It is made up of an inflated bladder covered with pebbled grain leather.

COLLEGE FOOTBALL

College football is one of America's most colorful and exciting sports. The National Collegiate Athletic Association (NCAA), which was founded in 1906, oversees college football today. There is no one tournament to determine the best team in college football. The national champion is chosen by several football polls, which sometimes disagree.

1994 TOP 10 COLLEGE TEAMS					
Chosen by the Associated Press Poll and the USA Today/CNN Poll.					
Rank	AP	USA Today/CNN	Rank	AP	USA Today/CNN
1.	Nebraska	Nebraska	6.	Miami	Miami
2.	Penn State	Penn State	7.	Florida	Florida
3.	Colorado	Colorado	8.	Texas A&M	Utah
4.	Florida State	Alabama	9.	Auburn	Ohio State
5.	Alabama	Florida State	10.	Utah	Brigham Young

THE BOWL GAMES

Post-season "bowl" games held on or near New Year's Day have become a great part of college football tradition. The Bowl Alliance, which includes the Sugar, Fiesta, and Orange Bowls, has been formed to try to get the best matchups in these Bowls, with the hope that one will determine the national champion. The Rose Bowl is the oldest bowl game, having been played first in 1902. It became an annual event in 1916. There are now some 18 post-season bowl games.

SOME 1994 SEASON MAJOR BOWL RESULTS
Rose Bowl (Pasadena, California): Penn State 38, Oregon 20
Orange Bowl (Miami, Florida): Nebraska 24, Miami 17
Cotton Bowl (Dallas, Texas): Southern Cal 55, Texas Tech 14
Sugar Bowl (New Orleans, Louisiana): Florida State 23, Florida 17

HEISMAN TROPHY. The Heisman Trophy is given to the most outstanding college football player in the United States. It was first presented in 1935. The **1994 Heisman Trophy Winner** was Rashaan Salaam from the University of Colorado, who became the fourth running back in Division I-A play to gain more than 2,000 yards in a single season.

▲ *Rashaan Salaam*

COLLEGE FOOTBALL HALL OF FAME

The College Football Hall of Fame was established in 1955 by the National Football Foundation. To be nominated, a player must be out of college 10 years and must have been a first team All-American pick by a major selector during his career. Coaches must be retired three years.
Address: 111 South St. Joseph Street, P.O. Box 11146, South Bend, Indiana 46634. **Phone:** (219) 235-9999.

GYMNASTICS

It takes a combination of strength, coordination, and grace to become a top gymnast. Although the sport goes back to ancient Greece, present-day gymnastics began in Sweden in the early 1800s. The sport has been part of the Olympic Games since 1896. An Olympic gold medal is the highest honor for a gymnast. There is also gymnastic competition for the World Championship. In 1994, fifteen-year-old Shannon Miller of the United States became the women's World Champion.

GYMNASTIC EVENTS

For Women
1. All-Around
2. Side Horse Vault
3. Asymmetrical (Uneven) Bars
4. Balance Beam
5. Floor Exercises
6. Team Combined Exercises
7. Rhythmic All-Around

For Men
1. All-Around
2. Horizontal Bar
3. Parallel Bars
4. Long Horse Vault
5. Side Horse (Pommel Horse)
6. Rings
7. Floor Exercises
8. Team Combined Exercises

Shannon Miller ▲

HOW ARE GYMNASTS JUDGED?
Gymnasts must do both compulsory and optional exercises during a routine. **Compulsory exercises** are rated for mechanical correctness, grace, rhythm, ease, form, continuity, posture, and timing. **Optional exercises** are judged for their difficulty, combination of movements, risk, originality, and execution. Scores range from 1 to a perfect 10. There are four or six judges at a competition. The highest and lowest scores are dropped, and the remaining scores are averaged for the contestant's mark.

ALL-AROUND CHAMPIONSHIP AT THE OLYMPICS
In women's Olympics competition, the All-Around championship is decided by adding the scores of four individual events (balance beam, floor exercise, uneven bars, vault). In men's competition, the All-Around is decided by adding the scores of six individual events (floor exercise, horizontal bar, parallel bars, pommel horse, rings, vault).

 DID YOU KNOW? Gymnastics is a sport in which teenage girls often excel.
☑ In 1972, the sports world was captivated by 4-foot 11-inch, 85-pound Olga Korbut of the Soviet Union. At 17, Olga won two Olympic gold medals.
☑ At the 1976 Olympics, 14-year-old Nadia Comanici of Romania became the first gymnast ever to receive a perfect score of 10 on both the uneven bars and the balance beam. Before the Olympics ended, she had been awarded seven perfect 10s. She also won three gold medals. Today, women must be at least 15 years of age to compete, and men must be at least 16.
☑ At the 1984 Olympics, 16-year-old Mary Lou Retton from Fairmont, West Virginia, became the first American woman to win the All-Around gold medal.

ICE HOCKEY

Ice hockey began in Canada in the mid-1800s. By the beginning of the 1900s, hockey was becoming a major Canadian sport. The National Hockey League was formed in 1916 and has been in operation ever since. In the 1994-1995 season, there were 26 teams in the NHL, 19 in the United States and 7 in Canada.

FINAL 1994-1995 STANDINGS. Because of a disagreement between players and team owners, the players were locked out by the owners at the beginning of the 1994-1995 season. Once the dispute was settled, the season was shortened to 48 games from the normal 84. Below are the final standings.

EASTERN CONFERENCE

Atlantic Division	W	L	T	Pts
Philadelphia Flyers	28	16	4	60
New Jersey Devils	22	18	8	52
Washington Capitals	22	18	8	52
N.Y. Rangers	22	23	3	47
Florida Panthers	20	22	6	46
Tampa Bay Lightning	17	28	3	37
N.Y. Islanders	15	28	5	35

Northeast Division	W	L	T	Pts
Quebec Nordiques	30	13	5	65
Pittsburgh Penguins	29	16	3	61
Boston Bruins	27	18	3	57
Buffalo Sabres	22	19	7	51
Hartford Whalers	19	24	5	43
Montreal Canadiens	18	23	7	43
Ottawa Senators	9	34	5	23

WESTERN CONFERENCE

Central Division	W	L	T	Pts
Detroit Red Wings	33	11	4	70
St. Louis Blues	28	15	5	61
Chicago Blackhawks	24	19	5	53
Toronto Maple Leafs	21	19	8	50
Dallas Stars	17	23	8	42
Winnipeg Jets	16	25	7	39

Pacific Division	W	L	T	Pts
Calgary Flames	24	17	7	55
Vancouver Canucks	18	18	12	48
San Jose Sharks	19	25	4	42
Los Angeles Kings	16	23	9	41
Edmonton Oilers	17	27	4	38
Anaheim Mighty Ducks	16	27	5	37

CONFERENCE FINALS:
> **Eastern Conference:** The New Jersey Devils defeated the Philadelphia Flyers, 4 games to 2.
> **Western Conference:** The Detroit Red Wings defeated the Chicago Blackhawks, 4 games to 1.

NHL CHAMPIONSHIP:
The New Jersey Devils and the Detroit Red Wings played for the Stanley Cup.

? DID YOU KNOW?
Wayne Gretzky, known as the "Great One," is the highest scorer in NHL history. On March 23, 1994, while playing for the Los Angeles Kings, he scored his 802nd goal, breaking Gordie Howe's record for the most goals in an NHL career.

▲ *Wayne Gretzky*

HOCKEY HALL OF FAME

The Hockey Hall of Fame was opened in 1961 to honor important hockey figures. **Address:** BCE Place, 30 Yonge Street, Toronto, Ontario, Canada M5E 1X8. **Phone:** (416) 360-7735.

ICE SKATING

People have enjoyed ice skating for hundreds of years. The first skates were made from animal bones ground to a smooth, flat surface. Wooden skates with iron blades appeared in the Netherlands around the 13th or 14th century. Steel skating blades appeared around 1860 and allowed skaters to move quickly and with more control.

FIGURE SKATING

There are two types of competitive ice skating—figure skating and speed skating. Figure skating, which is almost like ballet, is judged by the way the skaters perform certain turns and jumps and by the creative difficulty of their programs. There are singles competitions for both men and women, pairs skating, and ice dancing.

1995 World Championships

The figure skating World Championships took place in Birmingham, England, in March 1995. Below are the winners for the singles competition.

	Women's Singles	Men's Singles
Gold Medal:	Chen Lu (China)	Elvis Stojko (Canada)
Silver Medal:	Surya Bonaly (France)	Todd Eldredge (United States)
Bronze Medal:	Nicole Bobek (United States)	Philippe Candeloro (France)

America's Olympic Champions

Below are America's Olympic gold medalists in singles competition:

Men: Dick Button (1948, 1952), Hayes Alan Jenkins (1956), David Jenkins (1960), Scott Hamilton (1984), Brian Boitano (1988).

Women: Tenley Albright (1956), Carol Heiss (1960), Peggy Fleming (1968), Dorothy Hamill (1976), Kristi Yamaguchi (1992).

SPEED SKATING

Speed skating is a race around an oval track. The traditional track is 400 meters around with two lanes. The skaters, who skate two at a time, are racing the clock. The winner is the skater with the fastest time of any competitor. Speed skating for men became part of the Winter Olympics in 1924, for women in 1960. Men compete in five events: the 500 meters, 1,000 meters, 1,500 meters, 5,000 meters, and 10,000 meters. Women compete in five events: the 500 meters, 1,000 meters, 1,500 meters, 3,000 meters, and 5,000 meters.

 DID YOU KNOW? In the 1994 Winter Olympics at Lillehammer, Norway, America's Bonnie Blair won speed skating gold medals in the 500 and 1,000 meter races. It was her third straight Olympic gold in the 500 and second in the 1,000. Dan Jansen, also of the United States, ended a series of Olympic disappointments by taking the gold in the 1,000 meters.

▲ Bonnie Blair

SOCCER

Soccer, which is called football in many countries, is the number one sport worldwide. It is estimated that soccer is played by more than 100,000,000 people in over 150 countries. The first rules for the game were published in 1863 by the London Football Association. Since then, the sport has spread rapidly from Europe to almost every part of the world. The United States Youth Soccer Association runs age-group programs for more than one million kids all around the country.

THE WORLD CUP. The biggest soccer tournament is the World Cup. It is held every four years. Teams from more than 100 nations compete, and the top 24 teams represent their countries in a three-week long tournament. In 1994, the World Cup tournament was held in the United States for the first time.

1994 World Cup Results

Semifinals:	Brazil 1	Sweden 0
	Italy 2	Bulgaria 1
Championship:	Brazil 3	Italy 2
	(Game decided by penalty kicks)	

? DID YOU KNOW? His real name is Edson Arantes do Nascimento, but everyone knows him as Pele. A native of Brazil, he retired as a player in 1977, but may still be the greatest soccer player who ever lived. He helped Brazil win three World Cup titles (1958, 1962, 1970) and helped soccer become better established in the United States.

▲ *Pele*

SWIMMING

Competitive swimming as an organized sport began in the second half of the 19th century. When the modern Olympic Games began in Athens, Greece, in 1896, the only racing stroke was the breaststroke. Today, men and women at the Olympics swim the backstroke, breaststroke, butterfly, and freestyle, in events ranging from 50 meters to 1,500 meters.

SWIMMERS SWIM FASTER AND FASTER. When Johnny Weissmuller won the 100-meter freestyle at the 1924 Olympics, his winning time was 59.0 seconds. When Matt Biondi won it in 1988, his winning time was 48.63 seconds, more than 10 seconds faster than Weissmuller's. Swimming records continue to be broken nearly every year.

SOME GREAT U.S. OLYMPIC SWIMMERS

☑ **Johnny Weissmuller** won three gold medals at the 1924 and 1928 Games and later became even more famous playing Tarzan in movies.

☑ **Mark Spitz** won two gold medals in relays at the 1968 Games and returned in 1972 to make Olympic swimming history by winning seven gold medals.

☑ **Janet Evans**, at age 17, won three gold medals at the 1988 Olympics in Seoul, South Korea. In 1992, she won another gold and a silver in Barcelona, Spain.

☑ **Matt Biondi** won seven medals at the 1988 Olympics, including five golds.

TENNIS

The modern game of tennis began in 1873 when a British officer, Major Walter Wingfield, developed it from the earlier game of court tennis. In 1877, the first championship matches were held at the old Wimbledon Grounds near London. The United States Lawn Tennis Association was founded in 1881, and that same year the first United States men's championships were held at Newport, Rhode Island. Six years later the first women's championships took place in Philadelphia.

GRAND SLAM TOURNAMENTS

Today, professional tennis players from all over the world compete in dozens of tournaments. The four most important, called the **grand slam** tournaments, are the Australian Open, the French Open, the All-England (Wimbledon) Championships, and the United States Open. There are separate competitions for men and women in singles and doubles. There are also mixed doubles, where men and women team together.

Men's and Women's Singles Champions

1995 Australian Open Finals

Men: Andre Agassi (U.S.A.) defeated Pete Sampras (U.S.A.), 4-6, 6-1, 7-6, 6-4

Women: Mary Pierce (France) defeated Arantxa Sanchez Vicario (Spain), 6-3, 6-2

1994 Wimbledon Finals

Men: Pete Sampras (U.S.A.) defeated Goran Ivanisevic (Croatia), 7-6, 7-6, 6-0

Women: Conchita Martinez (Spain) defeated Martina Navratilova (U.S.A.), 6-4, 3-6, 6-3

1995 French Open Finals

Men: Thomas Muster (Austria) defeated Michael Chang (U.S.A.), 7-5, 6-2, 6-4

Women: Steffi Graf (Germany) defeated Arantxa Sanchez Vicario (Spain), 7-5, 4-6, 6,0

1994 United States Open Finals

Men: Andre Agassi (U.S.A.) defeated Michael Stich (Germany), 6-1, 7-6, 7-5

Women: Arantxa Sanchez Vicario (Spain) defeated Steffi Graf (Germany), 1-6, 7-6, 6-4

RANKINGS FOR 1994. The Association of Tennis Professionals (ATP) and the Women's Tennis Association (WTA) now keep computer rankings of all the players on the tour. The final top five rankings for men and women in 1994 were as follows.

Women

1. Steffi Graf, Germany
2. Arantxa Sanchez Vicario, Spain
3. Conchita Martinez, Spain
4. Jana Novotna, Czech Republic
5. Mary Pierce, France

Men

1. Pete Sampras, United States
2. Andre Agassi, United States
3. Boris Becker, Germany
4. Sergi Bruguera, Spain
5. Goran Ivanisevic, Croatia

DID YOU KNOW?
Jimmy Connors (109) and Martina Navratilova (167) of the United States have won the most singles titles in tennis history. Martina Navratilova also set a record by winning the Wimbledon singles championship nine times.

▲ Martina Navratilova

SPECIAL OLYMPICS

The Special Olympics is the world's largest program of sports training and athletic competition for children and adults with mental retardation. Founded in 1968, Special Olympics International has offices in all 50 U.S. states and Washington, D.C., and in many countries throughout the world. The organization offers year-round training and competition in 17 summer sports and 6 winter sports to nearly 1.5 million athletes in more than 140 countries.

The first Special Olympics competition was held in Chicago in 1968. After holding national events in individual countries, Special Olympics International holds World Games. The World Games alternate between summer and winter sports every two years. The 1995 Special Olympics World Summer Games were held in New Haven, Connecticut, in July.

SPECIAL OLYMPICS OFFICIAL SPORTS

Summer: aquatics, athletics (track and field), basketball, bowling, cycling, equestrian, gymnastics, roller skating, soccer, softball, tennis, volleyball

Demonstration sports: badminton, golf, poly hockey (similar to floor hockey), powerlifting, table tennis, team handball

Winter: alpine and cross-country skiing, figure and speed skating, floor hockey

WHERE TO GET MORE INFORMATION ON THE SPECIAL OLYMPICS

Anyone wanting more information on the Special Olympics can write to:
Special Olympics International Headquarters,
1350 New York Avenue NW, Washington, D.C. 20005.

SPORTS PUZZLE

How many of these can you find hidden in the letters below?
CHARGERS, GRAND SLAM, HEISMAN TROPHY, KRISTI YAMAGUCHI, LADY HUSKIES, LITTLE LEAGUE, MARTINA NAVRATILOVA, MICHAEL JORDAN, NADIA COMANICI, NINERS, OLYMPICS, PELE, SHAQUILLE O'NEAL, STANLEY CUP, SUPER BOWL, WAYNE GRETZKY

```
Q W E D F L I T T L E L E A G U E L S Y S M L P
Z X C K V M B N M L K J H P O I Y T H F T P A I
A M A R T I N A N A V R A T I L O V A G A B D K
G A S I D C F G A H J K H Q W E R O Q U N J Y P
R Z X S C H V B D S U P E R B O W L U M L T H O
A Q W T E A R T I Y C U I E P L O Y I A E J U H
N A S I D E F G A H H K S B C N F M L V Y G S T
D Z X Y C L V U C L A P M E O I R P L E C F K E
S P D A F J A S O D R G A C J N O I E M U D I Y
L A Z M X O C V M B G M N C S E N C O G P L E S
A R X A E R T I A Q E S T A L R K S N B V I S R
M A B G E D Q D N T R A R L K N I N E R S L C A
K L W U G A X A I Z S M O O P V B M A B D F D S
C L F C T N E N C W Y U P B J K P E L E L E R Y
U E T H Y B A J I T Q B H O P M H Y U R K A W D
T L R I E W S N B A W A Y N E G R E T Z K Y I L
```

What Are TIME ZONES?

The length of a day is 24 hours—the time it takes Earth to complete one rotation on its axis. The system we use to tell time is called **standard time**. In standard time, Earth is divided into 24 time zones. The time zones run north to south, from the North Pole to the South Pole. To figure out the time in a particular zone, you must count the number of zones east or west of the **prime meridian**, or 0 degrees, which runs through Greenwich, England. When it is midnight, or 0 hour, in Greenwich, it is 5 hours earlier in New York, because New York is 5 zones away. Forty-eight states of the United States are in 4 of the 24 time zones (Alaska and Hawaii are in different time zones).

WHEN IT IS 12 NOON IN NEW YORK, IT IS

12 noon in Atlanta, Georgia
11 A.M. in St. Louis, Missouri
11 A.M. in Dallas, Texas
10 A.M. in Denver, Colorado
9 A.M. in Los Angeles, California
8 A.M. in Juneau, Alaska
7 A.M. in Honolulu, Hawaii

Pacific Standard Time
Mountain Standard Time
Central Standard Time
Eastern Standard Time
Hawaii-Aleutian Standard Time
Alaska Standard Time

TRAVEL TIME

1492 — Christopher Columbus's first trip across the Atlantic Ocean from Spain to San Salvador took 70 days.

1650s — It took 50 days to sail from London, England, to Boston, Massachusetts.

1829 — The first Atlantic Ocean crossing by a ship powered in part by steam (*Savannah*, sailing from Savannah, Georgia, to Liverpool, England) took 29 days.

1917 — The first flight in a heavier-than-air craft was performed by Wilbur Wright at Kitty Hawk, North Carolina, and lasted for 59 seconds.

1927 — Charles Lindbergh flew from New York to Paris in 33 hours, 29 minutes, 30 seconds in the first nonstop flight across the Atlantic Ocean by one person.

1961 — The flight of the first U.S. satellite carrying an astronaut (Alan Shepard, Jr.) lasted 15 minutes.

1990s — Travel by supersonic plane, the Concorde, between London and New York now takes 3½ hours.

CALENDARS

WHAT IS A CALENDAR?
Calendars divide time into units, such as days, weeks, months, and years. Calendar divisions are based on movements of Earth and on the sun and the moon. A day is the average time it takes for one rotation of Earth on its axis (24 hours). A year is the average time it takes for one revolution of Earth around the sun (365.3 days).

EARLIEST CALENDAR: The Egyptian Calendar
In ancient times, calendars were based upon the movements of the moon across the sky. The ancient Egyptians were the first to develop a solar calendar, a calendar based on the movements of the sun.

ROMAN CALENDARS: The Julian and Gregorian Calendars
At first the ancient Romans had a calendar with a year of 304 days, but it was not a solar calendar and became confusing. Later, in 45 B.C., the emperor Julius Caesar decided to use a calendar based on the movements of the sun. This calendar, called the **Julian calendar,** fixed the normal year at 365 days and added one day every fourth year (leap year). The Julian calendar also established the months of the year and the days of the week.

The Julian calendar was used until A.D. 1582, when it was revised by Pope Gregory XIII, because the Julian calendar year was 11 minutes and 14 seconds longer than the solar year. Pope Gregory shortened the calendar year slightly to match the solar year. This new calendar, called the **Gregorian calendar,** is the one we use today in the United States.

OTHER CALENDARS: Jewish and Islamic Calendars
Other calendars are also used. The Jewish calendar, which starts in the year 3761 B.C., is the official calendar of the State of Israel. The year 1996 is equivalent to the year 5756-5757 on the Jewish calendar, beginning at Rosh Hashanah (New Year). The Islamic calendar starts counting years in A.D. 622. The year 1996 is equivalent to the year 1416-1417 on the Islamic calendar, beginning at Muharram (New Year).

? DID YOU KNOW?
Stonehenge, the ancient stone monument in Salisbury, England, is between 3,000 and 5,000 years old. Most scientists think it was used to predict the positions of the sun and moon—a kind of huge calendar.

BIRTHSTONES					
January	Garnet	May	Emerald	September	Sapphire
February	Amethyst	June	Pearl	October	Opal
March	Aquamarine	July	Ruby	November	Topaz
April	Diamond	August	Peridot	December	Turquoise

UNITED NATIONS

The United Nations—or UN for short—was 50 years old in 1995. It was established in 1945 after World War II to promote peace and cooperation throughout the world. The UN conducts its business in six official languages: Arabic, Chinese, English, French, Russian, and Spanish. The first members of the UN were the 50 countries that met and signed the Charter in 1945. By the end of 1994, 184 countries (most of the world) were members. For the names of the countries that belong to the UN, see the COUNTRIES section, pages 44-63.

What Are the UN's Goals?

☑ To keep worldwide peace and security.

☑ To develop friendly relations among countries.

☑ To help countries cooperate in solving economic, social, cultural, and humanitarian problems.

☑ To promote respect for human rights and basic freedoms.

☑ To be a center that helps countries to achieve these goals.

How the UN Is ORGANIZED

The work of the UN is carried out almost all over the world. It is done through six main organs, each with a different purpose. The Secretary-General is the Chief Officer of the UN.

GENERAL ASSEMBLY

The General Assembly can discuss any problem important to the world. The Assembly admits new members to the UN, appoints the Secretary-General, and decides the UN's budget. It meets once a year for three months, but emergency meetings can be called at any time.

Who Are Its Members? All members of the UN are represented in the General Assembly.

How Do Members Vote? When the General Assembly votes, each country—whether large or small, rich or poor—has one vote. Two thirds of the members must agree for a resolution to be decided.

SECURITY COUNCIL

The Security Council discusses questions of peace and security.

Who Are Its Members? It is made up of 5 permanent members (China, France, Great Britain, Russia, and the United States) and 10 members that are elected by the General Assembly for two-year terms.

How Do Members Vote? To pass a resolution, at least 9 of the 15 members, including all the permanent members, must vote "yes." If any permanent member vetoes (votes "no" on) the resolution, it is not passed.

UN SECRETARIES-GENERAL

The Secretary-General is the Chief Officer of the United Nations, appointed by the General Assembly for a five-year term. The Secretary-General can bring any problem that threatens world peace to the Security Council or the General Assembly.

1992-present	Boutros Boutros-Ghali, Egypt
1982-1991	Javier Perez de Cuellar, Peru
1972-1981	Kurt Waldheim, Austria
1961-1971	U Thant, Burma (Myanmar)
1953-1961	Dag Hammarskjold, Sweden
1945-1952	Trygve Lie, Norway

DID YOU KNOW? The headquarters for the UN is located in New York City, but the land and the buildings are not part of the United States. The United Nations is an international zone, with its own flag, post office, stamps, and security.

United Nations Day is celebrated every October 24th, because the UN Charter was officially approved on October 24, 1945, by 51 countries (50 countries that signed the original charter plus Poland).

Many countries send their soldiers to serve under the United Nations Command, not for war, but as unarmed observers or peace-keeping forces. They wear blue helmets so they can be easily identified. The "Blue Helmets" were awarded the Nobel Peace Prize in 1988.

To get more information about the United Nations, you can write to the Public Inquiries Unit, Room GA-57, United Nations, NY 10017 or call the UN at (212) 963-4475.

INTERNATIONAL COURT OF JUSTICE

The International Court of Justice, or World Court, is the highest court of law for legal disputes between countries. When countries have a dispute, they can take their case before the International Court of Justice, which is located at The Hague, Netherlands. Countries that come before the Court must promise to obey the decision of the judges.

Who Are Its Members? There are 15 judges on the Court, each from a different country, elected by the General Assembly and the Security Council.

SECRETARIAT

The Secretariat is the UN staff that carries out the day-to-day operations of the United Nations. Its head is the Secretary-General, currently Boutros Boutros-Ghali. Members of the Secretariat collect background information for the delegates to study and help carry out UN decisions.

ECONOMIC AND SOCIAL COUNCIL

The Economic and Social Council deals with world problems such as trade, economic development, industry, population, children, food, education, health, and human rights. The Council works closely with many commissions and special agencies, such as FAO (Food and Agriculture Organization), UNICEF (United Nations International Children's Fund), and WHO (World Health Organization).

Who Are Its Members? It has 54 member countries elected by the General Assembly for three-year terms.

TRUSTEESHIP COUNCIL

The Trusteeship Council was formed to watch over the people living in territories that were placed under UN trust until they could become independent.

Who Are Its Members? Its members are the permanent members of the Security Council.

United States: FACTS & FIGURES

AREA	Land: 3,536,278 square miles	Water: 251,041 square miles	Total: 3,787,319 square miles

POPULATION (1994): 260,341,000 **CAPITAL:** Washington, D.C.

LARGEST, HIGHEST, AND OTHER STATISTICS

Largest state: Alaska (656,424 square miles)
Smallest state: Rhode Island (1,545 square miles)
Northernmost city: Barrow, Alaska (71°17' north latitude)
Southernmost city: Hilo, Hawaii (19°43' north latitude)
Easternmost city: Eastport, Maine (66°59'02" west longitude)
Westernmost city: Atka, Alaska (174°20' west longitude)
Highest town: Climax, Colorado (11,560 feet)
Lowest town: Calipatria, California (185 feet below sea level)
Oldest national park: Yellowstone National Park (Idaho, Montana, Wyoming), 2,219,791 acres, established 1872
Largest national park: Wrangell-St. Elias, Alaska (4,852,773 acres)
Longest river: Mississippi (2,340 miles)
Deepest lake: Crater Lake, Oregon (1,932 feet)
Highest mountain: Mount McKinley, Alaska (20,320 feet)
Lowest point: Death Valley, California (282 feet below sea level)
Rainiest spot: Mt. Waialeale, Hawaii (average annual rainfall 460 inches)
Tallest building: Sears Tower, Chicago, Illinois (1,454 feet)
Tallest structure: TV tower, Blanchard, North Dakota (2,063 feet)
Longest bridge span: Verrazano-Narrows Bridge, New York (4,260 feet)
Highest bridge: Royal Gorge, Colorado (1,053 feet)

INTERNATIONAL BOUNDARY LINES OF THE U.S.

U.S.-Canadian border.....................................3,987 miles (excluding Alaska)
Alaska-Canadian border ....1,538 miles
U.S.-Mexican border (Rio Grande) ....1,933 miles
Atlantic coast..2,069 miles
Gulf of Mexico coast.....................................1,631 miles
Pacific coast ....7,623 miles
Arctic coast, Alaska......................................1,060 miles

TERRITORIAL SEA OF THE U.S. The territorial sea of the United States is the surrounding waters that the country claims as its own. A proclamation issued by President Ronald Reagan on December 27, 1988, stated that the territorial sea of the United States extends 12 nautical miles from the shores of the country.

SYMBOLS of the United States

THE MOTTO

The U.S. motto, "In God We Trust," was originally put on coins during the Civil War (1861-1865). Its use disappeared and reappeared on various coins until 1955, when Congress ordered it placed on all paper money and coins.

THE GREAT SEAL OF THE U.S.

The Great Seal of the U.S. shows an American bald eagle with a ribbon in its mouth bearing the Latin words "e pluribus unum" (one out of many). In its talons are the arrows of war and an olive branch of peace. On the back of the Great Seal is an unfinished pyramid with an eye (the eye of Providence) above it. The seal was approved by Congress on June 20, 1782.

THE FLAG

The flag of the United States has 50 stars (one for each state) and 13 stripes (one for each of the original 13 states). It is called unofficially the "Stars and Stripes." The first U.S. flag was commissioned by the Second Continental Congress in 1777 but did not exist until 1783, after the American Revolution. Historians are not certain who designed the Stars and Stripes. Many different flags are believed to have been used during the American Revolution.

The flag of 1777 was used until 1795. In that year President George Washington ordered that a new flag have 15 stripes, alternate red and white, and 15 stars on a blue field. In 1818, Congress directed that the flag have 13 stripes and that a new star be added for each new state of the Union. The last star was added in 1960 for the state of Hawaii.

| 1777 | 1795 | 1818 |

PLEDGE OF ALLEGIANCE TO THE FLAG

"I pledge allegiance to the flag of the United States of America and to the republic for which it stands, one nation under God, indivisible, with liberty and justice for all."

NATIONAL ANTHEM: THE STAR-SPANGLED BANNER

The Star-Spangled Banner was a poem written in 1814 by Francis Scott Key as he watched British ships bombard Fort McHenry, Maryland, during the War of 1812. It became the National Anthem of the United States by an act of Congress in 1931. Although it has four stanzas, the one most commonly sung is the first stanza. The music to the Star-Spangled Banner was originally a tune called "Anacreon in Heaven."

The U.S. GOVERNMENT And How It Works

THE U.S. CONSTITUTION: The Foundation of American Government

The Constitution is the document that created the present government of the United States. It was written in 1787 and went into effect in 1789. The Constitution establishes the three branches of the U.S. government, which are the executive (headed by the president), the legislative (the Congress), and the judicial (the Supreme Court and other federal courts). The first 10 amendments to the Constitution (the Bill of Rights) explain the basic rights of all American citizens.

The Preamble to the Constitution

The Constitution begins with a short statement called the **Preamble.** The Preamble states that the government of the United States was established by the people.

> "We, the people of the United States, in order to form a more perfect Union, establish justice, insure domestic tranquility, provide for the common defense, promote the general welfare, and secure the blessings of liberty to ourselves and our posterity do ordain and establish this Constitution for the United States of America."

The Articles

The original Constitution contained seven articles. The first three articles of the Constitution establish the three branches of the U.S. government.

Legislative Branch
ARTICLE 1 creates the Senate and House of Representatives and describes their functions and powers.

Executive Branch
ARTICLE 2 creates the Office of the President and the Electoral College and lists their powers and responsibilities.

Judicial Branch
ARTICLE 3 creates the Supreme Court and gives Congress power to create lower courts. The powers of the courts and certain crimes are defined.

The States
ARTICLE 4 discusses relationship of states to each other and to citizens. Defines powers.

Amending the Constitution
ARTICLE 5 describes how the Constitution may be amended (changed).

Federal Law
ARTICLE 6 makes the Constitution the supreme law of the land over state laws and constitutions.

Ratifying the Constitution
ARTICLE 7 establishes how to ratify (approve) the Constitution.

AMENDMENTS TO THE CONSTITUTION

The creators of the Constitution understood that the Constitution might need to be amended, or changed, in the future. Article 5 describes how the Constitution may be amended. In order to pass, an amendment must be approved by a two-thirds majority in the House of Representatives and a two-thirds majority in the Senate. An amendment must then be approved by three fourths of the states (38 states). Between 1791 and 1994 the Constitution was amended 27 times.

The Bill of Rights: The First 10 Amendments

The first ten amendments were adopted in 1791 and contain the basic freedoms Americans enjoy as a people. These amendments are known as the Bill of Rights. They are summarized below.

1. Guarantees freedom of religion, speech, and the press
2. Guarantees the right of the people to have firearms
3. Guarantees that soldiers cannot be lodged in private homes except with consent of the owner
4. Protects citizens against being searched or having their property searched or taken away by the government without a good reason
5. Protects rights of people on trial for crimes
6. Guarantees people accused of crimes the right to a speedy public trial by jury
7. Guarantees people the right to a trial by jury for other kinds of cases
8. Prohibits cruel and unusual punishments
9. States that specific rights listed in Constitution do not take away rights that may not be listed
10. Establishes that powers not granted specifically to the federal government are reserved for state governments or the people

Other Important Amendments

 13 (1865): Abolishes slavery in the United States

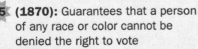 **14 (1868):** Establishes the Bill of Rights as protection against actions by a state government; guarantees equal protection under the law for all citizens

15 (1870): Guarantees that a person of any race or color cannot be denied the right to vote

19 (1920): Grants women the right to vote

22 (1951): Limits the president to two four-year terms of office

24 (1964): Outlaws the poll tax (a tax people had to pay before they could vote) in federal elections. (The poll tax had been used to keep African-Americans in the South from voting.)

25 (1967): Grants the president the power to appoint a new vice president, with the approval of Congress, if a vice president dies or leaves office in the middle of a term

26 (1971): Lowers the voting age to eighteen

The Executive Branch:
The PRESIDENT and the CABINET

The executive branch of the federal government is headed by the president of the United States. It also consists of the vice president, people who work for the president or vice president, the major departments of the government, and many special agencies. The president's cabinet is made up of the vice president, the heads of the major departments of the government, and a few other important people in the government. The cabinet meets when the president asks for its advice. As head of the executive branch of government, the president is responsible for enforcing the laws passed by Congress. The president is also commander in chief of all U.S. armed forces. The chart below shows the organization of the executive branch.

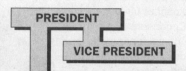

PRESIDENT

VICE PRESIDENT

CABINET DEPARTMENTS

State	Interior	Health and	Transportation
Treasury	Agriculture	Human Services	Energy
Defense	Commerce	Housing and Urban	Education
Justice	Labor	Development	Veterans Affairs

The Presidential Oath of Office The president is sworn into office on January 20, for a four-year term. At the inauguration, the president repeats the following oath of office as directed in the Constitution:

"I do solemnly swear (affirm) that I will faithfully execute the office of President of the United States, and will, to the best of my ability, preserve, protect, and defend the Constitution of the United States."

What Happens If the President Dies? If the president dies in office or cannot complete the term, Article 2 of the Constitution says that the vice president becomes president. If the president is disabled but still alive, the vice president can become acting president until the president is able to work again. The next person to become president after the vice president would be the Speaker of the House of Representatives.

The Judicial Branch:
The SUPREME COURT

The highest court in the United States is the **Supreme Court.** It consists of nine justices who are appointed for life by the president with the approval of the Senate. Eight of the nine members are called associate justices. The ninth is the chief justice, who presides over the Court's meetings.

What Does the Supreme Court Do? The Supreme Court's major responsibilities are to review federal laws, actions of the president, treaties of the United States, and laws passed by state governments to be sure that they do not conflict in any way with the U.S. Constitution. The Supreme Court carries out these responsibilities by deciding cases that come before it. This process is known as **judicial review.** If the Supreme Court finds that a law or action violates the Constitution, the justices declare it **unconstitutional.**

The Supreme Court's Decision Is Final. Most cases must go through other federal courts or state courts before they go to the Supreme Court. The Supreme Court is the final court for a case, and the justices usually decide which cases they will review. After the Supreme Court hears a case, it may agree or disagree with the decision by an earlier court. When the Supreme Court makes a ruling, its decision is final, and all people involved in the case must abide by it.

Who Is on the Supreme Court Now? Below are the nine justices who now sit on the Supreme Court.

Back row (from left to right): Ruth Bader Ginsburg, David H. Souter, Clarence Thomas, Stephen Breyer.
Front row (from left to right): Antonin Scalia, John Paul Stevens, Chief Justice William H. Rehnquist, Sandra Day O'Connor, Anthony M. Kennedy.

 DID YOU KNOW? In 1967, Thurgood Marshall became the first African-American to serve on the Supreme Court. In 1981, Sandra Day O'Connor became the first woman to serve on the Court.

The Legislative Branch: CONGRESS

The Congress of the United States is the legislative branch of the federal government. Congress's major responsibility is to pass the laws that govern the country. It is the president's responsibility to enforce them. Congress consists of two parts—the Senate and the House of Representatives. They are known as the houses of Congress.

THE SENATE

The Senate has 100 members, two from each state. Senators are elected for six-year terms. The framers (writers) of the Constitution created the Senate so that one house of Congress could provide equal representation for each state, whether the state is large or small. Thus, the state with the greatest population (California) has two senators as does the state with the smallest population (Wyoming).

In addition to passing laws, the Senate has the responsibility of approving people the president appoints for certain jobs, for example, cabinet members and Supreme Court justices. It also has the responsibility under the Constitution of trying federal officials who have been impeached (see box below) by the House of Representatives.

THE HOUSE OF REPRESENTATIVES

The House of Representatives has 435 members. The number of representatives a state has is determined by the state's population, so California has many more representatives than Wyoming. Each state is entitled to at least one representative— no matter how small its population. The first House of Representatives in 1789 had 65 members. As the country's population grew, the number of representatives increased. The total membership has been fixed at 435 since the 1910 census.

What Impeachment Means

A president, vice president, and other high-ranking officials of the United States (for example, federal judges) can be formally charged by the House of Representatives and removed from office for committing treason, bribery, or other serious crimes. Under the Constitution, the House of Representatives has the sole authority to impeach federal officials accused of crimes. "Impeachment" means that the House of Representatives formally charges a federal official with committing a crime. Once an official has been impeached (charged with a crime), he or she must be tried by the Senate. If the Senate finds the official guilty of the charges, he or she is then removed from office.

In 1868, the House impeached President Andrew Johnson, but he was acquitted (found not guilty) after a trial in the Senate. In 1974, a House committee recommended that the House of Representatives impeach President Richard Nixon, but before a vote was taken, President Nixon resigned.

The House of Representatives— STATE BY STATE

Each state has the following number of representatives in the House:

Alabama 7	Minnesota..............8	Texas.....................30
Alaska 1	Mississippi 5	Utah 3
Arizona 6	Missouri 9	Vermont...................1
Arkansas 4	Montana 1	Virginia 11
California 52	Nebraska 3	Washington 9
Colorado 6	Nevada 2	West Virginia 3
Connecticut.............6	New Hampshire 2	Wisconsin 9
Delaware 1	New Jersey.............13	Wyoming..................1
Florida 23	New Mexico 3	
Georgia..................11	New York..............31	
Hawaii 2	North Carolina........12	
Idaho.....................2	North Dakota 1	
Illinois 20	Ohio 19	
Indiana 10	Oklahoma 6	
Iowa 5	Oregon 5	
Kansas 4	Pennsylvania 21	
Kentucky..................6	Rhode Island...........2	
Louisiana.................7	South Carolina 6	
Maine 2	South Dakota...........1	
Maryland 8	Tennessee 9	
Massachusetts 10		
Michigan 16		

The District of Columbia (Washington, D.C.) has one nonvoting member of the House of Representatives.

How CONGRESS Makes LAWS

1. Senators and Representatives Propose a Bill.

A proposed law is called a bill. Any member of Congress may propose (introduce) a bill. A bill is introduced in each house of Congress. The House of Representatives and the Senate consider a bill separately. A member of Congress who introduces a bill is known as the bill's *sponsor*.

2. House and Senate Committees Consider the Bill.

The bill is then sent to appropriate committees for consideration. A committee is made up of a small number of members of the House or Senate. A bill relating to agriculture, for example, would be sent to the agriculture committees in the House and in the Senate. When committees are considering a bill, they hold hearings at which people can speak for or against the bill.

3. Committees Change the Bill.

The committees then consider the bill and change it as they see fit. They vote on the bill.

5. From the House and Senate to Conference Committee.

If the House and the Senate pass different versions of the same bill, the bill must then go to a "conference committee," where differences between the two versions must be worked out. A conference committee is a special committee made up of Senate and House members who meet to resolve the differences in versions of the same bill.

4. The Bill Is Debated in the House and Senate.

If the committees vote in favor of the bill, it goes to the full House and Senate, where it is debated and changed further. The House and Senate then vote on the bill.

8. What If the President Doesn't Sign the Bill?

Sometimes the president disapproves of the bill and refuses to sign it. This is called vetoing the bill. A bill that has been vetoed goes back to Congress, where the members can vote on it again. If the House and the Senate pass the bill again with a two-thirds majority vote, the bill becomes law. This is called overriding the president's veto.

6. Final Vote in the House and Senate.

The conference committee version is then voted on by the House and the Senate. In order for a bill to become a law, it must be approved in exactly the same form by a majority of members of both houses of Congress and signed by the president.

7. The President Signs the Bill Into Law.

If the bill passes both houses of Congress, it then goes to the president for his signature. Once the president signs a bill, it becomes law.

Major GOVERNMENT AGENCIES

Government agencies have a variety of functions. Some set rules and regulations or enforce laws. Others investigate or gather information. Some major agencies are listed below:

Central Intelligence Agency (CIA)

Gathers secret information on other countries and their leaders.

Commission on Civil Rights

Makes sure that the laws that protect people against discrimination are obeyed.

Consumer Product Safety Commission

Examines the products that people buy to be sure they are safe.

Environmental Protection Agency (EPA)

Enforces laws on clean air and water and is responsible for cleaning up hazardous waste sites.

Equal Employment Opportunity Commission (EEOC)

Makes sure that people are not discriminated against when they apply for a job and when they are at work.

Federal Communications Commission (FCC)

Issues licenses to radio and TV stations and makes broadcasting rules.

Federal Emergency Management Agency (FEMA)

Helps local communities recover from disasters such as hurricanes, earthquakes, and floods.

Federal Trade Commission (FTC)

Makes sure that businesses operate fairly and that they obey the law.

Library of Congress

The main library of the United States, collects most of the books published in the United States. It also has many historic documents and photographs.

National Archives and Records Administration

Stores major historic records of U.S. government.

National Foundation on the Arts and the Humanities

Gives government money to museums and artists.

Occupational Safety and Health Administration (OSHA)

Makes sure that places where people work are safe and will not harm their health.

Peace Corps

Sends American volunteers to foreign countries for two years to help with special projects such as teaching and farming.

Securities and Exchange Commission (SEC)

Makes sure that the stock market operates fairly and obeys the laws.

ELECTIONS: Electing the PRESIDENT and VICE PRESIDENT

You may be amazed to learn that the president and vice president of the United States are not really elected in November on Election Day. They are actually elected one month later, in December, by 538 people called the Electoral College.

WHAT IS THE ELECTORAL COLLEGE?

The system for electing presidents was established by the U.S. Constitution in 1789. Each state must choose a group of "electors," equal to the total number of Senators and Representatives the state sends to Congress. For example, the state of Missouri has 9 Representatives and 2 Senators and thus has 11 electors. The District of Columbia has 3 electors. Electors from the 50 states and the District of Columbia are called the Electoral College. Actually, they are not a college at all, but are a group of people (usually members of political parties) who officially elect the president and vice president.

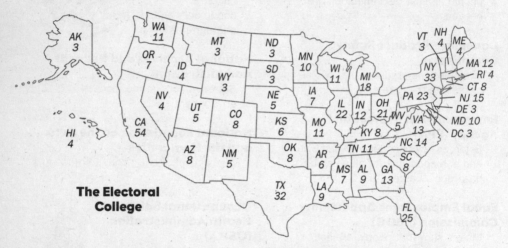

The Electoral College

HOW ARE THE PRESIDENT AND VICE PRESIDENT ELECTED?

Every four years on Election Day, in November, the names of the candidates for president and vice president appear on the voting machine or ballot, and voters select the people they prefer. Although the voter usually cannot see the names of the electors on the voting machine, when he or she pulls the lever for the president, the voter is really voting for a group of electors who have promised to support (are "pledged to") the voter's presidential candidate.

When the election polls close, each state then counts the votes cast for each presidential and vice presidential candidate. The electors in the Electoral College who are pledged to the candidate with the most votes in each state meet in their home state in December and officially cast their ballots for president and vice president. To be elected, a candidate must receive a majority of the Electoral College votes, or 270 votes. The results are announced in Congress the following January. If no candidate receives 270 electoral votes, the election goes to the House of Representatives, where the president is selected from the top three candidates.

How to VOTE:
Using a VOTING MACHINE

Although some people in the United States still vote on paper ballots, most people now vote on voting machines. There are different kinds of voting machines, but they all work in the same basic way. When the voter goes into the voting booth, he or she pulls a master lever that locks the machine. The voter sees the names of the candidates from different political parties and pulls a small lever next to the candidate the voter chooses for each office. The votes are then recorded in the machine when the voter pulls the master lever back into its original position.

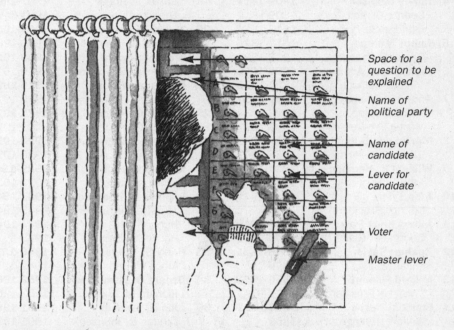

Space for a question to be explained

Name of political party

Name of candidate

Lever for candidate

Voter

Master lever

THE 1992 PRESIDENTIAL ELECTION

In the 1992 election, none of the Electoral College votes went to the independent candidate, Ross Perot. Even though he received nearly one-fifth of the total popular vote, he didn't win the most votes in any states and so did not win any electoral votes.

Election Year and Candidates	Popular Vote	Electoral Vote
1992 Bill Clinton (Democrat)	44,908,254	370
George Bush (Republican)	39,102,343	168
H. Ross Perot (Independent)	19,741,065	0

DID YOU KNOW? In the 1888 presidential election, Grover Cleveland received more popular votes than Benjamin Harrison. Cleveland received 5,540,050 votes, and Harrison received 5,444,337. But Harrison received 233 electoral votes (to 168 for Cleveland), and thus Benjamin Harrison became president.

PRESIDENTS and VICE PRESIDENTS
of the UNITED STATES

PRESIDENT / VICE PRESIDENT	TERM	PRESIDENT / VICE PRESIDENT	TERM
1 **George Washington**	**1789-1797**	22 **Grover Cleveland**	**1885-1889**
John Adams	1789-1797	Thomas A. Hendricks	1885
2 **John Adams**	**1797-1801**	23 **Benjamin Harrison**	**1889-1893**
Thomas Jefferson	1797-1801	Levi P. Morton	1889-1893
3 **Thomas Jefferson**	**1801-1809**	24 **Grover Cleveland**	**1893-1897**
Aaron Burr	1801-1805	Adlai E. Stevenson	1893-1897
George Clinton	1805-1809	25 **William McKinley**	**1897-1901**
4 **James Madison**	**1809-1817**	Garret A. Hobart	1897-1899
George Clinton	1809-1812	Theodore Roosevelt	1901
Elbridge Gerry	1813-1814	26 **Theodore Roosevelt**	**1901-1909**
5 **James Monroe**	**1817-1825**	Charles W. Fairbanks	1905-1909
Daniel D. Tompkins	1817-1825	27 **William Howard Taft**	**1909-1913**
6 **John Quincy Adams**	**1825-1829**	James S. Sherman	1909-1912
John C. Calhoun	1825-1829	28 **Woodrow Wilson**	**1913-1921**
7 **Andrew Jackson**	**1829-1837**	Thomas R. Marshall	1913-1921
John C. Calhoun	1829-1832	29 **Warren G. Harding**	**1921-1923**
Martin Van Buren	1833-1837	Calvin Coolidge	1921-1923
8 **Martin Van Buren**	**1837-1841**	30 **Calvin Coolidge**	**1923-1929**
Richard M. Johnson	1837-1841	Charles G. Dawes	1925-1929
9 **William H. Harrison**	**1841**	31 **Herbert Hoover**	**1929-1933**
John Tyler	1841	Charles Curtis	1929-1933
10 **John Tyler**	**1841-1845**	32 **Franklin D. Roosevelt**	**1933-1945**
No Vice President		John Nance Garner	1933-1941
11 **James Knox Polk**	**1845-1849**	Henry A. Wallace	1941-1945
George M. Dallas	1845-1849	Harry S. Truman	1945
12 **Zachary Taylor**	**1849-1850**	33 **Harry S. Truman**	**1945-1953**
Millard Fillmore	1849-1850	Alben W. Barkley	1949-1953
13 **Millard Fillmore**	**1850-1853**	34 **Dwight D. Eisenhower**	**1953-1961**
No Vice President		Richard M. Nixon	1953-1961
14 **Franklin Pierce**	**1853-1857**	35 **John F. Kennedy**	**1961-1963**
William R. King	1853	Lyndon B. Johnson	1961-1963
15 **James Buchanan**	**1857-1861**	36 **Lyndon B. Johnson**	**1963-1969**
John C. Breckinridge	1857-1861	Hubert H. Humphrey	1965-1969
16 **Abraham Lincoln**	**1861-1865**	37 **Richard M. Nixon**	**1969-1974**
Hannibal Hamlin	1861-1865	Spiro T. Agnew	1969-1973
Andrew Johnson	1865	Gerald R. Ford	1973-1974
17 **Andrew Johnson**	**1865-1869**	38 **Gerald R. Ford**	**1974-1977**
No Vice President		Nelson A. Rockefeller	1974-1977
18 **Ulysses S. Grant**	**1869-1877**	39 **Jimmy Carter**	**1977-1981**
Schuyler Colfax	1869-1873	Walter F. Mondale	1977-1981
Henry Wilson	1873-1875	40 **Ronald Reagan**	**1981-1989**
19 **Rutherford B. Hayes**	**1877-1881**	George Bush	1981-1989
William A. Wheeler	1877-1881	41 **George Bush**	**1989-1993**
20 **James A. Garfield**	**1881**	Dan Quayle	1989-1993
Chester A. Arthur	1881	42 **Bill Clinton**	**1993-**
21 **Chester A. Arthur**	**1881-1885**	Al Gore	1993-
No Vice President			

PRESIDENTS of the United States and their FAMILIES

1. GEORGE WASHINGTON (1789-1797)
Political Party: Federalist
Born: Feb. 22, 1732, at Wakefield, Westmoreland County, Virginia
Married: Martha Dandridge Custis (1732-1802); no children
Died: Dec. 14, 1799; buried at Mount Vernon, Fairfax County, Virginia
Early Career: Soldier; head of the Virginia militia; commander in chief of the Continental Army; chairman of Constitutional Convention (1787)

2. JOHN ADAMS (1797-1801)
Political Party: Federalist
Born: Oct. 30, 1735, in Quincy, Massachusetts
Married: Abigail Smith (1744-1818); 3 sons, 2 daughters
Died: July 4, 1826; buried in Quincy, Massachusetts
Early Career: Lawyer; delegate to Continental Congress; signer of the Declaration of Independence; first vice president

3. THOMAS JEFFERSON (1801-1809)
Political Party: Democratic-Republican
Born: Apr. 13, 1743, at Shadwell, Albemarle County, Virginia
Married: Martha Wayles Skelton (1748-1782); 1 son, 5 daughters
Died: July 4, 1826; buried at Monticello, Albemarle County, Virginia
Early Career: Lawyer; member of the Continental Congress; author of the Declaration of Independence; governor of Virginia; first secretary of state; author of the Virginia Statute on Religious Freedom

4. JAMES MADISON (1809-1817)
Political Party: Democratic-Republican
Born: Mar. 16, 1751, at Port Conway, King George County, Virginia
Married: Dorothea "Dolley" Payne Todd (1768-1849); no children
Died: June 28, 1836; buried at Montpelier, Orange County, Virginia
Early Career: Member of the Virginia Constitutional Convention (1776); member of the Continental Congress; major contributor to the U.S. Constitution; writer of the Federalist Papers; secretary of state

5. JAMES MONROE (1817-1825)
Political Party: Democratic-Republican
Born: Apr. 28, 1758, in Westmoreland County, Virginia
Married: Elizabeth Kortright (1768-1830); 2 daughters
Died: July 4, 1831; buried in Richmond, Virginia
Early Career: Soldier; lawyer; U.S. senator; governor of Virginia; secretary of state

6. JOHN QUINCY ADAMS (1825-1829)
Political Party: Democratic-Republican
Born: July 11, 1767, in Quincy, Massachusetts
Married: Louisa Catherine Johnson (1775-1852); 3 sons, 1 daughter
Died: Feb. 23, 1848; buried in Quincy, Massachusetts
Early Career: Diplomat; U.S. senator; secretary of state

7. ANDREW JACKSON (1829-1837)
Political Party: Democratic
Born: Mar. 15, 1767, in New Lancaster County, South Carolina
Married: Rachel Donelson Robards (1767-1828); no children
Died: June 8, 1845; buried in Nashville, Tennessee
Early Career: Lawyer; U.S. representative and senator; Indian fighter; general in the U.S. Army

8. MARTIN VAN BUREN (1837-1841)
Political Party: Democratic
Born: Dec. 5, 1782, at Kinderhook, New York
Married: Hannah Hoes (1783-1819); 4 sons
Died: July 24, 1862; buried at Kinderhook, New York
Early Career: Governor of New York; secretary of state; vice president

9. WILLIAM HENRY HARRISON (1841)
Political Party: Whig
Born: Feb. 9, 1773, at Berkeley, Charles City County, Virginia
Married: Anna Symmes (1775-1864); 6 sons, 4 daughters
Died: Apr. 4, 1841; buried in North Bend, Ohio
Early Career: First governor of Indiana Territory; superintendent of Indian affairs; U.S. representative and senator

10. JOHN TYLER (1841-1845)
Political Party: Whig
Born: Mar. 29, 1790, in Greenway, Charles City County, Virginia
Married: Letitia Christian (1790-1842); 3 sons, 5 daughters
Julia Gardiner (1820-1889); 5 sons, 2 daughters
Died: Jan. 18, 1862; buried in Richmond, Virginia
Early Career: U.S. representative and senator; vice president

11. JAMES KNOX POLK (1845-1849)
Political Party: Democratic
Born: Nov. 2, 1795, in Mecklenburg County, North Carolina
Married: Sarah Childress (1803-1891); no children
Died: June 15, 1849; buried in Nashville, Tennessee
Early Career: U.S. representative; Speaker of the House; governor of Tennessee

12. ZACHARY TAYLOR (1849-1850)
Political Party: Whig
Born: Nov. 24, 1784, in Orange County, Virginia
Married: Margaret Smith (1788-1852); 1 son, 5 daughters
Died: July 9, 1850; buried in Louisville, Kentucky
Early Career: Indian fighter; general in the U.S. Army

13. MILLARD FILLMORE (1850-1853)
Political Party: Whig
Born: Jan 7, 1800, in Cayuga County, New York
Married: Abigail Powers (1798-1853); 1 son, 1 daughter
Caroline Carmichael McIntosh (1813-1881); no children
Died: Mar. 8, 1874; buried in Buffalo, N.Y.
Early Career: Teacher; lawyer; U.S. representative; vice president

14. FRANKLIN PIERCE (1853-1857)
Political Party: Democratic
Born: Nov. 23, 1804, in Hillsboro, New Hampshire
Married: Jane Means Appleton (1806-1863); 3 sons
Died: Oct. 8, 1869, in Concord, New Hampshire
Early Career: U.S. representative, senator

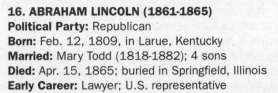

15. JAMES BUCHANAN (1857-1861)
Political Party: Democratic
Born: Apr. 23, 1791, near Mercersburg, Pennsylvania
Never Married
Died: June 1, 1868, in Lancaster, Pennsylvania
Early Career: U.S. representative; secretary of state

16. ABRAHAM LINCOLN (1861-1865)
Political Party: Republican
Born: Feb. 12, 1809, in Larue, Kentucky
Married: Mary Todd (1818-1882); 4 sons
Died: Apr. 15, 1865; buried in Springfield, Illinois
Early Career: Lawyer; U.S. representative

17. ANDREW JOHNSON (1865-1869)
Political Party: Republican
Born: Dec. 29, 1808, in Raleigh, North Carolina
Married: Eliza McCardle (1810-1876); 3 sons, 2 daughters
Died: July 31, 1875; buried in Greeneville, Tennessee
Early Career: State representative and senator; U.S. representative; governor of Tennessee; U.S. senator; vice president

18. ULYSSES S. GRANT (1869-1877)
Political Party: Republican
Born: Apr. 27, 1822, in Point Pleasant, Ohio
Married: Julia Dent (1826-1902); 3 sons, 1 daughter
Died: July 23, 1885; buried in New York City
Early Career: Army officer; commander of Union forces during Civil War

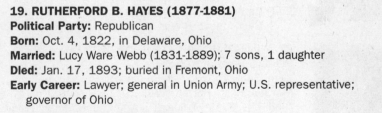

19. RUTHERFORD B. HAYES (1877-1881)
Political Party: Republican
Born: Oct. 4, 1822, in Delaware, Ohio
Married: Lucy Ware Webb (1831-1889); 7 sons, 1 daughter
Died: Jan. 17, 1893; buried in Fremont, Ohio
Early Career: Lawyer; general in Union Army; U.S. representative; governor of Ohio

20. JAMES A. GARFIELD (1881)
Political Party: Republican
Born: Nov. 19, 1831, in Orange, Cuyahoga County, Ohio
Married: Lucretia Rudolph (1832-1918); 4 sons, 1 daughter
Died: Sept. 19, 1881; buried in Cleveland, Ohio
Early Career: Teacher; Ohio state senator; general in Union Army; U.S. representative

21. CHESTER A. ARTHUR (1881-1885)
Political Party: Republican
Born: Oct. 5, 1830, in Fairfield, Vermont
Married: Ellen Lewis Herndon (1837-1880); 2 sons, 1 daughter
Died: Nov. 18, 1886; buried in Albany, New York
Early Career: Lawyer; vice president

22. GROVER CLEVELAND (1885-1889)
Political Party: Democratic
Born: Mar. 18, 1837, in Caldwell, New Jersey
Married: Frances Folsom (1864-1947); 2 sons, 3 daughters
Died: June 24, 1908; buried in Princeton, New Jersey
Early Career: Lawyer; mayor of Buffalo; governor of New York

23. BENJAMIN HARRISON (1889-1893)
Political Party: Republican
Born: Aug. 20, 1833, in North Bend, Ohio
Married: Caroline Lavinia Scott (1832-1892); 1 son, 1 daughter
Died: Mar. 13, 1901; buried in Indianapolis, Indiana
Early Career: Lawyer; general in Union Army; U.S. senator

24. GROVER CLEVELAND (1893-1897) See 22. above.

25. WILLIAM MCKINLEY (1897-1901)
Political Party: Republican
Born: Jan. 29, 1843, in Niles, Ohio
Married: Ida Saxton (1847-1907); 2 daughters
Died: Sept. 14, 1901; buried in Canton, Ohio
Early Career: Lawyer; U.S. representative; governor of Ohio

26. THEODORE ROOSEVELT (1901-1909)
Political Party: Republican
Born: Oct. 27, 1858, in New York City
Married: Anna Hathaway Lee (1861-1884); 1 daughter
　　　　　　 Edith Kermit Carow (1861-1948); 4 sons, 1 daughter
Died: Jan. 6, 1919; buried in Oyster Bay, New York
Early Career: Assistant secretary of the navy; cavalry leader in
　 Spanish-American War; governor of New York; vice president

27. WILLIAM HOWARD TAFT (1909-1913)
Political Party: Republican
Born: Sept. 15, 1857, in Cincinnati, Ohio
Married: Helen Herron (1861-1943); 2 sons, 1 daughter
Died: Mar. 8, 1930; buried in Arlington National Cemetery, Virginia
Early Career: Lawyer; judge; secretary of war

28. WOODROW WILSON (1913-1921)
Political Party: Democratic
Born: Dec. 28, 1856, in Staunton, Virginia
Married: Ellen Louise Axson (1860-1914); 3 daughters
　　　　　　 Edith Bolling Galt (1872-1961); no children
Died: Feb. 3, 1924; buried in Washington, D.C.
Early Career: Lawyer; college professor; governor of New Jersey

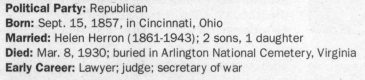

29. WARREN G. HARDING (1921-1923)
Political Party: Republican
Born: Nov. 2, 1865, near Blooming Grove, Ohio
Married: Florence Kling De Wolfe (1860-1924); no children
Died: Aug. 2, 1923; buried in Marion, Ohio
Early Career: Ohio state senator; U.S. senator

30. CALVIN COOLIDGE (1923-1929)
Political Party: Republican
Born: July 4, 1872, in Plymouth, Vermont
Married: Grace Anna Goodhue (1879-1957); 2 sons
Died: Jan. 5, 1933; buried in Plymouth, Vermont
Early Career: Massachusetts state senator, lieutenant governor, and governor; vice president

31. HERBERT HOOVER (1929-1933)
Political Party: Republican
Born: Aug. 10, 1874, in West Branch, Iowa
Married: Lou Henry (1875-1944); 2 sons
Died: Oct. 20, 1964; buried West Branch, Iowa
Early Career: Mining engineer; secretary of commerce

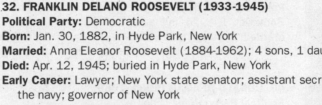

32. FRANKLIN DELANO ROOSEVELT (1933-1945)
Political Party: Democratic
Born: Jan. 30, 1882, in Hyde Park, New York
Married: Anna Eleanor Roosevelt (1884-1962); 4 sons, 1 daughter
Died: Apr. 12, 1945; buried in Hyde Park, New York
Early Career: Lawyer; New York state senator; assistant secretary of the navy; governor of New York

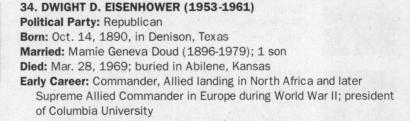

33. HARRY S. TRUMAN (1945-1953)
Political Party: Democratic
Born: May 8, 1884, in Lamar, Missouri
Married: Bess Wallace (1885-1982); 1 daughter
Died: Dec. 26, 1972; buried in Independence, Missouri
Early Career: Haberdasher (ran men's clothing store); judge; U.S. senator; vice president

34. DWIGHT D. EISENHOWER (1953-1961)
Political Party: Republican
Born: Oct. 14, 1890, in Denison, Texas
Married: Mamie Geneva Doud (1896-1979); 1 son
Died: Mar. 28, 1969; buried in Abilene, Kansas
Early Career: Commander, Allied landing in North Africa and later Supreme Allied Commander in Europe during World War II; president of Columbia University

35. JOHN FITZGERALD KENNEDY (1961-1963)
Political Party: Democratic
Born: May 29, 1917, in Brookline, Massachusetts
Married: Jacqueline Lee Bouvier (1929-1994); 1 son, 1 daughter
Died: Nov. 22, 1963; buried in Arlington National Cemetery, Virginia
Early Career: U.S. naval commander; U.S. representative and senator

36. LYNDON BAINES JOHNSON (1963-1969)
Political Party: Democratic
Born: Aug. 27, 1908, in Stonewall, Texas
Married: Claudia "Lady Bird" Alta Taylor (b. 1912); 2 daughters
Died: Jan. 22, 1973; buried in Stonewall, Texas
Early Career: U.S. representative and senator; vice president

37. RICHARD MILHOUS NIXON (1969-1974)
Political Party: Republican
Born: Jan. 9, 1913, in Yorba Linda, California
Married: Thelma Catherine Patricia Ryan (1912-1993); 2 daughters
Died: Apr. 22, 1994; buried in Yorba Linda, California
Early Career: Lawyer; U.S. representative and senator; vice president

38. GERALD R. FORD (1974-1977)
Political Party: Republican
Born: July 14, 1913, in Omaha, Nebraska
Married: Elizabeth Bloomer Warren (b. 1918);
      3 sons, 1 daughter
Early Career: Lawyer; U.S. representative; vice president

39. JIMMY (JAMES EARL) CARTER (1977-1981)
Political Party: Democratic
Born: Oct. 1, 1924, in Plains, Georgia
Married: Rosalynn Smith (b. 1927); 3 sons, 1 daughter
Early Career: Peanut farmer; Georgia state senator; governor
  of Georgia

40. RONALD REAGAN (1981-1989)
Political Party: Republican
Born: Feb. 6, 1911, in Tampico, Illinois
Married: Jane Wyman (b. 1914); 1 son, 1 daughter
      Anne Frances "Nancy" Robbins Davis (b. 1921);
      1 son, 1 daughter
Early Career: Film and television actor; governor of California

41. GEORGE BUSH (1989-1993)
Political Party: Republican
Born: June 12, 1924, in Milton, Massachusetts
Married: Barbara Pierce (b. 1925); 4 sons, 2 daughters
Early Career: U.S. navy pilot; businessman; U.S. representative; U.S.
  ambassador to the United Nations; vice president

42. BILL (WILLIAM JEFFERSON) CLINTON (1993-   )
Political Party: Democratic
Born: Aug. 19, 1946, in Hope, Arkansas
Married: Hillary Rodham (b. 1947); 1 daughter
Early Career: Arkansas state attorney general; governor of Arkansas

Presidential FACTS, FAMILIES, and FIRST LADIES

PRESIDENTIAL FACTS

Youngest president: Theodore Roosevelt, who was 42 when he was sworn in.

Oldest president: Ronald Reagan, who was 78 when he left office.

Only president to serve more than two terms: Franklin Delano Roosevelt

Only president to serve two terms that were not back to back: Grover Cleveland

Only president who was unmarried: James Buchanan. His niece acted as White House hostess for her uncle.

Presidents who died in office: Eight U.S. presidents have died while they served as president. Four of them were assassinated: Abraham Lincoln, James Garfield, William McKinley, and John F. Kennedy. The other four presidents who died in office were William Henry Harrison, Zachary Taylor, Warren G. Harding, and Franklin Delano Roosevelt.

FAMOUS FIRST FAMILIES

Adams family: John Adams was the 2nd president, and his son, John Quincy Adams, became the 6th president.

Harrison family: Benjamin Harrison, the 23rd president, was the great-grandson of Benjamin Harrison, a signer of the Declaration of Independence, and the grandson of William Henry Harrison, the 9th president of the United States.

Roosevelt family: Theodore Roosevelt was the 26th president and his 5th cousin, Franklin Delano Roosevelt, the 32nd. Franklin's wife, Eleanor Roosevelt, was also Theodore Roosevelt's niece.

FAMOUS FIRST LADIES

Martha Washington was the first First Lady. A wealthy widow when she married George Washington, she helped his position as a Virginia planter.

Abigail Adams, the wife of John Adams, was a thoughtful, outspoken woman. She wrote hundreds of letters in which she clearly expressed her opinions on the issues of the day.

Dolley Madison, James Madison's wife, was famous as a hostess and for saving a portrait of George Washington during the War of 1812, when the British were about to burn the White House.

Eleanor Roosevelt, wife of Franklin Delano Roosevelt, became a public figure herself after her husband became crippled by polio. She urged her husband to support civil rights and the rights of workers.

Jacqueline Kennedy, wife of John F. Kennedy, known for her elegance and style, restored the White House and made it a symbol the country could be proud of.

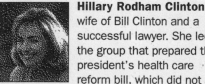

Hillary Rodham Clinton, wife of Bill Clinton and a successful lawyer. She led the group that prepared the president's health care reform bill, which did not come to a vote in Congress.

United States History Timeline

The First People in North America: Before 1492

40,000 B.C.-11,000 B.C.
First people (called Paleo-Indians) cross from Siberia to Alaska and begin to move into North America.

14,000 B.C.-11,000 B.C.
Paleo-Indians use stone points attached to spears to hunt big mammoths in northern parts of North America.

11,000 B.C.
Big mammoths disappear and Paleo-Indians begin to gather plants for food.

8000 B.C.-1000 B.C.
North American Indians begin using stone to grind food and to hunt bison and smaller animals.

1000 B.C.-A.D. 500
Woodland Indians, who lived east of the Mississippi River, bury people who have died under large burial mounds (which can still be seen today).

After A.D. 500
Anasazi peoples in the Southwestern United States live in homes on cliffs, called cliff dwellings. Anasazi pottery and dishes are well known for their beautiful patterns.

After A.D. 700
Mississippian Indian people in Southeastern United States develop farms and build burial mounds.

700-1492
Many different Indian cultures develop throughout North America.

Colonial America and the American Revolution: 1492-1783

1492
Christopher Columbus sails across the Atlantic Ocean and reaches an island in the Bahamas in the Caribbean Sea.

1513
Juan Ponce de León explores the Florida coast.

1524
Giovanni da Verrazano explores the coast from Carolina north to Nova Scotia, enters New York harbor.

1540
Francisco Vásquez de Coronado explores the southwestern United States north of the Rio Grande.

1565
St. Augustine, Florida, the first town established by Europeans in United States, is founded by the Spanish. Later burned by the English in 1586.

1607
Jamestown, Virginia, the first English settlement in North America, is founded by Captain John Smith.

1609
Henry Hudson sails into New York harbor and explores the Hudson River. Spaniards found Santa Fe, New Mexico.

1619
The first African slaves are brought to Jamestown. (Slavery is made legal in 1650.)

1620
Pilgrims from England arrive at Plymouth, Massachusetts, on the *Mayflower*.

1626
Peter Minuit buys Manhattan island for the Dutch from Man-a-hat-a Indians for $24. The island is renamed New Amsterdam.

1630
Boston is founded by Massachusetts colonists led by John Winthrop.

Benjamin Franklin (1706-1790) was a great American leader, printer, scientist, and writer. In 1732, he began publishing a magazine called *Poor Richard's Almanack*. Poor Richard was a make-believe person who gave advice about common sense and honesty. Many of Poor Richard's sayings are still known today. Among the most famous are "God helps them that help themselves" and "Early to bed, early to rise, makes a man healthy, wealthy, and wise."

Portion of The Declaration of Independence, July 4, 1776

"We hold these truths to be self-evident, that all men are created equal, that they are endowed by their Creator with certain unalienable rights, that among these are life, liberty, and the pursuit of happiness."

1634
Maryland is founded as a Catholic colony with religious freedom for all its settlers.

1664
The English seize New Amsterdam from the Dutch. The city is renamed New York.

1699
French settlers move into Mississippi and Louisiana.

1732
Benjamin Franklin begins publishing *Poor Richard's Almanack*.

1754-1763
French and Indian War between England and France. The French are defeated and lose their lands in Canada and the American Midwest.

1764-1767
England places taxes on sugar that comes from their North American colonies. England also requires colonists to purchase stamps to raise money to pay for the French and Indian War. Colonists protest and meet in the Stamp Act Congress.

1770
Boston Massacre: English troops fire on a group of people protesting English taxes.

1773
Boston Tea Party: English tea is thrown into the harbor to protest a tax on tea.

1775
Fighting at Lexington and Concord, Massachusetts, marks the beginning of the American Revolution.

1776
The Declaration of Independence is approved July 4 by the Continental Congress (made up of representatives from the American colonies).

1781
British General Cornwallis surrenders to the Americans at Yorktown, Virginia, ending the fighting in the Revolutionary War.

Who Attended the Convention?

The Constitutional Convention met in Philadelphia in the hot summer of 1787. Most of the great founders of America attended. Among those present were George Washington, James Madison, and John Adams. They met to form a new government that would be strong and, at the same time, protect the liberties that were fought for in the American Revolution. The Constitution they created is still the law of the United States.

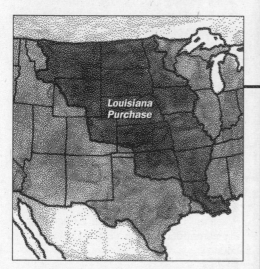

Louisiana Purchase

The New Nation: 1783-1900

1783

The Treaty of Paris ending the American Revolutionary War is signed by the United States and England. The English recognize U.S. independence.

1784

The first successful daily newspaper, the *Pennsylvania Packet & General Advertiser,* is published.

1787

The Constitutional Convention meets in Philadelphia to write a new Constitution for the United States.

1789

The new Constitution is approved by the states. George Washington is chosen as the first president of the United States.

1800

The federal government moves to a new capital, Washington, D.C.

1803

President Thomas Jefferson makes the Louisiana Purchase from France. Millions of square miles of territory are added to the United States.

1804

Lewis and Clark explore far into the northwestern United States.

1812-1814

War of 1812 with Great Britain: British forces burn the Capitol and White House. Francis Scott Key writes "The Star Spangled Banner."

1820

The Missouri Compromise in Congress bans slavery west of the Mississippi River and north of line 36°30' north latitude.

1823

The Monroe Doctrine (a statement by President Monroe) warns European countries not to interfere in North America.

1825

The Erie Canal opens in New York and links the east coast with the Midwest.

1831

The Liberator, a newspaper opposing slavery, is published in Boston.

"The Trail of Tears"

The Cherokee Indians living in Georgia were forced, by the state government of Georgia, to leave in 1838. They were sent to Oklahoma. On the long march, thousands died because of disease and the cold weather.

Uncle Tom's Cabin

Harriet Beecher Stowe's novel about the sufferings of slaves was an instant bestseller in the North and banned in most of the South. When President Abraham Lincoln met Stowe, he called her "the little lady who started this war" (the Civil War).

The Bloodiest War in U.S. History

The U.S. Civil War between the North and South lasted four years (1861-1865) and resulted in the deaths of more than 600,000 people—more than all other U.S. wars combined. Little was known at the time about the spread of diseases. As a result, many casualties were also the result of illnesses such as influenza, measles, and infections from battle wounds.

1836
Texans fighting for independence from Mexico are defeated by Mexican forces at the Alamo.

1838
Cherokee Indians are forced to move to Oklahoma, along "The Trail of Tears."

1844
The first telegraph line connects Washington and Baltimore.

1846-1848
U.S. war with Mexico: Mexico is defeated and the U.S. takes control of the Republic of Texas and of Mexican territories in the West.

1848
California "gold rush": The discovery of gold in California leads to a "rush" of more than 80,000 people to the West in search of gold.

1852
Uncle Tom's Cabin is published.

1858
Lincoln-Douglas debates during Senate campaign in Illinois: Abraham Lincoln and Stephen A. Douglas debate about slavery.

1860
Abraham Lincoln is elected president.

1861
The Civil War begins.

1863
President Lincoln issues the Emancipation Proclamation, freeing most slaves in the country.

1865
The Civil War ends as the South surrenders. Lincoln is assassinated.

1869
The first railroad connecting the east and west coasts is completed.

1878
The first telephone company begins operation.

1890
Battle of Wounded Knee is fought in South Dakota—the last major battle between Indians and U.S. troops.

1898
Spanish-American War: The U.S. defeats Spain and receives control of the Philippines and Puerto Rico.

The United States in the 20th Century

1903
The U.S. begins building the Panama Canal. The canal opens in 1914, connecting the Atlantic and Pacific oceans.

1908
Henry Ford introduces the Model T car, the first auto bought by thousands of people.

1916
The first woman—Jeanette Rankin of Montana—is elected to Congress.

1917-1918
The U.S. joins World War I on the side of the Allies against Germany.

1920
First licensed radio broadcast. Radio becomes extremely popular in 1920s.

1927
Charles A. Lindbergh becomes the first person to fly alone nonstop across the Atlantic Ocean.

1929
A stock market crash marks the beginning of the Great Depression.

1933
President Franklin D. Roosevelt's New Deal increases government help to people through programs such as Social Security.

1941
Japan attacks the U.S. navy base at Pearl Harbor, Hawaii. The U.S. enters World War II against Japan, Germany, and Italy.

1945
Germany and Japan surrender, ending World War II. Japan's surrender comes after the U.S. drops atomic bombs on Hiroshima and Nagasaki, Japan.

1950-1953
U.S. armed forces fight in the Korean War.

1954
The U.S. Supreme Court outlaws racial segregation in public schools.

1958
The first U.S. space satellite, *Explorer I,* goes into orbit.

1962
The U.S. forces the Soviet Union to pull its missiles out of Cuba (the Cuban missile crisis).

World War I
In World War I the United States fought with Great Britain, France, and Russia (the Allies) against Germany and Austria-Hungary. The Allies won the war in 1918.

The Great Depression
The stock market crash of October 1929 led to a period of severe hardship for the American people—the Great Depression. As many as 25 percent of all workers could not find jobs. The Depression lasted until the early 1940s. The Depression also led to a great change in politics. In 1932, Democrat Franklin D. Roosevelt was elected president. He served as president for 12 years, longer than any other president.

Watergate

In June 1972, six men were arrested in the Watergate building in Washington, D.C., for trying to bug the telephones in the offices of the Democratic Party. Some of the men worked for the committee to reelect President Nixon. In 1973, it was discovered that President Nixon had tape recorded his conversations in the Oval Office of the White House. One of the tapes revealed that Nixon knew about a plan to hide information about "Watergate." Facing impeachment, Nixon resigned the presidency.

1963
President John F. Kennedy is assassinated in Dallas, Texas.

1964
Congress passes the Civil Rights Act, which outlaws discrimination in voting and jobs.

1965
The U.S. sends large numbers of soldiers to fight in the Vietnam War.

1968
Civil rights leader Martin Luther King, Jr., assassinated in Memphis. Senator Robert F. Kennedy assassinated in Los Angeles.

1969
U.S. astronaut Neil Armstrong becomes first person to walk on the moon.

1973
U.S. participation in the Vietnam War ends.

1974
President Nixon resigns because of the Watergate scandal. He is the only U.S. president to resign from office.

1979
U.S. hostages are taken in Iran, beginning a 444-day crisis until their release in 1981.

1981
Sandra Day O'Connor becomes the first woman appointed to U.S. Supreme Court.

1985
U.S. President Ronald Reagan and Soviet leader Mikhail Gorbachev begin working together to improve relations between their countries.

1989
General Colin Powell becomes the first African-American to head the U.S. military forces.

1991
The Persian Gulf War in the Middle East: The U.S. and its allies force Iraq to withdraw its invading forces from neighboring Kuwait.

1993
Bill Clinton, a Democrat, is inaugurated as president of the United States. The Democratic Party controls both houses of Congress.

1994
The Republican Party wins majorities in both houses of Congress for the first time in 40 years.

1995
A government building in Oklahoma City is bombed. More than 165 people are killed.

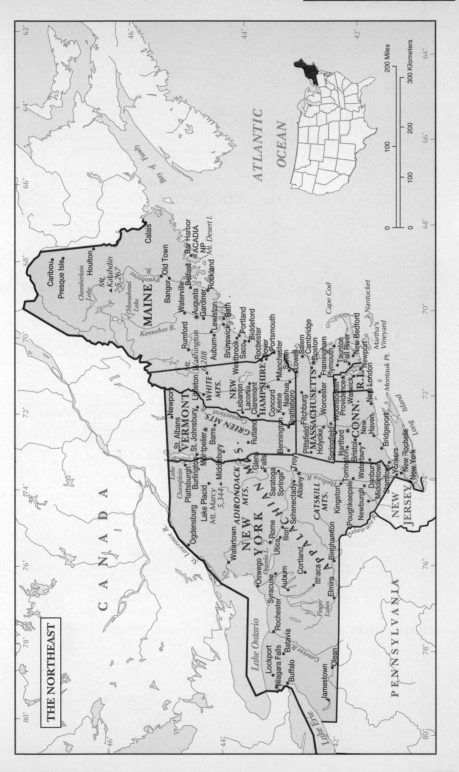

THE NORTHEAST

ATLANTIC OCEAN

CANADA

Bay of Fundy

Calais
Caribou
Presque Isle
Houlton
Mt. Katahdin 5,267
Chamberlain Lake
Moosehead Lake
Penobscot R.
Old Town
Bangor
Bar Harbor
ACADIA NP
Belfast
Mt. Desert I.
Rockland
Waterville
Augusta
Gardiner
MAINE
Kennebec R.
Rumford
Lewiston
Auburn
Brunswick
Bath
Portland
Saco
Biddeford
Westbrook
Rochester
Dover
Portsmouth
Mt. Washington 6,288
Littleton
WHITE MTS.
NEW HAMPSHIRE
Lebanon
Laconia
Concord
Manchester
Nashua
Lowell
Salem
Cambridge
Boston
Framingham
Cape Cod
Nantucket
Martha's Vineyard
Montauk Pt.
New Bedford
Taunton
Fall River
Plymouth
Worcester
Providence
Woonsocket
R.I.
Warwick
Newport
New London
CONN.
New Haven
Bridgeport
Long Island
Yonkers
New Rochelle
New York
NEW JERSEY
Delaware R.
Stamford
Danbury
Middletown
Waterbury
Bristol
Torrington
Hartford
Springfield
Holyoke
MASSACHUSETTS
Pittsfield
Fitchburg
Keene
Brattleboro
Claremont
Bennington
Rutland
Connecticut R.
GREEN MTS.
VERMONT
Newport
St. Albans
St. Johnsbury
Barre
Montpelier
Middlebury
Burlington
Plattsburgh
Lake Champlain
Ogdensburg
Lake Placid
Mt. Marcy 5,344
ADIRONDACK MTS.
Watertown
Glens Falls
Saratoga Springs
Schenectady
Troy
Albany
Hudson R.
CATSKILL MTS.
Kingston
Poughkeepsie
Newburgh
APPALACHIAN
NEW YORK
Oswego
Oneida L.
Rome
Utica
Iliot
Cortland
Binghamton
Ithaca
Elmira
Finger Lakes
Auburn
Syracuse
Rochester
Batavia
Lockport
Niagara Falls
Buffalo
Lake Erie
Jamestown
Olean
Genesee R.
Lake Ontario
St. Lawrence R.
PENNSYLVANIA

200 Miles
300 Kilometers
100
200
100
0

EASTERN SEABOARD

MICHIGAN

CANADA

Lake Ontario

NEW YORK

Lake Erie

Erie
Bradford

Oil City
Sharon
Williamsport
Wilkes-Barre
Scranton
Jersey City

PENNSYLVANIA
New Castle
State College
Altoona
Pottsville
Hazleton
Easton
Paterson
Newark
Elizabeth
New Brunswick
Bethlehem
Allentown

OHIO
Weirton
Pittsburgh
McKeesport
Johnstown
Lebanon
Harrisburg
Reading
Carlisle
Lancaster
Pottstown
Trenton
Wheeling
Uniontown
York
Philadelphia
Chester
Camden
Wilmington
Glassboro

Cumberland
Hagerstown
Newark
NEW
Atlantic City
Morgantown
Frederick
Middletown
Vineland
Fairmont
Martinsburg
Baltimore
JERSEY
Parkersburg
Winchester
Silver Spring
Milford
Rehoboth Beach
Clarksburg
Rockville
Annapolis
Elkins
Spruce Knob
4861
Arlington
Washington
D.C.
Seaford
Lewes
DEL.

WEST
VIRGINIA
Harrisonburg
Alexandria
SHENANDOAH
NP
Laurel
Georgetown
Ocean City
Huntington
Staunton
Fredericksburg
Salisbury
MARYLAND
St. Albans
Charleston
Oak Hill
Charlottesville
Chesapeake Bay
Beckley
James R.
Richmond
Princeton
Lynchburg
Petersburg
Hampton
KENTUCKY
Bluefield
Roanoke
VIRGINIA
Newport News
Norfolk
Blacksburg
Portsmouth
Virginia Beach
Martinsville
Suffolk
Chesapeake
Bristol
Danville
Elizabeth City

TENNESSEE
Winston-Salem
Greensboro
Burlington
Rocky Mount
High Point
Durham
Wilson
Mt. Mitchell
6684
Chapel Hill
Raleigh
Greenville
Hickory
Salisbury
Asheville
Concord
Goldsboro
Kannapolis
NORTH
CAROLINA
Kinston
GREAT SMOKY
MTNS NP
Gastonia
Charlotte
New Bern
Havelock
Spartanburg
Gaffney
Fayetteville
Jacksonville
Cape Hatteras
Easley
Greenville
Rock Hill
Clemson
Anderson
Florence
Greenwood
SOUTH
Lumberton
ATLANTIC
OCEAN
Columbia
CAROLINA
Sumter
Wilmington
Aiken
Orangeburg
Myrtle Beach
N. Augusta
Cape Fear
Summerville
Hanahan
GEORGIA
Charleston
Mount Pleasant
Beaufort
Hilton Head Island

APPALACHIAN
COASTAL
PLAIN
OUTER BANKS
Pamlico Sound
ATLANTIC

0   100   200 Miles
0   100   200   300 Kilometers

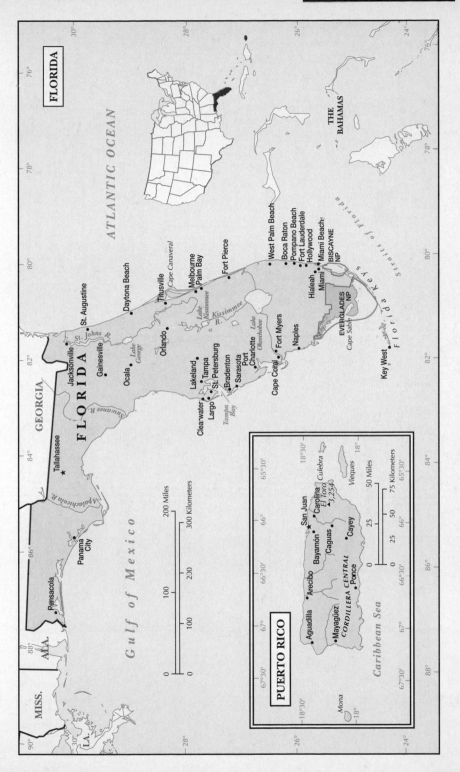

FLORIDA

ATLANTIC OCEAN

THE BAHAMAS

FLORIDA

GEORGIA

Tallahassee ★

Panama City

Pensacola

ALA.

MISS.

LA.

Gulf of Mexico

Apalachicola R.

Suwannee R.

Jacksonville

St. Augustine

Gainesville

Ocala

Daytona Beach

Titusville

Cape Canaveral

Melbourne

Palm Bay

Fort Pierce

Orlando

Lake George

St. Johns R.

Lake Kissimmee

Kissimmee R.

Lakeland

Tampa

St. Petersburg

Clearwater

Largo

Tampa Bay

Bradenton

Sarasota

Port Charlotte

Lake Okeechobee

Fort Myers

Cape Coral

Naples

West Palm Beach

Boca Raton

Pompano Beach

Fort Lauderdale

Hollywood

Miami Beach

Miami

Hialeah

BISCAYNE NP

EVERGLADES NP

Cape Sable

Key West

Florida Keys

Straits of Florida

200 Miles

300 Kilometers

100

200

100

0

0

PUERTO RICO

San Juan ★

Carolina

Culebra

El Toro ▲ 3,254

Bayamón

Caguas

Cayey

Vieques

Arecibo

Aguadilla

Mayagüez

CORDILLERA CENTRAL

Ponce

Caribbean Sea

Mona

50 Miles

75 Kilometers

50

25

25

0

0

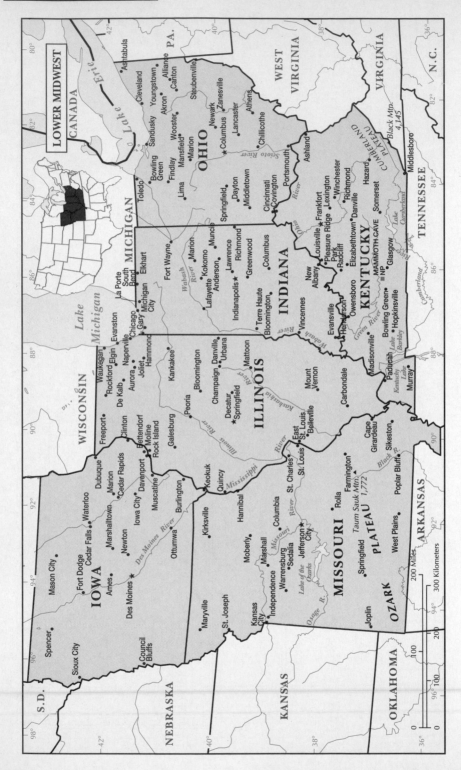

LOWER MIDWEST

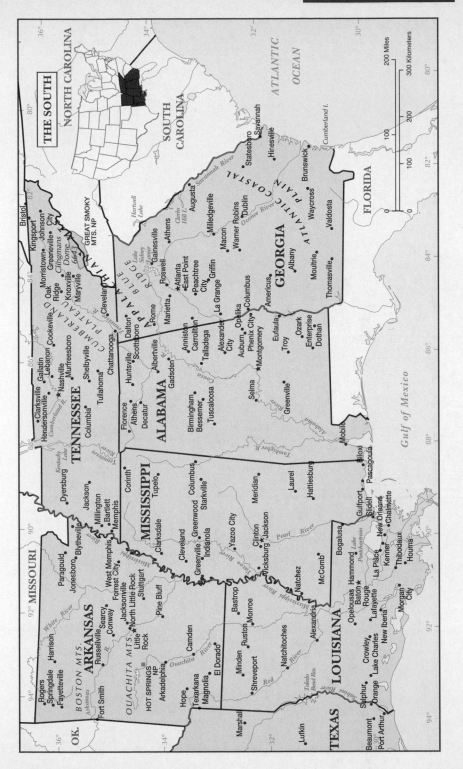

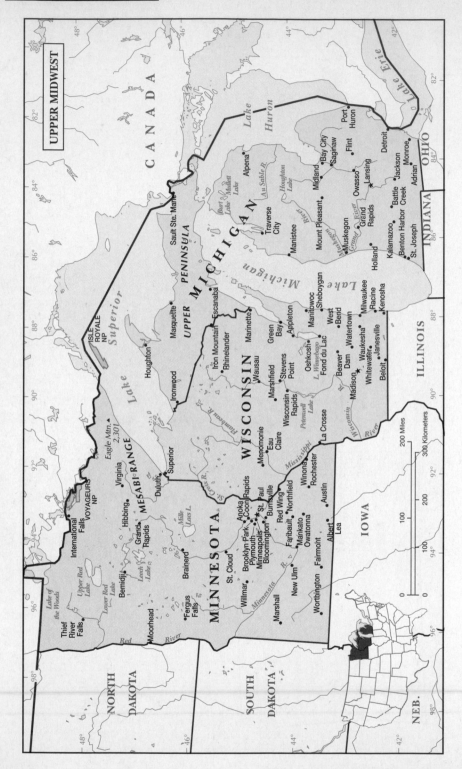

UPPER MIDWEST

CANADA

Lake Superior

Lake Erie

Lake Huron

Lake Michigan

ISLE ROYALE NP

VOYAGEURS NP

Eagle Mtn. ▲ 2,301

MESABI RANGE

UPPER PENINSULA

MICHIGAN

WISCONSIN

MINNESOTA

IOWA

ILLINOIS

INDIANA

OHIO

NORTH DAKOTA

SOUTH DAKOTA

NEB.

Lake of the Woods

Upper Red Lake

Lower Red Lake

Leech Lake

Mille Lacs L.

Lake Winnebago

Petenwell Lake

Houghton Lake

Burt Lake

Mullet Lake

Thief River Falls
International Falls
Bemidji
Moorhead
Fergus Falls
Brainerd
Hibbing
Virginia
Grand Rapids
St. Cloud
Willmar
Marshall
New Ulm
Worthington
Fairmont
Albert Lea
Austin
Mankato
Owatonna
Faribault
Northfield
Red Wing
Winona
Rochester
La Crosse
Anoka
Coon Rapids
St. Paul
Burnsville
Brooklyn Park
Plymouth
Minneapolis
Bloomington
Duluth
Superior
Ironwood
Houghton
Marquette
Sault Ste. Marie
Escanaba
Iron Mountain
Rhinelander
Marinette
Wausau
Marshfield
Stevens Point
Wisconsin Rapids
Eau Claire
Menomonie
Green Bay
Appleton
Oshkosh
Fond du Lac
Manitowoc
Sheboygan
West Bend
Beaver Dam
Watertown
Waukesha
Whitewater
Janesville
Beloit
Madison
Milwaukee
Racine
Kenosha
Manistee
Traverse City
Mount Pleasant
Midland
Bay City
Saginaw
Flint
Alpena
Muskegon
Grand Rapids
Holland
Kalamazoo
Battle Creek
Benton Harbor
St. Joseph
Owasso
Lansing
Jackson
Detroit
Port Huron
Monroe
Adrian

St. Croix R.

Chippewa R.

Wisconsin River

Mississippi River

Minnesota R.

Red River

Au Sable R.

Grand River

Muskegon River

0   100   200 Miles
0   100   200   300 Kilometers

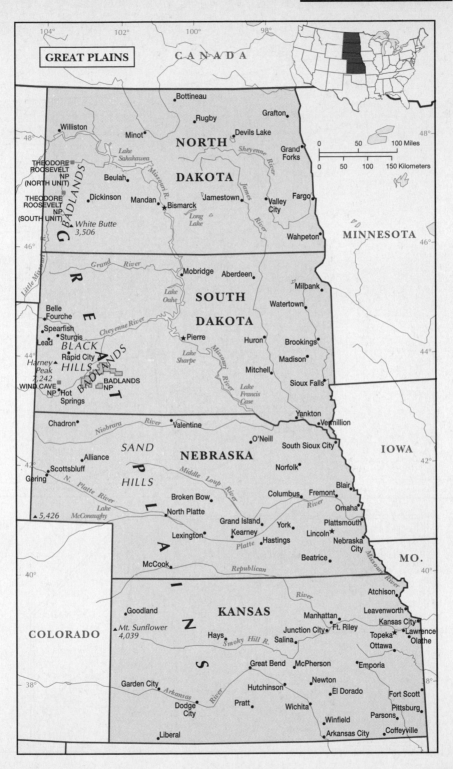

GREAT PLAINS

CANADA

NORTH DAKOTA

Bottineau
Rugby
Grafton
Williston
Minot
Devils Lake
Grand Forks
Lake Sakakawea
Sheyenne River
THEODORE ROOSEVELT NP (NORTH UNIT)
Beulah
THEODORE ROOSEVELT NP (SOUTH UNIT)
Dickinson
Mandan
Bismarck
Jamestown
James River
Valley City
Fargo
White Butte 3,506
Long Lake
Missouri R.
BADLANDS
Little Missouri River
MINNESOTA
Wahpeton

Grand River
Mobridge
Aberdeen
Milbank
SOUTH DAKOTA
Watertown
Lake Oahe
Belle Fourche
Cheyenne River
Spearfish
Sturgis
Pierre
Huron
Brookings
Lead
BLACK HILLS
Rapid City
Lake Sharpe
Madison
Harney Peak 7,242
Mitchell
WIND CAVE NP
Hot Springs
BADLANDS NP
Missouri River
Sioux Falls
Lake Francis Case
Yankton
BADLANDS
G R E A T

Chadron
Niobrara River
Valentine
Vermillion
IOWA
O'Neill
South Sioux City
SAND HILLS
NEBRASKA
Norfolk
Alliance
Scottsbluff
Blair
Gering
N. Platte River
Middle Loup River
Columbus
Fremont
Omaha
Lake McConaughy
5,426
Broken Bow
North Platte
Grand Island
York
Plattsmouth
Lexington
Kearney
Lincoln
Nebraska City
Platte
Hastings
McCook
Beatrice
Republican
MO.

Atchison
River
Goodland
Manhattan
Leavenworth
Kansas City
KANSAS
Junction City
Ft. Riley
Lawrence
Mt. Sunflower 4,039
Hays
Salina
Topeka
Olathe
Smoky Hill R.
Ottawa
P L A I N S
Great Bend
McPherson
Emporia
Garden City
Newton
Arkansas River
Hutchinson
El Dorado
Fort Scott
Dodge City
Pratt
Wichita
Pittsburg
Winfield
Parsons
Liberal
Arkansas City
Coffeyville
COLORADO

0   50   100 Miles
0 50 100 150 Kilometers

104° 102° 100° 98°
48°
46°
44°
42°
40°
38°

247

CRATER
LAKE
NP

OLYMPIC
NP
Seattle
Olympia
MT. RAINIER
NP
Portland
Salem

NORTH
CASCADES
NP

Columbia R.

WASHINGTON

GLACIER
NP

Missouri River

OREGON

IDAHO
Boise

Snake River

REDWOOD
NP

LASSEN
VOLCANIC
NP

Sacramento

Carson City

NEVADA

GREAT
BASIN
NP

San Francisco
San Jose
YOSEMITE
NP
KINGS CANYON
NP

SEQUOIA
NP

CALIFORNIA

DEATH
VALLEY
NP

Las Vegas

Los Angeles
Long Beach

Salton
Sea

JOSHUA
TREE
NP

San Diego

PACIFIC

OCEAN

MONTANA
Helena

ROOSEVELT NP
(SOUTH UNIT)

YELLOWSTONE
NP

GRAND TETONS
NP

WYOMING

Great
Salt
Lake

Salt Lake
City

Cheyenne

UTAH

ARCHES
NP

CAPITOL
REEF
NP

ZION
NP

BRYCE CANYON
NP

CANYONLANDS
NP

MESA
VERDE
NP

GRAND CANYON
NP

PETRIFIED
FOREST
NP

ARIZONA
Phoenix

Tucson

NORTH
DAKOTA

ROOSEVELT NP
(NORTH UNIT)

Bismarck

SOUTH
DAKOTA
Pierre

WIND
CAVE
NP

BADLANDS
NP

NEBRASKA

Platte River

ROCKY
MOUNTAINS
NP

Colorado R.

Denver

COLORADO

Arkansas River

KANSAS

ROCKY   MOUNTAINS

GREAT   PLAINS

Santa Fe

NEW MEXICO

Rio Grande

CARLSBAD
CAVERNS
NP

El Paso

GUADALUPE
MOUNTAINS NP

OKLAHOMA

Oklahoma
City

Red

TEXAS

Austin

San Antonio

Fort Wo

MEXICO

BIG
BEND
NP

Rio Grande

HAWAII

Kauai
Niihau
Oahu
Honolulu
Molokai
Lanai
Kahoolawe
Maui
HALEAKALA
NP

HAWAII
VOLCANOES
NP
Hawaii

0   100 Miles
0   200 Kilometers

ARCTIC OCEAN

GATES OF THE
ARCTIC NP & PRES

RUSSIA

KOBUK
VALLEY
NP

Yukon River

CANADA

ALASKA

DENALI
NP & PRES

WRANGELL-
ST. ELIAS
NP & PRES

Juneau

Bering Sea

LAKE
CLARK
NP & PRES

KENAI
FJORDS NP

GLACIER
BAY NP &
PRES

0   250   500 Miles
0   250   500   750 Kilometers

KATMAI NP
& PRES

Gulf of Alaska

ALEUTIAN ISLANDS

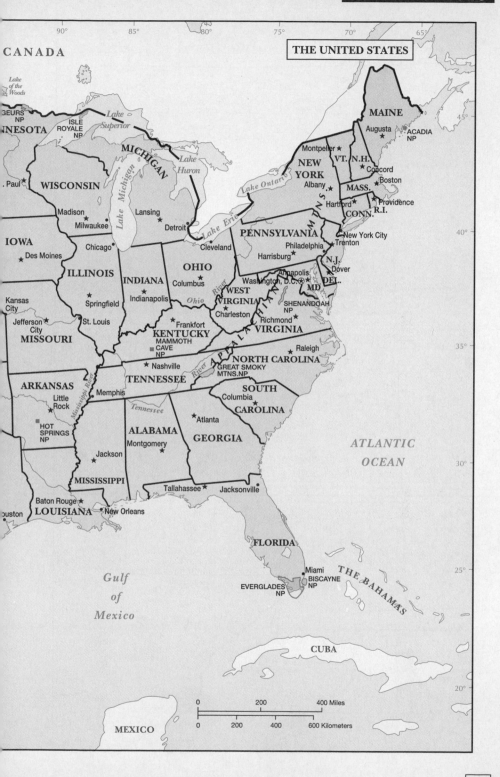

THE UNITED STATES

CANADA

Lake of the Woods

GEURS NP

MINESOTA

ISLE ROYALE NP

Lake Superior

MICHIGAN

Lake Huron

MAINE

Augusta ★

ACADIA NP

Montpelier ★
VT. N.H.
Concord ★

NEW YORK

Boston ★

WISCONSIN

St. Paul ★

Madison ★

Milwaukee ★

Lansing ★

Lake Michigan

Detroit ★

Lake Ontario

Albany ★

MASS.

Hartford ★
CONN. R.I.

Providence ★

IOWA

Des Moines ★

Chicago ★

Lake Erie

Cleveland ★

PENNSYLVANIA

Ohio River

Philadelphia ★

New York City

Trenton ★

ILLINOIS

Springfield ★

INDIANA

Indianapolis ★

OHIO

Columbus ★

Harrisburg ★

N.J.

Dover ★

Kansas City ★

St. Louis ★

Jefferson City ★

MISSOURI

Frankfort ★

KENTUCKY

MAMMOTH CAVE NP

WEST VIRGINIA

Charleston ★

Washington, D.C. ⊛

Annapolis ★

MD

DEL.

SHENANDOAH NP

Richmond ★

VIRGINIA

Raleigh ★

ARKANSAS

Little Rock ★

Nashville ★

TENNESSEE

Tennessee River

Memphis ★

Mississippi River

APPALACHIAN MTNS

NORTH CAROLINA

GREAT SMOKY MTNS. NP

HOT SPRINGS NP

Atlanta ★

SOUTH CAROLINA

Columbia ★

ALABAMA

Montgomery ★

GEORGIA

Jackson ★

MISSISSIPPI

Tallahassee ★

Jacksonville ★

Houston

Baton Rouge ★

LOUISIANA

New Orleans

Gulf of Mexico

FLORIDA

ATLANTIC OCEAN

Miami

BISCAYNE NP

EVERGLADES NP

THE BAHAMAS

CUBA

MEXICO

| 0 | 200 | 400 Miles |
| 0 | 200 | 400 | 600 Kilometers |

SOUTHERN ROCKIES

WYOMING

NEBRASKA

R O C K Y

ROCKY MOUNTAIN NP

Craig
Steamboat Springs
Fort Collins
Loveland
Sterling
Greeley
Longmont
Fort Morgan
Boulder
Lafayette
Arvada
Westminster
Lakewood
Aurora
Denver
Parker
Castle Rock
Limon

UTAH

FRONT RANGE

Glenwood Springs
Colorado River
Aspen
Grand Junction
Mt. Elbert 14,433
COLORADO
Gunnison R.

Montrose
Canon City
Pikes Peak 14,110
Colorado Springs
Fountain
Pueblo
La Junta
Lamar
Arkansas River

KS

KANSAS

COLORADO

San Juan Mts.
Cortéz
Durango
Alamosa
MESA VERDE NP
Trinidad

SANGRE DE CRISTO MTS.

Aztec
Raton

OKLAHOMA

Farmington
Bloomfield

PLATEAU

Wheeler Peak 13,161

M O U N T A I N S

Dumas

Espanola
Los Alamos
Santa Fe ★
Las Vegas
Conchas Res.
Canadian River
Lake Meredith
Amarillo

Gallup

Grants
Rio Rancho
Bernalillo
Alameda
Albuquerque
Belen
Tucumcari

ARIZONA

Rio Grande

Clovis
Portales
Plainview

NEW MEXICO

Socorro
Lubbock

LLANO

Rio

Roswell
Ruidoso
ESTACADO
Brownfield

Elephant Butte Res.
Truth or Consequences
Caballo Res.
Alamogordo
Lovington
Hobbs
Artesia

SACRAMENTO MTS.

Lake McMillan

Andrews
Big Spring
Midland
Odessa

Silver City
Lordsburg
Deming
Las Cruces
Carlsbad
Pecos

Guadalupe Peak 8,751
CARLSBAD CAVERNS NP
GUADALUPE MOUNTAINS NP

Sunland Park
El Paso
Socorro
Pecos River

TEXAS

Fort Stockton

MEXICO

Alpine

Rio Grande

0   100   200 Miles

0   100   200   300 Kilometers

BIG BEND NP

110°   108°   106°   104°   102°

250

SOUTHERN PLAINS

KANSAS

MO.
ARK.

Guymon
Woodward
Bartlesville
Miami
Ponca City
Enid
Claremore
Dumas
Stillwater
Keystone Lake
Tulsa
Broken Arrow
Pampa
Lake Meredith
Clinton
El Reno
Edmond
Sapulpa
Muskogee
Robert S. Kerr Lake
Amarillo
★ Oklahoma City
Okmulgee
Shawnee
Chickasha
Norman
Eufaula Lake

GREAT PLAINS

Canadian River

OKLAHOMA

Altus
Lawton
Ada
McAlester

LLANO
Plainview
Wichita Falls
Duncan
Ardmore
Lake Texoma
Durant
Paris
OUACHITA MTS

ESTACADO
Lubbock
Red River
Denison
Sherman
Texarkana

Brownfield
Denton
Plano
Greenville
Garland
Irving
Dallas
Marshall
Abilene
Fort Worth
Arlington
Mesquite
Longview
Tyler
Andrews
Big Spring
Sabine River
Midland
TEXAS
Corsicana
Nacogdoches
Odessa
Brownwood
Lufkin
San Angelo
Waco
Sam Rayburn Res.
Colorado River
Killeen
Brazos River
Fort Stockton
EDWARDS
Temple
Bryan
Huntsville
Lake Livingston
Pecos River
PLATEAU
College Station
Amistad Res.
Round Rock
Houston
Baytown
Austin ★
Del Rio
San Marcos
Pasadena
BIG BEND NP
New Braunfels
Seguin
Texas City
Galveston
Eagle Pass
San Antonio
Galveston Bay
MEXICO
Victoria
Freeport
Rio Grande
Nueces River
Matagorda Bay

Alice
Corpus Christi
Laredo
Kingsville
Gulf of Mexico
Falcon Res.
Padre Island
Edinburg
Mission
Pharr
Harlingen
McAllen
Weslaco
San Benito
Brownsville

0   100   200 Miles
0   100   200   300 Kilometers

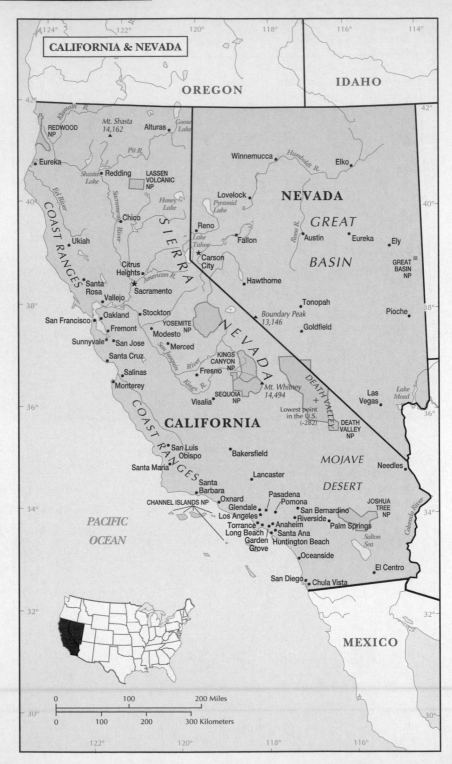

CALIFORNIA & NEVADA

OREGON

IDAHO

REDWOOD NP

Mt. Shasta 14,162 ▲

Alturas

Goose Lake

Klamath R.

Eureka

Pit R.

Winnemucca

Humboldt R.

Elko

NEVADA

Shasta Lake

Redding

LASSEN VOLCANIC NP

Sacramento River

Honey Lake

Lovelock

Pyramid Lake

GREAT

Chico

Reno

Lake Tahoe

Fallon

Austin

Eureka

Ely

BASIN

GREAT BASIN NP

Ukiah

El River

Citrus Heights

★ Carson City

Hawthorne

Santa Rosa

Vallejo

★ Sacramento

American R.

Tonopah

Pioche

San Francisco

Oakland

Stockton

YOSEMITE NP

Boundary Peak 13,146 ▲

Fremont

Modesto

Goldfield

Sunnyvale

San Jose

Merced

San Joaquin River

Santa Cruz

KINGS CANYON NP

Salinas

Fresno

Kings R.

Mt. Whitney 14,494 +

Las Vegas

Lake Mead

Monterey

Visalia

SEQUOIA NP

Lowest point in the U.S. (-282)

DEATH VALLEY NP

CALIFORNIA

San Luis Obispo

Bakersfield

MOJAVE

Needles

Santa Maria

Lancaster

DESERT

Santa Barbara

Oxnard

Pasadena

Pomona

JOSHUA TREE NP

CHANNEL ISLANDS NP

Glendale

San Bernardino

PACIFIC

Los Angeles

Torrance

Anaheim

Riverside

Palm Springs

Colorado River

OCEAN

Long Beach

Santa Ana

Garden Grove

Huntington Beach

Salton Sea

Oceanside

El Centro

San Diego

Chula Vista

COAST RANGES

SIERRA

NEVADA

DEATH VALLEY

MEXICO

0   100   200 Miles

0   100   200   300 Kilometers

ARIZONA & UTAH

WYOMING

NEVADA

Bear Lake
• Logan
• Brigham City
Roy • Ogden
• Clearfield
• Layton
Salt Lake City ★ • Bountiful
West Jordan • Murray
• Sandy
Tooele • Orem
• Provo
Utah Lake
• Payson

GREAT SALT LAKE DESERT

Great Salt Lake

RANGE

▲ Kings Peak 13,528
UINTA MTS
• Vernal

Green River

• Price

UTAH

WASATCH

Sevier Lake

• Richfield

• Green River
ARCHES NP ■
• Moab

Sevier River

CAPITOL REEF NP

CANYONLANDS NP

River

COLORADO

• Cedar City

BRYCE CANYON NP ■

Lake Powell

San Juan River

• Blanding

Saint George • ZION NP

• Page
• Kayenta

Colorado River

GRAND CANYON
GRAND CANYON NP

Lake Mead

PAINTED DESERT

Humphreys Peak 12,633 ▲
• Flagstaff
• Kingman
Bullhead City •

• Winslow
• Holbrook

PETRIFIED FOREST NP ■

NEW MEXICO

• Prescott
Cottonwood •

Verde R.

• Lake Havasu City

Lake Havasu

ARIZONA

CALIFORNIA

Colorado River

Peoria •
Glendale •
Phoenix ★ • Scottsdale
Tempe • • Mesa
Chandler •
Apache Junction •

Salt River

• Globe

Gila River

Casa Grande •
• Coolidge
• Eloy

Gila R.

• Safford

Yuma •

SONORAN DESERT

• Tucson

MEXICO

• Nogales

Sierra Vista •

Bisbee •
• Douglas

0   100   200 Miles

0   100   200   300 Kilometers

253

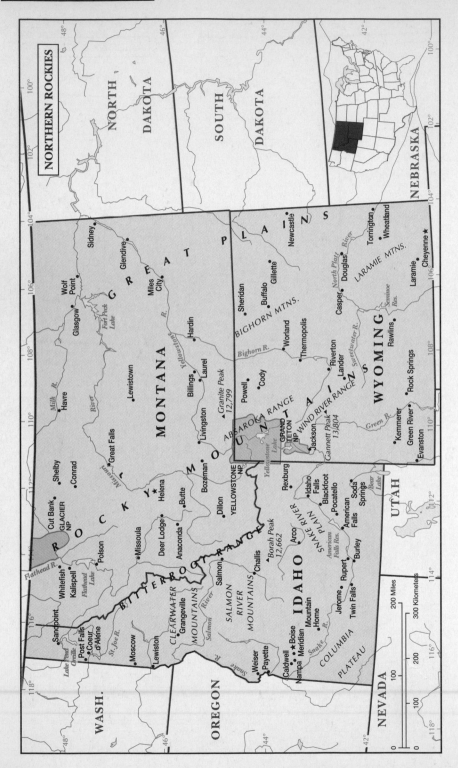

NORTHERN ROCKIES

NORTH DAKOTA

SOUTH DAKOTA

NEBRASKA

Sidney

Wolf Point

Glasgow

Glendive

G R E A T

Fort Peck Lake

Miles City

Havre

Milk R.

Hardin

Lewistown

Missouri R.

Great Falls

Shelby

Conrad

Cut Bank

GLACIER NP

Kalispell

Whitefish

Sandpoint

Post Falls

Coeur d'Alene

Lake Pend Oreille

Flathead Lake

Flathead R.

Polson

Missoula

Deer Lodge

Anaconda

Helena

Butte

Dillon

Bozeman

Livingston

Billings

Laurel

Yellowstone R.

Granite Peak 12,799

MONTANA

P L A I N S

Sheridan

Buffalo

Gillette

Newcastle

BIGHORN MTNS.

Bighorn R.

Worland

Thermopolis

Cody

Powell

Riverton

Lander

ABSAROKA RANGE

GRAND TETON NP

Jackson

Gannett Peak 13,804

WIND RIVER RANGE

YELLOWSTONE NP

Yellowstone Lake

Rexburg

Idaho Falls

Blackfoot

Pocatello

Soda Springs

American Falls

Bear Lake

North Platte River

Douglas

Torrington

Wheatland

LARAMIE MTNS.

Casper

Seminoe Res.

Sweetwater R.

WYOMING

Rawlins

Laramie

Cheyenne ★

Rock Springs

Kemmerer

Green River

Evanston

Green R.

UTAH

R O C K Y   M O U N T A I N S

Salmon

Salmon River

Challis

SALMON RIVER MOUNTAINS

Arco

Borah Peak 12,662

SNAKE RIVER PLAIN

Snake River

American Falls Res.

Burley

Rupert

Jerome

Twin Falls

COLUMBIA PLATEAU

BITTERROOT RANGE

CLEARWATER MOUNTAINS

Grangeville

Salmon R.

Moscow

Lewiston

St. Joe R.

Weiser

Payette

Caldwell

Nampa

Meridian

Boise ★

Mountain Home

IDAHO

WASH.

OREGON

NEVADA

200 Miles

300 Kilometers

200

100

100

200

100

0

0

254

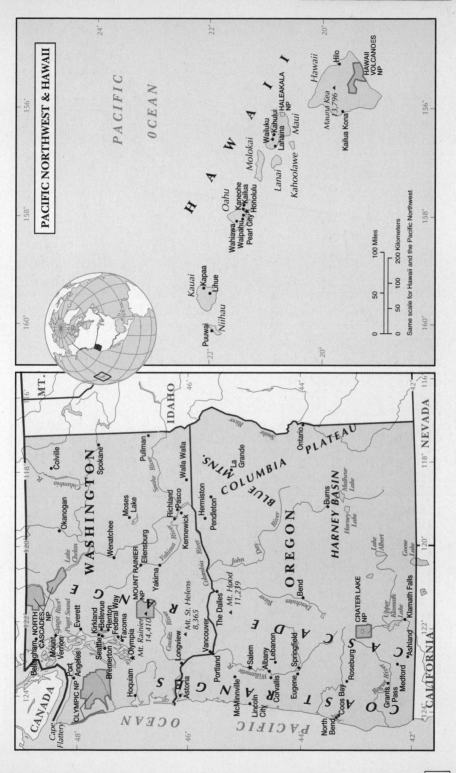

PACIFIC NORTHWEST & HAWAII

PACIFIC OCEAN

H A W A I I

Hawaii

Hilo

HAWAII VOLCANOES NP

Mauna Kea 13,796

Kailua Kona

Wailuku
Kahului
Lahaina
Maui

HALEAKALA NP

Molokai

Lanai

Kahoolawe

Oahu
Wahiawa
Waipahu
Pearl City
Kaneohe
Kailua
Honolulu

Kauai
Kapaa
Lihue

Puuwai
Niihau

100 Miles
50
0

200 Kilometers
100
50
0

Same scale for Hawaii and the Pacific Northwest

MT.

CANADA

Cape Flattery

IDAHO

Colville

Spokane

Pullman

Okanogan

Moses Lake

Wenatchee

Ellensburg

Walla Walla

Pasco

Richland

Kennewick

Hermiston

Pendleton

La Grande

BLUE MTNS.

COLUMBIA PLATEAU

Ontario

Snake River

Bellingham
Mount Vernon
Everett
Kirkland
Bellevue
Renton
Federal Way
Tacoma
Olympia

NORTH CASCADES NP

Lake Chelan

MOUNT RAINIER NP

Mt. Rainier 14,410

WASHINGTON

Seattle
Bremerton

Puget Sound

OLYMPIC NP
Port Angeles
Hoquiam

Yakima

Mt. St. Helens 8,365

Longview

Vancouver

The Dalles

Mt. Hood 11,239

Portland

Astoria

McMinnville

Lincoln City

Salem
Albany
Corvallis
Eugene
Springfield
Lebanon

OREGON

Bend

Deschutes River

John Day River

HARNEY BASIN

Burns

Harney Lake

Malheur Lake

Lake Albert

Goose Lake

North Bend
Coos Bay

Roseburg

Grants Pass
Medford
Ashland

Rogue River

Upper Klamath Lake

CRATER LAKE NP

Klamath Falls

C A S C A D E   R A N G E

C O A S T   R A N G E S

PACIFIC OCEAN

CALIFORNIA

NEVADA

Columbia River

Cowlitz River

Yakima River

Spokane River

Snake River

Columbia R.

Willamette River

NEVADA

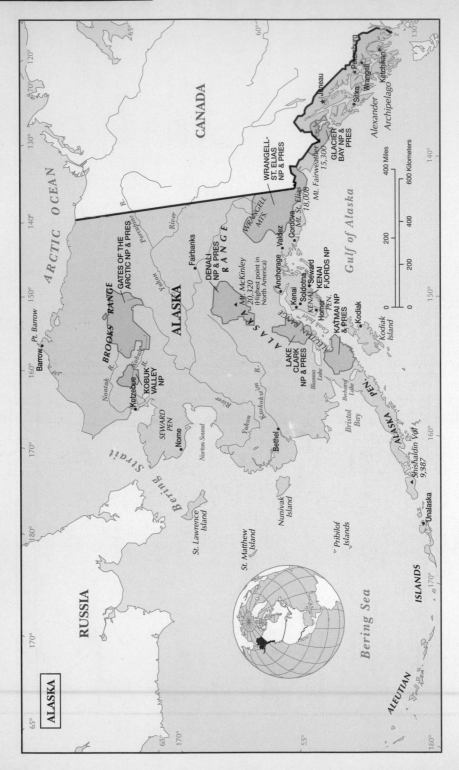

ALASKA

UNITED STATES

ARCTIC OCEAN

RUSSIA

CANADA

ALASKA

Bering Sea

Bering Strait

Gulf of Alaska

Bristol Bay

Norton Sound

BROOKS RANGE

ALASKA RANGE

ALEUTIAN RANGE

SEWARD PEN

ALASKA PEN

ALEUTIAN ISLANDS

Alexander Archipelago

WRANGELL MTS.

Pt. Barrow
Barrow
Kotzebue
Nome
Bethel
Fairbanks
Anchorage
Valdez
Cordova
Soldotna
Kenai
Seward
Homer
Kodiak
Juneau
Sitka
Petersburg
Wrangell
Ketchikan
Unalaska

GATES OF THE ARCTIC NP & PRES
KOBUK VALLEY NP
DENALI NP & PRES
WRANGELL-ST. ELIAS NP & PRES
GLACIER BAY NP & PRES
KENAI FJORDS NP
LAKE CLARK NP & PRES
KATMAI NP & PRES

Mt. McKinley 20,320 (Highest point in North America)
Mt. St. Elias 18,008
Mt. Fairweather 15,300
Shishaldin Vol. 9,387

Noatak R.
Kobuk R.
Porcupine R.
Yukon River
Kuskokwim R.
Iliamna Lake
Becharof Lake
Cook Inlet

St. Lawrence Island
St. Matthew Island
Nunivak Island
Pribilof Islands
Kodiak Island

400 Miles
600 Kilometers
400
200
200
0

FACTS About the STATES

The numbers in parentheses after Population, Area, and Entered Union show the ranking of the state compared with other states of the United States. For example, Alabama is the 22nd largest state in population, but it is the 30th largest state in area. It was the 22nd state to enter the Union.

ALABAMA

Heart of Dixie, Camellia State

Population (1994): 4,218,792 (22nd)
Area: 52,423 square miles (30th) (135,775 square kilometers)
Entered Union: December 14, 1819 (22nd)
Postal Abbreviation: AL
Flower: Camellia **Bird:** Yellowhammer
Tree: Southern pine **Song:** Alabama
Capital: Montgomery
Largest Cities (with population): Birmingham, 265,965; Mobile, 196,278; Montgomery, 187,543; Huntsville, 159,880
Important Products: clothing and textiles, metal products, transportation equipment, paper, industrial machinery, food products, lumber, coal, oil, natural gas, livestock, peanuts, cotton
Places to Visit: Alabama Space and Rocket Center, Huntsville; DeSoto State Park, near Fort Payne
DID YOU KNOW? Montgomery, Alabama, was the first capital of the Confederate States of America (1861). Alabama is a major center for rocket and space research.

ALASKA

The Last Frontier

Population (1994): 606,276 (48th)
Area: 656,424 square miles (1st) (1,700,139 square kilometers)
Entered Union: January 3, 1959 (49th)
Postal Abbreviation: AK
Flower: Forget-me-not **Bird:** Willow ptarmigan
Tree: Sitka spruce **Song:** Alaska's Flag
Capital: Juneau (population, 26,751)
Largest Cities (with population): Anchorage, 226,338; Fairbanks, 30,843
Important Products: oil, natural gas, fish, food products, lumber and wood products, fur
Places to Visit: Glacier Bay and Denali national parks, Mendenhall Glacier, Mount McKinley
DID YOU KNOW? Mount McKinley is the highest mountain in the United States. Alaska is the biggest and coldest state in the United States.

ARIZONA

Grand Canyon State

Population (1994): 4,075,052 (23rd)
Area: 114,006 square miles (6th) (295,276 square kilometers)
Entered Union: February 14, 1912 (48th)
Postal Abbreviation: AZ
Flower: Blossom of the Saguaro cactus **Bird:** Cactus wren
Tree: Paloverde **Song:** Arizona
Capital and Largest City: Phoenix (population, 983,392)
Other Large Cities (with population): Tucson, 405,371; Mesa, 288,104; Tempe, 141,993; Scottsdale, 130,075
Important Products: electronic equipment, transportation and industrial equipment, instruments, printing and publishing, copper and other metals
Places to Visit: Grand Canyon, Painted Desert, Petrified Forest, Hoover Dam
DID YOU KNOW? The Grand Canyon is the largest land gorge in the world and one of the world's natural wonders. It is 217 miles long and 4-18 miles wide at the rim.

ARKANSAS

Land of Opportunity

Population (1994): 2,452,671 (33rd)
Area: 53,182 square miles (29th) (137,742 square kilometers)
Flower: Apple blossom   **Bird:** Mockingbird
Tree: Pine   **Song:** Arkansas
Entered Union: June 15, 1836 (25th)
Postal Abbreviation: AR
Capital and Largest City: Little Rock (population, 175,727)
Other Large Cities (with population): North Little Rock, 61,829; Pine Bluff, 57,140
Important Products: food products, paper, electronic equipment, industrial machinery, metal products, lumber and wood products, livestock, soybeans, rice, cotton, natural gas
Places to Visit: Hot Springs National Park

DID YOU KNOW? Arkansas has the only working diamond mine on the continent of North America. President Bill Clinton was born in Arkansas and served as one of its governors.

CALIFORNIA

Golden State

Population (1994): 31,430,697 (1st)
Area: 163,707 square miles (3rd) (424,002 square kilometers)
Flower: Golden poppy   **Bird:** California valley quail
Tree: California redwood   **Song:** I Love You, California
Entered Union: September 9, 1850 (31st)
Postal Abbreviation: CA
Capital: Sacramento (population, 369,365)
Largest Cities (with population): Los Angeles, 3,485,398; San Diego, 1,110,554; San Jose, 782,248; San Francisco, 723,959
Important Products: transportation and industrial equipment, electronic equipment, oil, natural gas, motion pictures, milk, cattle, fruit and vegetables
Places to Visit: Yosemite Valley, Lake Tahoe, Palomar Observatory, Disneyland, San Diego Zoo, Hollywood, Sequoia National Park

DID YOU KNOW? California has more people, more cars, more schools, and more businesses than any other state in the United States. The oldest living things on earth are believed to be the Bristlecone pine trees in California's Inyo National Forest, estimated to be 4,700 years old. The world's tallest tree, 365 feet tall and 44 feet around, is a redwood tree in Humboldt County.

COLORADO

Centennial State

Population (1994): 3,655,647 (26th)
Area: 104,100 square miles (8th) (269,620 square kilometers)
Flower: Rocky Mountain columbine   **Bird:** Lark bunting
Tree: Colorado blue spruce   **Song:** Where the Columbines
Entered Union: August 1, 1876 (38th)   Grow
Postal Abbreviation: CO
Capital and Largest City: Denver (population, 467,610)
Other Large Cities (with population): Colorado Springs, 281,140; Aurora, 222,103; Lakewood, 126,481
Important Products: instruments and industrial machinery, food products, printing and publishing, metal products, electronic equipment, oil, coal, cattle
Places to Visit: Rocky Mountain National Park, Mesa Verde National Park, Dinosaur National Monument, old mining towns

DID YOU KNOW? The Grand Mesa in Colorado is the world's largest flat-top mountain. The highest bridge in the world (1,053 feet) is in Colorado—it is the suspension bridge over the Royal Gorge of the Arkansas River. Colorado has more mountains over 14,000 feet and more elk than any other state.

CONNECTICUT

Constitution State, Nutmeg State

Population (1994): 3,275,251 (27th)
Area: 5,544 square miles (48th) (14,358 square kilometers)
Flower: Mountain laurel   **Bird:** American robin
Tree: White oak   **Song:** Yankee Doodle
Entered Union: January 9, 1788 (5th)
Postal Abbreviation: CT
Capital: Hartford
Largest Cities (with population): Bridgeport, 141,686; Hartford, 139,739; New Haven, 130,474; Waterbury, 108,961; Stamford, 108,056
Important Products: aircraft parts and helicopters, industrial machinery, metals and metal products, electronic equipment, printing and publishing, instruments, chemicals, dairy products, stone
Places to Visit: Mystic Seaport and Marine Life Aquarium, in Mystic; P.T. Barnum circus museum, Bridgeport; Peabody Museum, New Haven

DID YOU KNOW? The first library for children opened in Salisbury, in 1803, and the first permanent school for the deaf opened in Hartford in 1817. The first woman to receive an American patent was Mary Kies of South Killingly, in 1809, for a machine to weave straw and silk or thread.

DELAWARE

First State, Diamond State

Population (1994): 706,351 (46th)
Area: 2,489 square miles (49th) (6,447 square kilometers)
Flower: Peach blossom   **Bird:** Blue hen chicken
Tree: American holly   **Song:** Our Delaware
Entered Union: December 7, 1787 (1st)
Postal Abbreviation: DE
Capital: Dover
Largest Cities (with population): Wilmington, 71,529; Dover, 27,630; Newark, 25,098
Important Products: chemicals, food products, instruments, chickens
Places to Visit: Rehoboth Beach, Henry Francis du Pont Winterthur Museum near Wilmington

DID YOU KNOW? Delaware was the first state to agree to the Constitution and thus became the first state of the United States. Delaware had the first log cabins in America.

FLORIDA

Sunshine State

Population (1994): 13,952,714 (4th)
Area: 65,756 square miles (22nd) (170,308 square kilometers)
Flower: Orange blossom   **Bird:** Mockingbird
Tree: Sabal palmetto palm   **Song:** Old Folks at Home
Entered Union: March 3, 1845 (27th)
Postal Abbreviation: FL
Capital: Tallahassee (population, 124,773)
Largest Cities (with population): Jacksonville, 672,971; Miami, 358,548; Tampa, 280,015; Saint Petersburg, 238,629
Important Products: electronic and transportation equipment, instruments, printing and publishing, food products, citrus fruits, vegetables, livestock, phosphates, fish
Places to Visit: Walt Disney World and Universal Studios, near Orlando; Sea World, Orlando; Busch Gardens, Tampa; Spaceport USA, at Kennedy Space Center, Cape Canaveral; Everglades National Park

DID YOU KNOW? St. Augustine, Florida, is the oldest city in the United States. Florida grows more citrus fruit than any other state. Also, Florida's warm, sunny climate attracts people from all over the country who are retired from their jobs. One out of every five people there is over the age of 65.

GEORGIA

Empire State of the South, Peach State

Population (1994): 7,055,336 (11th)
Area: 59,441 square miles (24th) (153,953 square kilometers)
Flower: Cherokee rose   **Bird:** Brown thrasher
Tree: Live oak   **Song:** Georgia on My Mind
Entered Union: January 2, 1788 (4th)
Postal Abbreviation: GA
Capital and Largest City: Atlanta (population, 394,017)
Other Large Cities (with population): Columbus, 179,278;
Savannah, 137,560; Macon, 106,612
Important Products: clothing and textiles, transportation equipment, food products, paper, chickens, peanuts, peaches, clay
Places to Visit: Stone Mountain Park, Six Flags Over Georgia, New Echota State Historic Site (eastern Cherokee capital) in Calhoun

 DID YOU KNOW? Georgia is the largest state east of the Mississippi River and has more woods than any other state. The first U.S. gold rush took place in Georgia. The first American Indian newspaper was published in Georgia by a Cherokee in 1828. The first radio station owned and operated by African-Americans started in Atlanta in 1949. Civil rights leader Martin Luther King, Jr. (1929-1968) and baseball player Jackie Robinson (1919-1972) were born in Georgia. Georgia's capital city, Atlanta, was selected to host the Olympic Games in 1996.

HAWAII

Aloha State

Population (1994): 1,178,564 (40th)
Area: 10,932 square miles (43rd) (28,313 square kilometers)
Flower: Yellow hibiscus   **Bird:** Hawaiian goose
Tree: Kukui   **Song:** Hawaii Ponoi
Entered Union: August 21, 1959 (50th)
Postal Abbreviation: HI
Capital and Largest City: Honolulu (population, 365,272)
Other Large Cities (with population): Hilo, 37,808; Kailua, 36,818; Kaneohe, 35,448
Important Products: food products, pineapples, sugarcane, printing and publishing, fish, stone
Places to Visit: Hawaii Volcanoes National Park; Haleakala National Park, Maui; Iolani Palace, Honolulu; U.S.S. *Arizona* Memorial, Pearl Harbor

 DID YOU KNOW? Hawaii is the only state made up entirely of islands, 122 of them. (People live on 7 of them.) Hawaii's Mauna Loa is the biggest active volcano in the United States.

IDAHO

Gem State

Population (1994): 1,133,034 (42nd)
Area: 83,574 square miles (14th) (216,456 square kilometers)
Flower: Syringa   **Bird:** Mountain bluebird
Tree: White pine   **Song:** Here We Have Idaho
Entered Union: July 3, 1890 (43rd)
Postal Abbreviation: ID
Capital and Largest City: Boise (population, 125,738)
Other Large Cities (with population): Pocatello, 46,080; Idaho Falls, 43,929
Important Products: potatoes, hay, wheat, cattle, milk, lumber and wood products, food products
Places to Visit: Sun Valley; Hells Canyon; Craters of the Moon, near Arco; Nez Percé National Historical Park, near Lewiston; ghost towns

 DID YOU KNOW? The first hydroelectric power plant built by the federal government was the Minidoka Dam on the Snake River in Idaho; the first unit started in 1909. Two thirds of all potatoes in the United States are grown in Idaho.

ILLINOIS

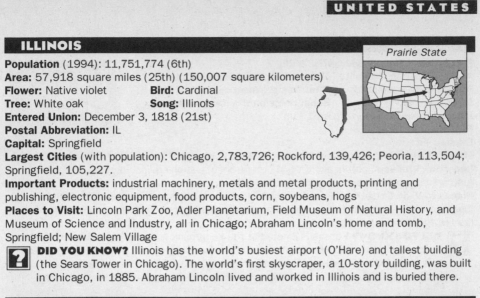

Prairie State

Population (1994): 11,751,774 (6th)
Area: 57,918 square miles (25th) (150,007 square kilometers)
Flower: Native violet   **Bird:** Cardinal
Tree: White oak   **Song:** Illinois
Entered Union: December 3, 1818 (21st)
Postal Abbreviation: IL
Capital: Springfield
Largest Cities (with population): Chicago, 2,783,726; Rockford, 139,426; Peoria, 113,504; Springfield, 105,227.
Important Products: industrial machinery, metals and metal products, printing and publishing, electronic equipment, food products, corn, soybeans, hogs
Places to Visit: Lincoln Park Zoo, Adler Planetarium, Field Museum of Natural History, and Museum of Science and Industry, all in Chicago; Abraham Lincoln's home and tomb, Springfield; New Salem Village

 DID YOU KNOW? Illinois has the world's busiest airport (O'Hare) and tallest building (the Sears Tower in Chicago). The world's first skyscraper, a 10-story building, was built in Chicago, in 1885. Abraham Lincoln lived and worked in Illinois and is buried there.

INDIANA

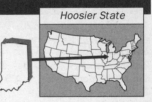

Hoosier State

Population (1994): 5,752,073 (14th)
Area: 36,420 square miles (38th) (94,328 square kilometers)
Flower: Peony   **Bird:** Cardinal
Tree: Tulip poplar   **Song:** On the Banks of the Wabash,
                              Far Away
Entered Union: December 11, 1816 (19th)
Postal Abbreviation: IN
Capital and Largest City: Indianapolis (population, 731,427)
Other Large Cities (with population): Fort Wayne, 173,072; Evansville, 126,272; Gary, 116,646; South Bend, 105,511
Important Products: transportation equipment, electronic equipment, industrial machinery, iron and steel, metal products, corn, soybeans, livestock, coal
Places to Visit: Children's Museum, Indianapolis; Conner Prairie Pioneer Settlement, Noblesville; Lincoln Boyhood Memorial, Lincoln City; Wyandotte Cave

 DID YOU KNOW? The first city to be lit with electricity was Wabash. Indiana's Lost River travels 22 miles underground. Indiana is the biggest basketball state and home of the famous Indianapolis 500 auto race.

IOWA

Hawkeye State

Population (1994): 2,829,252 (30th)
Area: 56,276 square miles (26th) (145,754 square kilometers)
Flower: Wild rose   **Bird:** Eastern goldfinch
Tree: Oak   **Song:** The Song of Iowa
Entered Union: December 28, 1846 (29th)
Postal Abbreviation: IA
Capital and Largest City: Des Moines (population, 193,187)
Other Large Cities (with population): Cedar Rapids, 108,751; Davenport, 95,333; Sioux City, 80,505
Important Products: corn, soybeans, hogs, cattle, industrial machinery, food products
Places to Visit: Effigy Mounds National Monument, Marquette; Herbert Hoover Birthplace, West Branch; Living History Farms, Des Moines; Adventureland; the Amana Colonies; Fort Dodge Historical Museum

DID YOU KNOW? The bridge built in 1856 between Davenport and Rock Island was the first bridge to span the Mississippi River. Frontiersman Buffalo Bill Cody (1846-1917) was born in Iowa.

KANSAS

Sunflower State

Population (1994): 2,554,047 (32nd)
Area: 82,282 square miles (15th) (213,110 square kilometers)
Flower: Native sunflower   **Bird:** Western meadowlark
Tree: Cottonwood   **Song:** Home on the Range
Entered Union: January 29, 1861 (34th)
Postal Abbreviation: KS
Capital: Topeka
Largest Cities (with population): Wichita, 304,011; Kansas City, 149,767; Topeka, 119,883
Important Products: cattle, aircraft and other transportation equipment, industrial machinery, food products, wheat, corn, hay, oil, natural gas
Places to Visit: Dodge City; Fort Scott and Fort Larned national historical sites; Dwight D. Eisenhower Museum and Home, Abilene; Kansas Cosmosphere and Space Discovery Center, Hutchinson

 DID YOU KNOW? Kansas is located at the geographical center of the United States (excluding Alaska and Hawaii). It is one of the two biggest U.S. wheat-growing states (the other is North Dakota). The carousel with jumping horses was invented in Kansas in 1898.

KENTUCKY

Bluegrass State

Population (1994): 3,826,794 (24th)
Area: 40,411 square miles (37th) (104,665 square kilometers)
Flower: Goldenrod   **Bird:** Cardinal
Tree: Kentucky coffee tree   **Song:** My Old Kentucky Home
Entered Union: June 1, 1792 (15th)
Postal Abbreviation: KY
Capital: Frankfort (population, 25,968)
Largest Cities (with population): Louisville, 269,063; Lexington 225,366
Important Products: coal, industrial machinery, electronic equipment, transportation equipment, metals, tobacco, cattle
Places to Visit: Mammoth Cave National Park; Lincoln Birthplace, Hodgenville; Cumberland Gap National Historical Park, Middlesboro

 DID YOU KNOW? Kentucky has the longest group of caves in the world (Mammoth Caves). Abraham Lincoln was born in Kentucky. Kentucky is also the home of the Kentucky Derby, the most famous horse race in America.

LOUISIANA

Pelican State

Population (1994): 4,315,085 (21st)
Area: 51,844 square miles (31st) (134,275 square kilometers)
Flower: Magnolia   **Bird:** Eastern brown pelican
Tree: Cypress   **Songs:** Give Me Louisiana;
                          You Are My Sunshine
Entered Union: April 30, 1812 (18th)
Postal Abbreviation: LA
Capital: Baton Rouge
Largest Cities (with population): New Orleans, 496,938; Baton Rouge, 219,513; Shreveport, 198,525
Important Products: natural gas, oil, chemicals, transportation equipment, paper, food products, cotton, fish
Places to Visit: French quarter in New Orleans; Jean Lafitte National Historical Park

 DID YOU KNOW? The busiest port in the United States is located in Louisiana. It's the second-biggest mining state (after Alaska). Louisiana is the home of New Orleans, known for its jazz and the colorful Mardi Gras festival.

MAINE

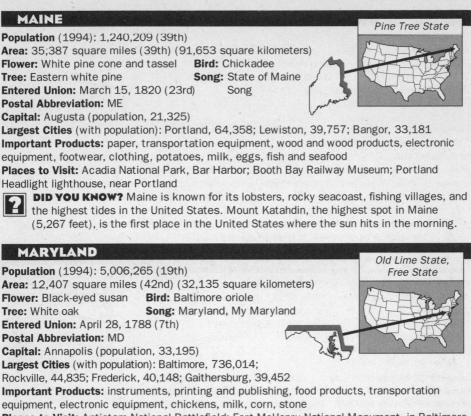

Pine Tree State

Population (1994): 1,240,209 (39th)
Area: 35,387 square miles (39th) (91,653 square kilometers)
Flower: White pine cone and tassel   **Bird:** Chickadee
Tree: Eastern white pine   **Song:** State of Maine
Entered Union: March 15, 1820 (23rd)   Song
Postal Abbreviation: ME
Capital: Augusta (population, 21,325)
Largest Cities (with population): Portland, 64,358; Lewiston, 39,757; Bangor, 33,181
Important Products: paper, transportation equipment, wood and wood products, electronic equipment, footwear, clothing, potatoes, milk, eggs, fish and seafood
Places to Visit: Acadia National Park, Bar Harbor; Booth Bay Railway Museum; Portland Headlight lighthouse, near Portland

 DID YOU KNOW? Maine is known for its lobsters, rocky seacoast, fishing villages, and the highest tides in the United States. Mount Katahdin, the highest spot in Maine (5,267 feet), is the first place in the United States where the sun hits in the morning.

MARYLAND

Old Lime State, Free State

Population (1994): 5,006,265 (19th)
Area: 12,407 square miles (42nd) (32,135 square kilometers)
Flower: Black-eyed susan   **Bird:** Baltimore oriole
Tree: White oak   **Song:** Maryland, My Maryland
Entered Union: April 28, 1788 (7th)
Postal Abbreviation: MD
Capital: Annapolis (population, 33,195)
Largest Cities (with population): Baltimore, 736,014; Rockville, 44,835; Frederick, 40,148; Gaithersburg, 39,452
Important Products: instruments, printing and publishing, food products, transportation equipment, electronic equipment, chickens, milk, corn, stone
Places to Visit: Antietam National Battlefield; Fort McHenry National Monument, in Baltimore harbor; U.S. Naval Academy in Annapolis

 **DID YOU KNOW?** Maryland is the narrowest state—near the town of Hancock, Maryland is only about one mile wide. The American flag on Fort McHenry during the War of 1812 inspired Francis Scott Key to write the "Star Spangled Banner," the national anthem.

MASSACHUSETTS

Bay State, Old Colony

Population (1994): 6,041,123 (13th)
Area: 10,555 square miles (44th) (27,337 square kilometers)
Flower: Mayflower   **Bird:** Chickadee
Tree: American elm   **Song:** All Hail to Massachusetts
Entered Union: February 6, 1788 (6th)
Postal Abbreviation: MA
Capital and Largest City: Boston (population: 574,283)
Other Large Cities (with population): Worcester, 169,759; Springfield, 156,983; Lowell, 103,439
Important Products: industrial machinery, electronic equipment, instruments, printing and publishing, metal products, clothing and textiles, fish, flowers and shrubs, cranberries
Places to Visit: Plymouth Rock, historical sites in Boston, and Minute Man National Historical Park; Children's Museum, Boston; Basketball Hall of Fame, Springfield; Old Sturbridge Village; Martha's Vineyard; Cape Cod

 DID YOU KNOW? The Pilgrims settled in Massachusetts in 1620 and celebrated the first Thanksgiving. Massachusetts is known for other American firsts: the first printing press (1639), the first public school paid for by taxes (1639), and the first college (Harvard, 1636). The American Revolution began in Massachusetts.

MICHIGAN

Great Lakes State, Wolverine State

Population (1994): 9,496,147 (8th)
Area: 96,705 square miles (11th) (250,465 square kilometers)
Flower: Apple blossom   **Bird:** Robin
Tree: White pine   **Song:** Michigan, My Michigan
Entered Union: January 26, 1837 (26th)
Postal Abbreviation: MI
Capital: Lansing (population, 127,321)
Largest Cities (with population): Detroit, 1,027,974; Grand Rapids, 189,126; Warren, 144,864; Flint, 140,761
Important Products: automobiles, industrial machinery, metals and metal products, printing and publishing, rubber and plastic products, chemicals, food products, milk, corn, natural gas, iron ore
Places to Visit: Greenfield Village and Henry Ford Museum, Dearborn; Detroit's "Art Center"; Isle Royal National Park; Pictured Rocks and Sleeping Bear Dunes national lakeshores; Mackinac Island

DID YOU KNOW? Michigan is known for manufacturing automobiles. Lake Michigan is the largest lake entirely in the United States.

MINNESOTA

North Star State, Gopher State

Population (1994): 4,567,267 (20th)
Area: 86,943 square miles (12th) (225,182 square kilometers)
Flower: Pink and white lady's-slipper   **Bird:** Common loon
Tree: Red pine   **Song:** Hail!
Entered Union: May 11, 1858 (32nd)   Minnesota
Postal Abbreviation: MN
Capital: St. Paul
Largest Cities (with population): Minneapolis, 368,383; St. Paul, 272,235
Important Products: industrial machinery, metal products, printing and publishing, food products, instruments, milk, hogs, cattle, corn, soybeans, iron ore
Places to Visit: Voyageurs National Park; Grand Portage National Monument; Minnesota Zoo; Fort Snelling; U.S. Hockey Hall of Fame, Eveleth

DID YOU KNOW? Minnesota is sometimes called the Land of 10,000 Lakes—it actually has more than 15,000 lakes. Minnesota is the second coldest state (Alaska is the coldest). The Mall of America, in Bloomington, is the largest shopping mall in the United States; it has space for 12,750 cars.

MISSISSIPPI

Magnolia State

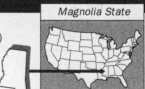

Population (1994): 2,669,111 (31st)
Area: 48,434 square miles (32nd) (125,443 square kilometers)
Flower: Magnolia   **Bird:** Mockingbird
Tree: Magnolia   **Song:** Go, Mississippi!
Entered Union: December 10, 1817 (20th)
Postal Abbreviation: MS
Capital and Largest City: Jackson (population, 196,637)
Other Large Cities (with population): Biloxi, 46,319; Greenville, 45,226
Important Products: transportation equipment, clothing and textiles, furniture, electronic equipment, wood and wood products, cotton, chickens, cattle, oil
Places to Visit: Vicksburg National Military Park; Natchez Trace Parkway; Old Capitol, Jackson; Old Spanish Fort and Museum, Pascagoula

DID YOU KNOW? Mississippi was the first state to celebrate Memorial Day (originally called Decoration Day) as a holiday, in 1866. Mississippi opened the first state-run college for women in Columbus in 1884. Jefferson Davis, president of the Confederate States of America, was born in Mississippi.

MISSOURI

Show Me State

Population (1994): 5,277,640 (16th)
Area: 69,709 square miles (21st) (180,546 square kilometers)
Flower: Hawthorn   **Bird:** Bluebird
Tree: Dogwood   **Song:** Missouri Waltz
Entered Union: August 10, 1821 (24th)
Postal Abbreviation: MO
Capital: Jefferson City (population, 35,481)
Largest Cities (with population): Kansas City, 435,146; St. Louis, 396,685; Springfield, 140,494; Independence, 112,301
Important Products: transportation equipment, metal products, printing and publishing, food products, cattle, hogs, milk, soybeans, corn, hay, lead
Places to Visit: Gateway Arch, St. Louis; Mark Twain Home and Museum, Hannibal; Harry S. Truman Museum, Independence; George Washington Carver Birthplace, Diamond

DID YOU KNOW? Missouri is a major center for shipping and railroads. President Harry S. Truman, agricultural scientist George Washington Carver, and poet Langston Hughes were born in Missouri. It has been said that the ice cream cone was first sold at a World's Fair in St. Louis, in 1904. Gateway Arch, in St. Louis, is the tallest monument (630 feet high) in the United States.

MONTANA

Treasure State

Population (1994): 856,047 (44th)
Area: 147,046 square miles (4th) (380,850 square kilometers)
Flower: Bitterroot   **Bird:** Western meadowlark
Tree: Ponderosa pine   **Song:** Montana
Entered Union: November 8, 1869 (41st)
Postal Abbreviation: MT
Capital: Helena (population, 24,559)
Largest Cities (with population): Billings, 81,151; Great Falls, 55,097; Missoula, 42,918; Butte, 33,941
Important Products: cattle, coal, oil, gold, wheat, hay, wood and wood products
Places to Visit: Yellowstone and Glacier national parks; Little Bighorn Battlefield National Monument, in Crow Agency

DID YOU KNOW? Montana is the fourth-biggest state, after Alaska, Texas, and California. The most famous Indian battle in history took place in Montana, at Little Bighorn in 1876.

NEBRASKA

Cornhusker State

Population (1994): 1,622,858 (37th)
Area: 77,358 square miles (16th) (200,358 square kilometers)
Flower: Goldenrod   **Bird:** Western meadowlark
Tree: Cottonwood   **Song:** Beautiful Nebraska
Entered Union: March 1, 1867 (37th)
Postal Abbreviation: NE
Capital: Lincoln
Largest Cities (with population): Omaha, 335,795; Lincoln, 191,932
Important Products: cattle, hogs, milk, corn, soybeans, hay, wheat, sorghum, food products, industrial machinery
Places to Visit: Oregon Trail landmarks; Stuhr Museum of the Prairie Pioneer, Grand Island; Agate Fossil Beds National Monument; Boys Town, near Omaha

DID YOU KNOW? Nebraska is not only a cattle state; it is the biggest meat-packing center in the world. It is also a farm state. Nebraska is the only state whose nickname comes from a college football team—the popular University of Nebraska Cornhuskers.

NEVADA

Sagebrush State, Battle Born State, Silver State

Population (1994): 1,457,028 (38th)
Area: 110,567 square miles (7th) (286,368 square kilometers)
Flower: Sagebrush   **Bird:** Mountain bluebird
Trees: Single-leaf piñon, bristlecone pine   **Song:** Home Means
Entered Union: October 31, 1864 (36th)   Nevada
Postal Abbreviation: NV
Capital: Carson City (population, 40,443)
Largest Cities (with population): Las Vegas, 258,295;
Reno, 133,850
Important Products: gold, silver, cattle, hay, metals and metal products, printing and publishing
Places to Visit: Great Basin National Park; Nevada State Museum, Carson City; Lake Mead
National Recreation Area; ghost towns

? DID YOU KNOW? It usually rains less in Nevada than in any other state. Between
1980 and 1990 the population of Nevada increased by more than one half, making it
the fastest-growing state. It also has the most wild horses.

NEW HAMPSHIRE

Granite State

Population (1994): 1,136,820 (41st)
Area: 9,351 square miles (46th) (24,219 square kilometers)
Flower: Purple lilac   **Bird:** Purple finch
Tree: White birch   **Song:** Old New Hampshire
Entered Union: June 21, 1788 (9th)
Postal Abbreviation: NH
Capital: Concord
Largest Cities (with population): Manchester, 99,567; Nashua, 79,662; Concord, 36,006
Important Products: industrial machinery, instruments, electronic equipment, metals and
metal products, rubber and plastic products, printing and publishing, paper, milk
Places to Visit: White Mountain National Forest; Mount Washington; Fort at Number 4 Living
History Museum, Charlestown; Old Man in the Mountain, Franconia Notch; Canterbury
Shaker Village

? DID YOU KNOW? Mount Washington is the highest mountain in the northeast. Its peak
is said to be the windiest spot on earth. The first town-supported, free public library in
the United States opened in New Hampshire in 1833

NEW JERSEY

Garden State

Population (1994): 7,903,925 (9th)
Area: 8,722 square miles (47th) (22,590 square kilometers)
Flower: Purple violet   **Bird:** Eastern goldfinch
Tree: Red oak   **Song:** none
Entered Union: December 18, 1787 (3rd)
Postal Abbreviation: NJ
Capital: Trenton (population, 88,675)
Largest Cities (with population): Newark, 275,221; Jersey City, 228,537;
Paterson, 140,891; Elizabeth, 110,002
Important Products: chemicals, printing and publishing, industrial machinery, instruments,
electronic equipment, metal products, stone, clothing and textiles, food products, milk,
tomatoes and vegetables
Places to Visit: ocean beaches; Edison National Historical Site, West Orange; Liberty State
Park; Pine Barrens wilderness area; Great Adventure amusement park

? DID YOU KNOW? The electric light bulb was invented in New Jersey by Thomas Edison
in 1879. The first ferryboat just for cars was built in New Jersey and placed in service
in 1926. New Jersey manufactures more flags than any other state.

NEW MEXICO

Land of Enchantment

Population (1994): 1,653,521 (36th)
Area: 121,598 square miles (5th) (314,939 square kilometers)
Flower: Yucca   **Bird:** Roadrunner
Tree: Piñon   **Song:** O, Fair New Mexico
Entered Union: January 6, 1912 (47th)
Postal Abbreviation: NM
Capital: Santa Fe
Largest Cities (with population): Albuquerque, 384,736; Las Cruces, 62,126; Santa Fe, 55,859
Important Products: natural gas, oil, copper, coal, potash, cattle, milk, hay, cotton, electronic equipment, instruments
Places to Visit: Carlsbad Caverns National Park; Palace of the Governors and Mission of San Miguel, Santa Fe; Chaco Canyon National Monument; cliff dwellings

 DID YOU KNOW? The oldest capital city in the United States is Santa Fe, New Mexico. Pueblo Indians had an advanced civilization in New Mexico a thousand years ago. The deepest cave in the United States is in New Mexico's Carlsbad Caverns. The first atom bomb was exploded in New Mexico, in a test on July 16, 1945.

NEW YORK

Empire State

Population (1994): 18,169,051 (3rd)
Area: 54,471 square miles (27th) (141,079 square kilometers)
Flower: Rose   **Bird:** Bluebird
Tree: Sugar maple   **Song:** I Love New York
Entered Union: July 26, 1788 (11th)
Postal Abbreviation: NY
Capital: Albany (population, 101,082)
Largest Cities (with population): New York, 7,322,564; Buffalo, 328,123; Rochester, 231,636; Yonkers, 188,082
Important Products: printing and publishing, instruments, electronic equipment, industrial machinery, clothing and textiles, transportation equipment, metal products, milk, cattle, hay, stone
Places to Visit: In New York City, museums, Empire State Building, United Nations, Bronx Zoo, Statue of Liberty and Ellis Island; Niagara Falls; National Baseball Hall of Fame, Cooperstown; Fort Ticonderoga; Franklin D. Roosevelt National Historical Site, Hyde Park

 DID YOU KNOW? New York City is the largest city in the United States. New York City was the first capital of the United States. The first pizza restaurant in the United States opened in New York City in 1895. The first children's museum opened in Brooklyn in 1899.

NORTH CAROLINA

Tar Heel State,
Old North State

Population (1994): 7,069,836 (10th)
Area: 53,821 square miles (28th) (139,397 square kilometers)
Flower: Dogwood   **Bird:** Cardinal
Tree: Pine   **Song:** The Old North State
Entered Union: November 21, 1789 (12th)
Postal Abbreviation: NC
Capital: Raleigh
Largest Cities (with population): Charlotte, 395,934; Raleigh, 207,951; Greensboro, 183,521; Winston-Salem, 143,485; Durham, 136,611
Important Products: clothing and textiles, tobacco and tobacco products, industrial machinery, electronic equipment, furniture, chemicals, foods, chickens, hogs, stone
Places to Visit: Great Smoky Mountains National Park; Cape Hatteras National Seashore; Wright Brothers National Memorial, at Kitty Hawk

DID YOU KNOW? The Wright Brothers took the first airplane ride in history in North Carolina. The first U.S. school of forestry was opened in North Carolina.

NORTH DAKOTA

Peace Garden State

Population (1994): 637,988 (47th)
Area: 70,704 square miles (19th) (183,123 square kilometers)
Flower: Wild prairie rose   **Bird:** Western meadowlark
Tree: American elm   **Song:** North Dakota Hymn
Entered Union: November 2, 1889 (39th)
Postal Abbreviation: ND
Capital: Bismarck
Largest Cities (with population): Fargo, 74,711; Grand Forks, 49,425; Bismarck, 49,256; Minot, 34,544
Important Products: wheat, barley, hay, sunflowers, sugar beets, cattle, milk, oil, coal, industrial machinery, food products
Places to Visit: Theodore Roosevelt National Park; Bonanzaville, near Fargo; Dakota Dinosaur Museum, Dickinson; International Peace Garden

DID YOU KNOW? North Dakota is one of the two biggest wheat-growing states in the United States (the other is Kansas). Theodore Roosevelt was a rancher here before he became president.

OHIO

Buckeye State

Population (1994): 11,102,198 (7th)
Area: 44,828 square miles (34th) (116,103 square kilometers)
Flower: Scarlet carnation   **Bird:** Cardinal
Tree: Buckeye   **Song:** Beautiful Ohio
Entered Union: March 1, 1803 (17th)
Postal Abbreviation: OH
Capital and Largest City: Columbus (population, 632,910)
Other Large Cities (with population): Cleveland, 505,616; Cincinnati, 364,040; Toledo, 332,943; Akron, 223,019; Dayton, 182,044
Important Products: metal and metal products, transportation equipment, industrial machinery, rubber and plastic products, electronic equipment, printing and publishing, chemicals, food products, coal, corn, soybeans, livestock, milk
Places to Visit: Mound City Group National Monuments, Indian burial mounds; Neil Armstrong Air and Space Museum; Cedar Point and King's Island amusement parks

DID YOU KNOW? Ohio was the birthplace of seven American presidents (Garfield, Grant, Harding, B. Harrison, Hayes, McKinley, Taft). Ohio was the home of the first professional baseball team, the Cincinnati Red Stockings. Ohio was the birthplace of the hot dog.

OKLAHOMA

Sooner State

Population (1994): 3,258,069 (28th)
Area: 69,903 square miles (20th) (181,049 square kilometers)
Flower: Mistletoe   **Bird:** Scissor-tailed flycatcher
Tree: Redbud   **Song:** Oklahoma!
Entered Union: November 16, 1907 (46th)
Postal Abbreviation: OK
Capital and Largest City: Oklahoma City (population, 444,719)
Other Large Cities (with population): Tulsa, 367,302; Lawton, 80,561; Norman, 80,071
Important Products: natural gas, oil, cattle, industrial machinery, transportation equipment, metal products, electronic equipment, rubber and plastic products, wheat, hay
Places to Visit: Indian City U.S.A., near Anadarko; Fort Gibson Stockade; National Cowboy Hall of Fame; White Water Bay and Frontier City theme parks; Cherokee Heritage Center

DID YOU KNOW? The American Indian nations called The Five Civilized Tribes (Cherokees, Chickasaws, Choctaws, Creeks, and Seminoles) settled in Oklahoma. Today, more Native Americans live in Oklahoma than in any other state.

OREGON

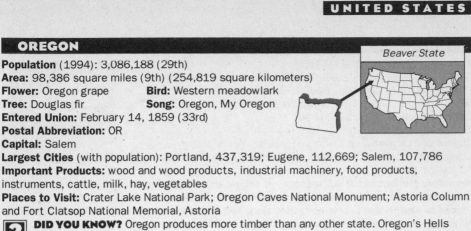

Beaver State

Population (1994): 3,086,188 (29th)
Area: 98,386 square miles (9th) (254,819 square kilometers)
Flower: Oregon grape   **Bird:** Western meadowlark
Tree: Douglas fir   **Song:** Oregon, My Oregon
Entered Union: February 14, 1859 (33rd)
Postal Abbreviation: OR
Capital: Salem
Largest Cities (with population): Portland, 437,319; Eugene, 112,669; Salem, 107,786
Important Products: wood and wood products, industrial machinery, food products, instruments, cattle, milk, hay, vegetables
Places to Visit: Crater Lake National Park; Oregon Caves National Monument; Astoria Column and Fort Clatsop National Memorial, Astoria

 DID YOU KNOW? Oregon produces more timber than any other state. Oregon's Hells Canyon, 7,900 feet deep at its maximum, is one of the deepest canyons in the world, and Crater Lake, which gets as deep as 1,932 feet, is the deepest lake in the United States.

PENNSYLVANIA

Keystone State

Population (1994): 12,052,367 (5th)
Area: 46,058 square miles (33rd) (119,291 square kilometers)
Flower: Mountain laurel   **Bird:** Ruffled grouse
Tree: Hemlock   **Song:** Pennsylvania
Entered Union: December 12, 1787 (2nd)
Postal Abbreviation: PA
Capital: Harrisburg (population, 52,376)
Largest Cities (with population): Philadelphia, 1,585,577; Pittsburgh, 369,879; Erie, 108,718; Allentown, 105,090
Important Products: iron and steel, coal, industrial machinery, printing and publishing, food products, electronic equipment, clothing and textiles, transportation equipment, milk, hay
Places to Visit: Independence Hall and other historic sites in Philadelphia; Franklin Institute Science Museum, Philadelphia; Valley Forge; Gettysburg; Hershey; Pennsylvania Dutch country, Lancaster County

DID YOU KNOW? Pennsylvania is known for the Liberty Bell in Philadelphia, which first rang after the signing of the Declaration of Independence. Philadelphia was also the U.S. capital for 10 years, from 1790 to 1800. The first hospital in the United States was established in Philadelphia in 1752.

RHODE ISLAND

Little Rhody, Ocean State

Population (1994): 996,757 (43rd)
Area: 1,545 square miles (50th) (4,002 square kilometers)
Flower: Violet   **Bird:** Rhode Island red
Tree: Red maple   **Song:** Rhode Island
Entered Union: May 29, 1790 (13th)
Postal Abbreviation: RI
Capital and Largest City: Providence (population, 160,728)
Other Large Cities (with population): Warwick, 85,427; Cranston, 76,060; Pawtucket, 72,644
Important Products: metals and metal products, instruments, clothing and textiles, printing and publishing, rubber and plastic products, industrial machinery, electronic equipment, fish
Places to Visit: Block Island; mansions, old buildings, and harbor in Newport; International Tennis Hall of Fame, Newport

 DID YOU KNOW? Rhode Island is the smallest state. The bluffs and islands of Rhode Island attract many tourists who like fishing and swimming. The oldest synagogue in the United States (Touro Synagogue, 1763) is in Newport.

SOUTH CAROLINA

Palmetto State

Population (1994): 3,663,984 (25th)
Area: 32,007 square miles (40th) (82,898 square kilometers)
Flower: Yellow jessamine   **Bird:** Carolina wren
Tree: Palmetto   **Song:** Carolina
Entered Union: May 23, 1788 (8th)
Postal Abbreviation: SC
Capital and Largest City: Columbia (population, 98,052)
Other Large Cities (with population): Charleston, 80,414; North Charleston, 70,218; Greenville, 58,282
Important Products: clothing and textiles, chemicals, industrial machinery, rubber and plastic products, electronic equipment, paper, metal products, livestock, tobacco, stone
Places to Visit: Grand Strand and Hilton Head Island beaches; Revolutionary War battlefields; historic sites in Charleston; Fort Sumter; Historic Camden

 DID YOU KNOW? More battles of the American Revolution took place in South Carolina than in any other state. The first shots of the Civil War were fired in South Carolina. Charleston Museum, established in 1773, is the oldest museum in the United States.

SOUTH DAKOTA

Mt. Rushmore State, Coyote State

Population (1994): 721,164 (45th)
Area: 77,121 square miles (17th) (199,743 square kilometers)
Flower: Pasqueflower   **Bird:** Ring-necked pheasant
Tree: Black Hills spruce   **Song:** Hail, South Dakota
Entered Union: November 2, 1889 (40th)
Postal Abbreviation: SD
Capital: Pierre (population, 12,906)
Largest Cities (with population): Sioux Falls, 100,814; Rapid City, 54,523
Important Products: cattle, hogs, milk, corn, hay, wheat, soybeans, food products, gold
Places to Visit: Mount Rushmore National Memorial; Crazy Horse Memorial; Jewel Cave; Badlands and Wind Caves national parks; Wounded Knee battlefield; Homestake Gold Mine

 DID YOU KNOW? South Dakota is best known for the faces of presidents carved on Mount Rushmore (Presidents Washington, Jefferson, Lincoln, and T. Roosevelt). Famous South Dakotans include Crazy Horse, Sitting Bull, and Wild Bill Hickok.

TENNESSEE

Volunteer State

Population (1994): 5,175,240 (17th)
Area: 42,146 square miles (36th) (109,158 square kilometers)
Flower: Iris   **Bird:** Mockingbird
Tree: Tulip poplar   **Song:** The Tennessee Waltz
Entered Union: June 1, 1796 (16th)
Postal Abbreviation: TN
Capital: Nashville
Largest Cities (with population): Memphis, 610,337; Nashville, 510,784; Knoxville, 165,121; Chattanooga, 152,466
Important Products: chemicals, clothing and textiles, industrial machinery, motor vehicles, food products, metal products, printing and publishing, electronic equipment, wood products and furniture, livestock, milk, soybeans, tobacco, stone
Places to Visit: Great Smoky Mountains National Park; the Hermitage, home of President Andrew Jackson near Nashville; Civil War battle sites; Grand Old Opry and Opryland, USA, theme park, Nashville; Graceland, home of Elvis Presley in Memphis

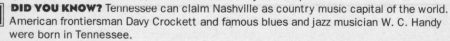 **DID YOU KNOW?** Tennessee can claim Nashville as country music capital of the world. American frontiersman Davy Crockett and famous blues and jazz musician W. C. Handy were born in Tennessee.

TEXAS

Lone Star State

Population (1994): 18,378,185 (2nd)
Area: 268,601 square miles (2nd) (695,676 square kilometers)
Flower: Bluebonnet   **Bird:** Mockingbird
Tree: Pecan   **Song:** Texas, Our Texas
Entered Union: December 29, 1845 (28th)
Postal Abbreviation: TX
Capital: Austin
Largest Cities (with population): Houston, 1,630,553; Dallas, 1,006,877; San Antonio, 935,933; El Paso, 515,342; Austin, 465,622; Fort Worth, 447,619
Important Products: oil, natural gas, cattle, milk, transportation equipment, chemicals, industrial machinery, electronic equipment, cotton, hay
Places to Visit: Guadalupe and Big Bend national parks; the Alamo, in San Antonio; Lyndon Johnson National Historic Site, near Johnson City; Six Flags Over Texas amusement park, Arlington

 DID YOU KNOW? Texas is the largest of the contiguous 48 states (the 48 states that border each other) and is second in size only to Alaska. One of the richest states in natural resources, Texas has more oil and natural gas than any other state and the most farmland. Texas is the only state with five major ports.

UTAH

Beehive State

Population (1994): 1,907,936 (34th)
Area: 84,904 square miles (13th) (219,902 square kilometers)
Flower: Sego lily   **Bird:** Seagull
Tree: Blue spruce   **Song:** Utah, We Love Thee
Entered Union: January 4, 1896 (45th)
Postal Abbreviation: UT
Capital and Largest City: Salt Lake City (population, 159,963)
Other Large Cities (with population): West Valley City, 86,976; Provo, 86,835
Important Products: transportation equipment, industrial machinery, instruments, food products, oil, coal, natural gas, copper, cattle, milk, hay
Places to Visit: Arches, Canyonlands, Bryce Canyon, Zion, and Capitol Reef national parks; Great Salt Lake; Temple Square (Mormon Church headquarters) in Salt Lake City, Indian cliff dwellings

 DID YOU KNOW? Utah's Great Salt Lake, which contains 6 billion tons of salt, is the largest lake in the United States outside of the Great Lakes. Rainbow Bridge in Utah is the largest natural arch or rock bridge in the world; it is 200 feet high and 270 feet wide.

VERMONT

Green Mountain State

Population (1994): 580,209 (49th)
Area: 9,615 square miles (45th) (24,903 square kilometers)
Flower: Red clover   **Bird:** Hermit thrush
Tree: Sugar maple   **Song:** Hail, Vermont!
Entered Union: March 4, 1791 (14th)
Postal Abbreviation: VT
Capital: Montpelier (population, 8,247)
Largest Cities (with population): Burlington, 39,127; Rutland, 18,230
Important Products: electronic equipment, industrial machinery, printing and publishing, metal products, wood and stone products, milk, hay, maple syrup, granite, marble
Places to Visit: Green Mountain National Forest; Shelburne Museum

 DID YOU KNOW? Vermont is famous for its granite, marble, scenery, and maple syrup. Vermont passed the first constitution (1777) to prohibit slavery and to allow all men to vote. The first ski tow in the United States was established in Vermont in 1934.

VIRGINIA

Population (1994): 6,551,522 (12th)
Area: 42,777 square miles (35th) (110,792 square kilometers)
Flower: Dogwood   **Bird:** Cardinal
Tree: Dogwood   **Song:** Carry Me Back to Old Virginia
Entered Union: June 25, 1788 (10th)
Postal Abbreviation: VA
Capital: Richmond
Largest Cities (with population): Virginia Beach, 393,069; Norfolk, 261,229; Richmond, 203,056; Newport News, 170,045
Important Products: transportation equipment, clothing and textiles, chemicals, printing and publishing, electronic equipment, food products, coal, livestock, milk, hay, tobacco
Places to Visit: Colonial Williamsburg; Busch Gardens, Williamsburg; Arlington National Cemetery; Mount Vernon (George Washington's home); Monticello (Thomas Jefferson's home); Shenandoah National Park

 DID YOU KNOW? Virginia was the birthplace of eight presidents (Presidents W. H. Harrison, Jefferson, Madison, Monroe, Taylor, Tyler, Washington, Wilson), more than any other state. The first permanent English settlement in the New World was in Virginia.

WASHINGTON

Population (1994): 5,343,090 (15th)
Area: 71,302 square miles (18th) (184,672 square kilometers)
Flower: Western rhododendron   **Bird:** Willow goldfinch
Tree: Western hemlock   **Song:** Washington, My Home
Entered Union: November 11, 1889 (42nd)
Postal Abbreviation: WA
Capital: Olympia (population, 33,840)
Largest Cities (with population): Seattle, 516,259; Spokane, 177,196; Tacoma, 176,664
Important Products: aircraft and aerospace equipment, lumber and wood products, food products, paper, industrial machinery, apples, wheat, cattle, milk, coal, fish
Places to Visit: Mount Rainier, Olympic, and North Cascades national parks; Mount St. Helens; Seattle Center, with Space Needle and monorail

 DID YOU KNOW? Washington's Grand Coulee Dam, on the Columbia River, is the world's largest concrete dam. Mount St. Helens is the tallest volcano in the contiguous 48 states and the only active one. Washington is known for its apples, timber, and fishing fleets.

WEST VIRGINIA

Population (1994): 1,822,021 (35th)
Area: 24,231 square miles (41st) (62,759 square kilometers)
Flower: Big rhododendron   **Bird:** Cardinal
Tree: Sugar maple   **Songs:** The West Virginia Hills, This Is My West Virginia, and West Virginia, My Home Sweet Home
Entered Union: June 20, 1863 (35th)
Postal Abbreviation: WV
Capital and Largest City: Charleston (population, 57,287)
Other Large Cities (with population): Huntington, 54,844; Wheeling, 34,882
Important Products: coal, natural gas, metal and metal products, chemicals, stone, clay, and glass products, industrial machinery, cattle, hay
Places to Visit: Harpers Ferry National Historic Park; Grave Creek Mound, Moundsville; Monongahela National Forest

 DID YOU KNOW? West Virginia's mountain scenery and mineral springs attract many tourists. The state is one of the biggest coal states. West Virginia was part of Virginia until West Virginians decided to break away, in 1861.

WISCONSIN

Badger State

Population (1994): 5,081,658 (18th)
Area: 65,499 square miles (23rd) (169,642 square kilometers)
Flower: Wood violet **Bird:** Robin
Tree: Sugar maple **Song:** On, Wisconsin!
Entered Union: May 29, 1848 (30th)
Postal Abbreviation: WI
Capital: Madison
Largest Cities (with population): Milwaukee, 628,088; Madison, 191,262; Green Bay, 96,466; Racine, 84,298; Kenosha, 80,352
Important Products: industrial machinery; paper; metal products; milk, cheese, beer, packed meat, and other foods; printing and publishing; corn, hay, and vegetables
Places to Visit: Dells of the Wisconsin; Cave of the Mounds, near Blue Mounds; Milwaukee Public Museum; Circus World Museum, Baraboo; National Railroad Museum, Green Bay

DID YOU KNOW? Wisconsin is known as America's Dairyland; more recently it has also become a major manufacturing state. The first kindergarten in America was opened in Wisconsin in 1865.

WYOMING

Equality State

Population (1994): 475,981 (50th)
Area: 97,818 square miles (10th) (253,349 square kilometers)
Flower: Indian paintbrush **Bird:** Meadowlark
Tree: Cottonwood **Song:** Wyoming
Entered Union: July 10, 1890 (44th)
Postal Abbreviation: WY
Capital and Largest City: Cheyenne (population, 50,008)
Other Large Cities (with population): Casper, 46,742; Laramie, 26,687
Important Products: oil, coal, natural gas, clays, oil and coal products, cattle, hay
Places to Visit: Yellowstone and Grand Teton national parks; Fort Laramie; Buffalo Bill Historical Center, in Cody

DID YOU KNOW? Wyoming is the home of the first U.S. national park (Yellowstone). Established in 1872, Yellowstone has 10,000 geysers, including the world's tallest active geyser (Steamboat Geyser).

PUERTO RICO

Puerto Rico

History: Christopher Columbus landed in Puerto Rico in 1493. Puerto Rico was a Spanish colony for centuries, then fell to the United States in 1898 after the Spanish-American War. In 1952, still associated with the United States, Puerto Rico became a commonwealth with its own constitution.
Population estimate: 3,522,000
Area: 3,492 square miles (9,044 square kilometers)
National Anthem: La Borinqueña
Became a Self-Governing Commonwealth: July 25, 1952
Postal Abbreviation: PR
Capital and Largest City: San Juan (population, 426,832)
Other Large Cities (with population): Bayamón, 202,103; Carolina, 162,404; Ponce, 159,151
Important Products: chemicals, food products, electronic equipment, clothing and textiles, instruments, industrial machinery, coffee, vegetables, sugarcane, dairy products
Places to Visit: San Juan National Historic Site; beaches and resorts

DID YOU KNOW? Puerto Ricans have most of the rights of American citizens, but they cannot vote in U.S. presidential elections and do not pay federal income tax.

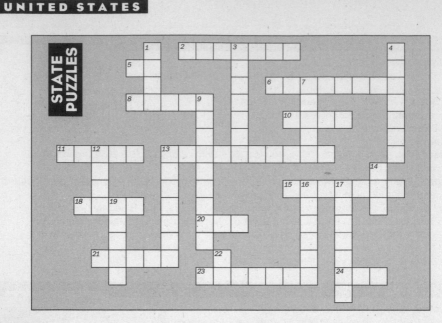

STATE PUZZLES

ACROSS

2. The chief crop in North Carolina.
5. Postal abbreviation for the northeastern state with the first ski tow.
6. This red bird is the state bird of Ohio, Kentucky, and Illinois.
8. This grain is the chief crop in Kansas and North Dakota.
10. Large amounts of this fuel are mined in Kentucky, Pennsylvania, and West Virginia.
11. A state in the west known for its potatoes. Its capital is Boise.
13. These fruits are a major product of Hawaii.
15. This president lived and worked in Illinois and is buried there.
18. This valuable mineral is Nevada's most important product.
20. Colorado has more of these wild animals than any other state.
21. The biggest state except for Alaska. Known for its cattle and oil.
23. The state tree of California.
24. The state tree of Iowa.

DOWN

1. The Great Salt Lake is in this western state.
3. The biggest city in Georgia.
4. Nickname for the state of Louisiana.
7. The smallest state (first word only).
9. Nashville, the world's country music capital, is located in this state.
12. Indianapolis, Indiana, is famous for this kind of racing.
13. These fruits are a major product of Georgia.
14. The state tree of North Dakota (second word only).
16. The smallest state (second word only).
17. This president was born in Arkansas and became governor there.
19. There are more than 15,000 of these in Minnesota.
22. Postal abbreviation for the first state to join the United States. Wilmington is its largest city.

(Answers are on page 305.)

To the right are the names of five states, their capital city, and one chief product—scrambled up. Can you unscramble each word? If you need help, look back at the Facts About the States.

STATE	CAPITAL	PRODUCT
SAKALA	EAUJUN	LOI
LARINAFIOC	SAMENCRATO	VOMIES
DRAFILO	SEEATALLHAS	RANGOES
GICHINMA	SINGLAN	BILESMOTOAU
MAHOLOAK	KOMAHALO TCIY	TLECAT

(Answers are on page 305.)

WASHINGTON, D.C.:
The Capital of the United States

Area: 69 square miles
Population: (1992): 588,620

Flower: American beauty rose
Bird: Wood thrush

HISTORY. Washington, D.C., became the capital of the United States in 1800, when the U.S. government moved there from Philadelphia. The city of Washington was especially designed and built to be the capital. It was named after George Washington, the first president of the United States. Today, Washington is a city of wide, tree-lined boulevards and impressive buildings. Many of its major sights are located on the Mall, an open grassy area that runs from the Capitol to the Potomac River.

The Capitol, which houses the United States Congress, is at the east end of the Mall, on Capitol Hill. The dome of the Capitol's rotunda can be seen from many parts of the city.

Jefferson Memorial, a circular marble building located near the Potomac River. At night, it is floodlit and very impressive.

Lincoln Memorial, at the west end of the Mall, is built of white marble and styled like a Greek temple. Inside is a large, seated statue of Abraham Lincoln, whose Gettysburg Address is carved on one wall. From the Lincoln Memorial, you can look down the Mall to the Washington Monument and the Capitol.

National Archives, on Constitution Avenue, is the place to see the Declaration of Independence, the Constitution, and the Bill of Rights.

National Gallery of Art, on the Mall, is one of the world's great art museums. Older paintings and sculptures are housed in the West Building, while 20th-century art is housed in the newer East Building.

Smithsonian Institution has 14 museums, including the National Air and Space Museum and the Museum of Natural History. The Smithsonian Information Center, located in "the Castle" on the Mall, is a good place to start a visit. The Smithsonian also has museums outside of Washington.

Vietnam Veterans Memorial has a black-granite wall shaped like a V. The names of the more than 58,000 Americans who lost their lives in the Vietnam War are inscribed on the wall.

Washington Monument, a white marble pillar, or obelisk, standing on the Mall and rising to over 555 feet. From the top, there are wonderful views of the city.

White House, at 1600 Pennsylvania Avenue, has been the home of every U.S. president except George Washington, who chose its site in 1790 and supervised its construction. Only the public rooms can be visited.

▲ White House

How the STATES

Alabama comes from *Alibamu*, which was the name of the town of a Creek Indian tribe.

Alaska comes from *alakshak*, the Aleutian (Eskimo) word meaning "mainland" or "land that is not an island."

Arizona comes from an American Indian word meaning "little spring" or "little spring place."

Arkansas is a variation of *Quapaw*, the name of a Sioux Indian tribe. *Quapaw* means "downstream people."

California is the name of an imaginary island in a Spanish story. It was named by Spanish explorers of Baja California, a part of Mexico.

Colorado comes from a Spanish word meaning "reddish." It was first given to the Colorado river because of its reddish color.

Connecticut comes from an Algonquin Indian word meaning "beside the long tidal river."

Delaware is named after Lord De La Warr, the English governor of Virginia in colonial times.

Florida, which means "flowery" in Spanish, was named by the explorer Ponce de Leon, who landed there during the Spanish flower festival.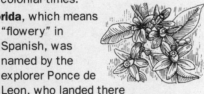

Georgia was named after King George II of England, who granted the right to create a colony there in 1732.

Hawaii probably comes from *Hawaiki,* or *Owhyhee*, the native Polynesians' name for their homeland.

Idaho's name is of uncertain origin, but it may come from an Apache name for the Comanche Indians.

Illinois is the French version of *Illini,* an Algonquin Indian word meaning "men" or "warriors."

Indiana means "land of the Indians."

Iowa comes from the name of an American Indian tribe that lived on the land that is now the state.

Kansas comes from a Sioux Indian word that possibly meant "people of the south wind."

Kentucky comes from an Iroquois Indian word, possibly meaning "meadowland."

Louisiana, which was first settled by French explorers, was named after King Louis XIV of France.

Maine means "the mainland." English explorers called it that to distinguish it from islands nearby.

Maryland was named after Queen Henrietta Maria, wife of King Charles I of England, who granted the right to establish an English colony there.

Massachusetts comes from an Algonquin Indian word meaning "at the big hill."

Michigan comes from the Chippewa Indian words *mici gama*, meaning "great water" (referring to Lake Michigan).

Minnesota got its name from a Sioux Indian word meaning "cloudy water" or "sky-tinted water."

Mississippi is probably derived from two Chippewa Indian words meaning "great river" or "father of the waters," or from an Algonquin word.

Missouri comes from an Algonquin Indian term meaning "people of the big canoes."

Montana comes from a Spanish word meaning "mountainous."

Got Their NAMES

Nebraska comes from "flat water," an Omaha or Otos Indian name for the Platte River.

Nevada means "snowy or "snow-covered" in Spanish. Spanish explorers gave the name to the Sierra Nevada Mountains.

New Hampshire was named by an early settler after his home county of Hampshire, in England.

New Jersey was named for the English Channel island of Jersey.

New Mexico was given its name by a Spanish explorer in Mexico.

New York, first called New Netherland, was renamed for the Duke of York and Albany after the English took it from Dutch settlers.

North Carolina, the northern part of the English colony of Carolana, was named for King Charles I.

North Dakota comes from a Sioux Indian word meaning "allied tribes."

Ohio is the Iroquois Indian word for "fine or good river."

Oklahoma comes from a Choctaw Indian word meaning "red people."

Oregon may have come from *Ouaricon-sint,* a name on a French map for the Wisconsin River, and mistakenly given to the Columbia River. The name of the Columbia River was changed, but the state kept the name.

Pennsylvania, meaning "Penn's woods," was the name given to the colony founded by William Penn.

Rhode Island may have come from the Dutch Roode Eylandt (red island) or may have been named after the Greek island of Rhodes.

South Carolina, the southern part of the English colony of Carolana, was named for King Charles I.

South Dakota comes from a Sioux Indian word meaning "allied tribes."

Tennessee comes from the name the Cherokee Indians gave to their ancient capital. The name was given to the Tennessee River. The state was named after the river.

Texas comes from a word meaning "friends" or "allies," used by the Spanish to describe some of the American Indians living there.

Utah comes from Ute, the name of a Shoshone Indian tribe.

Vermont comes from two French words, *vert* (green) and *mont* (mountain).

Virginia was named in honor of Queen Elizabeth I of England, who was known as the Virgin Queen because she never married.

Washington was named after George Washington, the first president of the United States.

West Virginia got its name from the people of western Virginia, who formed their own government during the Civil War.

Wisconsin comes from an Algonquin Indian name for the state's principal river. The word, meaning "the place where the waters come together," was once spelled *Ouisconsin.*

Wyoming comes from an Algonquin Indian word meaning "at the big plains" or "large prairie place."

NATIONAL PARKS

Most national parks are large and naturally beautiful and have a wide variety of scenery. They are visited by millions of people each year. The world's first national park was Yellowstone, established in 1872 in the northwestern United States. Since then, the American government has set aside a total of 53 national parks. Fifty-one of those in the United States are listed below. Two outside the United States are in the Virgin Islands and American Samoa. The National Park Service oversees the national parks and tries to keep them unspoiled.

Acadia (Maine)
  41,972 acres; established 1929
  Rugged coast and granite cliffs; seals, whales, and porpoises; highest land along the East Coast of the U.S.

Arches (Utah)
  73,379 acres; established 1971
  Giant natural sandstone arches, including Landscape Arch, over 100 feet high and 291 feet long

Badlands (South Dakota)
  242,756 acres; established 1978
  A prairie where, over centuries, the land has been formed into many odd shapes with a variety of colors

Big Bend (Texas)
  801,163 acres; established 1935
  Desert land and rugged mountains, on the Rio Grande River; dinosaur fossils

Biscayne (Florida)
  172,924 acres; established 1980
  A water-park on a chain of islands in the Atlantic Ocean, south of Miami, with beautiful coral reefs

Bryce Canyon (Utah)
  35,835 acres; established 1928
  Odd and very colorful rock formations carved by centuries of erosion

Canyonlands (Utah)
  337,570 acres; established 1964
  Sandstone cliffs above the Colorado River; rock carvings from an ancient American Indian civilization

Capitol Reef (Utah),
  241,904 acres; established 1971
  Sandstone cliffs cut into by gorges with high walls; old American Indian storage huts

Carlsbad Caverns (New Mexico)
  46,766 acres; established 1930
  A huge cave system, not fully explored, with the world's largest underground chamber, called "the Big Room"

Channel Islands (California)
  249,354 acres; established 1980
  Islands off the California coast, with sea lions, seals, and sea birds

Crater Lake (Oregon)
  183,224 acres; established 1902
  The deepest lake in the United States, carved in the crater of an inactive volcano; lava walls up to 2,000 feet high

Death Valley (California)
  over 3 million acres; established 1994
  Largest national park outside Alaska. Vast hot desert, rocky slopes and gorges, huge sand dunes; hundreds of species of plants, some unique to the area; variety of wildlife, including desert foxes, bobcats, coyotes

Denali (Alaska)
  4,741,910 acres; established 1980
  Huge park, containing America's tallest mountain, plus caribou, moose, sheep

Dry Tortugas (Florida)
64,700 acres; established 1992
Colorful birds and fish; a 19th-century
fort, Fort Jefferson

Everglades (Florida)
1,506,499 acres; established 1934
The largest subtropical wilderness
within the U.S.; swamps with
mangrove trees, rare birds, alligators

Gates of the Arctic (Alaska)
7,523,888 acres; established 1980
The largest national park; huge tundra
wilderness, with rugged peaks and
steep valleys

Glacier (Montana)
1,013,572 acres; established 1940
Rugged mountains, with glaciers,
lakes, sheep, bears, and bald eagles

Glacier Bay (Alaska)
3,225,284 acres; established 1910
Glaciers moving down mountainsides
to the sea; seals, whales, bears, eagles

Grand Canyon (Arizona)
1,217,158 acres; established 1919
Mile-deep expanse of multicolored
layered rock, a national wonder

Grand Teton (Wyoming)
309,992 acres; established 1929
Set in the Teton Mountains; a winter
feeding ground for elks

Great Basin (Nevada)
77,180 acres; established 1986
From deserts to meadows to tundra;
caves; ancient pine trees

Great Smoky Mountains
(North Carolina, Tennessee)
520,269 acres; established 1926
Forests, with deer, fox, and black bears,
and streams with trout and bass

Guadalupe Mountains (Texas)
86,416 acres; established 1966
Remains of a fossil reef formed 225
million years ago

Haleakala (Hawaii)
28,099 acres; established 1960
The largest crater of any inactive
volcano in the world

Hawaii Volcanoes (Hawaii)
229,177 acres; established 1961
Home of two large active volcanoes,
Mauna Loa and Kilauea, along with a
desert and a tree fern forest

Hot Springs (Arkansas)
5,543 acres; established 1921
47 hot springs that provide warm
waters for drinking and bathing

Isle Royale (Michigan)
571,790 acres; established 1931
On an island in Lake Superior; woods,
lakes, many kinds of animals—and
no roads

Joshua Tree (California)
559,955 acres; established 1994
Large desert with rock
formations and
unusual desert
plants, including
many Joshua
trees; fossils
from pre-
historic
times;
wildlife,
including
desert bighorn

Katmai (Alaska)
3,716,000 acres; established 1980
Contains the Valley of Ten Thousand
Smokes, which was filled with ash
when Katmai Volcano erupted in 1912

Kenai Fjords (Alaska)
669,541 acres; established 1980
Fjords, rain forests, the Harding
Icefield; sea otters, seals; a breeding
place for many birds

Kings Canyon (California)
461,901 acres; established 1940
Mountains and woods and the highest
canyon wall in the U.S.

Kobuk Valley (Alaska)
1,750,736 acres; established 1980
Located north of the Arctic Circle, with
caribou and black bears; archeological
sites indicate that humans have lived
there for over 10,000 years

Lake Clark (Alaska)
2,636,839 acres; established 1980
Lakes, waterfalls, glaciers, volcanoes,
fish and wildlife

Lassen Volcanic (California)
106,372 acres; established 1916
Contains Lassen Peak, a volcano that
began erupting in 1914, after being
dormant for 400 years

Mammoth Cave (Kentucky)
52,419 acres; established 1941
The world's longest known cave
network, with over 300 miles of
mapped passages

Mesa Verde (Colorado)
52,122 acres; established 1906
A plateau covered by woods and
canyons; the best preserved ancient
cliff dwellings in the U.S.

Mount Rainier (Washington)
235,612 acres; established 1899
Home of Mount Rainier, a volcano dormant since 1870; thick forests, glaciers

North Cascades (Washington)
504,781 acres; established 1968
Rugged mountains and valleys, with
deep canyons, lakes and glaciers

Olympic (Washington)
922,651 acres; established 1938
Rain forest, with woods and
mountains, glaciers, and rare elk

Petrified Forest (Arizona)
93,533 acres; established 1962
A large area of woods turned into
stone; American Indian pueblos and
rock carvings

Redwood (California)
110,232 acres; established 1968
Groves of ancient redwood trees, the
world's tallest trees

Rocky Mountain (Colorado)
265,727 acres; established 1915
Located in the Rockies, with gorges,
alpine lakes, and 59 mountain peaks
at least 12,000 feet high

Sequoia (California)
402,482 acres; established 1890
Groves of giant sequoia trees, the
world's tallest living things; Mount
Whitney (14,494 feet), highest peak in
the lower 48 states

Shenandoah (Virginia)
196,466 acres; established 1926
Located in the highest part of the Blue
Ridge Mountains, overlooking the
scenic Shenandoah Valley

Theodore Roosevelt (North Dakota)
70,447 acres; established 1978
Scenic badlands and a part of the old
Elkhorn Ranch that belonged to
Theodore Roosevelt

Voyageurs (Minnesota)
218,035 acres; established 1971
Forests with wildlife and many scenic
lakes for canoeing and boating

Wind Cave (South Dakota)
28,295 acres; established 1903
Limestone caverns in the Black Hills; a
prairie with colonies of prairie dogs

Wrangell-Saint Elias (Alaska)
4,852,773 acres; established 1980
The biggest national park, with
mountain peaks over 16,000 feet high

Yellowstone (Idaho, Montana, Wyoming)
2,219,791 acres; established 1872
The first national park and world's
greatest geysers; waterfalls and
canyons; bears and moose

Yosemite (California)
751,236 acres; established 1890
Yosemite Valley; highest waterfall in
North America; mountain scenery

Zion (Utah)
146,598 acres; established 1919
Deep, narrow Zion Canyon and other
canyons in different colors; Indian cliff
dwellings over 1,000 years old

Naming HURRICANES

For many years, violent storms have been given names. Until early in the 20th century, people named storms after saints. Then, in 1953, the U.S. government began to use women's names for hurricanes. Men's names began to be used in 1978. Today, there are six sets of names for both Atlantic and Pacific hurricanes. These lists of names are used again every six years (1996 names will be used again in 2002). Representatives of countries that often have hurricanes agree upon hurricane names at meetings of the World Meteorological Organization, an agency of the United Nations.

HURRICANE NAMES FOR 1996	In the North Atlantic:	In the Eastern Pacific:
	Arthur, Bertha, Cesar, Dolly, Edouard, Fran, Gustav, Hortense, Isidore, Josephine, Kyle, Lili, Marco, Nana, Omar, Paloma, Rene, Sally, Teddy, Vicky, and Wilfred.	Alma, Boris, Cristina, Douglas, Elida, Fausto, Genevieve, Hernan, Iselle, Julio, Kenna, Lowell, Marie, Norbert, Odile, Polo, Rachel, Simon, Trudy, Vance, Winnie, Xavier, Yolanda, and Zeke.

The SPEED of WIND

In 1805, Sir Francis Beaufort, an admiral in the British Navy, developed a system for describing wind speeds at sea. Later the scale was adapted for use on land. Called the Beaufort Scale, it uses the numbers 0 to 12. The numbers get higher as the winds increase in speed.

0 Calm

4 Moderate Breeze

0	Calm	(under 1 mph)
1	Light Air	(1-3 mph)
2	Light Breeze	(4-7 mph)
3	Gentle Breeze	(8-12 mph)
4	Moderate Breeze	(13-18 mph)
5	Fresh Breeze	(19-24 mph)
6	Strong Breeze	(25-31 mph)
7	Near Gale	(32-38 mph)
8	Gale	(39-46 mph)
9	Strong Gale	(47-54 mph)
10	Storm	(55-63 mph)
11	Violent Storm	(64-72 mph)
12	Hurricane	(73 or above mph)

8 Gale

12 Hurricane

The U.S. Weather Service also uses the numbers 13 to 17 for winds of hurricane speed.

WEATHER WORDS

air mass
A large amount of air at a certain temperature and humidity.

atmospheric pressure
Pressure on the surface of the earth from the weight of the atmosphere. Rising atmospheric pressure usually means calm, clear weather. Falling pressure usually leads to storms.

A **low** or **cyclone** or **depression** is an area of low atmospheric pressure.

A **high** is an area of high atmospheric pressure.

climate
Average weather conditions for an area over a long time period.

front
Boundary, or dividing line, between two air masses.

humidity
Amount of water vapor (water in the form of a gas) in the air.

meteorologist
A person who studies the atmosphere, weather, and weather forecasting.

PRECIPITATION

precipitation
The word for the different forms of water that fall from clouds—like rain, snow, hail, and sleet.

rain
Liquid water falling in drops that measure more than two hundredths of an inch across.

drizzle
Liquid water droplets that measure less than two hundredths of an inch across.

freezing rain
Liquid water that freezes as it hits the ground and other surfaces at temperatures below freezing.

sleet
Drops of water that freeze in cold air and reach the ground as ice.

hail
Frozen raindrops that are kept in the air by upward-blowing air currents. Water keeps freezing on the surface of the hailstone until the hailstone is so heavy that it falls to the ground.

snow
Ice crystals that form in clouds and fall to the ground.

STORMS

cyclone
General word for a circulating storm that forms over warm tropical oceans. It is also the name for a hurricane in the Indian Ocean.

hurricane
A circulating storm with wind speeds of 73 miles per hour or more. This type of storm is called a *hurricane* when it occurs in the Atlantic Ocean, a *typhoon* when it occurs in the Pacific Ocean, and a *cyclone* when it occurs in the Indian Ocean.

monsoon
A system of winds that changes direction between seasons.

thunderstorm
A storm with thunder and lightning.

tropical storm
A circulating storm with wind speeds from 39 to 73 mph; can develop into a hurricane.

tornado
Violently circulating winds of more than 200 miles per hour form a dark funnel reaching from the cloud to the ground.

Taking TEMPERATURES

HOW TO MEASURE TEMPERATURE

Two systems for measuring temperature are commonly used in weather forecasting. One is Fahrenheit (abbreviated F). The other is Celsius (abbreviated C). Another word for Celsius is Centigrade. Zero degrees (0°) Celsius is equal to 32 degrees (32°) Fahrenheit. Temperatures can be easily converted from one system to the other by following these steps:

To Convert Fahrenheit to Celsius:
1. Subtract 32 from the Fahrenheit temperature value.
2. Then multiply by 5.
3. Then divide the result by 9.
   Example: To convert 75 degrees Fahrenheit to Celcius, 75 – 32 = 43; 43 x 5 = 215; 215 ÷ 9 = 23.9 or 24

To Convert Celsius to Fahrenheit:
1. Multiply the Celsius temperature by 9.
2. Then divide by 5.
3. Then add 32 to the result.
   Example: To convert 24 degrees Celsuis to Fahrenheit, 24 x 9 = 216; 216 ÷ 5 = 43.1 or 43; 43 + 32 = 75

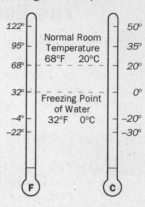

THE HOTTEST AND COLDEST PLACES IN THE WORLD

Below are the highest and lowest temperatures recorded on each continent.

CONTINENT	HIGHEST RECORDED TEMPERATURE	LOWEST RECORDED TEMPERATURE
Africa	Azizia, Libya, 136°F (58°C)	Ifrane, Morocco, -11°F (-24°C)
Antarctica	Vanda Station, 59°F (15°C)	Vostok, -129°F (-89°C)
Asia	Tirat Zevi, Israel, 129°F (54°C)	Oymyakon and Verkhoyansk, Russia, -90°F (-68°C)
Australia	Cloncurry, Queensland, 128°F (53°C)	Charlotte Pass, New South Wales, -8°F (-22°C)
Europe	Sevilla, Spain, 122°F (50°C)	Ust Shchugor, Russia, -67°F (-55°C)
North America	Death Valley, California, 134°F (57°C)	Northice, Greenland, -87°F (-66°C)
South America	Rivadavia, Argentina, 120°F (49°C)	Sarmiento, Argentina, -27°F (-33°C)

HOTTEST PLACES ON RECORD IN THE U.S.			COLDEST PLACES ON RECORD IN THE U.S.		
State	**Temperature**	**Year**	**State**	**Temperature**	**Year**
California	134°F	(1913)	Alaska	–80°F	(1971)
Arizona	127°F	(1905)*	Montana	–70°F	(1954)
Nevada	122°F	(1990)*	Utah	–69°F	(1985)
* Tied with a record set earlier					

WEIGHTS AND MEASURES

The Earliest MEASUREMENTS

We use weights and measures all the time—you can measure how tall you are, or how much gasoline a car needs. Ancient people developed measurements to describe the amounts or sizes of things. These units are called **weights** and **measures**. The first measurements were based on the human body and on activities.

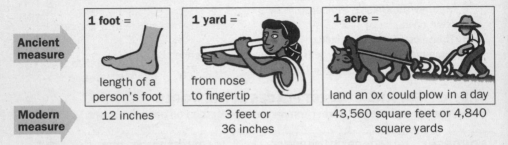

	1 foot =	1 yard =	1 acre =
Ancient measure	length of a person's foot	from nose to fingertip	land an ox could plow in a day
Modern measure	12 inches	3 feet or 36 inches	43,560 square feet or 4,840 square yards

Measurements Used in the United States

The system of measurement used in the United States is called the **U.S. Customary System**. Most countries use a system called the **metric system**. A few metric measurements are also used in the United States, such as for soda, which comes in 1-liter and 2-liter bottles. In the tables below, when a unit has an abbreviation, the abbreviation appears in parentheses the first time the unit is mentioned.

LENGTH, HEIGHT, and DISTANCE	AREA
The basic unit of **length** in the U.S. System is the **inch**. Length, width, depth, thickness, and the distance between two points all use the inch or larger related units.	**Area** is used to measure a section of a flat surface like the floor or the ground. Most area measurements are given in **square units**. Land is measured in **acres**.
1 foot (ft.) = 12 inches (in.) 1 yard (yd.) = 3 feet or 36 inches 1 rod (rd.) = 5½ yards 1 furlong (fur.) = 40 rods or 220 yards or 660 feet 1 mile (mi.) (also called statute mile) = 8 furlongs or 1,760 yards or 5,280 feet 1 league = 3 miles	1 square foot (sq. ft.) = 144 square inches (sq. in.) 1 square yard (sq. yd.)= 9 square feet or 1,296 square inches 1 square rod (sq. rd.) = 30¼ square yards 1 acre = 160 square rods or 4,840 square yards or 43,560 square feet 1 square mile (sq. mi.) = 640 acres

CAPACITY

Units of **capacity are used** to measure how much of something will fit into a container. **Liquid measure** is used to measure liquids, such as water or gasoline. **Dry measure** is used with large amounts of solid materials, like grain or fruit.

Dry Measure. Although both liquid and dry measures use the terms "pint" and "quart," they mean different amounts and should not be confused. Look at the lists below for examples.

> 1 quart (qt.) = 2 pints (pt.)
> 1 peck (pk.) = 8 quarts
> 1 bushel (bu.) = 4 pecks

Liquid Measure. Although the basic unit in liquid measure is the **gill** (4 fluid ounces), you are more likely to find liquids measured in pints or larger units.

> 1 gill = 4 fluid ounces
> 1 pint (pt.) = 4 gills or 16 ounces
> 1 quart (qt.) = 2 pints or 32 ounces
> 1 gallon (gal.) = 4 quarts = 128 ounces

☑ For measuring most U.S. liquids,
  1 barrel (bbl.) = 31½ gallons
☑ For measuring oil,
  1 barrel (bbl.) = 42 gallons

Cooking measurements. Cooking measure is used to measure amounts of solid and liquid foods used in cooking. The measurements used in cooking are based on the **fluid ounce**.

> 1 teaspoon (tsp.) = ⅙ fluid ounce
>   (fl. oz.)
> 1 tablespoon (tbsp.) = 3 teaspoons or ½
>   fluid ounce
>   1 cup = 16 tablespoons or 8
>   fluid ounces
>   1 pint = 2 cups
>   1 quart = 2 pints
>   1 gallon = 4 quarts

VOLUME

The amount of space taken up by an object (or the amount of space available within an object) is measured in **volume**. Volume is usually expressed in **cubic units**. If you wanted to buy a room air conditioner and needed to know how much space there was to be cooled, you could measure the room in cubic feet.

1 cubic foot (cu. ft.) =
  1,728 cubic inches (cu. in.)
1 cubic yard (cu. yd.) = 27 cubic feet

DEPTH

Some measurements of length are used to measure ocean depth and distance.

> 1 fathom = 6 feet
>   1 cable = 120 fathoms or 720 feet
> 1 nautical mile = 6,076.1 feet or
>   1.15 statute miles

WEIGHT

Although 1 cubic foot of popcorn and 1 cubic foot of rock take up the same amount of space, they wouldn't feel the same if you tried to lift them. We measure heaviness as **weight**. Most objects are measured in **avoirdupois weight** (pronounced a-ver-de-POIZ), although precious metals and medicines use different systems.

> 1 dram (dr.) = 27.344 grains (gr.)
> 1 ounce (oz.) = 16 drams or
>   437.504 grains
> 1 pound (lb.) = 16 ounces
> 1 hundredweight (cwt.) = 100 pounds
> 1 ton = 2000 pounds
> (also called short ton)

Rock ▶

▲ Popcorn

The METRIC System

Do you ever wonder how much soda you are getting when you buy a bottle that holds 1 liter? Or do you wonder how long a 50-meter swimming pool is? Or how far from Montreal, Canada, you would be when a map says "8 kilometers"?

Every system of measurement uses a basic unit for measuring. In the U.S. Customary System, the basic unit for length is the inch. In the metric system, the basic unit for length is the **meter**. The metric system also uses **liter** as a basic unit of volume or capacity and the **gram** as a basic unit of weight. The related units are made by adding a prefix to the basic unit. The prefixes and their meanings are:

milli- = $\frac{1}{1,000}$	deci- = $\frac{1}{10}$	hecto- = 100
centi- = $\frac{1}{100}$	deka- = 10	kilo- = 1,000

For example:

millimeter (mm) = $\frac{1}{1,000}$ of a meter   milligram (mg) = $\frac{1}{1,000}$ of a gram
centimeter (cm) = $\frac{1}{100}$ of a meter   centigram (cg) = $\frac{1}{100}$ of a gram
decimeter (dm) = $\frac{1}{10}$ of a meter   decigram (dg) = $\frac{1}{10}$ of a gram
dekameter (dm) = 10 meters   dekagram (dg) = 10 gram
hectometer (hm) = 100 meters   hectogram (hg) = 100 gram
kilometer (km) = 1,000 meters   kilogram (kg) = 1,000 grams

To get a rough idea of what measurements equal in the metric system, it is helpful to know that a liter is a little more than a quart. A meter is a little more than a yard. And a kilometer is less than a mile.

☑ A bottle of soda that holds 2 liters holds a little more than two quarts (2.1 quarts to be exact).
☑ A football field is 100 yards long. It is a little more than 90 meters (91.4 meters to be exact).

 DID YOU KNOW? Did you know that the metric system is used for measurements in the Olympic Games? Here are a few Olympic Game measurements and what they are equal to in U.S. Customary units.

☑ A 50-meter swimming pool is 54.7 yards long. A 400-meter freestyle swimming race is 437 yards.
☑ A 10-kilometer relay race is 6.2 miles. A 50-kilometer relay race is 31.2 miles.
☑ A 1,000-meter speed-skating race is six-tenths of a mile, which is a little over half a mile. A 5,000-meter speed-skating race is a little more than 3 miles. (Remember that 1,000 meters = 1 kilometer, so a 1,000-meter race would be the same as a 1-kilometer race, and a 5,000-meter race would be the same as a 5-kilometer race.)

> You can check these numbers by using the conversion charts on the following page. A calculator will be a big help with this. For example, if you multiply 50 meters (the length of an Olympic swimming pool) by 1.0936, you get 54.68 yards. When rounded off, that becomes 54.7 yards.

Converting U.S. Measurements to Metrics and Metrics to U.S. Measurements

If you want to convert feet to meters or miles to kilometers, you need to know how many meters there are in one foot or how many kilometers there are in one mile. The tables below show how to convert U.S. Customary units to metric units and how to convert metric units to U.S. Customary units. If you want to convert numbers from one system to the other, a calculator can help with the multiplication.

CONVERTING U.S. CUSTOMARY UNITS TO METRIC UNITS			CONVERTING METRIC UNITS TO U.S. CUSTOMARY UNITS		
If you know the number of	Multiply by	To get the number of	If you know the number of	Multiply by	To get the number of
inches	2.54	centimeters	centimeters	.3937	inches
inches	.0254	meters	centimeters	.032808	feet
feet	30.48	centimeters	meters	39.37	inches
feet	.3048	meters	meters	3.2808	feet
yards	.9144	meters	meters	1.0936	yards
miles	1.6093	kilometers	kilometers	.6214	miles
square inches	6.4516	square centimeters	square centimeters	.155	square inches
square feet	.0929	square meters	square meters	10.764	square feet
square yards	.8361	square meters	square meters	1.1960	square yards
acres	.405	hectares	hectares	2.471	acres
cubic inches	16.387	cubic centimeters	cubic centimeters	.06102	cubic inches
cubic feet	.02832	cubic meters	cubic meters	35.315	cubic feet
cubic yards	.7646	cubic meters	cubic meters	1.3080	cubic yards
quarts (liquid)	.946	liters	liters	1.057	quarts (liquid)
ounces	28.35	grams	grams	.03527	ounces
pounds	.4536	kilograms	kilograms	2.205	pounds

Highlights of WORLD HISTORY

The section on World History is divided into five parts. Each part is a major region of the world: the Middle East, Africa, Asia, Europe, and the Americas. Major historical events from ancient times to the present are found under the headings for each region.

THE ANCIENT MIDDLE EAST   4000 B.C. - 4 B.C.

4000-3000 B.C.

1. The world's first cities are built by the Sumerian peoples in Mesopotamia, southern Iraq.
2. Egyptians develop a kind of writing called hieroglyphics.
3. Sumerians develop a kind of writing called cuneiform.

2700 B.C.

Egyptians begin building the great pyramids in the desert. The pharaohs' (kings') bodies are mummified (preserved), and they are buried in the pyramids.

1792 B.C.

First written laws are created in Babylonia. They are called the Code of Hammurabi.

Some Achievements of Peoples of the Ancient Middle East

The early peoples of the Middle East are responsible for many great achievements. They:

1. Studied the stars (astronomy).
2. Invented the wheel.
3. Created alphabets from picture drawings (hieroglyphics and cuneiform).
4. Established the 24-hour day.
5. Studied medicine and mathematics.

1200 B.C.

Hebrew people settle in Canaan in Palestine after escaping from slavery in Egypt. They are led by the prophet Moses.

The Ten Commandments

Unlike most early peoples in the Middle East, the Hebrews believed in only one God (monotheism). They believed their faith was given to Moses in the Ten Commandments on Mount Sinai when they fled Egypt.

1000 B.C.

King David unites the Hebrews in one strong kingdom.

Ancient Palestine

Ancient Palestine was invaded by many different peoples after 1000 B.C., including the Babylonians, the Egyptians, the Persians, and the Romans. It came under Arab Muslim control in the 600s and remained mainly under Muslim control until the 1900s.

336 B.C.

Alexander the Great, King of Macedonia, builds an empire from Egypt to India.

4 B.C.

Jesus Christ, the founder of the Christian religion, is born in Bethlehem. He is crucified about A.D. 30.

ANCIENT AFRICA 3500 B.C. - A.D. 900

Ancient Africa

In ancient times, especially from 3500 B.C. to A.D. 100, northern Africa was dominated by the Egyptians, Greeks, and Romans. However, we know very little about the lives of ancient people in Africa south of the Sahara Desert (sub-Saharan Africa). The people of Africa south of the Sahara did not have written languages in ancient times. What we learn about them comes from such things as weapons, tools, and other items that have been found in the earth.

500 B.C.

The Nok culture becomes strong in Nigeria, in West Africa. The Nok use iron for tools and weapons. They are also known for their fine terra-cotta sculptures of heads.

300 B.C.

Bantu-speaking peoples in West Africa begin to move into eastern and southern Africa.

A.D. 100

The Kingdom of Axum in northern Ethiopia is founded by traders from Arabia and becomes a wealthy trade center for ivory.

400

Ghana, the first known state south of the Sahara Desert, rules the upper Senegal and Niger river region. It controls the trade in gold being sent from the southern parts of Africa north to the Mediterranean Sea.

Islam: A New Religion for Africa and the Middle East

570

The prophet Muhammad is born in Mecca in Arabia. Muhammad creates a new religion called Islam, which spreads from Arabia to North Africa. The followers of Islam are also called Muslims.

The Koran

The holy book of Islam is called the Koran. It was dictated by Muhammad beginning in 611. The Koran gives rules that Muslims must follow. For example, it tells how many times a day they must pray.

661-900

Islam begins to spread to the west into Africa and Spain under the Arab rulers known as the Omayyads.

The Spread of Islam

The Arab armies that went across North Africa brought great change:

1. The people who lived there were converted to Islam.
2. The Arab language replaced many local languages that had been spoken before. Islam changed North Africa. It is still an Arab region and Islam is the major faith.

Achievements of Arab Muslims

The Muslim Arab empire that stretched across Africa and the Middle East is known for many great achievements. Arab Muslims:

1. Studied math and medicine.
2. Translated the works of other peoples, including the Greeks and Persians.
3. Created governments throughout the empire.
4. Wrote great works on religion and philosophy.

THE MIDDLE EAST 600s - the 1990s

632
Muhammad dies. By now, Islam is accepted in Arabia as a religion.

641
Arab Muslims conquer the Persians.

1071
The Muslim Seljuk Turks conquer the city of Jerusalem. Europeans try to take back Jerusalem for Christians during the Crusades (campaigns by European Christians to take the Middle East from the Muslims).

The Ottoman Empire: 1300-1900s
The Ottoman Turks, who were Muslims, created a huge empire beginning in 1300, covering the Middle East, North Africa, part of Eastern Europe. The Ottoman Empire fell apart gradually. European countries took portions of North Africa and the Middle East away from the Ottoman Turks beginning in the 1800s.

1914-1918
World War I begins in 1914. By its end, the Ottoman Empire has been broken apart. Most of the Middle East falls under British and French control.

1921
Two new Arab kingdoms are created: Transjordan and Iraq. The French take control of Syria and Lebanon.

1922
Egypt becomes independent from Britain.

Jews Migrate to Palestine
Jewish settlers from Europe began migrating to Palestine in the 1880s. They wanted to return to the historic homeland of the Hebrew people. In 1945, after World War II, many Jews who survived the Holocaust migrated to Palestine. Arabs living in the region opposed the Jewish immigration. In 1948, after the British left, war broke out between the Jews and the Arabs.

1948
The state of Israel is created.

The Arab-Israeli Wars
Israel's Arab neigbors (Egypt, Jordan, and Syria) attack the new country in 1948 but fail to destroy it. Israel and its neighbors fight wars again in 1956, 1967, and 1973. Israel wins each war. In the 1967 war, Israel captures the Sinai Desert from Egypt and the area known as the West Bank from Jordan.

1979
Egypt and Israel sign a peace treaty. Israel gradually returns the Sinai to Egypt.

The Middle East and Oil
Much of the oil we use to drive our cars, heat our homes, and run our machines comes from the Arabian peninsula in the Middle East. For a brief time in 1973-1974, Arab nations would not let their oil be sold to the United States because of its support of Israel. Although the U.S. still buys much of its oil from the Middle East, the government has tried to reduce the amount by drilling for more oil at home and by buying oil from other regions.

The 1990s
1. In 1991, the United States and its allies go to war with Iraq. Iraq had invaded neighboring Kuwait in 1990. The conflict, known as the Persian Gulf War, lasts only a few weeks. Iraq's army is defeated and is forced to withdraw from Kuwait.
2. After many years of conflict, Israel and the Palestine Liberation Organization (PLO) agree to work toward peace in the area in 1993. In 1994, Israel signs a peace treaty with Jordan. Some Palestinians and Israelis do not want peace, however, and the region continues to be tense.

AFRICA   900s - the 1990s

900
Arab Muslims begin to settle along the coast of East Africa. Their contact with Bantu people produces the Swahili language, which is still spoken today.

1050
The Almoravid Kingdom in Morocco, North Africa, is powerful from Ghana as far north as Spain.

1230
The beginning of the Mali Kingdom in North Africa. Timbuktu, a center for trade and learning, is its main city.

1464
The Songhai Empire becomes strong in West Africa. By 1530, it has destroyed Mali. The Songhai are remembered for their bronze sculptures.

1505-1575
The beginning of Portuguese settlement in Africa. Portuguese people settle in Angola and Mozambique.

The African Slave Trade
Once Europeans began settling in the New World, they needed people to harvest their sugar. The first Africans were taken as slaves by European traders across the Atlantic to the Caribbean. Later, slaves were taken to South America and the United States. The slaves were crowded on to ships and many died during the long journey. Shipping of African slaves to the United States lasted until the early 1800s.

1770-1835
1. Dutch settlers arrive in southern Africa. The Dutch in South Africa are known as the Boers.
2. Shaka the Great forms a Zulu Empire in eastern Africa. The Zulus are warriors.
3. The "Great Trek" (march) of the Boers north. They defeat the Zulus at the Battle of Bloody River.

1880s: European Colonies in Africa
European settlers start moving into the interior of Africa and forming colonies in the mid-1800s. The major European countries with colonies in Africa were:

1. **Great Britain:** East and central Africa, from Egypt to South Africa.
2. **France:** Most of West Africa and North Africa.
3. **Spain:** Parts of Northwest Africa.
4. **Portugal:** Mozambique (East Africa) and Angola (West Africa).
5. **Italy:** Libya (North Africa) and Somalia (East Africa).
6. **Germany:** East Africa, Southwest Africa.

1899: Boer War
The beginning of the South African War between Great Britain and the Boers. It is also called the Boer War. The Boers accept British rule but are allowed a role in government.

1948
The white South African government creates the policy of apartheid, the total separation of blacks and whites.

1950s: African Independence
African colonies begin to receive their independence in the 1950s. European countries could no longer afford to keep colonies, and the peoples of Africa demanded their independence.

1983
Droughts (water shortages) lead to starvation over much of Africa.

The 1990s
During the 1990s many African countries struggle with poverty and political unrest. The South African government officially ends apartheid. Nelson Mandela, a black freedom fighter, becomes South Africa's first black president.

ANCIENT ASIA 4000 B.C. - 1 B.C.

4000 B.C.
Communities of people settle in the Indus River Valley of India and Pakistan and the Yellow River Valley of China.

2500 B.C.
Cities of Mohenjo-Daro and Harappa in Pakistan become centers of trade and farming.

1600 B.C.
Shang peoples in China build walled towns and use a kind of writing based on pictures. This writing develops into the writing Chinese people use today.

1500 B.C.
The Hindu religion (Hinduism) begins to spread throughout India.

1027 B.C.
Chou peoples in China overthrow the Shang and control large territories.

700 B.C.
Beginning of a 500-year period in China in which many warring states fight each other.

563 B.C.
The birth of Prince Siddhartha Gautama in India. He becomes known as the Buddha—which means the "Enlightened One"—and is the founder of the Buddhist religion (Buddhism).

551 B.C.
Birth of the Chinese philosopher Confucius. His teachings— especially the rules and morals about how people should treat each other and get along—spread throughout China and are still followed today.

Two Important Asian Religions
Many of the world's religions began in Asia. Two of the most important were:
1. **Hinduism.** Hinduism began in India and has spread to other parts of southern Asia and to parts of the Pacific region.
2. **Buddhism.** Buddhism also began in India and spread to China, Japan, and Southeast Asia.
Both Buddhism and Hinduism are still followed by millions of people in Asia, but their followers also live all over the world.

320-264 B.C.: India
1. Northern India is united under the emperor Chandragupta Maurya.
2. Asoka, emperor of India, begins to send Buddhist missionaries throughout southern Asia to spread the Buddhist religion.

221 B.C.
The Chinese ruler Shih Huang Ti makes the Chinese language the same throughout the country.

215 B.C.
Chinese begin building the Great Wall of China. It is 1,500 miles long and was meant to keep invading peoples from the north out of China. The Great Wall is still visited by people today.

202 B.C.
The Han people in China overthrow Shih Huang Ti.

Chinese Achievements under the Han
During the rule of the Han, the Chinese:
1. Invented paper.
2. Invented gunpowder.
3. Studied astronomy.
4. Studied engineering.
5. Invented acupuncture to treat illnesses.

ASIA A.D. 1 - 1700s

320
The Gupta Empire controls northern India. The Guptas are Hindus. They drive the Buddhist religion out of India.The Guptas are well known for their advances in the study of mathematics and medicine.

618
The beginning of the Tang dynasty in China. The Tang are famous for inventing the compass and for advances in surgery and the arts. They trade silk, spices, and ivory as far away as Africa.

932
The Chinese begin to make books in large numbers by using wood blocks for printing.

960
The Northern Sung Dynasty in China is known for advances in banking and paper money.

1000
The Samurai, a warrior people, become powerful in Japan. They live by a code of honor called bushido.

1180
Angkor Empire is powerful in Cambodia. The empire is known for its beautiful temples.

1215
The Mongol people of Asia are united under the ruler Genghis Khan. He builds a huge army and creates an empire that stretches all the way from China to India, Russia, and Eastern Europe.

1264
Kublai Khan, the grandson of Genghis Khan, rules China as emperor from his new capital at Beijing.

1368
The Ming Dynasty comes to power in China. The Ming drive the Mongols out of China.

1467-1603: War and Peace in Japan
1. Civil war breaks out in Japan. The conflicts last more than 100 years.
2. Peace comes to Japan under the military leader Hideyoshi.
3. Beginning of the Shogun period in Japan, which lasts until 1868. Europeans are driven out of the country and Christians are persecuted.

1526-1556: The Moguls in India
1. Beginning of the Mogul Empire in India under Babur. The Moguls are Muslims who invade and conquer India.
2. Akbar, the grandson of Babur, becomes Mogul emperor of India. He attempts to unite Hindus and Muslims but is unsuccessful.

1644
The Ming Dynasty in China is overthrown by the Manchu peoples. They allow more Europeans to trade in China.

1739
Nadir Shah, a Persian warrior, conquers parts of western India and captures the city of Delhi.

Achievements of Indian Civilizations
Many civilizations grew in India over thousands of years of history. Among the many achievements of Indian civilizations are:

1. Great literature, especially Sanskrit literature and language.
2. Great architecture, for example, the Taj Mahal, a mausoleum (tomb) built in 1629 under the Moguls.
3. Great world religions, including Hinduism and Buddhism.

MODERN ASIA 1800s - 1990s

1839
The Opium War in China between the Chinese and the British. The British and other Western powers want to control trade in Asia. The Chinese want the British to stop selling opium to the Chinese. Britain wins the war.

1858
The French begin to take control of Indochina (Southeast Asia).

1868
The end of the Shogunate dynasty in Japan. The new ruler is Prince Meiji. Western ideas begin to influence the Japanese.

The Japanese in Asia
Japan became a powerful country during the early 20th century. It was a small country with few raw materials. For example, Japan had to buy oil from other countries. The Japanese army and navy took control of the government during the 1930s. Japan soon began to invade some of its neighbors. The U.S. thought Japan was a threat to its own safety. By 1941 the two nations were at war in World War II, after Japan attacked the U.S. Navy at Pearl Harbor, Hawaii.

1945
Japan is defeated in World War II after the U.S. drops atomic bombs on the Japanese cities of Hiroshima and Nagasaki.

1947
India and Pakistan become independent from Great Britain, which had ruled them as colonies since the mid-1800s.

1949
China comes under the rule of the Communists led by Mao Zedong.

China Under the Communists
The Communists brought great changes to China. Private property was abolished, and the government took over all businesses and farms. China became more isolated and had poor relations with the United States.

1950-1953: The Korean War
The Communist country North Korea invades South Korea. The U.S. and other nations join to fight the invasion. China joins North Korea. The Korean War ends in 1953. Neither side wins, but the North Korean army is forced out of South Korea.

1954-1975: The Vietnam War
The French are defeated in Indochina in 1954 by the Vietminh. The Vietminh are Vietnamese fighters under the leadership of the Communists headed by Ho Chi Minh. The U.S. sends troops to fight in the Vietnam War in 1965 on the side of South Vietnam against Ho Chi Minh and Communist North Vietnam. The U.S. withdraws from the war in 1973. In 1975, South Vietnam is defeated and taken over by North Vietnam.

1972
President Richard Nixon visits Communist China. A new period of better relations between China and the United States begins.

1989
Chinese students protest for more democracy but the protests are crushed by the army.

The 1990s
By the 1990s many nations in Asia have become economically strong. Japan is a major economic power, producing a large amount of the world's automobiles and electronic equipment. South Korea, Taiwan, and China also become important trading nations, producing many different products sold around the world.

ANCIENT EUROPE 4000 B.C. - 300 B.C.

4000 B.C.

People in many parts of Europe start building large stone tombs called megaliths. Examples of megaliths can still be seen today.

The Minoans and the Mycenaeans
2500 B.C.-1200 B.C.

1. People on island of Crete (Minoans) in the Mediterranean Sea built great palaces and became sailors and traders.
2. People in the city of Mycenae in Greece built stone walls and a great palace.
3. Mycenaean people invaded Crete and destroyed the power of the Minoans.

The Trojan War

The Trojan War was a conflict between invading Greeks and the people of Troas (Troy) in Southwestern Turkey in 1200 B.C. Although little is known today about the real war, it has become a part of Greek mythology. According to the Greek poet Homer, the Greek soldiers hid inside a huge wooden horse. The horse was pulled into the city of Troy. Then the soldiers jumped out of the horse and conquered Troy.

1200 B.C.

Celtic peoples in Northern Europe settle in farms and villages and learn to mine for iron ore.

Some Achievements of the Greeks

The early Greeks were responsible for many great achievements. They include:

1. The first governments elected by people. Greeks invented democratic government.
2. Great writers such as the poet Homer, who wrote the Iliad, a long poem about the Trojan War.
3. Great philosophers such as Socrates, Plato, and Aristotle.
4. Great architecture, like the Parthenon in Athens, which can still be seen (see below).

700 B.C.

Etruscan peoples rule most of Italy until 400 B.C. They build many cities and become traders.

431 B.C.

Beginning of the Peloponnesian Wars between the Greek cities of Athens and Sparta. The wars end in 404 B.C. when Sparta wins.

338 B.C.

King Philip II of Macedonia in northern Greece unites the cities of Greece and defeats Sparta.

336 B.C.

Philip's son Alexander becomes king. He conquers lands and makes an empire from the Mediterranean Sea to India. He is known as Alexander the Great.
For the next 300 years, Greek culture dominates this vast area.

EUROPE 300 B.C. - A.D. 800s

264 B.C.- A.D. 476: Roman Empire

The city of Rome in Italy begins to expand and captures surrounding lands. The Romans gradually build a great empire and control all of the Mediterranean region. At its height, the Roman Empire includes Western Europe, Greece, Egypt, and much of the Middle East. The Roman Empire lasts until A.D. 476.

Some Achievements of the Romans

1. Roman law. Many of our laws today are based on Roman law. For example, Romans invented independent judges and protected the rights of women and children.
2. Great roads to connect their huge empire. The Appian Way, south of Rome, is a Roman road that is still in use today.
3. Aqueducts to bring water to the people living in large cities.
4. Great sculpture. Roman statues can still be seen in Europe.
5. Great architecture. The Colosseum, which still stands in Rome today, is an example of great Roman architecture (see below).

45 B.C.

Julius Caesar becomes the leader of Rome but is murdered one year later by rivals in the Roman army.

29 B.C.

Octavian becomes the first emperor of Rome. He takes the name Caesar Augustus. A peaceful period of almost 200 years begins.

The Christian Faith

Christians believe that Jesus Christ is the Son of God. The history and beliefs of Christianity are found in the New Testament of the Bible. Christianity spread slowly throughout the Roman empire. The Romans tried to stop the spread of the new religion and persecuted the Christians. They were forced to hold their services in hiding, and some were crucified. Eventually, more and more Romans became Christian.

337

The Roman Emperor Constantine the Great becomes a Christian. He is the first Roman emperor to be a Christian.

410

The Visigoths and other barbarian tribes from northern Europe invade the Roman Empire and begin to take over its vast territories.

476

The last Roman emperor is overthrown.

The Byzantine Empire, centered in modern-day Turkey, was made up of the eastern half of the old Roman empire. Byzantine rulers extended their power into western Europe. The great Byzantine Emperor Justinian ruled parts of Spain, North Africa, and Italy. The city of Constantinople (today Istanbul, Turkey) became the capital of the Byzantine Empire in 520.

768

Charlemagne becomes king of the Franks in northern Europe. He rules a kingdom that includes parts of France, Germany and northern Italy.

800

Feudalism becomes important in Europe. Feudalism means that poor farmers are allowed to farm a lord's land in return for certain services to the lord.

EUROPE 800s - 1500s

898
Magyar peoples from lands east of Russia found Hungary.

900
Viking warriors and traders from Scandinavia begin to move into the British Isles, France, and parts of the Mediterranean. They remain for 200 years.

Viking ship ▶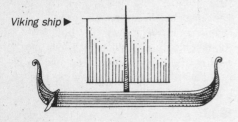

989
The Russian state of Kiev becomes Christian.

1066
William of Normandy, in France, successfully invades England and makes himself king. He is known as William the Conqueror.

The Crusades: 1095-1291
In 1095 Christian European kings and nobles sent armies to the Middle East to try to capture the city of Jerusalem from the Muslims. Between 1095 and 1291 there were about ten Crusades. The Europeans briefly recaptured Jerusalem. But in the end, the Crusades did not recapture the Holy Land for Christians. One of the most important results of the Crusades was that trade increased between the Middle East and Europe.

The Magna Carta: 1215
The Magna Carta is a document signed by King John of England and the English nobility. The English king agreed that he did not have absolute power and had to obey the laws of the land. The Magna Carter is considered an important step in the beginning of English democracy.

1290
The beginning of the Ottoman Empire. It is controlled by Turkish Muslims who conquer lands in the eastern Mediterranean and the Middle East.

War and Plague in Europe
1337-1453
1. The start of the Hundred Years' War (1337) in Europe between France and England. The war lasts until 1453 when France wins. England gives up all claims to govern France.
2. The beginning of the bubonic plague in Europe in 1348. The plague is also called the Black Death. It is a deadly disease caused by the bite of infected fleas. Perhaps as much as one third of the people of Europe die in the plague.

1453
The Ottoman Turks capture Constantinople and rename it Istanbul.

The Reformation: 1517
The Reformation resulted in the breakup of the Christian church into Protestant and Roman Catholic branches in Europe. The German priest Martin Luther broke away from the Catholic church. He opposed the power of the pope (the leader of the Catholic church) and believed people should read the Bible themselves and not be guided by priests.

1534
King Henry VIII of England breaks away from the Catholic church. He names himself head of the English (Anglican) church.

1558
The beginning of the reign of King Henry's daughter Elizabeth I in England. During her long reign, England's power grows.

1588
The Spanish Armada (fleet of warships) is defeated by the English navy as Spain tries to invade England.

MODERN EUROPE 1600s - 1990s

1600
The Ottoman Turks attack central Europe. They take control of territories in the Balkans region of southeastern Europe.

1618
The beginning of the Thirty Years' War in Europe. The war is fought over religious issues. Much of Europe is destroyed in the conflict, which ends in 1648.

1642
The English civil war. King Charles I fights against the Parliament (legislature). The king's forces are defeated and he is executed in 1649. But his son, Charles II returns as king in 1661.

1762
Catherine the Great becomes the Empress of Russia. She allows religious freedom and extends the Russian empire.

The French Revolution: 1789
The French Revolution ended the rule of kings in France and was the beginning of democracy there. Before democracy was won, however, there were wars, much bloodshed, and times when dictators took control. King Louis XVI and Queen Marie Antoinette were overthrown and later executed in 1793.

1804
Napoleon Bonaparte, an army officer, declares himself Emperor of France. Under his rule, France conquers most of Europe by 1812.

1815
Napoleon's forces are defeated by the British and German armies at Waterloo (in Belgium). Napoleon is exiled.

1848
Revolutions break out in countries of Europe. People force their rulers to make more democratic changes.

World War I in Europe: 1914-1918
The start of World War I in Europe (1914). Germany and Austria-Hungary opposed England, France, and Russia (the Allies). The United States joined the war in 1917 on the side of the Allies. The Allies won in 1918.

1917
The Russian Revolution. The czar (emperor) is overthrown. The Bolsheviks (communists) under Vladimir Lenin take control of the government. The country is now called the Soviet Union. After Lenin's death, Josef Stalin becomes dictator.

1933
Adolph Hitler becomes the dictator of Germany. He persecutes Jews and tries to take the territory of neighboring countries.

World War II in Europe: 1939-1945
Germany and Italy fought against England, France, the Soviet Union, and the United States (the Allies) in Europe. Germany surrendered in May 1945 after much of Europe was destroyed. During the war, the Germans killed almost 6 million Jews (the Holocaust).

1945
The beginning of the Cold War. The Cold War is a 45-year period of tension between the United States the Soviet Union. Both countries build up their armies and make thousands of nuclear weapons but never go to war.

The 1990s
Europe in the 1990s experiences great changes. Communist governments in Eastern Europe that were allied with the Soviet Union are overthrown and replaced by democratic governments. In 1991, the Soviet Union itself breaks apart into a number of different countries. The biggest, Russia, gets rid of communism and holds democratic elections.

THE AMERICAS 4000 B.C. -A.D. 1600s

4000 B.C.
People in North America gather plants for food and hunt animals using stone-pointed spears.

3000 B.C.
People in Central America begin growing corn and beans for food.

1500 B.C.
Mayan people in Central America begin to live in small villages.

500 B.C.
People in North America begin to hunt buffalo for meat and skin for clothing.

100 B.C.
City of Teotihuacán founded in Mexico. It becomes the center of a huge empire extending from central Mexico to Guatemala. Teotihuacán contains many large pyramids and temples.

A.D. 150
Mayan people in Guatemala build many centers for religious ceremonies. They create a calendar and learn mathematics and astronomy.

900
Toltec warriors in Mexico begin to invade lands of Mayan people. Mayans leave their old cities and move to Yucatan Peninsula of Mexico.

1000
Native Americans in Southwestern United States begin to live in settlements called pueblos. They learn to farm.

1325
Mexican Indians known as Aztecs create huge city of Tenochtitlán and rule a large empire in Mexico. They are warriors who practice human sacrifice.

Europeans Arrive in the New World
(See page 300 for map of American Indians from 1500 to 1800.)

1492
Christopher Columbus sails from Europe across the Atlantic Ocean and lands in the Bahamas, in the Caribbean. This is the first step toward European settlements in the Americas.

1510
The first Africans are brought to the Americas as slaves.

1519
The Spanish conqueror Hernán Cortes travels into the Aztec empire in search of gold. The Aztecs are defeated in 1521 by Cortes. The Spanish take control of Mexico.

Why Did the Spanish Win?
How did the Spanish defeat the powerful Aztec empire in such a short time? One reason is that they had better weapons than the Indians. Another is that the Aztecs became sick and died from diseases brought by the Spanish. Because the Indians had not had these illnesses before, they became sick from contact with Europeans.

1532
Portuguese explorers first settle in Brazil. The Portuguese establish colonies in this part of South America.

1534
Jacques Cartier of France explores Canada.

1583
The first English colony in North America is set up in Newfoundland, Canada.

1607
English colonists led by Captain John Smith settle in Jamestown, Virginia.

1682
The French explorer Robert La Salle sails down the Mississippi River. The area is named Louisiana after the French King Louis XIV.

THE AMERICAS 1700s

European Colonies in the Americas

By 1700, most of the Americas are under the control of Europeans:

Spain: Florida, southwestern United States, Mexico, Central America, western South America.
Portugal: eastern South America.
France: central United States, parts of Canada.
England: eastern United States, parts of Canada.
Holland: New York.

1700

European colonies in North and South America begin to grow in population and wealth.

1775-1783: American Revolution

The American Revolution begins in 1775 when the first shot is fired in Lexington, Massachusetts. The thirteen British colonies in North America become independent under the Treaty of Paris in 1783.

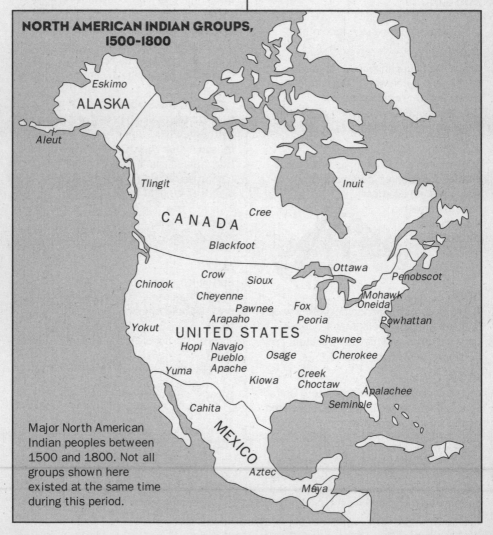

NORTH AMERICAN INDIAN GROUPS, 1500-1800

Eskimo
ALASKA
Aleut
Tlingit
Inuit
CANADA
Cree
Blackfoot
Crow
Sioux
Ottawa
Penobscot
Chinook
Cheyenne
Mohawk
Oneida
Pawnee
Fox
Arapaho
Peoria
Powhattan
Yokut
UNITED STATES
Shawnee
Hopi Navajo
Pueblo
Osage
Cherokee
Yuma Apache
Kiowa
Creek
Choctaw
Apalachee
Cahita
Seminole
MEXICO
Aztec
Maya

Major North American Indian peoples between 1500 and 1800. Not all groups shown here existed at the same time during this period.

THE AMERICAS 1800s - the Present

Simón Bolívar: Liberator of South America

Simón Bolívar was a South American revolutionary who led a revolt against the Spanish starting in 1810. He fought for more than 10 years against the Spanish and became president of the independent country of Greater Colombia in 1824. As a result of his leadership, 10 South American countries had become independent by 1830. Simón Bolívar is honored today as South America's greatest hero.

South American Colonies Become Independent

Most countries of South America became independent in the early 1800s. The following are the dates each country became independent of European control.

Argentina	1816
Bolivia	1825
Brazil	1822
Chile	1818
Colombia	1819
Ecuador	1830
French Guiana[1]	
Guyana	1966[2]
Paraguay	1811
Peru	1824
Suriname	1973[3]
Uruguay	1825
Venezuela	1821

1. French Guiana is an overseas territory governed by France.
2. Guyana was a British colony until it became independent in 1966.
3. Suriname was governed by the Netherlands until it became independent in 1973.

1810-1910: Mexico's Independence and Revolution

Mexico first revolts against Spanish rule in 1810 and finally wins independence in 1821. In 1846, Mexico and the United States go to war. Mexico is defeated and loses parts of the Southwest and California to the Americans. A revolution in 1910 overthrows Porfirio Diaz.

1867

The Canadian provinces are united as the Dominion of Canada.

1898: The Spanish-American War

Spain and the United States fight a brief war in 1898. The U.S. victory results in Spain losing its colonies of Cuba and Puerto Rico in the Caribbean and the Philippines in the western Pacific.

U.S. Power in the Americas: 1900-1995

Throughout the 1900s the United States was a powerful influence in the affairs of countries in Central America and the Caribbean. For example, troops were sent to Mexico (1916-1917), Nicaragua (1912- 1925), Haiti (1915-1934; 1994-1995), the Dominican Republic (1965), Grenada (1983), and Panama (1989). In 1962, the United States nearly went to war with the Soviet Union because that country had put missiles on the island of Cuba, only 90 miles from American territory. The U.S. wanted to remain powerful in the Americas, but it also wanted to bring democratic reforms to the countries of the region.

The 1990s: Economic Cooperation

In 1994 the United States, Canada, and Mexico become partners in the North American Free Trade Agreement (NAFTA), which makes it easier for these countries to trade with each other.

ANSWERS TO PUZZLES

ANIMALS

Page 22: HABITAT PUZZLE

1. DESERTS
2. TROPICAL FORESTS
3. GRASSLANDS
4. POLAR REGIONS
5. OCEANS
6. MOUNTAINS

Page 25: ENDANGERED SPECIES PUZZLE

```
Q V N A H L M B S F Q X C U S A I F S H C O Z A
U P A O P A I L K D R A K E R N T B E F A G N Y
L E O P A R D H L E W R Y O U R A O V O L R C A N
M Z L O R P F O I N I G T P W R I A E R I O A T
A G A R U I B W E S K I M O C U R L E W F C V A
T R S W I N C L V E C R J U L E S T M X O K E R
T I M A S E W E S T A F R I C A N O S T R I C H
E Z O E N T H R N Y L F O R T I L D E S N B R P
S Z T L U A Y M V B W F W E R T Y U I O I L A D E
D L I N D I G O M A C A W C V B N M J H A F Y E
P Y K I J L V N I U M S B G R T Y C I O C Q F M
A B D F N E X K N V B W W I L D Y A K R O M I O
D E R E P D Q E A D R E W E R T H E Y O N R S T
O A E C R S X Y I H A B I T L R V E N T D O H L
C R E A M E R I C A N C R O C O D I L E O Z E U
K J H D R I W I N W E R T G H J P A L Y R T L N
A S I A N E L E P H A N T I L K J H S D G B V X
```

COMPUTERS

Page 42: BINARY PUZZLE

1. **bug byte**
2. **mouse pad**
3. **hard drive**

COUNTRIES

Page 64: MIXED-UP COUNTRIES

MCOXEI = MEXICO
ANGEINRTA = ARGENTINA
TEKYUR = TURKEY

ATRUAALIS = AUSTRALIA
SNRWETLDAIZ = SWITZERLAND
ZIREA = ZAIRE
NELPA = NEPAL

Page 64:
CAPITAL CITY CROSSWORD

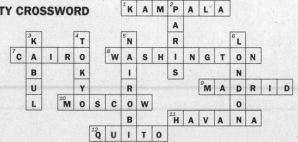

ENERGY AND NATURAL RESOURCES
Page 86: **ENERGY PUZZLE**
  1. United States   **2.** India   **3.** Great Britain

ENVIRONMENT
Page 95: **TEST YOUR TREE SMARTS: TRUE OR FALSE?**
  1. **T** Because changes in climate affect how much a tree grows each year, scientists can tell what the climate was like in years past (in some cases 4,000 years!) by examining a tree's annual rings.
  2. **F** Some trees, such as the northern red oak and the juniper, resist pollution better than others.
  3. **F** Only 5% of the original forests in the lower 48 states still stand. Most of this old growth forest is in the Pacific Northwest (Washington, Oregon, and northern California).
  4. **T** The tropical forests have more types of plants and animals than all the other parts of the world combined.
  5. **T** Paper in the form of newsprint, catalogs, packaging, and the white paper used by schools and businesses makes up over 40% of our trash.
Scoring: 5 right, a tree genius; 3-4 right, a tree whiz; 1-2 right, a forest friend.

GEOGRAPHY
Page 104: **GEOGRAPHY CROSSWORD PUZZLE**

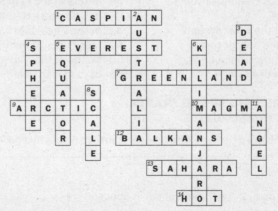

LANGUAGE
Page 120: **ACRONYM PUZZLE**
  1. **c.**   2. **e.**   3. **a.**   4. **f.**   5. **b.**   6. **d.**

Page 122: **WORD PUZZLE**
  3-letter words: act, cat, cop, cot, hat, hip, hit, hop, hot, lap, lip, lit, lot, oat, pal, pat, ply, pot, sap, sat, sip, sly, sty, tap, yap, yip
  4-letter words: cast, chat, chip, chop, clap, clay, clip, clop, coal, coat, colt, cool, coop, coot, cost, halt, hoop, hoot, host, itch, last, loop, loot, lost, pail, past, path, play, pool, post, sail, ship, shop, slap, slop, slip, slit, spit, spat, spot, stay, stop, tail, this, toil, tool
  5-letter words: clasp, coast, latch, patch, patsy, pitch, plait, scoop, shoot, sloop, stool, spoil, stoop
  6-letter word: school

Page 123: **IDIOM PUZZLE: Mixing Colors**   1. **d.**   2. **e.**   3. **b.**   4. **a.**   5. **c.**

Page 125: **SCRAMBLED MENU PUZZLE**

1. OTTMAO <u>T</u> <u>O</u> <u>M</u> <u>A</u> <u>T</u> <u>O</u>
            1   4

3. HILCI <u>C</u> <u>H</u> <u>I</u> <u>L</u> <u>I</u>
                    5

2. ZEMIA <u>M</u> <u>A</u> <u>I</u> <u>Z</u> <u>E</u>
        3   6

4. ACCOO <u>C</u> <u>O</u> <u>C</u> <u>O</u> <u>A</u>
                      2

<u>T</u> <u>A</u> <u>M</u> <u>A</u> <u>L</u> <u>E</u>
1 2 3 4 5 6

NUMBERS
Page 150: **ROMAN NUMERALS** The year 1996 in Roman numerals: MCMXCVI

Page 153: **CALCULATORS CAN SPELL TOO**
1. 7738: BELL
2. 5318804: HOBBIES
3. 0.7734: HELLO
4. 77345: SHELL
5. 4614: HIGH
6. 710: OIL
7. 7108: BOIL
8. 317.618: BIG LIE

Page 153: **MAGIC SQUARE**

4	9	2
3	5	7
8	1	6

Page 153: **NUMBERS COUNT**

5 players on a basketball team	26 letters in the English alphabet
7 continents	27 amendments to the U.S. Constitution
9 planets in the solar system	32 ounces in a quart
11 players on a soccer team	42 presidents of the United States
13 stripes on the American flag	50 states of the United States
24 hours in a day	366 days in leap year

PLANETS, STARS, AND SPACE TRAVEL
Page 163: **SPACE TRAVEL PUZZLE**

The first American woman and African-American man went into space on the shuttle
<u>C</u> <u>H</u> <u>A</u> <u>L</u> <u>L</u> <u>E</u> <u>N</u> <u>G</u> <u>E</u> <u>R</u>.
1   **2**

The name of the first American woman in space is
<u>S</u> <u>A</u> <u>L</u> <u>L</u> <u>Y</u>   <u>R</u> <u>I</u> <u>D</u> <u>E</u>.
   3

The Hubble Space Telescope was launched from
<u>D</u> <u>I</u> <u>S</u> <u>C</u> <u>O</u> <u>V</u> <u>E</u> <u>R</u> <u>Y</u>.
    4

The Russian space station is called <u>M</u> <u>I</u> <u>R</u>.
                       5

<u>E</u> <u>N</u> <u>T</u> <u>E</u> <u>R</u> <u>P</u> <u>R</u> <u>I</u> <u>S</u> <u>E</u> is the name of the first space shuttle.
6   **7**

The upcoming Saturn probe is called <u>C</u> <u>A</u> <u>S</u> <u>S</u> <u>I</u> <u>N</u> <u>I</u>.
                        1 2 3 4 5 6 7

SCIENCE
Page 185: **ELEMENTS PUZZLE**

Element	Element Is Named After
Curium	French chemists Marie and Pierre Curie
Einsteinium	Nobel Prize winner Albert Einstein
Neptunium	the planet Neptune
Nobelium	Swedish inventor Alfred Nobel
Plutonium	the planet Pluto
Promethium	Greek god Prometheus
Thorium	Norse god Thor
Uranium	the planet Uranus

SPORTS
Page 209: **SPORTS PUZZLE**

```
Q W E D F L I T T L E L E A G U E L S Y S M L P
Z X C K V M B N M L K J H P O I Y T H F T P A I
A M A R T I N A N A V R A T I L O V A G A B D K
G A S I D C F G A H J K H Q W E R O Q U N J Y P
R Z X S C H V B D S U P E R B O W L U M L T H O
A Q W T E A R T I Y C U I E P L O Y I A E J U H
N A S I D E F G A H H K S B C N F M L V Y G S T
D Z X Y C L V U C L A P M E O I R P L E C F K E
S P D A F J A S O D R G A C J N O I E M U D I Y
L A Z M X O C V M B G M N C S E N C O G P L E S
A R X A E R T I A Q E S T A L R K S N B V I S R
M A B G E D Q D N T R A R L K N I N E R S L C A
K L W U G A X A I Z S M O O P N B M A B D F D S
C L F C T N E N C W Y U P B J K P E L E L E R Y
U E T H Y B A J I T Q B H O P M H Y U R K A W D
T L R I E W S A W A W A Y N E G R E T Z K Y I L
```

UNITED STATES
Page 274: **STATE PUZZLES**

Crossword answers:

2 Across: TOBACCO
5 Down: VT... VA...
6 Across: CARDINAL
8 Across: WHEAT
10 Across: COAL
11 Across: IDAHO
13 Across: PINEAPPLES
15 Across: LINCOLN
18 Across: GOLD
20 Across: ELK
21 Across: TEXAS
23 Across: REDWOOD
24 Across: OAK

SCRAMBLED STATES

State:	ALASKA	CALIFORNIA	FLORIDA	MICHIGAN	OKLAHOMA
Capital:	JUNEAU	SACRAMENTO	TALLAHASSEE	LANSING	OKLAHOMA CITY
Product:	OIL	MOVIES	ORANGES	AUTOMOBILES	CATTLE

INDEX

The names of the sections are in boldface.

ILLUSTRATION AND PHOTO CREDITS

ILLUSTRATION
Bernard Adnet; Janice Edelman-Lee; Arthur Friedman;
Image Club Graphics, Inc., 800-387-9193; Sophia Lato; George Ulrich

PHOTOGRAPHY
13: Helen Huang, Chris Lee. **14:** Hubble Telescope, NASA. **15:** Chen Lu, Focus On Sports Inc.; Steve Young, Courtesy of the San Francisco 49ers.
16: Jim Carrey in *The Mask*, © 1994, New Line Productions, Inc. All rights reserved. Photo by B. Little. Photo appears courtesy of New Line Productions, Inc.; Sheryl Crow, Photo: Naomi Kaltman. **18:** *Anne Frank: The Diary of a Young Girl* book jacket, Courtesy of Bantam Doubleday Dell Publishing Group, Inc. **139:** *The Starship Enterprise*, Courtesy of Paramont Pictures. **140:** *Home Improvement*, Bob D'Amico/ABC, Inc. **145:** Ace of Base, Thomas Eriksson/ARISTA; Whitney Houston, ARISTA. **147:** *A Chorus Line* poster, Courtesy of *A Chorus Line*; *The Fantasticks* poster, Courtesy of *The Fantasticks*. **174:** Scene from *Forrest Gump*, Courtesy of Paramount Pictures. **175:** The Tony Award, Photofest. **176:** Yasir Arafat, Siaud/Stills/Retna Ltd.; Yitzhak Rabin, Steve Granitz/Retna Ltd.; Shimon Peres, Daniel Root/Retna Ltd.; F. W. de Klerk and Nelson Mandela, Robert King Camera Press 26806-7 London (1994)/ Retna Ltd. **177:** Maya Angelou, Dwight Carter/Random House. **178:** *Walk Two Moons* book jacket, Courtesy of HarperCollins Publishers. **194:** Olympic Torch Bearer, J. Patronite/AllSport USA. **196:** Major League Baseball logo, Courtesy of Major League Baseball. **197:** Frank Thomas, Stephen Dunn/ AllSport USA. **199:** NBA logo, The NBA logo reproduced in this publication is the exclusive property of NBA Properties, Inc., is being used under license from NBA Properties, Inc. and may not be used without the written conscent of NBA Properties, Inc.; Michael Jordan, Focus On Sports Inc. **200:** Rebecca Lobo, Courtesy of the University of Connecticut Athletic Communications. **201:** AFC and NFC logos, Courtesy of NFL Properties, Inc. **202:** Barry Sanders, Stephen Dunn/AllSport USA. **203:** Rashaan Salaam, Courtesy of University of Colorado at Boulder. **204:** Shannon Miller, Dave Black/USA Gymnastics Federation. **205:** Wayne Gretzky, Wen Roberts/Photography Ink. **206:** Bonnie Blair, Jonathan Daniel/AllSport USA. **207:** Pele, Bill Davila, Retna Ltd. **208:** Martina Navratilova, Simon Bruty/AllSport USA. **218:** Clinton Inaugural, Courtesy of the White House. **219:** Supreme Court Justices, Courtesy of the Supreme Court Historical Society. **221:** Capitol Building, PhotoDisc Inc. **227-232:** United States Presidents 1-36, © 1967 by Dover Publications, Inc. **232:** President Nixon, Courtesy of Richard Nixon Library; President Ford, Courtesy of the Gerald R. Ford Museum; President Carter, Courtesy of the Jimmy Carter Library; President Reagan, Courtesy of the Ronald Reagan Library; President Bush, Courtesy of Bush Presidential Materials Project; President Bill Clinton, Courtesy of the White House. **233:** Martha Washington, Abigail Adams, Dolley Madison, Eleanor Roosevelt, Jacqueline Kennedy, © 1967 by Dover Publications, Inc.; Hillary Rodham Clinton, Courtesy of the White House.

COVER
Illustration: Todd Cooper
Photography: Globe, NASA; Mazda Miata, John Crall/FPG; Shaquille O'Neal, Tim Defrisco/Allstock; Puu Oo Eruption, Greg Vaughan/Allstock; Tutankhamen Sarcophagus, Art Resource.